HOLLYWOOD v. HARD CORE

JON LEWIS

HOLLYWOOD v. HARD CORE

How the Struggle over Censorship Saved
the Modern Film Industry

New York University Press • *New York and London*

NEW YORK UNIVERSITY PRESS
New York and London

An earlier version of chapter 1 appeared as "We Do Not Ask You to Condone This: How the Blacklist Saved Hollywood," *Cinema Journal* 39, no. 2 (winter 2000): 3–30. © 2000 by University of Texas Press. Reprinted by permission of University of Texas Press.

Library of Congress Cataloging-in-Publication Data
Lewis, Jon, 1955–
Hollywood v. hard core : how the struggle over censorship saved the modern film industry / Jon Lewis.
p. cm.
Includes bibliographical references and index.
ISBN 0-8147-5142-3 (acid-free paper)
1. Motion pictures—Censorship—United States—History.   I. Title: Hollywood versus hard core. II. Title.
PN1995.62 .L47 2000
363.3'1'0973—dc21   00-010741

New York University Press books are printed on acid-free paper, and their binding materials are chosen for strength and durability.

Manufactured in the United States of America

10 9 8 7 6 5 4 3 2 1

For my father, Robert Guy Lewis

Contents

Acknowledgments

There are a lot of people to thank here, first and foremost Dana Polan and Mike Oriard. Their reading of early drafts of the manuscript helped immeasurably to shape its structure and style.

The two Erics—Smoodin and Zinner—were there from the start as well. They provided smart advice and years' worth of encouragement. I tend to move forward and fast anyway, but their confidence and friendship kept me on track.

Four colleagues—Jim Foster, Kevin Sandler, Eric Schaefer, and Justin Wyatt—generously provided unpublished manuscripts and research materials that saved me a whole lot of time and trouble. Ron Scott, my first and to date only research assistant, did some of the early library legwork. Much later in the project, Scott Curtis generously helped me navigate the MPAA files at the Margaret Herrick Library of the Academy of Motion Picture Arts and Sciences. When I finally decided that it was impossible to write a film history without actually talking about specific films, Mike Conrad at Downtown Video here in Corvallis tracked down some key titles.

My old classmate and friend, *Cinema Journal* editor Frank Tomasulo, helped work out the kinks in chapter 1. A shorter and slightly less audacious version of the chapter appeared in the winter 2000 issue of the journal. Big thanks to Frank and the folks at the University of Texas Press for their permission to reprint the essay.

I got a whole lot of mileage out of otherwise casual conversations over pizza with Ralph Rodriguez, at parties and conferences with Suzanne Clark, and on the telephone with my sister, Joanne Lewis, and David Stowe.

There is often little distinction between the pleasures of work and the pleasures of play for me. I watch movies for a living, after all. Still, I've got more of a perspective than I had ten years ago and I have my parents, my sister and her new family, and all those in-laws (there are so many of you!) to thank for that. I have come to understand and appreciate the greater pleasures of family and that has helped me take pleasure in the work I've done here.

This book took shape over several years and benefited from several semiformal rehearsals. Early drafts of chapters 1, 3, 4, 5, and 6 were trotted out at professional conferences—SCS, MLG, PNASA, and the MLA—and for guest spots at USC and North Texas State. I learned a lot from conversations with colleagues after those presentations. Especially memorable is a little exchange I had in the summer of 1998 with Mike Sprinker, the last person on earth to call me "kid." Mike died last year before I could tell him how much he's meant to me over the years. This will have to do.

My colleagues in the English Department, especially my two chairs (Bob Frank and Bob Schwartz), have from my arrival in Corvallis been generous and supportive. The Center for the Humanities and its director Pete Copek provided time and space for this research. Thanks again.

I do most of my writing and reading at home, which greatly restricts what the rest of my family can do while I'm "trying to work." There were a lot of times during the past few years when they thought it might be better for me to work elsewhere, but I can't. Frankly, I like the interruptions, the wrestling and boxing bouts, the necessary snacks, drinks, runs up and around and through the house. When I'm working, I like to know that Martha and the boys, Guy and Adam, are around, poised to distract or better yet to rescue me. It's their love that makes the work worth doing.

Acronyms

ACLU   American Civil Liberties Union
AFAA   Adult Film Association of America
AIP   American International Pictures
ARI   Audience Research Institute
CARA   Code and Rating Administration; after 1977: Classification and Rating Administration
CP   Communist Party
CPI   Columbia Pictures Industries
CSU   Conference of Studio Unions
FCC   Federal Communications Commission
FTC   Federal Trade Commission
HUAC   House Committee on Un-American Activities
IATSE   International Alliance of Theatrical and Stage Employees
IFIDA   International Film Importers and Distributors of America
LCA   Licensing Corporation of America
MPAA   Motion Picture Association of America
MPEA   Motion Picture Export Association
MPPC   Motion Picture Patents Company
MPPDA   Motion Picture Producers and Distributors of America
MPTOA   Motion Picture Theater Owners Association
NATO   National Association of Theater Owners
NCOMP   National Catholic Office of Motion Pictures
NLRB   National Labor Relations Board
OWI   Office of War Information
PCA   Production Code Administration
SAG   Screen Actors Guild
UA   United Artists
UMPI   United Motion Picture Industry
WAP   Women Against Pornography
WAVAW   Women Against Violence Against Women
WCI   Warner Communications Incorporated

Introduction

Late July 1999. The New York film critics have just had their first look at the release version of Stanley Kubrick's *Eyes Wide Shut*. The new version is different from the so-called director's cut screened earlier in the week. And the critics don't much like the changes. Now they're anxious to tell their readership, the film's distributor, Warner Brothers, Jack Valenti, the longtime chief of the Motion Picture Association of America (MPAA), and anyone else who will listen, why.

The director's cut received an NC-17 rating from the Motion Picture Association of America's Classification and Rating Administration (CARA). The release version secured an R, though it features only one significant change. Hooded figures have been digitally inserted into the film's orgy scene and block what was previously a clear view of some of the action. It's a silly little change in a silly and long scene. But so far as the New York critics are concerned (and they're right on this score), specific content in a specific scene is beside the point.

In a letter to Warner Brothers chairman Terry Semel, copies of which were sent to several major newspapers and the industry trades, the New York Film Critics Circle expressed disappointment at Semel's reluctance to protect the film. But the critics know precisely why Semel did what he did and wrote their letter only to make public their frustration at studio business as usual. Semel is, after all, just a studio executive and in this case he was just doing his job.

Semel's press release in response to the critics' letter was succinct and unsurprising. The studio did not file an appeal challenging the decision because it did not have to. Warner Brothers' primary commitment, Semel reminded the reviewers, was not to Kubrick, his fans, or film history, but to the film distributor's parent company, Time Warner, and that company's stockholders. "We're not in the NC-17 business," Semel wrote. "NC-17 is a whole industry. It includes triple-X-rated porno films. So to us that's just not a business that we're in."

Semel's press release reveals the contemporary film industry's all too industrial bottom line. The flap over *Eyes Wide Shut*, as Semel coolly implied, is not really about the integrity of the film itself, or of films in general. Nor is it really about the practice of film censorship, which has persisted in the United States in a variety of forms since before the turn of the twentieth century. It's about box office and ancillary revenues. It's about the generation of profits and the complex ways cine-regulation (engineered in this and most other such cases by the MPAA) is designed primarily to serve the studios' best interests.

Like all the other MPAA member studios, Warner Brothers is committed to "box office friendly" movies. Studio executives do not necessarily like such fare, but that is beside the point. Semel's refusal to finance the release of an NC-17 cut of *Eyes Wide Shut* has nothing much to do with his respect or lack of respect for Kubrick. And Kubrick's willingness to comply with the conditions of the standard studio contract he signed with Warner Brothers, which required him to deliver an R-rated print, tells us nothing about his personal or working relationship with the studio executive. Both men understood the rules going in.

The Classification and Rating Administration's objection to the orgy scene in the director's cut was anticipated and was consistent with its classification of other similar scenes in other studio films. Kubrick made the film knowing that the orgy scene would most likely be cut to suit the industry censors. He understood that when the CARA board listed certain changes he might make to secure an R rating, Warner Brothers would force him to make the cuts or find someone else to do it for him.

That said, it was well worth Warner Brothers' time and money to let Kubrick shoot the scene and the film the way he wanted. From the start, Semel could plan on two versions of the film: an American release version cut to suit CARA and a director's cut, suitable for general release in Europe. The NC-17 version is now available stateside on video, laserdisk, and DVD. Now we can see the orgy scene intact. Now we can see a film a second time that was not very good the first time we saw it. And that's fine with the MPAA, Semel, and the executives and shareholders at Time Warner.

I begin this book with this little industry story for a reason. It reminds us how film censorship only incidentally and superficially regards specific film content. *Eyes Wide Shut* is a Warner Brothers film and Warner Brothers is not, as Semel told the press, in the NC-17 business (with regard to theatrically released motion pictures, at least). Warner Brothers' primary commitment is to the shareholders of its parent company. The parent company's primary interest is in the long-term health of the industry. That's why Kubrick, Semel, and Time Warner chairman Gerald Levin have played along with the MPAA.

The MPAA supervises the regulation of film content solely to protect studio products in the marketplace. Cooperation with the MPAA is a practical as well as symbolic gesture. In the very act of adding those robed figures in the orgy scene, Warner Brothers expressed its continued commitment to the network of relationships that constitute the MPAA. Semel got Kubrick to alter his film because the network of relationships (between studios and other studios, between studios and the vast majority of American theater owners) that is maintained by the MPAA is and always will be more important than the integrity of a single movie.

The New York critics' letter called attention to the ways such a practical business policy might have a larger cultural or political dimension. Their letter to Semel described the CARA board as "a punitive and restrictive force [that] effectively tramples the freedom of American filmmakers." The studios' collective commitment to the economic imperatives of a safe and sensible movie culture (as envisioned by the MPAA) has engendered, in the critics' words, a "kneejerk Puritanism." The network of cooperative and collusive arrangements between the MPAA, CARA, and the member studios has, the critics contend, stifled creativity and has required of filmmakers and studio executives alike the delivery of watered-down, dumbed-down products. The principal and sole virtue of such a system is that it insures that all MPAA films move freely and profitably through the vast entertainment marketplace. Thanks to the MPAA, the art of cinema is institutionally subsumed by and/or rendered secondary to commerce. It's a matter of policy and standard business procedure.

A separate letter protesting the cuts to *Eyes Wide Shut* penned by the Los Angeles Film Critics Association was addressed directly to Jack Valenti and the MPAA. It was met with a swift, succinct, and decidedly undiplomatic response. In a widely circulated press release, Valenti dismissed the West Coast critics as "a small band of constant whiners [who] talk to each other, write for each other, opine with each other and view with lacerating contempt the rubes who live Out There, west of Manhattan and east of the San Andreas fault." "Out There," after all, is where all films these days must play. As the New York film critic Armond White so vividly describes it, "those who disagree" have but one alternative: they "can kiss Jack Valenti's ass."[1]

ORDER FROM CHAOS: WHERE THERE ARE NO RULES, THERE ARE NO GUARANTEES

Hollywood is a place of great irony at all times.
—Mark Canton, former chairman, Sony/Columbia Pictures

According to the industrial economist Art DeVany, Hollywood is a place perpetually "poised between order and chaos."[2] So much is riding on the success of a single product, executives are disinclined to take risks. Their jobs, which pay astonishingly well, hinge to an extent on short-term indicators at the box office but much more importantly are governed by long-term indicators on *the street*, where studio stock values have long been the industry's real bottom line. To protect their position(s), executives are quite practically attracted to what DeVany calls "simple rules" that enhance or promise predictability and stability. These rules are more or less shared by other similarly neurotic and frightened executives at "rival" studios.

"Simple rules" regulating workforce compensation and utility, trust and antitrust, and production standards are instituted and managed by the studio industry's governing body, the Motion Picture Association of America. These regulations provide a cooperative framework for an industry that has for the entirety of its history thrived only when all the major parties have agreed to work together.

DeVany characterizes Hollywood as "a complex adaptive system." The film business conducted there is affected by political, economic, and social forces that are difficult to predict, let alone control. Predicting the future in the film business, DeVany quips, is like forecasting the weather . . . next year.[3] Censorship and regulation, however inhibiting in the short term, offer long-term structure to this uncertain and unpredictable business and offer the illusion of certainty and security to studio executives whose jobs hinge on the measurable success of their studio's product lines.

The enormous sums invested in movies these days significantly raise the stakes. Every big motion picture is potentially an executive's undoing. As the former studio executive Lynda Obst describes it,

> Personal humiliation and career dashing confrontations are endemic, impersonal, constant. This is the flip side of ambition: debilitating exhaustion and the constant threat of defeat. Therefore every crisis can't be taken too seriously or you won't survive. . . . The only way they

know you're a player is when you respond to a disaster by behaving as though nothing has happened. Denial also works. It's a terrific advantage if you actually feel nothing, as opposed to having to anesthetize. This is clearly why the best full-time deniers of all—sociopaths—do so very well in Hollywood.[4]

Obst's pointed remarks apply to the old Hollywood as well as the new. In his incisive (and alas incomplete) old Hollywood novel, *The Love of The Last Tycoon*, F. Scott Fitzgerald captures this pervasive uncertainty in an early scene aboard an airplane. Fitzgerald's ill-fated hero, Monroe Stahr, enters the cockpit of the plane. Alone with the pilots, he poses a hypothetical:

> Suppose you were a railroad man. . . . You have to send a train through [a mountain range] somewhere. Well, you get your surveyors, reports, and you find there's three or four or half a dozen gaps, and not one is better than the other. You've got to decide—on what basis? You can't test the best way—except by doing it. So you just do it.

Upon reflection, the pilots consider Stahr's narrative "valuable advice."[5] After all, pilots and movie executives must "fly by the seat of their pants"—they must appear decisive under all circumstances.

Fitzgerald based Stahr on a real-life mogul, Irving Thalberg, with whom the author spoke just once in the commissary at MGM. In Fitzgerald's working notes for the novel, one finds an earlier version, by Thalberg, of the story about the road through the mountains, the various blueprints, and the necessity for someone in charge to select a route and stick to it. "When you're planning a new enterprise on a grand scale," Thalberg told the novelist, "the people under you mustn't ever know or guess that you're in any doubt."[6]

Though today's industry is differently organized, with assets more complexly integrated and diversified and products significantly less likely to lose money than ever before, executives are nonetheless judged as harshly as Stahr and Thalberg. Hollywood is still in many ways an uncertain little place. Those in charge must behave as if they have things under control. But they don't.

Case in point: at the end of 1989, when Sony was finalizing a deal to purchase Columbia Pictures, Akio Morita, the firm's CEO, asked NHK (TV) president Keiji Shima what he thought of the deal. Shima was candid: "Morita-san, you're making a big mistake. . . . Making movies is different; it's a special kind of business. You don't understand Hollywood. You're asking for trouble. You're getting into a business you won't be able to control. Don't do it."[7] In Hollywood, or so goes the industry adage, nobody knows anything.

Morita went ahead with the purchase despite his friend's advice because he was attracted to the glamour and gamble of Hollywood. Like Stahr, Morita figured he'd find the right route through the mountains, he'd be the one to predict the weather next year.

FILM CONTENT IS MOSTLY BESIDE THE POINT

The objective of [the MPAA], which has never varied, is to make sure that American movies can move freely and unhobbled around the world.

—Jack Valenti, MPAA president and CEO

Content regulation, the various systems by which films are granted a seal of approval or are classified in advance of their arrival into the marketplace, has been a part of the public distribution and exhibition of cinema since before the turn of the twentieth century. Such regulation significantly inhibits artistic freedom and certainly dumbs down the final product, but the rationale for such regulation only incidentally stems from predictable, political, elitist assumptions about the mass audience and the persuasive, potentially dangerous impact of film on them.

As I will argue throughout this book, the political and social utility of film censorship is altogether secondary to its economic function. Like other forms of industrial regulation, content censorship functions to secure the long-term health of the industry as a whole. That the content of so many films has been changed in service of such a corporate agenda reveals just how little art matters in the film business.

For over a hundred years, film producers and distributors have publicly regarded production codes as a necessary evil. The industry self-regulates, we have been told time and again by the studios in Hollywood, in order to prevent the government from doing it for them. But the government is not now nor has it ever been all that interested in censoring films; it would be a hazardous and litigious process. For the past forty years, the only films the government could legally ban or seize are those that fit the fairly specific criteria of hard-core pornography. The Hollywood studios don't now nor did they ever produce films that fall under such a legal definition. But the MPAA regulates studio product lines anyway.

Content censorship works not because it is legally binding; it's not. It works because all the studios have agreed to abide by the MPAA's rules, even when the rules (and specific rulings) function to an individual studio's short-term disadvantage.

In Hollywood, content regulation does have its political dimension. But the political is subsumed by or conflated with the economic. The studios self-regulate because they are convinced that self-regulation is good for business. The motivation behind and function of content regulation reveal the truth in the old Hollywood adage "When they tell you it's not about the money . . . it's about the money."

Successful studio response to the chaotic economic and social system into which their products are released (a perfectly chosen industry term) continues to depend on the effectiveness of industry self-regulation. Specific content in specific scenes of specific films, which comes to mind first when one thinks about self-regulation in Hollywood, is of secondary significance. The policing of images onscreen rarely concerns the images themselves, the morality or immorality of their content. It derives instead from concerns about box office, about how to make a product that won't have *problems* in the marketplace.

Censorship in any of its various forms targets free artistic expression. But such a creative freedom, let alone creative autonomy, is hardly a Hollywood priority. Compliance with at times burdensome regulations—for example, production code decisions that end up dramatically altering a film's plot and theme—serves the far more significant big picture of industry and commerce. In the very enforcement of censorship codes, certain important relationships (between management and talent, between studio distributors and film exhibitors) are solidified and secured. Censorship codes and regulations are in many ways what binds the various competing agencies in the film business together. When it all works as it should, everyone who plays by the rules makes money.

In 1908, well before the first feature film was unspooled, the principal producers and distributors of filmed entertainment in America formed a trust in order to exploit its members' control over certain industrial patents. The Motion Picture Patents Company (MPPC) assured the feds that the intra-industry accord was the best way to establish and maintain production and print quality. Exclusive use of certain key patents "protected consumers." The patents also enabled the trust companies to make a whole lot of money. In the process of regulating film length and content, the trust established a system of intra-industry cooperation and collusion, a model for the successful management of the business of film that persists today.

Production codes, at least from the 1930s on, have been legally unenforceable because they do not comply with specific constitutional guarantees. Content regulation in the film business is, technically, voluntary. Studios comply even though they don't have to. Compliance confirms studio/industry confidence in the MPAA and the rules it adopts and enforces. Self-regulation requires that all parties regard voluntary commitments as binding agreements. Standard operating procedure in the film business, responsiveness if not submission to the rules and regulations of the MPAA and its subsidiary, CARA, guarantees cooperation and collusion. Cooperation and collusion protect the studios against the vagaries of the marketplace, the American zeitgeist, and all those so-called independent producers and distributors.

There are several histories at stake in this book. The first and foremost of these regards the 1968 MPAA film rating system, as a production code as well as an intra- and interindustry agreement, and how it has made the new Hollywood not only possible but inevitable. It's a complex story and begins a lot better than it ends.

Despite complex ties to the studio system and to the studio-controlled MPAA, the rating system accompanied and seemed at least at first to encourage a glorious new Hollywood, a place dominated by terrific filmmakers: auteurs like Francis Coppola, Martin Scorsese, and Robert Altman. These directors presided over something like a golden age in American film, ten years or so during which a whole lot of terrific movies were made and the studios finally and fully emerged from a twenty-five-year box office slump.

Though I'd like to believe that the auteur seventies saved Hollywood because there were so many good films being made there—just make a good movie and people will pay to see it!—we all know where the story goes next. The auteur renaissance was short-lived and ended while the more interesting directors were still making good films. In its place, a second new Hollywood emerged, run by attorneys, agents, and conglomerate yes-men. The conglomerate-owned studios now make fewer and bigger films, spectacles of American excess and illiteracy. Theirs is a formula for navigating the industrial and cultural chaos grounded in the cold hard world of American commerce and capital.

In working out the significance of the rating system, I found myself more and more interested in industry regulation in general, more and more convinced that it was unreasonable to talk about content regulation as if it evolved or existed independently of workforce or industrial (antitrust) regulation. What began as a fairly compact little history of the 1968 MPAA film rating system became the expansive political, legal, and social history of American cinema I present here.

Hollywood v. Hard Core is a history of Hollywood policy and procedure. While my primary interest is in content censorship, I argue throughout that Hollywood's dealings with sex on screen are part of a larger history concerning the evolution of American moviemaking into a big, indeed very Big Business. Like much of my previous work, this study presents a narrative of the formation of today's Hollywood out of the conflicts of the past.[8] The Hollywood history I tell is comprised of a series of industrial problems and solutions, some more dramatic than others. In every circumstance, the studios have responded collectively and collusively, emerging stronger with each adaptation.

The book begins with a chapter each on the blacklist and the *Paramount* decision and tells these histories more or less from start to finish before it gets to the more glamorous stuff about dirty movies. The discussion of content regulation, which makes up the final five chapters, is fairly ambitious. I look back briefly to the end of the nineteenth century and then forward again through the summer of 1999.

The history I tell throughout this book is synchronous and elliptical. It is structured less like an academic history than a novel. There is a cast of fascinating characters here (heroes and more often villains), plot suspense, and narrative reversals. Hollywood history, I am pleased to say, is never dull.

There is a point in this book, as in any good novel, at which the various narratives meet. It takes a while to get there, but the payoff is well worth the wait. The climax in this narrative marks the precise moment at which the new Hollywood begins, a moment I would never have given a second look had I not taken the route I've taken here.

I've spent the better part of three years tracing the long and chaotic history of Hollywood regulation. What I have found at the end of all this research is that at a particularly crucial moment the fate of the new Hollywood hinged on a strange little confrontation, the solution of which perplexed and frustrated the MPAA. Between 1968 and 1973, despite a revolutionary new film rating system, the studios' box office woes persisted. The principal competition came from an unlikely place, a body of independently produced and distributed films rated X, films that proved at once disreputable and for a moment at least irresistible, even chic.

Then the studios caught a break. In 1973 the so-called Nixon (Supreme) Court stepped in and on one fateful day virtually eliminated the competition posed by hard core. Hollywood regained control of the theatrical marketplace and hasn't looked back since.

Hollywood is luxuriating these days in the aftereffects of this strange and significant skirmish. As I write this introduction, it's hard to believe that once upon a time not so long ago the studios were not making any money. They are now. And they have a lucky victory over hard-core pornography to thank for it.

1

How the Blacklist Saved Hollywood

WHEN THE HOUSE Committee on Un-American Activities (HUAC)
first convened in the fall of 1947, the film industry was on the verge of
some very big changes.[1] The stability and profitability of theatrical
exhibition were severely threatened by the shift in population out of
the big cities (prompting a decrease in revenues at the studios' first-
run deluxe theaters), the Justice Department's rekindled interest in
breaking up the studio trusts, and the development of a competitive
audiovisual pop culture on television.[2] Talent agents exploiting
movie stars' growing independence from the contract system and the
threat of job actions from the various industry guilds and unions
made the business of producing and distributing motion pictures increasingly expensive and complicated. By 1947 the studios' relations
with exhibitors and the industry workforce had become profoundly
adversarial.

Beginning in 1947, HUAC provided the studios with lists of union-
ized writers, actors, and directors who, despite National Labor Relations Board (NLRB) protections, could for reasons of national security
be fired without cause, without severance, and in a number of cases
without concern for previously earned wages or option fees. In doing
so, the committee helped the studios better manage an uncertain labor
situation; moreover, it helped them cut expenses and payrolls in preparation for a widely predicted postwar box office decline. The so-called
free market got a whole lot less free during the blacklist era because the
studios discovered that they could circumvent the spirit of the various
antitrust decrees, keep production costs down, and control the industry
guilds if they just learned to work better together. The new Hollywood
we see in place today—a new Hollywood that rates and censors its own
and everyone else's films, flaunts its disregard for antitrust legislation
and federal communications and trade guidelines, and has reduced
filmmaking to a science of market and product research is very much
the product, the still-evolving legacy, of the blacklist.

To fully understand the complex history of regulation in the post-war film industry, we have to view the blacklist as not just an ideological struggle. Of course the Red Scare was political, but in Hollywood it is difficult to separate the ideological from the industrial. The studios' cooperation with HUAC featured ample anticommunist rhetoric. But at the same time, the industry blacklist was designed as, or evolved into, a complex and collusive business strategy that diminished the threat of further federal regulation of the business of making movies and censorship of film content. The blacklist may well have reflected shifting political alliances among studio ownership, management, and the industry's celebrity workforce. But it also enabled the studios to establish a new way of doing business that solved several larger, long-term problems that were plaguing them at the time.

Two parallel dramas emerge once we begin to look at the blacklist as a fiscal as well as an ideological struggle. The first involves a residual, pervasive postwar anti-Semitism that got HUAC interested in (Jewish) Hollywood in the first place. The committee members' efforts to clean up the film business focused in large part on the industry's workforce, which in their minds was overrepresented by American Jews. That HUAC also set in motion larger changes in the management of the industry proved an added bonus. The New York offices—the mostly non-Jewish, old money corporate owners—of the West Coast studios exploited postwar anti-Semitism not only to combat the unions but to force out the first-generation Jewish studio moguls. In doing so, they put an end to an entrepreneurial system run by charismatic but inefficient self-made businessmen, a system that seemed suddenly out of step with postwar American capitalism. Impending market deregulation and the resulting industry-wide panic prompted change, and the Red Scare made it all not only possible but easy. In the final analysis, the blacklist did not save America from films promoting communism, liberalism, or humanitarianism. Instead, it encouraged studio ownership to develop and adopt a corporate model more suited to a future new Hollywood, one in which studio ownership, exploiting stricter self-regulation, might maintain profitability and control.

The shift from the entrepreneurial model that seemed to prevail in the time of the moguls to the more anonymous conglomerate model that is in evidence today involved a complex assimilation of one sort of business into another. The 1948 *Paramount* decision put an end to the contract system that supported the entrepreneurial model. The blacklist enabled the MPAA to establish in its place a system far better suited for

business in postindustrial, postwar America and far more suitable eth-
nically and politically for doing business with the federal government,
as would become increasingly necessary in the forties and fifties.

A second story involves the Motion Picture Association of America,
which allied with HUAC seemingly against its own best interests, only
to emerge from the fray as a powerful industry gatekeeper. In 1947 the
MPAA was little more than a new name for the old and fraying MPPDA
(Motion Picture Producers and Distributors of America). It got its charter in 1945 at the very moment the Justice Department resumed its antitrust suit against the studios. The studio membership of the MPAA
used the Waldorf Statement in 1947 (which made public their intention
to cooperate with HUAC) to establish an identity and moreover to assert studio unity in the face of a seeming ideological and very real fiscal
crisis. Over the years, the MPAA has done well to downplay its roots in
the Red Scare. But its power today seems very much indebted to right-
wing congressional support at its inception and the collusive strategies
it by necessity developed during the late 1940s and 1950s.

The Hollywood guilds and unions that had gained so much power
and influence in the thirties and forties lost their momentum during the
blacklist and have never recovered. In the new Hollywood, the guilds
are so weak that strikes afford little hope for even celebrity talent. For
example, in 1980 the Screen Actors Guild (SAG) organized a strike to establish residual pay scales for films reproduced for and exhibited in the
home box office market (including videocassette sales and rentals and
cable television). The studios responded by locking out the entire union
workforce. Universal announced in the trades its intention to invoke the
force majeure clause in its contracts with talent, effectively suspending all
projects on film and television. Other studios, it was fair to assume at
the time, were inclined to follow suit. SAG leadership, which had timed
the strike to coincide with the beginning of the fall television season,
underestimated the extent of studio collusion and misunderstood how
little filmmaking mattered in the new Hollywood. What the guild members discovered in 1980 was that the studios were so well diversified,
their entertainment industry interests so extensive and lucrative, they
no longer needed to make movies or TV shows to make money. Such is
the legacy of the Red Scare in Hollywood.

The decline in the effectiveness of the industry guilds has been accompanied by dramatic growth at the MPAA. The very antitrust regulations that promised to break up the studios in the late forties are no
longer enforced: witness Time Warner Turner, Disney/Capital Cities/

ABC, Viacom/Paramount. The regulation of film content, formerly complicated by grassroots organizations like the Legion of Decency, and state and local censorship boards, is now wholly supervised by the MPAA. Through its rating system, first adopted in 1968, the MPAA not only self-regulates its various product lines, it monitors all participation in the legit theatrical and home box office markets.

The operative roots of the MPAA's Classification and Rating Administration (CARA), which supervises and enforces the film rating system, lay in the various industry modes of self-regulation that preceded it. The Production Code Administration (PCA), its industry predecessor, was rooted in anti-Semitic assumptions about the dangers of movies and the men who made them. Joseph Breen, one of the cofounders of the PCA and its chief censor for much of its existence, was a Catholic procensorship activist before he became an industry player. His mission to regulate Hollywood cinema can be traced in large part to his dislike and distrust of the Jews who seemed to run the business. "These Jews seem to think of nothing but money making and sexual indulgence," Breen wrote in a letter to a fellow Catholic activist. "They are, probably, the scum of the scum of the earth."[3]

As a business practice, the rating system dates most immediately and directly to 1947, when the studio membership of the MPAA began to understand and exploit the complex relationship between censorship and other forms of industrial regulation. What the studio ownership discovered was that self-regulation in compliance with HUAC and grassroots pressure to make less political, less meaningful films enabled them to better control the industry workforce and exploit the increasingly international postwar theatrical marketplace.

When the House Committee on Un-American Activities made its recommendation to indict Alvah Bessie, Herbert Biberman, Lester Cole, Edward Dmytryk, Ring Lardner Jr., John Howard Lawson, Albert Maltz, Samuel Ornitz, Adrian Scott, and Dalton Trumbo, the so-called Hollywood Ten, for contempt of Congress, the MPAA at first assured those under investigation that it would oppose government regulation. "Tell the boys not to worry," MPAA president Eric Johnston remarked on October 18, 1947. "There'll never be a blacklist. We're not going to go totalitarian to please this committee."[4]

But just twelve days later—five days before the full House of Representatives was scheduled to vote on the contempt citations—Johnston issued a stunning public reversal: "We did not defend them. We do not defend them now. On the contrary, we believe they have done a tremen-

Some of the more famous "unfriendlies" and their attorneys, October 27, 1947. *Front row, left to right:* Lewis Milestone, Dalton Trumbo, John Howard Lawson, and Bart Crum; *center row, left to right:* Gordon Kahn, Irving Pichel, Edward Dmytryk, and Robert Rossen; *third row, left to right:* Waldo Salt, Richard Collins, Howard Koch, Albert Maltz, Herbert Biberman, Lester Cole, Ring Lardner Jr., and Martin Popper (UPI, 1947).

dous disservice to the industry which has given them so much material rewards [*sic*] and an opportunity to exercise their talents."[5] Indictments, incarcerations, and an industry-wide blacklist followed, all with the co-operation and much of it under the supervision of the MPAA.

This sudden change in policy at the MPAA was a source of consid-erable speculation at the time. The hearings were a public relations nightmare, but capitulation was not the most fiscally prudent way for the studios to deal with the situation. Reliable polls revealed that pub-lic opinion was split especially with regard to the way HUAC treated the unfriendly witnesses. The results of a Gallup poll were released on November 29, 1947. The poll highlighted two questions, the first of which focused on the conduct of the committee: "What is your opinion of the investigation—do you approve or disapprove of the way it was handled?" 37 percent approved, 36 percent disapproved, and 27 percent had no opinion. A second question regarded the jail time sought as a consequence of the ten's refusal to answer questions: "Do you think the Hollywood writers who refused to say whether or not they were members of the Communist Party should be punished or not?" 47 percent maintained that they should be punished, 39 percent that they should not be punished, and 14 percent had no opinion.

Close examination of the Gallup poll results revealed a relationship between public opinion and educational experience. College graduates voted 54 percent to 34 percent *against* punishment; high school grads were split 43 percent against, 44 percent in favor of punishment. Citizens with just a grammar school education were 53 percent to 31 percent in favor of punishment. The congressional vote was 346 to 17 in support of the contempt indictments, which works out to approximately 80 percent in favor, 8 percent against, and 12 percent either abstaining or absent.

The Audience Research Institute (ARI), a Gallup unit formed to perform market research for the studios, produced data that complicated matters further. The ARI data revealed that the *moviegoing* public was evenly split over the conduct of the committee. Only 10 percent of those polled believed that there were all that many communists in the film business. The majority of those who believed HUAC's contention that communism posed a significant threat in the motion picture business were not regular moviegoers before or during the Red Scare.[6]

Several big city newspapers, including the *New York Times* and the *Washington Post*, openly criticized the way HUAC conducted the hearings. While skirting the central ideological issues—anticommunism, patriotism, anti-Semitism, antiunionism—editorials in major newspapers across the nation highlighted the committee's seeming disregard for due process and its apparent disinterest in the civil rights of the unfriendly witnesses.

Gordon Kahn, one of the original nineteen, attempted to explain the MPAA reversal by alleging that the Hollywood Ten were sacrificed as part of a complicated deal between the feds and studio ownership.[7] "[The MPAA's] surrender was the result of a deal," Kahn wrote in 1948 in *Hollywood on Trial*. "They would immolate on the altar of hysteria and reaction . . . they would purge other writers, directors, producers and actors from the industry . . . in return for all of this, [HUAC chair J. Parnell] Thomas would promise to call off any further investigation of Hol-

lywood."[8] Attractive as Kahn's theory was at the time, no such conspiracy ever existed and no such bargain was ever struck. Thomas and his
successors (after Thomas's conviction and incarceration) continued to
investigate and terrorize the liberal and radical Left in Hollywood
through the end of the 1950s.[9] But Kahn was right about the industry-
wide panic, the roots of which lay not, as is commonly assumed, solely,
or even primarily, in the politics of patriotism.

In the fall of 1947 studio executives had something bigger than
HUAC to worry about: *United States v. Paramount Pictures,* an antitrust
case before the Supreme Court that had turned decidedly against their
interests (see chapter 2).[10] The government's eventual victory in the
Paramount case in 1948 put an end to the distribution/exhibition guarantees that supported the old studio system.

In the fall of 1947, the House Committee on Un-American Activities
benefited from and capitalized on studio panic over the impending and
inevitable decision in the *Paramount* case by offering a means by which
the studios might continue to control their workforce despite divestiture
and despite the unions. The working relationship between the MPAA
and the committee was less a concession vis-à-vis control of a product
line than a strategy on the part of the studio establishment to regain control over the marketplace, itself in the process of postwar privatization.

When HUAC began its investigation of the movie industry, a new
Hollywood seemed imminent. In concert with the forthcoming decision
in the *Paramount* case, this new Hollywood promised or threatened to
be a place in which talent, suddenly organized, seemingly radicalized,
and soon to be further empowered by the free market engendered by
divestiture, held significant power. It was thus in the best interests of
studio management to find a way to control the industry workforce before it controlled them.

THE JEWS

Please get me the names of the Jews. You know, the big Jewish contributors. . . . Could we please investigate some of those cocksuckers.
—Richard Nixon, former HUAC member,
on the campaign trail, 1972

The Hollywood Ten hearings revealed a tendency on the part of
HUAC and those who shared its politics to conflate communism with

unionism and antiracism. Since the union and civil rights movements were, in the committee's peculiar view of things, Jewish causes, they further conflated communism with Jewishness. HUAC members steadfastly refused to view films or review screenplays, claiming, in a bizarre twist of logic, that communists and by association Jews were smart and insidious and thus the political messages they inserted into films were very difficult (for non-Jews, noncommunists) to discern. The logical extension of such an argument—that the mass audience would be unable to recognize such subtle political content and thus unlikely to be poisoned by such propaganda—never seemed to cross their minds. Or maybe it did. The committee could not explicitly set out to ban films with civil libertarian leanings; it could not legally prohibit or call for the censorship of films about unions or Jews or African Americans. What made the blacklist so effective was that it offered a means by which the government (or by proxy, the MPAA) could censor film content without ever reading a script or viewing a movie.

Six of the Hollywood Ten were Jews: Lawson, Maltz, Bessie, Ornitz, Biberman, and Cole. Of the four who were not, two (Scott and Dmytryk) were responsible (as producer and director) for *Crossfire*, a 1947 antiracist, anti–anti-Semitic film eventually nominated for best picture, best director, and best screenplay Academy Awards.

Crossfire was an important Hollywood film for a number of reasons. It was a provocative and political movie. And it struck a lot of people on the Right as a harbinger of things to come.

Crossfire proved to be the film that most interested the House Committee on Un-American Activities, but its development was quick and untroubled and its production posed few problems for the industry censors. Once the studio gave the project a green light, RKO production chief Dore Schary took the screenplay to Joseph Breen, head of the PCA, which censored films at the time. Breen, a conservative and an anti-Semite, did not express a single concern about the picture's politics. In a memo to Schary, he requested the usual stuff: minimize the drinking, be careful not to condone prostitution, and insert a speech by an army major noting that the killer (a serviceman named Monty) is not typical of army personnel. Otherwise Breen gave the film his okay.

Crossfire tells the story of a vicious, racist serviceman who murders a Jew in what today would be termed a hate crime. Adrian Scott pitched *The Brick Foxhole*, later retitled *Crossfire*, in a 1946 memo to the RKO studio executives William Dozier and Charles Korner as a modest-budget suspense picture prepackaged with A talent. (Already on board were

A scene from the film that most interested HUAC in 1947: *Crossfire*, produced by Adrian Scott and directed by Edward Dmytryk (RKO, 1947).

the screenwriter John Paxton and the director Edward Dmytryk.) After presenting the package to Dozier and Korner, Scott moved on to describe some key changes from story to screenplay: "This is a story of personal fascism as opposed to organized fascism. . . . In the book [on which the film is based] Monty hates fairies, Negroes, Jews and foreigners. In the book Monty murders a fairy. He could have murdered a foreigner or a Jew. It would have been the same thing. In the picture he murders a Jew."[11]

A number of those blacklisted who actually belonged to the Communist Party in the thirties and forties have since remarked that they first turned to the Party because it seemed to support the civil rights movement to a degree that the Democrats and Republicans did not at the time.[12] With *Crossfire*, such a civil rights (if not explicitly Communist Party) agenda was at stake from the start, as Scott himself reveals at the end of the memo: "Dmytryk, Paxton and I want to make this picture for two reasons. First, we are ambitious. We want to make fine pictures. This will make a fine picture. Secondly, and more important, is this: anti-Semitism is not declining as a result of Hitler's defeat . . .

anti-Semitism and anti-Negroism will grow unless heroic measures can be undertaken to stop them. This picture is one such measure."[13]

Dozier and a third RKO executive, Peter Rathvon, responded positively to the film's anti–anti-Semitic message—perhaps cynically, since Hollywood was abuzz with news about Fox's production of a similarly themed picture, *Gentleman's Agreement*. Rathvon concluded his response to Scott's memo by lamenting "the sterility" of "general motion picture production," implying an impatience with the usual Hollywood escapist fare and by extension, the PCA's tendency to censor controversial political content. RKO production chief Dore Schary, himself a former Screen Writers Guild member, expressed interest in financing the film *because* it was politically meaningful.[14]

Schary was an interesting cold war Hollywood player.[15] On October 29, 1947, he was called to testify before HUAC because of his role in the development and production of *Crossfire*. He conceded that RKO had no standing policy concerning the hiring of communists and then went on to say that so long as party membership was not against the law, he saw no reason to develop one: "Up until the time it is proved that a Communist is a man dedicated to the overthrow of the government by force or violence, or by any illegal methods, I cannot make any determination of his employment on any basis except whether he is qualified best to do the job I want him to do." Asked if he would employ Scott and Dmytryk again, Schary stunned the committee by saying yes. So long as they were not proven to be foreign agents, Schary concluded, they would be welcome to pitch their work to him again.

After the Waldorf Statement was issued, the MPAA held a meeting to officially bring the bad news about the blacklist to the membership of the Screen Writers Guild. To soften the blow, Johnston chose Schary to speak on behalf of management. Schary's first words that night, "We do not ask you to condone this . . ." at the time implied his sympathy for his former fellow guild members. But in retrospect we can see that Schary, a Hollywood liberal and a major industry player, risked little by expressing his condolences. For their role in the production of *Crossfire*, Scott and Dmytryk were jailed and blacklisted. Schary continued to find work at the top levels of studio management. Even after his testimony before HUAC, Schary remained in charge of production at RKO. A massive, cost-cutting shakeup at the studio in the spring of 1948 set in motion by RKO's new owner, Howard Hughes, forced Schary's exit. But Schary had little trouble finding a top executive position at a far more healthy studio, MGM, which was run at the time by Nicholas Schenck, who, like Hughes, was an anticommunist and a staunch supporter of the blacklist.[16] Schenck's willingness to work with Schary at a time when one's political affiliations and public statements were so important supports my contention here that the blacklist was only partly about politics. At least where skilled managers were concerned, Schenck was willing to work with a self-proclaimed liberal and blacklistee sympathizer so long as the films he produced made money for the studio.

Though neither Scott nor Dmytryk was Jewish, *Crossfire* proved to be an important film because it seemed so much a product of a Jewish industry. Hollywood, of course, has long suffered its reputation as an industry run by Jews. Efforts to control American cinema date back to the very beginning of commercial production and have often focused on the Jewish question. The Motion Picture Patents Company trust, for example, was formed in 1908 in part to regulate and limit foreign-born Jewish ownership and management in the industry.

In 1920 an item with a Washington, D.C., dateline appeared in newspapers across the country. It spoke for a number of the grassroots censorship organizations active at the time, many of which were affiliated with Catholic or Protestant churches: "The lobby of the International Reform Bureau, Dr. Wilbur Crafts presiding, voted tonight to rescue the motion pictures from the hands of the Devil and 500 un-Christian Jews."[17]

The so-called propaganda hearings of 1941, convened at the urging of two conservative, isolationist senators, Burton Wheeler of Montana and North Dakota's Gerald Nye, revealed the trenchant anti-Semitism that lay at the root of much of the government's interest in regulating the film industry in the 1940s.[18] Encouraged by the Justice Department's early successes in challenging the studio trusts, Wheeler and Nye railed against a Hollywood "propaganda machine" and studios "operated by a central agency." Senate hearings were convened on September 9, 1941, with attention focused on seventeen "war-mongering features," including Charles Chaplin's *Great Dictator* and *Foreign Correspondent*, directed by Alfred Hitchcock and produced by Walter Wanger.[19] The liberal Republican Wendell Willkie was hired by the studios to speak for the MPPDA. Willkie quickly lured Nye into an embarrassing diatribe against the industry's Jews. Nye claimed that the seventeen pictures at issue served the agenda of the Hollywood elite, which consisted, he claimed, exclusively of foreign-born Jews. When Nye added, "If anti-Semitism exists in America, the Jews have themselves to blame," Willkie took the offensive. He argued that Nye and Wheeler had planned to exploit the hearings to discourage "accurate and factual pictures on Nazism" and to "divide the American people in discordant racial and religious groups in order to disunite them over foreign policy."[20]

Willkie successfully embarrassed Wheeler and Nye and in doing so put off further federal scrutiny of the Hollywood product. Wheeler and Nye's anti-Semitism, which fueled their doubts about Hollywood management's patriotism, was poorly concealed and badly timed—the Japanese attacked Pearl Harbor during the hearings' extended Thanksgiving recess and the United States was at war with Germany before the anti-Semitic senators could regroup and respond. But the "propaganda hearings" foreshadowed and foregrounded HUAC's far more successful disruption of studio production and its Jewish workforce after the war.

Wheeler and Nye focused specifically on the apparent political messages in leftist, politically progressive movies. Their concerns about the ideological and economic ramifications of the growing number of social realist films in Hollywood were shared by HUAC as well as grassroots organizations like the Catholic Legion of Decency, the Catholic Knights of Columbus, and the American Legion. As the fight to clean up Hollywood took off again after the war, the Production Code Administration took much of the heat. Unfortunately for the MPAA, the PCA's vague charter—"to uphold the larger moral responsibility of the motion pictures"—sounded good, but regarded fairly narrow issues about film content. Moreover, as an administrative body, the PCA had no authority over the workforce, the ultimate if not ostensible target of cold war film regulation.

A key to Wheeler and Nye's call for political censorship of American films in 1941 was a growing distrust of the PCA, which seemed unable to attend to even the narrowest interpretation of its charter. For example, the 1939 Warner Brothers release *Confessions of a Nazi Spy*, a potent antifascist melodrama, was developed, produced, and released despite PCA opposition.[21] Breen and his fellow censors viewed the project as "a portentous departure" because it was so unlike the usual Hollywood spy picture and also because the talent behind the project was notoriously left-wing: the film was directed by Anatole Litvak, written by John Wexley, and starred Paul Lukas and Edward G. Robinson.[22] After some negotiation, the PCA gave in to Warners and, despite its objections, gave the film its production seal only to have its worst fears realized as a wave of anti-Nazi, antifascist films soon found their way into the marketplace: *The Great Dictator, Pastor Hall, The Mortal Storm, I Married a Nazi.*

Breen had little sympathy for the politics of these films and disliked the men who made them, many of whom were active in the Hollywood anti-Nazi movement.[23] But his opposition to the production of these films did not end (or perhaps even begin) there. Breen was concerned about the impact of these antifascist films in the worldwide marketplace. A film like *Confessions of a Nazi Spy* could not play in Germany, Spain, or Italy in 1939 and complicated matters for other, less political studio films in those same markets. The official PCA memo to Jack and Harry Warner concerning the original script for *Confessions of a Nazi Spy* read as follows:

> Hitler and his government are unfairly represented in this story in violation of the Code. . . . To represent Hitler ONLY as a screaming madman and a bloodthirsty persecutor and *nothing else* is manifestly unfair. . . . *Are we ready to depart from the pleasant and profitable course of entertainment to engage in propaganda, to produce screen portrayals arousing controversy.* . . . Where's the line to be drawn? Why not make [pictures about] the Stalin purges, the Japanese rape of China, the Terror of Spain, etc.[24]

So long as the United States was not (yet) at war, Breen saw no reason why MPPDA films could not still make money overseas. Moreover, Breen foresaw problems with congressional isolationists like Nye and Wheeler and feared that antifascist, interventionist films risked larger, long-term problems with federal regulators, grassroots organizations, and local censorship boards. Breen certainly agreed with Nye and Wheeler about the war and about Hollywood's Jews, but he did not agree with their contention that the government should have a say in the regulation of film production.

Breen appreciated the fact that much of the criticism resulted from a series of well-publicized battles between himself and some well-known producers. A number of films reached the marketplace with the memory of these confrontations fresh in his critics' minds. The release of these antifascist/proto-leftist films seemed to indicate that the PCA had lost its authority or nerve in its efforts to maintain control over studio production.

The PCA's problems were not limited to political films. For example, when Breen refused to grant a seal for the 1941 adult western *The Outlaw*—primarily due to suggestive camera placements that emphasized Jane Russell's breasts—its producer, Howard Hughes, bitterly complained about the proposed censorship as a restraint of trade and criticized the MPPDA code apparatus for prohibiting member studios from distributing movies denied a code seal. Hughes used his battle with Breen to keep *The Outlaw* in the news and successfully brought to light the relationship between the self-regulation of content and the studios' monopoly control of the marketplace. Throughout a two-year battle with the PCA and then still after the film finally got released to some success, Hughes continued to embarrass Breen and the PCA by highlighting (in the press, in ads for the film) the various ridiculous problems he had had with the censors.

Somewhat less ridiculous and a whole lot more problematic were the battles between Breen and a more mainstream industry player, David Selznick, during the development and production of *Gone with the Wind* and *Rebecca*, two big studio films released to huge box office numbers and critical success. Both films reached theaters only after the PCA backed down on several disputed scenes. Selznick's success at the box office with both films suggested that concessions might have to be made again (and again) when big studio money and potentially big profits were at stake.

In a 1939 letter to the *New York Times*, the producer Walter Wanger spoke for many independent and studio producers when he complained that the PCA's "formulated theory of pure entertainment [made] impossible the honest handling of important truths and ideas." Will Hays, president of the MPPDA, responded to Wanger's letter in terms oddly suggestive of Nye and Wheeler's. Indeed, we can see the roots of MPAA cooperation with HUAC in Hays's insistence on maintaining the moral imperative of the production code, despite rogue producers, writers, and directors. "The screen has handled successfully themes of contemporary thought in dramatic and vivid form," Hays remarked, "and presented the subject matter in a splendid entertainment, rather than propaganda."

Eight years later, and just weeks after the Waldorf Statement was issued, Eric Johnston echoed Hays's sentiments, lending his and the MPAA's continued support to apolitical film entertainment. Fully embracing the leverage the PCA attained as a consequence of MPAA cooperation with the feds, Johnston boldly announced, "There will be no more *Grapes of Wrath*, we'll have no more *Tobacco Roads*."[25]

The Jews who managed the studios throughout the thirties and forties were for the most part politically conservative. Nye and Wheeler targeted them anyway, but lost in large part because their timing was bad and because the moguls had the support of the workforce. In contrast, the Jewish producers and screenwriters targeted by HUAC in its various incarnations after 1947 were not so lucky. The very assumptions that characterized Nye and Wheeler's failed confrontation with industry management, the conflation of anti-Nazism with anti-Americanism and procommunism, reemerged in the peculiar logic that underscored the postwar blacklist.

The primary target of the House investigation was a segment of the Hollywood creative community made up in large part of Jews. Jewish managers tried to distance themselves from the fray, but did so at the expense of their faith and ethnicity. The blacklisted playwright and screenwriter Edward Chodorov contends that the relationship between studio management and the Hollywood workforce became strained because the moguls refused to acknowledge their faith and heritage and in doing so seemed to abandon their own. "I became angry," Chodorov writes in retrospect, "at my studio [MGM] and all the studios who insisted that business as usual must go on in Europe [in the 1930s] and that it was none of our business. It was unthinkable to me that Louis B. Mayer, who was a Jew, knew what was happening in Germany . . . unthinkable to me that he would insist nothing was wrong."[26] Such a frustration prompted Chodorov to join the Anti-Nazi League in the 1930s, an affiliation that was enough for HUAC and the MPAA to brand him a communist ten years later.

Nye and Wheeler's claims in the late thirties that Hollywood Jews were pushing us into the war in Europe had fairly wide support in Congress and with the general public. The ever-pragmatic Jewish moguls were as a consequence all the more careful not to make their ethnicity an issue in their films or in their public lives. In 1939 a group of Jewish film actors and actresses, writers, and directors held a press conference and spoke out against Hitler. The only mogul to sign their manifesto was Carl Laemmle, who was very ill and did not live out the year. The other moguls had been warned by the U.S. ambassador to Great Britain, Joseph Kennedy, to keep their politics (and ethnicity) private. The executives' decision not to sign petitions brought to them by talent active in the various anti-Nazi organizations revealed the extent of their fear of anti-Semitism, but it also evidenced their growing distrust of the industry labor force, which was by then in the early stages of organizing. The membership of these newly formed guilds included many of the Jewish film actors and actresses, writers, and directors who spoke out against Hitler. As HUAC would later contend, many of these Jewish film actors and actresses, writers, and directors were either members of or had interests in common with the Communist Party.

The blacklist engaged the subject of patriotism in a number of ways. For the assimilated first-generation American Jewish moguls, many of whom no longer practiced the rituals of their faith, there was no question in their minds that they were Americans first and foremost. A 1998 cable television special based in large part on Neil Gabler's research on the history of the Jews in Hollywood examined just how easily that patriotism was undermined in the late 1940s.[27] The show ends with a sentimental vignette about the last days of the legendary movie mogul Louis B. Mayer, who, after his ouster at MGM, spent his days aimlessly pacing the floor in his house, no studio to run, no idea how it all happened. Though it is hard to feel all that sorry for Mayer, who was a hard man to work for and whose support of HUAC never wavered, the show's parting gesture is apt: once Mayer's ethnicity became an issue, he became a liability to the New York moneymen who controlled the studio's access to production and distribution financing. All Mayer wanted to be, the show contended, was an American. But in the end, the WASP establishment in New York and the American public at large insisted that he was just a Jew.[28]

The moguls' inability to fully assimilate into American WASP culture is an important aspect of this book's story of the decline of the old studio system and the emergence, in its place, of a more anonymous, more corporate new Hollywood. The public perception of Hollywood's Jewishness was for the studios' New York ownership during the cold war essentially a public relations problem. The most efficient way to solve the problem was for the MPAA (with a whole lot of help from HUAC) to enable a purge not only of Jewish union workers but of old-Hollywood Jewish moguls as well.

The Red Scare was a particularly complex and difficult time for American Jews because they were targeted ostensibly for who they were as opposed to what they did. In "Reading the Rosenberg Letters," an essay on two of the most celebrated casualties of cold war anti-Semitism and anticommunist hysteria, Andrew Ross examines just how and why attempts at assimilation provided so little safety for Jews during the Red Scare. The Rosenbergs contended throughout their very public trial that they were just an ordinary American couple. But the feds and the public didn't buy it. At issue from start to finish was, Ross argues, the Rosenbergs' "Jewishness, [which was] still massively identified in the public mind with unpatriotic behavior and opinions." Years before he was indicted, Julius Rosenberg dabbled in Talmudic scholarship; in his youth he had been fairly religious. But by the time he was accused of espionage, he had long since rearticulated his religious beliefs in far more secularized, albeit leftist/communist, terms.

Throughout his jailhouse letters to his wife, Ethel, Julius Rosenberg ruminated over the various connections between his ethnic heritage, his religious training, and the ideology of the American Left. All three sites, Rosenberg argued, extolled the virtues of social and economic justice.[29] The confluence, then, between Jewishness and Communist Party affiliation was less conspiratorial than many at the time believed. Though Ross would hardly draw a parallel between Rosenberg and Hollywood management (someone like Louis B. Mayer, for example), his account of the government's treatment of Julius Rosenberg sheds light on the plight of the Jewish writers, producers, and directors targeted by HUAC and then by the MPAA. Communists and Jews shared some basic precepts about racial and economic justice. Drawing distinctions between the two groups, for the committee and the MPAA, was a matter of semantics, a matter hardly worth worrying about during a time of apparent political and economic crisis.

Ross explores the foundation of anti-Semitism and by extension anticommunism through an extended discussion of Robert Coover's comic novel *The Public Burning*, in which the Rosenberg execution takes on all the hideous splendor of a C. B. DeMille epic.[30] At one point in the tour de force, Richard Nixon contemplates Julius's Death House letters and compares them to his own famous "Checkers speech." Nixon finally rejects the comparison, deciding that his speech was at least the truth—wasn't it? Even he's not really sure. Nixon shrugs, then accedes to the obvious. He doesn't really understand the Rosenbergs at all; Julius and Ethel, Nixon muses, "hung out with people Pat and I wouldn't know how to talk to."[31]

A deft and revealing analysis of the Jewish question in late 1930s Hollywood is laid out in the last few pages of F. Scott Fitzgerald's unfinished Hollywood novel, *The Love of the Last Tycoon*. Monroe Stahr, the studio mogul based loosely on Irving Thalberg, is at one point in the novel depicted as a product of an ethnic heritage: Stahr has "an intense respect for learning, a racial memory of the old shuls."[32] Like a lot of moguls in that era, Stahr has a thing for non-Jewish women, the most recent of whom is a woman named Kathleen Moore, whom he meets during an earthquake. Moore eventually jilts him in a cold-blooded telegram, which Stahr gets to read only after he has perused a stack of other, we gather less important, messages: "At two o'clock when he came from luncheon there was a stack of telegrams—a company ship lost in the Arctic, a star was in disgrace, a writer was suing for one million dollars, Jews were dead miserably beyond the sea."[33] The cable regarding the Holocaust offers ironic counterpoint to Kathleen's terse telegram: "I WAS MARRIED AT NOON TODAY GOOD-BYE." But it also sets up Stahr's next move, a self-destructive meeting with a Communist Party member, as he decides to meet "one of [the] organizers, from New York."[34]

The meeting is reluctantly arranged by Cecelia Brady, the daughter of a rival at the studio. She predicts that the meeting will be a disaster. And it is. The emergence of the CP and the union movement in Hollywood, Fitzgerald accurately predicts, spelled the end for the old tycoons. Stahr, the last tycoon mentioned in the title, has a terminal disease; he will be dead within a year's time. But he is dying in a larger, metaphorical sense; he invites the confrontation with the CP organizer because he knows it's a bad idea. Fitzgerald died before he could write the end of the novel, but his notes project a future Hollywood in which someone quite unlike Stahr, someone less charismatic, less instinctively brilliant, less Jewish, takes over.

Brimmer, the party organizer, arrives only after Stahr has researched the CP first by viewing Russian films from the twenties and then by rereading a two-page treatment of Marx's *Communist Manifesto* penned by someone in the studio's story department. (It is at once comic and revealing that Stahr comes to understand the world almost entirely through the movies and notes handed to him by his staff.) While Stahr maintains the studio's bottom line, Brimmer focuses on two issues: the studio's unsuccessful negotiations with the Writers Guild and the moguls' reluctance to support the Anti-Nazi League. When Brimmer asks Stahr why the producers, most of whom were Jewish, decided not to back the Anti-Nazi League, Stahr bristles and responds, "Because of you people."[35] Stahr has other things on his mind besides Nazis (who are incarcerating and incinerating Jews "beyond the seas"). He knows that if he and his fellow moguls fail to control the CP, someone else (the New York office, the feds) will.

As the meeting gets more tense, Stahr continues to insist that his opposition to the CP is not ideological. The CP and the unions are bad for business, Stahr maintains. Concessions to creative labor will only lead to problems with the various local ratings boards, the Catholic Legion of Decency, and the feds. Stahr presses his point by telling Brimmer a story:

> The best director in Hollywood—a man I never interfere with—has some streak in him that wants to slip a pansy into every picture or something on that order. Something offensive. He stamps it in deep like a watermark so I can't get it out. Every time he does it the Legion of Decency moves a step forward and something has to be sacrificed out of an honest film. . . . It's an endless battle. So now this director tells me [I can't edit his films] because he's got a Directors Guild and I can't oppress the poor.[36]

Stahr's monologue reveals Fitzgerald's keen awareness of the ways labor relations in Hollywood affect other parallel relationships. In this case, a concession to the union causes problems with local and grassroots censorship activists. Stahr is not anxious about increased creative freedom; he has always left good directors alone. He's just convinced that as unions compel management to give *all* writers and directors and actors (more) creative freedom, (self-)regulation of film content becomes more difficult to manage. What the unions want, Stahr suggests, is bad for business, bad not only for management but in the long run for the creative artists as well.

For Stahr, the problems posed by the CP and the unions he assumes are held under its influence concern a battle for control: over himself (he and Brimmer indeed come to blows and Stahr loses the fight and maybe the studio as well), over the product (specific films authored by directors and writers backed by powerful unions), and over the workforce (from directors on down). Fitzgerald cleverly depicts Stahr as at once desperate and insightful. Stahr overreacts, just as the moguls would overreact throughout the forties and early fifties. But Stahr is right about Brimmer and his cronies who are playing a political game that will not only have dire consequences for Stahr and his ilk, but in the end will do little for "the working man."

And he's right in citing the absurdity of well-paid directors, writers, and actors preaching the party line on the poor and unfortunate. Stahr sees the CP and the party/union organizers not so much as dangers to the nation but dangers to the stability of the film industry.[37] As Stahr predicted, organized leftist and in certain instances Communist writers, producers, and directors during and after the war, whether they were Jewish or not, began to develop projects with antiracist themes: *Hangmen Also Die, Cornered, Confessions of a Nazi Spy, None Shall Escape* (scripted by Lester Cole), *Crossfire, Gentleman's Agreement* (directed by the onetime leftist and eventual fink Elia Kazan), and *Pride of the Marines* (scripted by Albert Maltz).

The year 1947 proved to be a watershed not only because of the HUAC hearings but because the 1947 Oscars seemed to celebrate politically themed, serious, antiracist filmmaking: *Gentleman's Agreement* won best picture, best director, and best supporting actress (Celeste Holm), beating out *Crossfire* for the two top awards. The production of Jewish-themed films called attention to Hollywood's Jewishness and as Fitzgerald (via Stahr) predicted, such an affirmation of creative Hollywood's politics and ethnicity prompted swift and firm federal regulation of the studio product.

All ten of the unfriendly witnesses called to appear before the House Committee on Un-American Activities in 1947 requested permission to read a statement into the record. But only two were admitted into evidence.[38] Of the eight statements that were suppressed, five explicitly identified anti-Semitism as a motive behind the inquisition. Virtually all the suppressed statements cited similarities between the committee and (anti-Semitic) fascists in 1930s and 1940s Europe.

When John Howard Lawson took the stand, a heckler audibly grumbled, "Jew." It was an uncomfortable but apt prelude. His statement, which was suppressed, included the following: "What are J. Parnell Thomas and the Un-American interests he serves, afraid of? They want to cut living standards, introduce an economy of poverty, wipe out labor rights, attack Negroes, Jews, and other minorities."[39]

Samuel Ornitz made anti-Semitism an issue in his opening sentence:

> I wish to address the committee as a Jew because one of its leading members [Rankin] is the outstanding anti-Semite in the congress and

revels in this fact. . . . It may be redundant to repeat that anti-Semitism and anti-Communism were the number one poison weapon used by Hitler. . . . I am struck forcibly by the fact that this committee has subpoenaed the men who made *Crossfire*. . . . Is it a mere coincidence that you chose to subpoena and characterize as *unfriendly* the men who produced, wrote, directed or acted in the following feature length pictures and short subjects, which attacked anti-Semitism or treated Jews and Negroes sympathetically: *Pride of the Marines, The House I Live In, Don't Be a Sucker, None Shall Escape, Of Mice and Men, The Brotherhood of Man, The Commington Story, Freedom Road, Body and Soul, New Orleans, The Master Race,* and *The Al Jolson Story*. . . . Therefore, I ask as a Jew, based on the record, is bigotry this committee's yardstick of Americanism and its definition of subversive?[40]

When the committee chairman, J. Parnell Thomas, perused Adrian Scott's opening statement in front of the newsreel and newspaper cameras it left him momentarily speechless; it was, as Thomas himself would describe it, from start to finish a vilification. "I would like to speak about the cold war now being waged by the committee of [*sic*] Unamerican Activities against the Jewish and Negro people," Scott's statement began.

Individually a member of this committee may protest that he is not anti-Semitic. He may say some of his best friends are Jews. . . . Let the committeeman say he is not anti-Semitic. But let the record show he does the work of anti-Semites. . . . This is a cold war being waged by the Committee on Unamerican Activities against minorities. The next phase—total war against minorities—needs no elaboration. History has recorded what has happened in Nazi Germany.[41]

Robert Stripling, the attorney who conducted most of the interrogations, opened his questioning of Scott by referring to the producer as Mr. Dmytryk, a slip that suggests that *Crossfire* was more at issue than the precise identity of the two Hollywood players who produced and directed it.

The analogy to Nazi Germany and to the anti-Semitic political platform that supported the Holocaust appears in several of the suppressed statements, most powerfully and memorably in the closing paragraph of Dalton Trumbo's prepared (and suppressed) remarks:

Already the gentlemen of this Committee and others of like disposition have produced in this capital city a political atmosphere
which is acrid with fear and repression; a community in which
anti-Semitism finds safe refuge behind secret tests of loyalty; a city
in which no union leader can trust his telephone; a city in which
old friends hesitate to recognize one another in public places; a
city in which men and women who dissent even slightly from the
orthodoxy you seek to impose, speak with confidence only in
moving cars and in the open air. You have produced a capital city
on the eve of its Reichstag fire. For those who remember German
history in the autumn of 1932 there is the smell of smoke in this
very room.[42]

When the committee moved unanimously to seek indictments for
contempt of Congress against all ten unfriendly witnesses and brought
the issue to the House floor, Mississippi representative John Rankin,
who had been on the campaign trail in an unsuccessful bid for reelection and had not attended the interrogations, spoke on behalf of the
committee. He opened his remarks by referring to the few congressmen
who spoke in defense of the ten as "traitor(s) to the government of the
United States." He then segued into a brief speech on Hollywood's "attempt to smear and discredit the white people of the Southern States,"
and then produced a petition signed by a number of Hollywood lumi-
naries, condemning the committee. "They sent this petition to Congress," Rankin announced,

and I want to read some of the names. One of the names is June
Havoc. We found from the motion picture almanac that her real
name is Joan Hovick. Another one was Danny Kaye, and we found
out that his real name was David Daniel Kaminsky. . . . Another one
is Eddie Cantor, whose real name is Edward Iskowitz. There is one
who calls himself Edward Robinson. His real name is Emmanuel
Goldberg. There is another one here who calls himself Melvyn Douglas, whose real name is Melvyn Hesselberg. There are others too
numerous to mention. They are attacking the Committee for doing
its duty in trying to protect this country and save the American people from the horrible fate the Communists have meted out on the
unfortunate Christian people of Europe.[43]

The Congress voted 346 to 17 to indict.

ONLY VICTIMS

There is more than one way to lose your liberty. It can be torn out of your hands by a tyrant—but it can also slip away, day by day, while you're too busy to notice, or too confused, or too scared.
—Gregory Peck, actor, 1948

In January 1946, President Truman appointed six Americans to the joint Anglo-American Committee of Inquiry into Palestine. One of them was a prominent Catholic, liberal-Republican attorney named Bart Crum, who a year later would appear at the HUAC hearings representing Adrian Scott and Edward Dmytryk. A veteran of the Committee Against Nazi Persecution (founded by Henry Wallace), the Joint Anti-Fascist Refugees Committee, Citizens for Harry Bridges, the Scottsboro Boys Fund, Independent Citizens Committee of the Arts and Sciences, and founding member and onetime president of the National Lawyers Guild (all Communist front organizations, according to Congressman Thomas), Crum, like the unfriendly witnesses brought before HUAC, had a long and complex history of joining political organizations.

A prevailing political theory at the time, espoused most elegantly by C. Wright Mills, held that while individuals were isolated from real political power by big business and the mass media, some hope for political participation could still be found in collective action—individuals pooling their resources (both intellectual and financial) into what Mills called "publics."[44] Though the members of the committee were hardly devotees of Mills, they seemed very interested in breaking up progressive publics, especially those with access to the mass media in Hollywood or to state power in Washington.

Crum was a politically active attorney and represented a number of prominent left-wing clients: the legendary labor organizer Harry Bridges, and as cocounsel with Wendell Willkie, the CP president William Schneiderman. The committee and the FBI, which hounded the attorney until his suicide in 1959, failed to acknowledge that Crum also represented William Randolph Hearst, Safeway, Pepsi, and Godfrey Schmidt (who with Robert Kennedy's financial and political support tried, unsuccessfully, to wrest the teamsters away from Jimmy Hoffa). The committee and the FBI drew inferences from Crum's more liberal political affiliations, charitable contributions, and legal defenses mounted in criminal and civil actions. (Both Schneiderman and Bridges were hounded by law enforcement for their political activism.)

Additionally alarming to the FBI was Crum's activity on behalf of European Jewish refugees after the war. The FBI got interested in Crum's activity overseas, even though he was sent there by Truman, because it feared growing sentiment in liberal circles on behalf of the Zionist cause—especially in the entertainment industry, where Crum was taking on some high-profile clients, including Rita Hayworth. With Zionism, Hollywood Jews found themselves again compelled to either affirm or deny their Jewishness in public. Rankin's roll call of names reveals his prejudice. But he *was* onto something. Jewish entertainers did change their names. They did hide their Jewishness to fit in.[45]

Zionism was hardly supported by a public mandate in 1947, certainly not in the non-Jewish public. Many Americans were tired of the Jewish question after fighting a war (at least in part) on *their* behalf. The British, our allies who at the time had considerable economic interests in the Middle East, rejected the joint committee's suggestions out of hand (as Albert Einstein, called before the Anglo-American Committee to testify on behalf of Europe's expatriated Jews, had predicted they would).[46] Truman, who set up the committee knowing full well that the British would never agree to any land or sovereignty deal setting up a Jewish state in the Middle East, used the committee to court the Jewish vote, which advisors had told him was essential to victory in the 1948 election.

Crum returned from Great Britain scandalized. After making passionate speeches exposing the horrible conditions in the refugee camps, he earned an inaccurate but indicative label in the press as "a powerful Jewish lawyer." The FBI shared such a sentiment even though the biographical and genealogical data suggested otherwise. As the FBI files read, "[subject Crum] is most certainly a communist or a hidden communist . . . subject always refers to himself as a Catholic or a Republican; obviously a double alibi."[47]

I bring up Crum here because he offers a sobering reminder that what mattered at the time was the public perception of one's private beliefs and values. The most dangerous perception, the most dangerous accusation, regarded Jewishness, actual Jewishness (by blood, by birth, by ethnicity, by belief) as well as membership in the sorts of organizations that fronted for Jewish tendencies or sympathies (membership in the CP and/or the Screen Writers Guild, practicing law, supporting Zionism, having liberal humanist politics).

Though he became a target of the same repressive tactics—blacklisting, surveillance—Crum was, by all available evidence, not only not

Jewish, but not a fellow traveler either. His two Hollywood Ten clients, Scott and Dmytryk, were, at least at the time of the committee hearings, not members of the Communist Party.[48] As liberal activists but not party members, Crum and his clients were conspicuously absent at the party members–only evening sessions when Ben Margolis and other Communist Party attorneys decided that the Ten should refuse to answer questions about party and union membership.

Crum opposed Margolis's legal strategy because he believed that the unfriendly witnesses' refusal to answer questions raised rather than allayed suspicions about alleged conspiracies. Moreover, Crum was suspicious of the party's motives, especially since Margolis seemed content to martyr the Hollywood Ten. Margolis's strategy, Crum correctly concluded, guaranteed contempt citations, and it left Scott and Dmytryk with a difficult choice: they could either tell the committee that they were not members of the party (and in doing so indirectly affirm the committee's right to demand an answer to questions about party affiliation) or go along with a legal strategy that hardly served their interests.

As Patricia Bosworth, Crum's daughter, recounts in her memoir, *Anything Your Little Heart Desires,*

> Just before Eddie Dmytryk took the stand, he and Adrian Scott met hastily with my father. "It had gotten so crazy by then," Dmytryk remembered, "It was out of control—the hearings, the Committee . . . I was disillusioned. I couldn't support it. I told Bart, I just want to stand up there and tell the truth and so does Adrian. And Bart said 'That is wonderful!' We met with the other lawyers and he [Crum] argued passionately about how our silence was going to prolong the anguish. He tried to convince Margolis and the others that we be allowed to break rank, but he was argued down again."[49]

Ironically, neither Dmytryk nor Scott had time to say much of anything on the stand, and both of their statements were suppressed and never entered into the congressional record. When Dmytryk tried to explain his position, he was interrupted by Thomas; the chairman systematically interrupted any testimony that seemed to him to be unresponsive or ideological. When Dmytryk persisted, he was shouted down and cited for contempt.

After serving his prison sentence, Dmytryk broke ranks and testified, the only one of the ten to do so. Both he and Crum were vilified by the CP. Just before his death, Crum also (secretly) named names in a final, desperate attempt to get the FBI off his back and to ingratiate himself with Robert Kennedy, for whom he did some secret business. Dmytryk, who appeared again before the committee on April 25, 1951, named twenty-six names. Included were fellow Hollywood nineteen defendants Adrian Scott, Alvah Bessie, Herbert Biberman, Lester Cole, Gordon Kahn, John Howard Lawson, and Albert Maltz, the director Jules Dassin (*Naked City*), and the writer John Wexley (*Angels with Dirty Faces* and, in collaboration with Bertolt Brecht, *Hangmen Also Die*).[50] Crum named just two names, both CP attorneys: Martin Popper and the architect of the legal strategy for the Hollywood Ten, Ben Margolis.

Liberal (especially civil rights) activism and Communist Party membership were viewed by the committee as crimes distinguished mostly by degree. The CP exploited this point of view often at the expense of the liberal Hollywood Left. Trumbo's legendary "Only Victims" speech, delivered to the Writers Guild of America in 1970, contended that blacklisted artists and informers alike each "reacted as his nature, his needs, his convictions, and his particular circumstances compelled him to . . . [that there was] bad faith and good, honesty and dishonesty, courage and cowardice, selflessness and opportunism, wisdom and stupidity, good and bad on both sides." In the spirit of Christian forgiveness, Trumbo concluded that "in the final tally we were all victims because almost without exception each of us was compelled to say things he did not want to say, to do things he did not want to do, to deliver and receive wounds he did not want to exchange. None emerged from that long nightmare without sin."[51]

Trumbo's speech was meant to be conciliatory, but the implication that the Communist Party had to answer for its role in the wholesale scuttling of the Hollywood Left prompted an immediate reaction from, among others, party hard-liner Albert Maltz: "To say, 'None of us emerged from that long nightmare is without sin' is to me ridiculous. . . . What did people suffer for?"[52] While the question Maltz posed was meant to be rhetorical, it begged an answer several blacklisted Hollywood artists are now anxious to provide. As Paul Jarrico, second in command to Lawson in the Hollywood section of the CP when HUAC first convened, reflected in 1987,

> We underestimated the amount of fear and the quickness with which [the blacklist] spread. . . . I do think there was a fundamental mistake made in the defense of the Ten. Their stand that they were defending

the constitution was justified. But their failure to identify themselves as Communists—those of them who were—certainly let the liberals who had been led to believe that they would identify themselves if they were Communists, off the hook. It gave them a rationale for deserting the ship. But it was a ship they were sailing on too . . . the liberals suffered as much under McCarthyism as the Communists did, in that they lost their freedom to write liberal scripts, even though they themselves were not blacklisted.[53]

THE MPAA

After the shooting [in World War II] stops . . . Hollywood naturally will go back to the business of making films strictly for profit. But it will also do something else. Now that Hollywood has grown up, it knows it must play a role in creating the world of tomorrow, just as it has helped to destroy the world desired by the enemy.
—Robert St. John, *Look* magazine, 1945

The selection of Eric Johnston to run the postwar MPAA revealed just how much the studios were concerned about federal regulation. Like his successor Jack Valenti, Johnston was a Washington, D.C., player, a four-time president of the U.S. Chamber of Commerce. When he was hired to replace Will Hays in 1945 he promised not only to continue Hays's policy of endorsing American business and the capitalist interests that supported and profited from that business, he publicly took the initiative in the evolving cold war. During a well-publicized visit to the USSR as a member of the Economic Policy Subcommittee of the State Department, Johnston told his hosts that "in economic ideology and practice my country is not only different from yours . . . it is more different from yours than any other country in the world. . . . we are determined to remain so—and even to become more so."[54]

With the European theatrical market ripe for the taking in the immediate aftermath of the war, with the ideological cold war for the hearts and minds of free Europe in the balance, Johnston encouraged the studios to develop products that might capture the interest of film-starved audiences across the Atlantic. Johnston believed that film was "the greatest conveyor of ideas—the most revolutionary force in the world," and sought to match a corporate strategy of "dynamic capitalism" to an ideological agenda promoting the American way of life.[55]

In his first year in charge of the MPAA, Johnston established the Motion Picture Export Association (MPEA), a trade organization that merged industry interests in foreign film distribution with the federal government's overseas branch of the Office of War Information (OWI). While the studios had come to expect few easy alliances with the feds at home, the MPEA enjoyed full cooperation from the OWI because it so clearly served the agency's cold war political agenda. The role of the PCA as a subsidiary organization of the MPAA that censored politically unacceptable content in films was paramount to this relationship.

The social problem films that raised the ire of HUAC after the war—*Crossfire, Gentleman's Agreement*, and *The Best Years of Our Lives*—were also the sorts of films that were bad for business *and* public relations abroad. Efforts to curb production of these films and to focus instead on more entertaining and less disturbing and meaningful pictures conceded ground to the committee and the grassroots censorship organizations that demanded that the studios more effectively regulate their product. But these efforts also served the studios' financial interests.

In the first years after the war, studio profits declined from $119 billion in 1946 to $30.8 billion in 1950. Studio revenues decreased by 21 percent, reflecting declining attendance, especially for A features in first-run houses, where the studios made most of their money.[56] Over the same period, Hollywood films dominated the world theatrical market. By 1949, studio income abroad exceeded $100 million. Despite widespread protectionism, especially in Europe, in 1949, 38 percent of the studios' gross revenues came from overseas.[57]

It is no wonder, then, that Johnston embraced the ideological war waged during the blacklist era; simply put, it was good for business. Sold out in the process of waging that war was a workforce exceedingly well represented by Jews; Hollywood in the 1940s was indeed managed (but not owned or controlled) by Jews, and the creative workforce, especially the Screen Writers Guild (the target of HUAC more often than not), included a large percentage of Jewish members. The battle lines were drawn between the feds (fronted by a committee that included two anti-Semites: Rankin and Nixon) and the Hollywood creative community *and* more importantly between the WASP/New York/Wall Street establishment that in all practical economic terms ran Hollywood at the time and a frightened, dare we suggest self-loathing Jewish managerial class afraid of losing their jobs, their six-figure salaries, their women, their tables at posh restaurants.[58]

What was at stake in the blacklist era was control over the film industry. That seemed clear enough at the time, but the press, much of which was critical of HUAC even as it conducted its investigation, more often than not focused on the notion that the government actually wanted to censor films. Maybe it did, but the feds never had to because Johnston and the MPAA (through the PCA) were all too happy to do it for them.

In 1947 the MPAA was farsighted enough to understand that its cooperation in HUAC's ideological witch hunt was a means toward an end. As the Waldorf Statement so clearly reveals, battle lines were never drawn between the MPAA and HUAC. Instead, HUAC afforded the means by which the MPAA could deal with its problems with talent and by extension the guilds, agents, and lawyers who represented talent. More important, HUAC set the stage for a confrontation between the New York offices (which supported the MPAA and its president, Eric Johnston, whom they handpicked) and the erstwhile moguls who no longer could be trusted with control over an industry with so much potential but so many problems (with the Justice Department, with competing popular audiovisual media, with its notoriously politicized workforce).

Some members of the press understood the stakes as early as 1947. Writing for the *New York Times*, the film critic Bosley Crowther wrote: "It should be fully realized that this action [the MPAA's capitulation to HUAC] was engineered by the major New York executives, the industry's overlords, and not the Hollywood producers, who form a different and subordinate group."[59]

The studios' complicity and collusion with HUAC and with each other in the late forties seems a first and important affirmation of a growingly conglomerized and multinationalized new Hollywood. A quick look at Moody's Index (of corporate holdings and interests) reveals that in 1947 the studios were in partnership with and ostensibly answerable to big business. Paramount ran on Coca-Cola money; RKO on funds from United Fruit; Fox on capital from General Foods.[60] The Hollywood Ten were sacrificed because they were bad for business—a business that was no longer (just) about making movies.

THE UNIONS

Ninety-nine percent of us are pretty well aware of what is going on.
—Ronald Reagan, HUAC hearings testimony, 1947

In 1945 a tense and ultimately violent conflict between the Hollywood workforce and management took place at the Warner Brothers studio. Two years later Jack Warner testified as a friendly witness before the House Committee on Un-American Activities. Lawson, Trumbo, Maltz, and Scott (four of the Hollywood Ten) all publicly supported the striking workers in the confrontation at Warners. Lawson so infuriated Jack Warner that when the executive testified before the committee, he introduced into evidence a picture of Lawson talking to strikers on the line.

During the 1930s labor disputes were largely handled in-house; contracts were subject to "a basic agreement" overseen by the Motion Picture Academy.[61] If an actor, for example, filed a grievance for breach of contract, the Actors' Adjustment Committee (manned by four prominent actors and one industry executive) or an actor-producer relations representative mediated the case. The system was set up less to protect either side from the other than to protect the industry from poor public relations. Few cases won by labor were ever appealed by management (a total of eight in five years). As academy president William C. DeMille remarked in 1930, the committee maintained a four-to-one split in favor of labor in order to show support for and confidence in the mostly equitable relationship between labor and management. The studios were willing to live with the arrangement because they believed that few actors, directors, and writers would ever want or need to seek contract arbitration.

Critics of the Hollywood Ten and the Communist Party in Hollywood in the thirties are quick to point out that the CP was first attracted to the movie business not so much because it was interested in using films for propaganda purposes but because it had failed to exert its influence virtually everywhere else. The relatively late emergence of unions in such a high-profile and lucrative industry provided the CP with an opportunity it simply could not afford to miss. In a scathing review of Victor Navasky's well-respected blacklist study, *Naming Names*, Richard Schickel (who produced the highlight reel of Elia Kazan's films screened on Oscar night 1999) argues,

> In those days, when the economy was smaller—when Hollywood was, compared to other industrial complexes, larger and perhaps more significant than it is now (in the Thirties it was always in the top ten, from the point of view of sales, right up there with steel, autos and

other heavyweights)—its unions were a great prize. If, through a strike you could bring so rich and visible an industry to its knees, then a faction like the Communists could look to be more powerful than it actually was.

The industry's most successful and important "friendly witness," Elia Kazan, clutching his 1954 best director Oscar for *On the Waterfront*, a film that implausibly celebrates the nobility of ratting out your friends.

Its insinuation into the labor movement in Hollywood, Schickel argues, was something of a last stand for the party that ended once and for all with the HUAC hearings in 1947.[62]

Schickel argues throughout the review that work on the blacklist tends to be politically myopic, that historians tend to focus on two over-simplified images: the heroic martyr and the self-serving fink. He agrees with Trumbo that there were "only victims," then adds that on both sides there were also victimizers. Schickel contends that the party undermined the Hollywood Left through its insistence on secrecy: "If a group is open about its membership, it is damned difficult to persuade people it is conspiratorial, let alone subversive . . . [the CP's] insistence on inviolable secrecy about their activities had as much to do with creating the blacklist (lending credence to the argument that they must have been up to something nasty) as the Committee itself did."[63]

Movie executives understood that organized labor posed a distinct threat to the basic agreement and the system of self-regulation the Motion Picture Academy had managed so quietly and effectively. That someone or some political party from outside the industry might want to disrupt labor relations significantly complicated an already complex moment for the studios. Several of the "friendly witnesses" who testified before HUAC expressed concern about "outside agitators" stirring things up.[64] Industry management at the time was so desperate to hang on, they were willing to deal, even though it seemed to invite federal censorship of their product, even though it forced the moguls into complicity with a profoundly anti-Semitic congressional committee.

But it wasn't the CP or union activists or any other outside agitators who first precipitated the abandonment of the basic agreement. The academy system first showed signs of vulnerability as early as 1933 during the Bank Moratorium declared by President Roosevelt.[65] This first big fissure in worker-management relations, this first big break in faith, came not as a result of outside agitation or workforce organization, but from panicked short-term thinking on the part of studio ownership.

The Great Depression made even routine banking a difficult enterprise, particularly bad news for an industry so dependent on credit. The Bank Moratorium seemed to foreshadow an even more desperate crisis: the possibility that for an indeterminate period of time, the studios would be unable to secure short-term loans to finance production and distribution. Moreover, film executives had reason to believe that the Bank Moratorium was just a first step toward increased federal regulation from the Roosevelt administration. After all, Roosevelt was hardly shy about interfering with other lucrative industries and had displayed an interest in using the media to hawk the ideology of the New Deal.

Supporters of Roosevelt administration policies and members of political organizations who supported or were sympathetic to that administration were the first and easiest targets of HUAC. Studio executives encouraged such a payback. They supported the committee's attack on FDR's legacy because they believed that the New Deal had been bad for business: it made banking more complex and difficult, it supported the breakup of the studio trusts, and it protected workers' collective action and unionization.

When Roosevelt introduced the moratorium, the Motion Picture Academy instituted an arrangement between management and labor by which, from March 4 to April 30, 1933, fees and salaries were deferred or reduced. The agreement required the studios to resume full pay for full-time work after the eight-week moratorium expired, but once the moratorium went into effect, executives began to hedge on the time line. An unidentified executive admitted to the trades that "there is little chance of any of the slashed salary percentages being returned until the country's box offices reflect a decided up movement."[66]

Between 1931 and 1933, studio payrolls were cut 60 percent, from $156 million to $50 million. Approximately ninety thousand employees lost their jobs.[67] The moratorium was designed to give ailing businesses time to develop new strategies. The studios used the time-out to breach existing employment, option, and development agreements with actors, directors, and writers. Studio employees appreciated that in the absence of enforceable contracts, they would be unable to recover fees in the event that studio management continued to cut payrolls and costs. To protect labor against such a likely management strategy, the Motion Picture Academy empowered its Emergency Committee to compel a studio, if a survey of its books warranted it, to resume full payment of salaries and fees before the eight-week moratorium period was up. The accounting firm of Price, Waterhouse and Company, eventually made famous on telecasts of the Academy Awards, was retained to audit the studios' books. But when Price, Waterhouse recommended to the Emergency Committee that Warners should resume full payments in advance of the eight-week moratorium date, studio ownership, in direct opposition to studio management, refused to comply with the Emergency Committee's decision.

Conrad Neagle, the academy president at the time, was aware of the ramifications of Warners' refusal and sought a compromise. He prevailed on Will Hays, himself a veteran of studio deals involving self-regulation, to intervene. But the appeasement strategy backfired; the labor force at Warners understandably resisted any deal that diminished the power of the academy's Emergency Committee. Neagle resigned in disgrace and Darryl Zanuck, the legendary production chief at Warners, quit and withdrew his membership from the academy.[68] Zanuck recognized that the studios were powerful and profitable primarily because competition within the industry was so carefully and completely (self-)regulated. The contract system worked only because *all* the studios agreed to participate and follow a mutually advantageous set of rules.

When Warners refused to pay up after an impartial audit suggested it should, the studio undermined the academy and the collusive industry the basic agreement protected. When the academy proved too weak to protect its interests, industry labor sought alternatives, many of which leaned way to the Left, many of which, once and for all, redefined talent as labor and industry relations between labor and management as adversarial.

The lone exception to Hollywood labor's move to the Left in the early 1930s was the Screen Actors Guild (SAG). From its beginnings, SAG was a very different sort of movie industry union. Unlike the Screen Writers Guild, which mostly consisted of anonymous screenwriters, the leadership of the Actors Guild was made up of movie stars, larger-than-life celebrities who made astronomically high salaries. Early on, SAG benefited from its celebrity leadership. By 1937 SAG got the studios to agree to a 90 percent closed shop and established employment standards designed to protect lower-paid actors. A few years later, SAG established a fully closed shop; all studio features were cast entirely with union actors.[69]

SAG's success with studio management was from the start tied directly to the box office clout of its celebrity leadership. The rank and file—actors who had little bargaining power on their own—were as a result dependent on stars to bargain on their behalf. After the war, as box office problems loomed, star actors became even more indispensable to studio production and star agents emerged to exploit the situation for their star clients. These agents replaced SAG as the primary means of protecting the interests of the most powerful, productive, and influential screen actors.

As SAG became less and less useful to star actors in their negotiations with studio management, star actors used SAG primarily for public (as opposed to industrial) relations. They did so for pragmatic and selfish reasons. Much like the studio executives who paid them, star actors had a lot riding on box office revenues; indeed, by 1947 agents had begun tying star compensation to box office grosses. The first in a series of sellouts by SAG's postwar leadership involved an alliance with the promanagement, (at one time) mob-run International Alliance of Theatrical and Stage Employees (IATSE). The alliance put SAG at odds with the other independent unions in Hollywood, all of which had allied with the Conference of Studio Unions (CSU), and placed SAG leadership at odds with its rank and file as well.

From 1946 to 1947, beginning with the armistice and ending with the HUAC hearings, IATSE was purged, or at least appeared to purge itself, of mob involvement. By the time Thomas convened the HUAC hearings, the leadership of IATSE was much like SAG's: devoutly anticommunist, antistrike (IATSE members signed a no-strike pledge in 1945), and promanagement.

The HUAC apologist Ronald Reagan, along with other SAG board members Robert Montgomery, George Murphy, and Leon Ames, complied with the committee from the start because they shared its ideology and also because they accepted the larger argument that cooperation with the committee was good for business. As SAG board member Leon Ames so starkly put it at the time, "I believe we must approve [the termination of studio contracts with the Hollywood Ten, as elaborated in the Waldorf Statement] from a public relations standpoint, if nothing else." For Ames, it was up to the guild's celebrity actors to "protect the economic welfare of the industry."[70]

Reagan was no less cognizant of the public relations crisis set in motion by HUAC. When he took the stand as a friendly witness at the committee hearings, Reagan took the opportunity to extol the virtues of the anticommunist "majority" in the industry and cast the problem posed by Hollywood communists and leftists as a threat to democracy and the free enterprise of the movie business:

> within the bounds of democratic rights, we have done a pretty good job in our business of keeping those [communist] activities curtailed. . . . We have exposed their lies when we came across them, we have exposed their propaganda, and I can certainly testify that in the case of the Screen Actors Guild we have been eminently successful in

preventing them from, with their usual tactics, trying to run a major-ity organization [SAG] with a well organized minority.[71]

The 1945 strike at Warners highlighted the increasingly bitter struggle between the two powerful industry "unions": the CSU (run by Herb Sorrell, a much-named name during the HUAC hearings) and IATSE (led from its inception by gangsters like Willie Bioff; in 1945, IATSE was managed by Roy Brewer, a Reagan compadre and vocal anticommunist). When the CSU organized the strike at the Warner Brothers studio, IATSE helped management hire scabs and then supported the studio's use of tear gas and high-powered water hoses on picketing strikers. The strike dragged on for eight months. As the strike fund depleted, some members of the CSU joined IATSE in order to get back to work. The strike not only pitted labor against management, but laborer against laborer.

Two years later, when the MPAA established the blacklist, it did so with the support and organizational help of Roy Brewer and IATSE. Brewer and SAG president Ronald Reagan became close friends and political allies during the blacklist era. In 1984, despite (or because of) Brewer's history of complicity with industry blacklisting and strike-breaking, President Reagan appointed Brewer chairman of the Federal Service Impasse Panel, which arbitrated disputes between federal agen-cies and unions representing federal workers.[72] The larger political legacy of the blacklist can be found first in the so-called silent majority of the Nixon era and then again in the steady move to the Right during the Reagan-Bush years.

When Jack Warner appeared as a friendly witness before HUAC, his presence alone revealed his support of the investigators. But his tes-timony was pretty hard to follow. It is worth a look anyway because it includes a hilarious digression about the Warner Brothers film *Mission to Moscow*, the development of which Jack blamed on his brother Harry.[73] A far more useful witness was Walt Disney, himself also the vic-tim of a bitter strike at the start of the 1940s. After a long review of Dis-ney's resume—as if anyone in America at the time needed to be intro-duced to their Uncle Walt—HUAC cocounsel H. A. Smith cut to the chase: "As a matter of fact, Mr. Disney, you experienced a strike at your studio." Following Smith's cue, Disney named names: Herbert Sorrell and the animator Dave Hilberman, the two men who organized Disney animators.

For six months in 1922, Hilberman attended the prestigious Leningrad Art Theater, which Disney vaguely remembered as the Moscow Art Theater. That educational experience, along with his membership in the union and professional meetings with Sorrell, proved enough to get Hilberman fired at Disney, blacklisted in the industry, and hounded by the FBI into the early 1960s. Disney used his testimony not only to get back at Hilberman but to offer commentary on the labor movement.[74] "I know I have been handicapped," Disney mused, "out there in fighting it[75] because [the communists] have been hiding behind this labor set up, they get themselves closely tied up in the labor thing, so that if you try to get rid of them they make a labor case out of it."[76] Arthur Babbitt, a senior animator and pro-unionist, did just that. When Disney attempted to fire him for his union activity, Babbitt took his case to the NLRB. Disney was ultimately forced to pay Babbitt back wages plus a hefty penalty.

The nine-week strike at Disney was a turning point for the company.[77] The negative publicity attending the strike mitigated against long-held notions of amiable relations between supposedly dedicated animators and their Uncle Walt. It also, as things played out, marked the end of the studio's golden age; the animation unit never regained its prominence, at least during Walt's lifetime. Walt Disney's subsequent moves into theme park operations and television—a harbinger of things to come in the entertainment industry—were driven as much by necessity as creative vision. Once he was forced to capitulate to the Cartoonists Guild, Disney lost interest in making movies.[78]

For those who participated in the strike, for those who knew Disney during the war years, his testimony at HUAC came as no surprise. As the biographer Marc Eliot depicts him, Disney was a vindictive boss with decidedly reactionary right-wing politics. Along with his attorney Gunther Lessing, throughout the 1930s Disney attended meetings held at the houses of American Nazi Party members and appeared at rallies for "America First," posing for photographs alongside the group's figurehead, the Nazi sympathizer Charles Lindbergh. Leni Riefenstahl told Eliot that Disney told her he admired her work and briefly considered hiring her. Eliot reports on a meeting between Henry Ford and Disney at which the automobile executive praised Disney for his success in a business otherwise dominated by Jews. According to Eliot, Ford advised Disney to sell his company outright before considering a public offering (of stock), because Wall Street was controlled by Jewish investment interests. During the war years, Disney made animated films in support of the war effort. And while Disney would later exaggerate his contribution to the cause, Eliot maintains that Disney resented every second he had to deal with "that Jew," secretary of the treasury Henry Morgenthau, whose job it was to oversee the budgets on films made for the War Department.[79] At a time when affiliations, memberships, friendships, even casual conversations defined who you were in all sorts of important ways, Disney's record in the 1930s and 1940s speaks volumes.

Less than two months after the Disney strike was settled in labor's favor, the California state legislature mounted the so-called Little HUAC hearings. When the hearings were convened by California state senator Jack Tenney in July 1941, the first witness called to testify was CSU president Herbert Sorrell, the man responsible for unionizing the Disney studio workers.

The unfair labor practices at the Disney studios resulted from a paternalistic system in which rewards and punishments were distributed according to the whim of Walt Disney. When more senior and in some cases fairly well paid animators like Babbitt and Hilberman joined the strike force, Disney viewed their action not in terms of labor relations but as a personal betrayal. It is important to understand that Disney viewed his workers as children not so much or not only because he felt he knew what was best for them, but because he was, like the Jewish moguls who managed the other studios, an entrepreneurial capitalist. The unions ushered in a new way of doing business that at once professionalized labor relations and rendered obsolete the more personal, entrepreneurial, paternalistic style that characterized management at virtually all the studios. Like the other moguls (most of whom he despised), Disney found that his way of doing business came abruptly to an end in the 1940s.

The Red Scare did not mark the beginning of increased federal regulation of Hollywood. To the contrary, the last four decades in the entertainment business have seen a systematic erosion of antitrust regulation and enforcement and the evolution of a rating system, supervised by the MPAA, that with little concern for free trade, regulates participation in the various markets now routinely exploited by the conglomerate-owned studios.[80] The blacklist taught the studio membership of the MPAA that when they worked together they could turn a sow's ear—how else can we describe the HUAC hearings?—into a silk purse. And they have never looked back since.

The brief Waldorf Statement delivered on behalf of the MPAA on November 24, 1947, the very day the House voted to approve contempt indictments for the Hollywood Ten, revealed the economic bottom line of the blacklist: "we will forthwith suspend without compensation those in our employ and we will not re-employ any of the ten until such time he is acquitted or has purged himself of contempt and declares under oath that he is not a Communist."[81] MGM immediately suspended Trumbo and refused to pay him $60,000 in fees (per his contract). Lardner was fired by Fox and Dmytryk and Scott were dumped by RKO. All told, over three hundred writers, directors, producers, and actors were blacklisted between 1947 and 1957.[82]

The breaking of contracts, the refusal to pay fees for scripts that were optioned, developed, and/or produced before the fall of 1947 prompted a number of civil suits that dragged on well into the 1950s and 1960s and helped establish the very acrimonious relationship between Hollywood management and talent that continues to today.

Hollywood is an industry run by agents and lawyers; it's a common lament these days. It's true. And one need only look back to 1947 to understand why.

2

Collusion and Conglomeration in the Movie Business

THE 1948 *PARAMOUNT* decision briefly broke up the studios' monopoly control over the production, distribution, and exhibition of motion pictures. It forced the studios to sell off some of their theaters, thus making it more difficult for them to place or license their films for exhibition. The theaters were in themselves valuable real estate. Selling the theaters not only affected industry policy and procedure, it significantly hampered the studios' ability to borrow money (to make movies). The theaters were collateral even in the worst of times. New movies, even in the best of times, were not.

By the fall of 1947, the studios were convinced that they were going to lose the *Paramount* case. Their panic in Washington, their capitulation to HUAC, revealed a desperate economic situation that seemed to require a significant albeit temporary and symbolic ideological concession to certain key players in the federal government.

The new regulations proposed in the government's suit against the studios could not have come at a worse time. Market research, much of it financed by the studios after the war, heralded significant expansion in the leisure/entertainment industry. But while such an expansion promised good times for the larger American economy, the studios' inability to expand—their inability to even maintain control over certain segments of their own sector of the entertainment industry—suggested that such a prosperity might come at their expense. For the studios, postwar prosperity promised increasing competition from better-run and -financed concerns in the recording, radio, publishing, and television industries.

Just how much the regulations forthcoming in the *Paramount* case would hamper their ability to compete was the single biggest question facing studio ownership and management at the very moment the House Committee on Un-American Activities issued its first subpoena. Because the economic situation was complex if not dire, the stakes of the coincident ideological cold war were raised. Gordon Kahn, one of the "Hollywood nineteen," suggested as early as 1948 that widespread fear of divorcement/divestiture was a prime motivator in the MPAA's decision to implement a blacklist. "[The] owners and controllers of the motion picture industry [the New York executives] may be frightened men too," Kahn surmised. "They are frightened of change and their fear is a cold, calculated fear." Kahn predicted that the imminent economic crisis would dramatically affect product supply and prompt stricter regulation of (especially politically charged) film content. "The real controlling interests of this industry," Kahn concluded, alluding to Adorno and the prevailing Frankfurt School Marxist line on pop culture, "[are] interested first in making money from films. But they are also interested, and perhaps increasingly so, in using films as both a medium to protect their privileges and their plans for expanded markets, and as a soporific or escape valve for people who might otherwise read or think at home, or talk over high prices and what to do about them with neighbors or fellow-workers."[1]

Kahn's conflation of business and ideology reveals his Communist Party ties. But he nonetheless fairly accounts for the fact that the *Paramount* decision was about more than just market share and industry (self-)regulation. The government's effort to break up industry trusts compelled the studios to redefine themselves and in the process develop new modes of doing business. The *Paramount* decision threatened what Kahn termed the studios' "basic motivation" to establish and maintain monopoly control over motion picture production, distribution, and exhibition. The apparent "retreat of the motion picture industry" during the 1940s—its capitulation to the committee, its surrender of market share to other pop culture industries and to smaller film companies, its abandonment of the studio system after the emergence of the industry guilds and talent agencies—was in Kahn's view "not a retreat at all, but a ruthless, aggressive advance, against all that the people want and expect of Americanism and democracy."[2]

Kahn's sense of drama reveals the heat of the moment and his screenwriter's imagination. But his account proved prescient nonetheless. While divestiture briefly interrupted studio operations and forced the majors to regroup, it made not only possible but necessary new ways of thinking about and implementing production and distribution. These intellectual and methodological changes at the studios made possible and ultimately inevitable the multinational, conglomerate, monopoly system that we now call the new Hollywood.

The blacklist, a dramatic and ugly instance of workforce regulation, was in large part an effort by the studios to control one aspect of the business at the very moment another aspect—industry operations/relations—was in the process of radical restructure. It is important to remember that both the blacklist and the *Paramount* case were rooted in prewar America. The blacklist took shape in large part as a reaction *against* the New Deal. The *Paramount* case seemed only to finish a job begun by a Justice Department appointed by and working with the support of President Franklin D. Roosevelt.

Throughout his tenure in office, Roosevelt not only encouraged the Justice Department's efforts to break up the studio trusts, he also supported workers' collective action and unionization, the ostensible problems solved by HUAC and the MPAA-enforced blacklist. When Roosevelt died in office just as the war was coming to an end, the studios had reason to fear that their relationship with the federal government might even get worse. Harry Truman, who succeeded Roosevelt, had led a Senate investigation of the major studios, one closely tied to the Justice Department's case against Paramount.

The Justice Department's resumption of the *Paramount* case under Truman was part of a larger federal regulatory effort to combat studio consolidation and expansion after the war. Television promised a new delivery system and exhibition format for audiovisual product. In an effort to keep the studios from (more) freely accessing this new medium, the FTC and FCC refused as a matter of policy to grant TV licenses to the studios. The federal agencies contended that any sort of studio ownership or control over television exhibition would inevitably result in a restraint of free and fair trade.

The FTC and FCC bans on film studio intrusion into the television industry were based on the notion that television was primarily an alternative or second-run exhibition format. In direct and obvious ways, the FTC and FCC operated in concert with the Justice Department and its efforts to force the studios to divest their interests in theatrical, first-run motion picture exhibition.

The war's end brought with it the promise of a new Hollywood, the shape of which in 1947 seemed to depend on an increasingly complex and profoundly unstable relationship between the studios and the federal government. This was not altogether bad news. The industry's failure to make peace with the feds at home was accompanied by a strategic and harmonious relationship abroad.[3]

The studios resumed foreign distribution of their movies in 1944, well before the war was over. By war's end, the same federal agencies that had overseen the production and distribution of wartime propaganda films cooperated with the MPAA to establish for the studios an ideological and industrial presence abroad. It is ironic that by war's end the Wheeler and Nye hearings into movie propaganda seemed all but a distant memory; so long as the propaganda was of the sort endorsed by the government, the studios enjoyed little federal interference in their overseas operations.

But the lessons learned during the war years about the persuasive power of the cinema fueled domestic censorship efforts during the late 1940s and 1950s. The PCA's Joseph Breen, the industry's chief censor, had sided with senators Nye and Wheeler in 1941 because he agreed with them. Nye and Wheeler were anti-Semitic and so was he. Nye and Wheeler railed against politically controversial pictures because they were bad for America; Breen tried to obstruct the release of the very same films because they were bad for business.

After the war, an even greater priority was placed on establishing a position in foreign markets. The Office of War Information (OWI) made life easy for the MPAA overseas so long as the PCA made sure that the studios continued to make the sorts of films the OWI could endorse. The MPAA's subsidiary organization, the Motion Picture Export Association (MPEA) earned the nickname "Little State Department."

Like Breen, MPAA president Eric Johnston appreciated the importance of foreign markets after the war. He also understood the value of a continued good relationship with the OWI and the State Department. Johnston attempted to exploit MPEA and PCA cooperation with the OWI in the industry's ongoing conflict with the Justice Department, the FCC, and the FTC. There is no evidence that Johnston had much success with the Justice Department, but the MPEA/OWI relationship proved to be a very successful venture for the studios in the first years after the war. Foreign distribution accounted for a significant percentage of overall industry profits, an especially important consideration given the decline in domestic studio revenues after 1948.

The relationships fostered by the MPEA with the Commerce Department and the Justice Department came at a price. The complex network of political relationships that seemed necessary to industry profitability made film content vulnerable to government regulation. The key question then is, how important was film content to the studios anyway? As a matter of policy the PCA, which was overseen by the MPPDA and then by the MPAA, censored overtly political films.

Industry wisdom at the time was that "anti-American" pictures did little business at the box office and made for poor public relations at home and abroad. It is important to remember that Johnston, Breen, and many of the New York executives and stockholders who controlled the studios were as fervently anticommunist and anti-unionist as the House Committee on Un-American Activities. The seeming surrender of creative freedom during the cold war jibed with industry interests. The political censorship that resulted from the congressional hearings was a matter of quid pro quo.

HUAC's interest in regulating political content on film coincided with PCA policy at the time. Breen's vigilance with regard to politically sensitive material implied the PCA's willingness to do the committee's dirty (and busy) work for it. In exchange for PCA vigilance, the committee effectively criminalized organized labor and political activism in the workplace, briefly solving workforce problems set in motion by the collapse of the studio system in the last years before the war. MPAA complicity with HUAC enabled the studios to appear patriotic at the very moment the Justice Department was insisting that their business practices and products were bad for the country and the postwar economy.

UNITED STATES v. PARAMOUNT PICTURES

Let me give you some facts of life. . . . Every Friday, the front door of this studio opens and I spit a movie out onto Gower Street. . . . If that door opens and I spit and nothing comes out, it means a lot of people are out of work—drivers, distributors, exhibitors, projectionists, ushers, and a lot of other pricks. . . . I want one good picture a year . . . and I won't let an exhibitor have it unless he takes the bread and butter product, the *Boston Blackies*, the *Blondies*, the low-budget westerns, and the rest of the junk we make.

— Harry Cohn, head of production, Columbia Studios

The film industry has been controlled by monopoly interests since 1908, when the Motion Picture Patents Company (MPPC) linked the interests of ten production companies: Edison, Biograph, Vitagraph, Essanay, Kalem, Selig Polyscope, Lubin, Star Film, Pathé Freres, and Kleine Optical.[4] The trust effectively exploited Edison's and Biograph's respective patents on motion picture technology to fix prices, restrict the distribution and exhibition of foreign-made pictures, regulate domestic production, and control film licensing and distribution. The trust was supported by an exclusive contract with the Eastman Kodak company, the principal and at the time only dependable provider of raw film stock.

The MPPC deal with Kodak was announced on December 18, 1908, the same day the MPPC agreement was formalized. The MPPC became possible—it became immediately effective—because it presented not only a vertical but also a horizontal monopoly. By the end of 1908, the MPPC companies owned and controlled the technology and maintained exclusive access to the raw material necessary to make movies.

The MPPC trust enabled the early cinema production companies to expand and enhance their facilities; in 1909 virtually all the MPPC members built bigger and better studios, updated their labs, and streamlined production. The trust guaranteed profits for the MPPC membership and at the same time standardized their product lines. The MPPC provided a hint of things to come—of trust arrangements and industry collusion in general that would come to characterize the studio era.

The first big problem for the MPPC arose in February 1911, when Kodak, a key player from the start but one without a distinct profit interest in the trust, exploited a clause in the original agreement and began to sell film stock to independents. These independents were by then also organized into a combine of sorts: the Motion Picture Distributing and Sales Corporation (the Sales Company). Carl Laemmle, William Fox, and Adolph Zukor, who headed this second wave of movie entrepreneurs, attacked the MPPC trust on a number of fronts. Laemmle et al. established affiliations with rival film exchanges (the Sales Company colluded with the Greater New York Film Exchange, the MPPC with General Film), they introduced an alternative product (the Sales Company backed feature-length motion pictures, the MPPC maintained strict reel and time limits on its short-film productions),[5] and they challenged in court the exclusive patent control and the various related, collusive arrangements between the MPPC and other industry groups.

In August 1912 the first of a series of suits challenging the MPPC's business operation was decided in the independents' favor as the Supreme Court overthrew the Latham Loop patent formerly controlled by the Biograph company.[6] The decision enabled the independents to use formerly restricted equipment; as a result, their product could look as good and as professional as the MPPC's. The opinion handed down by Justice Learned Hand implied that other similar patent restrictions exploited by the MPPC might not survive a legal challenge either.

Later in 1912, Fox filed suit against the MPPC, charging restraint of trade. The suit was eventually settled out of court. At the start of the following year, the U.S. Justice Department filed a similar suit. The government's petition went directly to the point: "On or about April 1910, defendants set out to monopolize the business of all rental exchanges in the United States, their purpose being to drive out of business all persons so engaged and to absorb to themselves the profits theretofore made therein."[7]

The suit dragged on. By the time the Court decided the case in 1918, Kalem, Star Film, General Film, Biograph, and Edison were all pretty much out of business and the so-called independents, who themselves had gained power through collusion and vertical and horizontal integration and monopoly agreements, became the dominant players in the marketplace.

A second pivotal court case, *Binderup v. Pathe Exchange*, attending this second generation of motion picture trusts reached the Supreme Court in 1923.[8] *Binderup* struck many in the industry at the time as similar to a 1922 case, *Federal Baseball Club of Baltimore, Inc. v. National League of Professional Baseball Clubs*. In the baseball case, the Court held that because major league baseball "was neither interstate in nature nor commerce in the constitutional sense" it was exempt from antitrust regulations. But to the moguls' surprise and disappointment, in *Binderup v. Pathe Exchange* the justices concluded that the studio film industry was significantly different from the sports entertainment business and thus held that federal antitrust laws were fully applicable.[9]

United States v. Paramount Pictures was first filed in July 1938 in federal district court in New York. The government held that the studios systematically maintained monopoly control over every aspect of the development, production, distribution, and exhibition of motion pictures. The suit, however, focused on fairly narrow issues with regard to industry ownership and collusion in theatrical exhibition.

The Supreme Court's eventual decision in the government's favor some ten years later compelled the studios to divest their interests in movie theaters and to cease certain industry practices that unfairly inhibited free and fair trade in the presentation of their films to the public. This divestiture, or divorcement, came at a significant cost. Throughout the thirties and most of the forties, the studios made a whole lot of money and ably protected their products in the marketplace through ownership and manipulation of movie theaters. By the time the case reached the Supreme Court in the late 1940s, the so-called Big Five studios—MGM, Paramount, RKO, Twentieth Century Fox and Warner Brothers—held controlling interest in about 2,600 theaters nationwide. Their holdings accounted for 17 percent of the national total, and it was the *right* 17 percent. The Big Five controlled or owned approximately 80 percent of the urban first-run theaters where a vast majority of the money was made on their pictures. All told, in 1947 the big studios controlled exhibition in seventy-three of the top ninety-five American cities, where they not only screened their own pictures but cut collusive deals to showcase choice films produced and distributed by their competitors.[10]

The urban theaters were also valuable as real estate, and the Big Five studios routinely used that value as collateral in the financing of film production and studio operations. The government's threat to studio ownership of these theaters thus involved more than just the loss of exhibition revenues and the loss of control over which theaters would screen studio product. It also promised to undermine their primary means of attaining financing, indirectly and eventually forcing the studios to find other sources of capital through arrangements (mergers, for example) with better-capitalized, better-diversified companies.

A January 1939 article in the *Wall Street Journal* proclaimed that the studios' "high, wide and handsome days [were] coming to a close."[11] Even this early on, the studios seemed inclined to agree. From the start, their defense strategy in the *Paramount* case had little to do with the issues at hand. Instead, the studios endeavored to stall, to put off the decision for as long as they could. In the first twelve months after the Justice Department's filing, industry attorneys secured thirteen trial postponements, after which the Big Five and the Justice Department agreed to sign an interim "consent decree" to further forestall the inevitable.

The decree, signed on October 29, 1940, suspended the government's suit. It addressed certain inequities in the marketplace and put in place a system by which conflicts between theater owners and the Big Five studios could be arbitrated. But as the government came to understand, and as the independent theater owners of the Motion Picture Theater Owners Association (MPTOA) repeatedly pointed out to them, the 1940 decree did little to undermine the studios' monopoly control of the marketplace.

While a brief domestic box office surge after the U.S. entrance into the war kept independent theater owners happy and quiet, government attorneys quickly lost enthusiasm for the first consent decree and started to question whether "discrimination" against independent theater owners could be "remedied by measures short of divorcement."[12] Their answer to that question was revealed in the asking: no.

As the decree neared the end of its first year, the studios were hit with a series of setbacks. First, they hoped that the *Paramount* case would continue to be suspended and the ineffective consent decree maintained as part of a government policy to exempt from antitrust regulations those industries cooperative in the war effort. But attorney general Thurman Arnold, who seemed to understand how little the consent decree actually accomplished, announced that such a policy would not include the film industry. The studios then negotiated with the MPTOA on their own and hammered out an agreement, the United Motion Picture Industry (UMPI or Unity) plan. The plan closely resembled the consent decree, though it was a little more complicated and seemed to afford theater owners a bit more choice. Arnold summarily rejected it. Insisting that "more and more competition must be shown," Arnold allowed the 1940 consent decree to expire.[13]

Significantly worse news for the studios came in 1944, when the Supreme Court rendered its decision in a case involving the Crescent Theater circuit.[14] The suit alleged that the Crescent Theater chain monopolized exhibition in a five-state area and colluded with the majors for favorable terms on big films. Two other suits—one against the Griffith and another against the Schine chains—hinged on the decision in the case against Crescent. In all three cases the larger antitrust and restraint of trade issues concerned standard operating procedure for theater chains and the major studios in virtually every U.S. metropolitan area. These issues were also relevant to the ongoing negotiations between the Justice Department and the Big Five studios to find a compromise in the *Paramount* case. When the Supreme Court upheld the decision of the lower court and insisted on the breakup of the Crescent circuit of theaters, it implied its support for the basic premises of the government's argument in the *Paramount* case and thus significantly diminished the attorney general's interest in settling with the studios for anything short of divestiture.

In December 1945 Paramount was named in another antitrust suit as the Justice Department challenged the studio's proposed expansion into television. This proposed expansion into a parallel, potentially lucrative exhibition format prompted the attorney general to accuse the studio of attempting to "[create] a world cartel and domestic monopoly." The FCC, which moved swiftly to block Paramount's expansion, defended its position by citing its authority to pull licenses and refuse applications from companies "found in violation of antitrust laws." But as the studio's attorneys pointed out, their clients had not yet been found in violation of antitrust laws. The government's argument in the Paramount TV case, they noted, seemed to take as a foregone conclusion a decision in their favor in *United States v. Paramount Pictures*.[15]

At the very moment Paramount decided to fight the FCC, a three-judge panel made a preliminary ruling that unsettled things significantly, albeit temporarily. To pretty much everyone's astonishment, the court agreed only in part with the Justice Department and took issue with the attorney general's contention that exhibition was necessarily the problem. "It would seem unlikely," the court concluded, that the studios, "having aggregate interests of little more than one-sixth of all the theaters in the United States are exercising such a monopoly of the motion picture business that they should be subjected to the drastic remedy of complete divestiture in order to effect a proper degree of free competition."[16]

The preliminary decision seemed to encourage the studios to invest even more in exhibition; it called for them to make clear their interests in urban theaters, to either sell off the theaters they owned in part or purchase them in full. Competitive bidding was mandated and price fixing was outlawed.

Despite its booking policy restrictions, the preliminary decision was much better than the studios had come to expect. The key issue of theater ownership was decided in their favor; the bottom line, after all, was the value of the theaters as property, as capital. The court seemed to share the Justice Department's larger argument that the studios were in fact trusts and went fairly far in its decision to insist on free, or at least freer, trade in the licensing process for the exhibition of movies nationwide. But the possibility that the government's suit had focused on the wrong sector of the industry certainly made things more interesting when attorney general Tom Clark finally took the case to the U.S. Supreme Court.

The panel's surprise finding ran counter to a series of related decisions in suits filed by independent theater owners against the major theater chains and by extension the studios that either owned or conspired with those theaters to restrain free trade. The Jackson Park Theater in Chicago, for example, was awarded treble damages in its suit against the major theater circuit in that city. A similar ruling was issued in a case filed by the William Goldman Theater against the Warner-Stanley chain in Philadelphia. The decisions were bad news for the studios for a number of reasons, not the least of which was that other independent the- aters in Detroit, Baltimore, Memphis, and St. Louis were so encouraged by the rulings that they too filed suit against the studios and/or the the- ater chains that engaged in restrictive trade practices.[17]

In 1948 came the realization of the much predicted postwar box of- fice slide, especially in the urban, first-run market. The timing, for the studios at least, could not have been worse. In the spring of 1948, just as the disappointing box office numbers were first made public in the trades, the Supreme Court agreed to hear arguments in the *Paramount* case. Two closely related suits filed by independent exhibitors (*United States v. Griffith* and *Schine Chain Theaters v. United States*) finally found their way onto the Court calendar as well.[18] The spring term of 1948 promised to be significant for the industry; after ten years of stalling and a little give and take, the fate of the studio trusts seemed once and for all in the balance.

In decisions handed down on May 3, 1948, the Court decided against studio interests in *United States v. Paramount Pictures, United States v. Griffith,* and *Schine Chain Theaters v. United States.* Justice William O. Douglas's opinion in the *Paramount* case made clear the Court's view that the studios were indeed trusts and that the only avail- able remedy to the situation was divestiture.[19] The Court found that the defendants in the case (Paramount, RKO, Warner Brothers, Fox, Loew's/MGM, Columbia, and Universal, which produced and distrib- uted films to selected theaters owned "independently," and United Artists, which at the time just distributed films) had indeed "conspired to restrain and monopolize and had restrained and monopolized inter- state trade in the distribution and exhibition of films."

The Court focused first on price fixing, finding that two forms of this practice persisted: "a horizontal one between all the defendants" and "a vertical one between each distributor defendant and its li- censees." Consistent with its findings in *Binderup v. Pathe Exchange* in 1923, the Court chose to view the movie business as fundamentally like other big industries in which restraints of trade were all too com- monplace and illegal. For example, in his discussion of price fixing, Douglas cited a related case involving the gypsum industry. In *United States v. Gypsum Co.,* the Court maintained that "the rewards which flow from the patentee and his licensees from the suppression of com- petition through the regulation of an industry [price fixing] are not reasonably and normally adapted to secure pecuniary reward for the patentee's monopoly."[20] The same was true, Douglas concluded, of the rewards of the copyright owners and their licensees in the *Paramount* case: "For here too the licenses are but a part of the general plan to suppress competition."

The "incontestable" consequence of price fixing, the regulation of minimum prices for each run in a film's general release, was viewed as a restraint of trade, "a concert of action" that clearly violated the spirit and letter of the Sherman (Antitrust) Act. "It is enough that a concert of action is contemplated," Douglas concluded, "and that the defendants conformed to the arrangement."

Run clearances, a standard industry practice that favored first-run houses by assuring them first and regionally exclusive access to big studio films, were found to be unlawful. The various pooling agreements between affiliates—arrangements under which ostensible competitor-exhibitors operated in collusion in order to share in the profits of a given film's run—were also found to be unlawful because they too, as Douglas put it, enabled the players to act "collectively rather than competitively."

At the time of the decision, Paramount owned joint interest (with so-called independents) in 993 theaters, hence its name was listed first in the suit. Warner Brothers owned 20, Fox 66, RKO 187, and Loew's/MGM 21. Additionally, the studios jointly owned theaters with each other: Paramount-Fox owned 6, Paramount-Loew's 14, Paramount–Warner Brothers 25, Paramount-RKO 150, Loew's-RKO 3, Loew's–Warner Brothers 5, Fox-RKO 1, Warner Brothers–RKO 10.[21] The Big Five held interests in 3,137 out of 18,076 theaters nationwide. In the ninety-two cities with populations exceeding 100,000, over 70 percent of the first-run theaters were affiliated with the Big Five.[22] These holdings and the various pooling arrangements were used to maintain the system of run-zone clearances as well as widespread price fixing in the first-run marketplace. Douglas referred to these various pooling relationships as the "fruits of monopolistic practices or restraints of trade" and concluded that nothing short of divestiture would remedy the situation.

Writing for the Court, Douglas also outlawed "formula deals" or "master (franchise) agreements," the pooling arrangements in which theater chains paid a single guarantee for a film and then spread that expense among a number of affiliated theaters showing the same picture.[23] Formula deals operated to the distinct advantage of the circuits.

A theater chain got access to choice studio features for a lump sum guarantee (to be shared by all its theaters) that easily exceeded what an independent could pay to screen the film at a single venue. The studios benefited as well, as they could book a picture at a number of first-run theaters under one simple agreement.

Block booking, the licensing of one (choice) feature on the condition that the exhibitor also license a number of other features distributed by the studio over a specified period of time, was regulated but not outlawed in preliminary consent decrees. The 1940 decree, for example, limited blocks to five (studio-selected) features; the UMPI compromise allowed blocks of twelve under a revised system in which theaters could select films from a list supplied by the studio. The *Paramount* decision outlawed the practice entirely, enjoining the defendants "from performing or entering into any license in which the right to exhibit one feature is conditioned upon the licensees taking one or more other features."

Block booking was integral to the collusive relationship between the studios and the circuits. It unfairly disadvantaged the independent theater owners and thus made them all the more dependent on whatever informal, extralegal relationship they might be able to establish with the studios. The independents could not compete with chains paying pooled guarantees for blocks of pictures. Nor could they refuse to enter into block booking arrangements for fear of getting cut off by any one of the studios. The chains, on the other hand, guaranteed the studios a range of screening options across a specific region. Many of the circuits virtually controlled key geographic areas. So long as the circuits could pool their resources, the studios routinely "cleared" their films first with the chains before offering them to the independents.

Columbia Pictures, which produced and distributed movies but did not own any theaters, petitioned the court for an exemption from block booking restrictions. Justice Douglas's response to the petition revealed the extent of his distrust of the studio system as a whole and his refusal to view studio collusion in terms of degree: "Columbia Pictures makes an earnest argument that enforcement of the restriction as to block booking will be very disadvantageous to it and will greatly impair its ability to operate profitably. But the policy of the anti-trust laws is not qualified or conditioned by the convenience of those whose conduct is regulated."

The Court was also troubled by the studios' creative accounting of revenues earned from block booking deals. Because films were booked as a package, revenues earned by the initially more attractive films in a given block were difficult to distinguish from revenues earned by less desired or desirable films included as part of the multi-picture arrangement. The Court, which continued to view movies as primarily if not exclusively a mode of commerce instead of art, maintained that the measure of quality, of success, of a given film was simply a matter of performance in the marketplace.

Block booking, Douglas opined, gave inferior products unfair advantage: "Where a high quality film greatly desired is licensed only if an inferior one is taken, the latter borrows quality from the former." The notion of "borrowed quality" is key here, as Douglas was far less interested in artistic quality than earning power. In the late forties, stars were increasingly contracted to receive a percentage of, or "points" on, the profits of certain films. Block booking deals spread profits among the specified group of films and thus made percentage calculations difficult and often inaccurate. Such creative accounting not only affected specific percentage deals, it undermined future negotiations. Star fees depend on previous box office records, on a star's proven ability to "open" or "carry" a film. When revenues were shared by a group of films, stars and their agents had trouble proving the star's worth to the studio.

The more general, ruminative sections of Douglas's opinion reveal a contempt for the conspiratorial and collusive relationships that prevailed in Hollywood at the time. Though Douglas conceded that "the judiciary is unsuited to affairs of business management," he concluded that it would be far worse to leave "the management of the system to the discretion of those who had the genius to conceive the present conspiracy and to execute it with the subtlety which this record reveals."[24]

The Justice Department raised a First Amendment argument in its brief for the case. Douglas, a strict civil libertarian especially on free speech, welcomed the opportunity to write on the subject even though he found the argument at best tangential: "The question here is not *what* the public will see, or *if* the public will be permitted to see certain features. It is clear that under the present system the public will be denied access to none." At issue then was where and when a feature might be screened—in what sort of theater, in what sort of run—and how its exhibition might come to define, prefigure, or somehow regulate audience reception. Block booking and pooling arrangements, according to Douglas, unfairly skewed the marketplace but at the same time established a system in which choice features as well as films released without much studio enthusiasm had relatively equal chances with the national audience. Block booking assured virtually all the films in a given block access to screenings at first-rate, first-run theaters.[25]

Free speech, Douglas cannily observed, was in cinema a matter of access (products to venues, venues to patrons, etc.). In his opinion in the *Paramount* case, Douglas weighed the importance of commercial divorcement against the ways the block booking system guaranteed free access and, ironically, free trade and speech for lesser or at least less enthusiastically promoted studio films. Douglas believed that cinema was mostly a form of commerce and thus gave priority to commercial regulation.

Douglas understood that in a more competitive market the studios would be compelled to treat different films differently—to secure first-rate venues only for films *they* liked best. But he could take heart that as an immediate consequence of the *Paramount* decision, studio and ex-hibitor commitment to the production code diminished. The produc-tion code worked because all the studio members of the MPPDA/MPAA agreed to follow the PCA's "advice." Theater owners, before 1948 at least, participated in the PCA-studio arrangement because they were tied to the studios through either ownership, collusion, or de-pendency. Independent theaters who contracted studio products were prohibited from screening movies that did not have a PCA seal. The penalty for defying the prohibition was a $25,000 fine (levied by the MPAA, a studio-run public relations organization that had no direct power over and operated independently of any input from the nation's exhibitors).

In his opinion, Douglas deemed these fines unconstitutional on an-titrust as opposed to First Amendment grounds, though both seemed to apply. The vast majority of the films released without a PCA seal, Dou-glas understood, were independently produced and distributed. The practice of fining theaters booking these films significantly inhibited the screening of pictures produced and distributed outside the studio sys-tem. The PCA fine system, Douglas logically concluded, amounted to a restraint of trade.

Whether the production code itself was constitutionally pro-tected—whether the studios could legally defend their system on First Amendment grounds—was left for another day (though Douglas's po-sition on that subject was available for any who would listen). The more narrow commercial issues in play in the Court's decision in the *Para-*

mount case implied that so long as the code depended on industry collusion and restrained free and fair trade it could not be enforced should
a theater, newly made independent through compulsory studio divestiture, want to screen films that either could not or did not receive a
PCA seal. The PCA, which operated only so long as collusive arrangements were maintained between one studio and another and between
the studios and the nation's theater owners, became after 1948 significantly less effective as a means of regulating film content and the daily
operation of the film business.

In the concluding section of the opinion, Douglas dismissed industry claims that the studio system was not devised or designed (primarily) with monopoly control in mind. Douglas argued that "specific intent" was beside the point so long as "monopoly results as a necessary
consequence of what was done."

"Size is itself an earmark of monopoly power," Douglas wrote, "for
size carries with it an opportunity for abuse." Such a conclusion continues to ring true with regard to the huge conglomerates that control
the industry today far more completely and effectively than their 1948
predecessors ever did.

ON TV

It seems as if you can't even go to the bathroom in Hollywood without
asking MCA's permission. What upsets me most is the way people tell
me that MCA says, "Nobody in Washington can touch us."
                                        —Frederick W. Ford, FCC commissioner

The implementation or enforcement of the *Paramount* decision coincided with a steady decline in box office revenues, a 43 percent drop
from a high of $1.7 billion in 1946 to $955 million in 1961. Over the same
period, television revenues increased significantly. By 1961 the TV signal reached almost 90 percent of the population.[26] Because it was accompanied by bad times at the box office and the emergence of a competitive new medium, the precise economic aftershock of divestiture remains difficult to chart.

The box office decline surprised no one in the industry. It was worse
than most expected, but that had much more to do with shifting demographics, vastly expanded leisure, competitive pop culture industries

(TV and then rock and roll music and the various youth-oriented industries that accompanied it), and moribund studio production (of films no one seemed to want to see) than with divestiture.

Though the FTC closely regulated investment in the television industry, by the mid-1950s the studios began to establish a variety of commercial relationships with the networks. By 1955, MGM, Twentieth Century Fox, Warner Brothers, and the Walt Disney Company all produced shows for television. The shows put to use otherwise dormant production space on the studio lots and moreover helped increase the studios' visibility. Each show carried its studio's name in its title: *The MGM Parade*, *The Twentieth Century Fox Theater*, *Warner Brothers Presents*, and *Disneyland* (later retitled *Walt Disney Presents*). The studios used the television shows to advertise forthcoming features, merchandise, and amusement parks.

Disney's move into television seems especially significant and interesting. After the 1941 strike and the studio's continuing labor problems after the war, Walt Disney endeavored to diversify. Though he did so in exasperation after losing a number of his more senior animators to post-strike acrimony and HUAC, the move proved timely. In 1952 Walt asked his brother Roy, who managed the money for the studio, to help him convince the corporate board to finance a new sort of amusement park: Disneyland. Roy was against the project from the start and came back from his meeting with the board with just ten thousand dollars. In order to finance the building of the park, independently of his brother and the Disney company board, Walt formed a strategic alliance with the smallest of the three TV networks, ABC, which agreed to back the Disneyland amusement park project in exchange for a percentage of its future profits and a weekly television show. The ABC/Disney deal was one of the first industry agreements to cross media lines. The establishment of connections between three different entertainment venues— film, television, and amusement parks—suggested that potentially lucrative ancillary markets, or at least ancillary venues, awaited the studios at the very moment box office revenues were in decline.[27]

Having lost their first-run theaters, the studios found in television an opportunity to effectively control or at least successfully contract for subsequent, second-run screenings of their movies. Features released before 1948, most of which would not have been screened again in theaters anyway, were offered to the networks under fairly simple licensing or sales agreements. These agreements worked very much to the advantage of the studios. Few pre-1948 contracts (with talent, with independent producers) were drawn up with ancillary exhibition in mind.

In post–*Paramount* decision Hollywood, stars became even more important to a film's (and by extension, a studio's) success, but they were no longer necessarily under contract to a specific studio. To attract stars to a movie project, studios negotiated deals with agents, who increasingly demanded profit-sharing points for their clients. Once sales to TV were a matter of routine, residual schedules were drawn up so that stars got a piece of the TV action as well.

The obligation to pay residuals seemed like bad news at first. But the evolving postwar studios quickly came to use television contracts and residual schedules as a negotiating tool, as a means of securing and compensating talent, and as a means of financing and developing motion pictures. The promise of future residuals—and moreover the promise of a television sale (at a time when the networks so needed product they bought virtually anything)—provided the studios with a means of deferring payment to stars and guaranteeing revenue at the end of a film's initial run.

By the time television was well enough produced and available in enough households to provide any real competition to the studios, the two media were inextricably integrated. Today, virtually all the studios have their own TV divisions; their products move freely and fluidly from one medium to another, making money for the parent company at every stop along the way. While the *Paramount* decision compelled the studios to divest their interests in urban first-run theaters, it encouraged them to establish new sorts of synergies, to view the larger entertainment marketplace in much the same way they had viewed the movie business before 1948.

The loss of their theaters, the development of complex new ways to finance films, and the necessity to establish working, synergistic relationships with other media required more capital than the studios had on hand and a far more expansive corporate vision than studio management seemed able to muster at the time. Diversified conglomerates that were in the process of expanding into new markets had the capital to secure the sorts of relationships necessary to reestablish the industry's profitability. These companies had executives with the vision to see film production and distribution as part of a larger and potentially more lucrative entertainment landscape.

Though industry revenues were down, the value of the studios was fairly high, especially to these outside investors. The studios' film libraries, long thought of as just inventory, after 1948 could be exploited on television. Studio lots were valuable as real estate, especially in booming Los Angeles. The studios had little or no debt; films were routinely financed on short-term money and repaid out of film revenues. And thanks to HUAC and the various consent decrees, studio stock prices were down. Companies interested in expanding their holdings were presented with a rare opportunity in a time of economic boom to take advantage of an undervalued stock.[28]

The first in what became a series of corporate buyouts involved MCA/Revue Productions and Universal. MCA, which was founded by Jules Stein in the 1920s, began as a music talent agency.[29] In the early 1940s, largely under the direction of Stein's ambitious protégé Lew Wasserman, MCA began representing movie stars. By 1950 Wasserman had more talent under contract to MCA than any studio. As a result, Wasserman was in a position to package films. He developed movie projects, attached MCA talent to them, and then sold his product to the highest bidder. For his trouble, Wasserman got a percentage of every MCA client's pay and, in the case of stars, a percentage (of the client's percentage) of the profits of the MCA packaged film.[30]

Just as Wasserman and MCA were emerging as forces to be reckoned with in Hollywood, Universal CEO J. Cheever Cowdin retired and a struggle for control of the publicly traded studio began. Victory came fast and first to Decca Records president Milton Rackmil, who planned from the start to institute synergies (collusive, monopoly relationships) between Decca's holdings in the music industry and Universal's interests in film.

But Decca's control over the studio was short-lived. In February 1959, MCA bought Universal City (the studio facility formerly owned by Universal Studios), ostensibly in order to streamline television production for the MCA subsidiary Revue Productions. At the time, Revue produced approximately a third of NBC's prime-time lineup. These TV shows featured, for the most part, MCA talent, an arrangement that proved profitable for the agency. The MCA purchase of Universal City was a mixed blessing for Decca and Universal Studios. The deal brought much-needed cash to support studio production, but it made Universal vulnerable to takeover and dependent on MCA for production facilities, which the agency leased to its former owner.

MCA eventually bought out Decca in 1962 and in its first year in control, the former agency sported record profits. Wasserman ably exploited strategic relationships between a variety of media to establish profitability for the studio. The Justice Department, which opposed MCA's purchase of the studio, forced Wasserman and MCA to divest its interests in the talent agency business. But by then, MCA-Universal no longer needed its talent base. By the time it took over Universal, MCA had become a model for the new studio system as it sported a variety of synergistic relationships. Under Wasserman's direction, MCA-Universal was a film and television production plant, a motion picture distribution company, a familiar trademark, but more so it was a multimedia company that fully exploited a larger vision of the entertainment marketplace.

The MCA-Universal deal set in motion a tide of conglomerate investment in Hollywood. Gulf and Western Industries bought Paramount in 1966. Charles Bluhdorn, the legendary CEO of Gulf and Western, established relationships between various entertainment divisions: film, television, book and magazine publishing, and professional athletics. But the bulk of his holdings was in other industries. Through its first few years in operation, the entertainment companies accounted for only 11 percent of the multinational's gross revenues.[31]

Both Warner Brothers and United Artists turned to conglomerate ownership in 1967. Warner Brothers merged first with Seven Arts (a Canadian film and television distributor) and then with Kinney National Service to form Warner Communications. United Artists followed Paramount's lead and sold out to a non–entertainment industry conglomerate, Transamerica, a San Francisco–based insurance company.

As the conglomerates swept into Hollywood, they swiftly instituted a variety of corporate practices that were consistent with their non-film holdings—a dependence on market research, the development of fewer, more predictably profitable product lines (fewer, blockbuster-style films)—which exploited relationships with various other conglomerate holdings (merchandising, publishing, TV). When people finally got back into the habit of going to the movies in the 1970s, the top four studios in terms of market share were Warner Brothers, Paramount, Universal, and United Artists, the first four companies to secure conglomerate ownership.[32]

UNITED STATES v. CAPITOL SERVICE

In [the] communication [business] if your company does not grow and consolidate with others, then you run the risk of lacking the outlets to justify spending for a quality product. By consolidating, you can sell your product to your network, to your cable channel, as reruns, as merchandise, as overseas product. There are now so many more ways to get paid.

—Alan Schwartz, investment banker, on the Disney acquisition of Capital Cities/ABC

Despite dramatic industry expansion and diversification through the 1970s and the first half the 1980s, the Justice Department maintained keen interest in protecting the basic, if narrow, restrictions established in the landmark *Paramount* decision. In 1985 these protections came once again under scrutiny in *United States v. Capitol Service.*[33] The case involved a civil antitrust action filed against four theater chains—Capitol Service, Kohlberg, Marcus, and United Artists—which together controlled 90 percent of the exhibition business in the Milwaukee area. The four theater companies entered into a collusive arrangement in which they agreed not to bid on certain films in order to maintain exclusive runs for choice titles in specified geographic zones. In industry parlance this was called a "split agreement," because it involved the split or allocation of negotiation rights for films. Such splits effectively reduced—in the case of the Milwaukee area, eliminated—competition, thus insuring licensing terms advantageous to the exhibitor.

The *Capitol Service* case was important to the conglomerate studios. This time around, their interests were actually served by the government's case. The anticompetitive scheme maintained by the Milwaukee split resulted in regional price fixing, which operated very much to the studios' collective disadvantage.

The stakes in the case involved more than just the Milwaukee pooling arrangement or even the larger practice of splitting elsewhere in the United States. The case was in many ways a showdown between the divorced theater circuits, many of which were struggling, and the conglomerate studios, which were making money as never before. The Milwaukee split was on its surface an anticompetitive scheme. But as such it betrayed the desperation of the exhibitors, all of whom seemed to agree that the only way for them to make money was to pool their resources.

The government's argument in the suit was similar to the one that prevailed in the *Paramount* case. The Justice Department argued that the split (which established its own zone clearances and skewed the bidding process) was collusive in nature and represented a restraint of trade. The breakup of the split, the government argued as it did in 1948, would open up the theatrical marketplace, increase competition, and by extension create the sort of product differentiation that would benefit the filmgoing public.

A United States circuit court decided the *Capitol Service* case in the government's (and the studios') favor, agreeing with the lower court decision that splits deny the studio distributor "a chance of entering into meaningful negotiations for the licensing of a film at a theater other than the split designee because other theaters have been designated for other films."[34] The decision explicitly outlawed the practice of splitting nationwide and drove a wedge between the studios and the theaters. It also seemed to suggest that while the Justice Department and the courts were still prepared to tackle antitrust issues in certain film industry sectors, they were either unaware of or unwilling to tackle far larger and more obvious violations perpetrated by the conglomerate owners of the new Hollywood studios.

The decision in the *Capitol Service* case proved devastating for the nation's exhibitors. In 1986 alone, 4,357 screens changed hands, and the studios were involved in a vast majority of the purchases. In a two-year period—1986–87—MCA/Universal purchased the Plitt, Septum, Essaness, Sterling, and Neighborhood Theater chains as well as a 50 percent stake in the huge Cineplex Odeon chain—a total of over 2,500 screens. Columbia purchased the Walter Reade Theaters; Tri-Star (owned in part by Columbia Pictures Industries) picked up the Loew's, Music Makers, and United Artist Theaters; and Gulf and Western/Paramount bought the Trans-Lux, Festival, and Mann Theaters (which it added to its ownership of the Famous Players chain and its coownership, with MCA, of Cinema International).[35] Despite its success in outlawing the theater circuit splits and its apparent continued concern for the regulation of theatrical exhibition, the Justice Department announced in July 1986 that it would not oppose the studios' move back into the movie theater business.[36]

The announcement fueled further expansion in the industry. By the end of 1987, ten companies controlled over 50 percent of the first-run, showcase screens, a situation reminiscent of the good old days before the first consent decree in 1940.[37] As Richard Trainor concluded in *Sight and Sound* at the end of 1987, "Representatives of the new Hollywood may insist that monopoly is the last thought on their minds, but many independent producers and exhibitors remain skeptical. They see further theater acquisitions on the horizon, fewer independently produced and distributed pictures, a re-establishment of the majors' power over all aspects of the industry."[38]

The government's perseverance in the *Capitol Service* suit suggested a continued interest in protecting the film exhibition market from collusive/monopoly arrangements, but as things played out, only with regard to companies within the sector. The *Capitol Service* decision made the theater chains vulnerable to acquisition and the conglomerate studios took full advantage of the situation. Exactly why the Justice Department failed or refused to challenge the studios' move back into theatrical exhibition is a question I wish I could answer here. The effect of its failure or refusal is, alas, far easier to chart.

THE KERKORIAN DECISION

[Kerkorian] seems to view a written contract as the beginning of a negotiation.

—Fay Vincent, former executive, Columbia Pictures

People call me a raper and a pillager, and that's not how I want to be thought of.

—Kirk Kerkorian, entrepreneur, 1996

On April 25, 1979, *Variety* published a piece tracking a series of fairly confusing stock moves by MGM CEO Kirk Kerkorian.[39] First, Kerkorian sold 297,000 shares of his MGM stock. Then, with the proceeds of the sale, Kerkorian secured a $38 million loan, which he then used to finance the purchase of a block of stock (amounting to 24 percent of the publicly trading shares) in a rival studio, Columbia Pictures Industries (CPI). The moves enabled Kerkorian to become the largest shareholder in two of the six major studios at the same time.[40]

Kerkorian insisted from the start that he had no interest in running Columbia Pictures; he was just making an investment in a company that, like another company he owned and controlled, just happened to make movies. Management at CPI and attorneys in the antitrust division of the U.S. Justice Department saw Kerkorian's stock moves in a far different light. Citing antitrust as well as federal trade violations, the Justice Department filed suit in federal court. The suit set in motion a confrontation between federal regulatory agencies and a very new sort of Hollywood player, the outcome of which changed the movie business in dramatic and so far it seems irreversible ways.[41]

The Justice Department suit called for Kerkorian to divest interest in one of the two film companies. On August 7, 1979, the opening day of the trial, Judge Andrew Hauk set the government attorneys back on their heels by challenging them to prove "actual Kerkorian intent to meddle in Columbia's affairs," something that the government attorneys were unprepared and unable to do.[42]

The key to the Justice Department's argument was that Kerkorian's purchase of such a large block of CPI stock amounted to a hostile move on the company and that his potential dual ownership of both MGM and CPI created a "diminution of competition" that promised to significantly disadvantage exhibitors. But when pressed by Judge Hauk, none of the exhibitors brought in by the Justice Department to testify could cite a single example in the four months after Kerkorian's stock move to suggest such an anti-competitive scheme. In fact, the exhibitors testified that they had little choice with regard to product in any event, no matter who owned or controlled the major studios.

Columbia CEO Herbert Allen proved of little use to the government case either. While other Columbia executives like Fay Vincent (who eventually left Columbia to become the commissioner of major league baseball) and Frank Price vented their frustration with Kerkorian in the trades, Allen was more philosophical. When called to testify, Allen downplayed the significance of Kerkorian's stock purchase, remarking that while he would have preferred a standstill agreement (an agreement not to buy any additional stock) that held for ten as opposed to just three years, he felt confident that Kerkorian had no "current anti-competitive scheme." Allen then pointed out that the primary problem was not with Kerkorian's dual ownership, but rather with how that dual ownership was perceived by talent, independent producers, and others in less stable and powerful positions within the industry. "In the motion picture business," Allen remarked, "perception is often more important than reality."

The most telling blow to the government's case came when Judge Hauk called on two expert witnesses, University of California professors of economics, Robert Clower and Fred Weston. Both academics dismissed the government's argument regarding the antitrust implications of Kerkorian's stock purchase. Clower's testimony proved particularly damaging. He argued that even an outright merger of MGM and CPI "would not significantly lessen competition in any line of commerce" and added that even if two of the more successful studios were to merge, "you still should have five or six major distributors, thus a reasonably competitive environment."[43]

Judge Hauk concurred and on August 22 decided in Kerkorian's favor. In his decision, Hauk admonished the government attorneys for pursuing the case in the first place. In a single phrase, Hauk dismissed the government's argument in the very process of acknowledging the corporate structure and operation of the new Hollywood: "How on earth the government can arrive at the thought that there will be *a diminution of non-existent competition* is beyond me."[44]

Whether or not Kerkorian appreciated the larger historic significance of the decision is anybody's guess; what he did understand was that the victory put him one step closer to taking over Columbia Pictures. In September 1980 Kerkorian made a tender offer to purchase an additional one million shares of CPI stock (via call options to be exercised once the standstill agreement expired). The proposed purchase promised to raise his total stake in CPI to 35 percent. The CPI board labeled the move "an outrageous assault" and, though they should have known better, "a blatant violation of anti-trust laws."[45]

In order to block Kerkorian's apparent takeover attempt, Columbia issued more stock via a convertible debenture.[46] The stock move promised to put the shares in the friendly hands of Ray Stark, an in-house studio producer (who, Kerkorian alleged, was running the studio anyway), thereby diminishing Kerkorian's stake in the company.[47] Kerkorian responded by declaring the standstill agreement null and void and then, to cull shareholder support, turned to the press and accused CPI management of all sorts of corporate misadventures, highlighting the stock deal with Stark and a one-million-dollar underwriting fee paid by CPI to its CEO Herbert Allen's brokerage firm. Just as Kerkorian prepared to mount a proxy fight for control of the company, a fight he seemed poised to win, he was sidetracked by a catastrophic fire at his MGM Grand Hotel in Las Vegas. Sufficiently distracted, Kerkorian allowed Allen to buy him off. In exchange for yet another standstill agreement, Kerkorian sold his Columbia stock, netting a cool $137 million.

Four months later Kerkorian made an offer to buy Chris Craft Industries' 22 percent stake in Fox. He was ultimately outbid by Marvin Davis, whom management preferred at first but lived to despise as he sold off pieces of the studio to service his debt. Kerkorian emerged a few years later as a principal in Saul Steinberg's leveraged move on Disney, which led to yet another huge greenmail payoff.[48]

Kerkorian spent the better part of the 1980s trying to unload MGM (and the eventually annexed United Artists), first to Ted Turner, then to the producers Peter Guber and Jon Peters, then to the Australian multinational Quintex, and finally (and successfully) in a very questionable deal with Giancarlo Parretti. In less than a year's time, amid accusations of fraud and mismanagement leveled against both Parretti and Kerkorian, Parretti was forced to relinquish control of the company to the French bank, Crédit Lyonnais, which maintained control of the studio until July 1996, when Frank Mancuso engineered a management buyout financed by—who else—Kirk Kerkorian.[49] Though he generally goes unmentioned in contemporary film history, Kerkorian was the eighties' most interesting and perplexing industry player. Through the course of the decade, he held significant stock positions at MGM, Columbia, and United Artists; negotiated distribution deals and thus integrated MGM Filmco with United Artists, Paramount, and Universal; and made tender offers for Columbia, Fox, Disney, and United Artists.

TIME WARNER

Arbitrageurs are in a stock for the next two days—they're not building America. I am.
                    —Steve Ross, CEO, Warner Communications

Hollywood changed significantly in the wake of the decision in the Kerkorian-CPI case. Today, an elite set of multinational players—the News Corporation's Rupert Murdoch and Seagram's Edgar Bronfman Jr., to name just two—use their assets to control an astonishingly lucrative, extremely well integrated entertainment industry. The majors all now exploit synergistic relationships in a wide variety of ancillary markets: cable and network television, videocassettes and laserdisks, toy manufacture, and book and magazine publishing. Most of the studios own their own theaters now and though they don't use them to show their own product exclusively, they could anytime they want or need to. In seeming preparation for the next new Hollywood—one in which the film market may well be even more dependent on "home box office" and more integrated with the vaunted information-entertainment superhighway—the studios have begun to establish strategic relationships with computer software providers like Microsoft and cable and telephone hardware providers like TCI (which in 1996 owned almost a fourth of the voting stock in Turner Broadcasting), Viacom (which owns Paramount and CBS-TV), Nynex (a partner in a number of Viacom/Paramount ventures), and US West (a partner in Time Warner Entertainment).

The ability to coordinate and exploit different media outlets has enabled the big studios to better insulate themselves against the ever unpredictable American box office. These new media conglomerates are not threatened by the economic shifts that virtually shut down the B movie industry at the end of the seventies.[50] So much money can be made in such a variety of markets that it is hard to imagine that any film these days actually loses money. Even films like *Waterworld* or *Last Action Hero*—well-publicized flops at the domestic box office—earn out their investment because the studios have access to first money revenues in so many ancillary markets.

The high profitability of the "film business"—or, more accurately, the diversified entertainment industries of which motion pictures are a part—continues to support increased conglomeration and monopolization. To understand how the companies themselves view this new Hollywood, consider the following three paragraphs excerpted from the 1989 annual report published by the newly formed Time Warner. Note the references to "profound political and economic changes," ostensibly referring to Reaganomics and deregulation (which followed the Kerkorian decision), and the conspicuous omission, the conspicuous irrelevance of such outmoded notions as divestiture and free trade:

> In the Eighties we witnessed the most profound political and economic changes since the end of the Second World War. As these changes unfolded, Time Inc. and Warner Communications Inc. came independently to the same fundamental conclusion: globalization was rapidly evolving from a prophecy to a fact of life. No serious competitor could hope for any long term success unless, building on a secure home base, it achieved a major presence in all of the world's important markets.
>
> With this goal in mind, Time and Warner began discussions on joint ventures. The more we talked—the more we learned about each other—the more obvious it became that the most significant and exciting possibility was a synthesis that would lift us to a position neither could achieve alone.

In a season of history when technology has combined with political and social change to open vast new markets, we are a company equipped to reap the greatest benefits.[51]

The Time Warner merger was finalized at a moment of record prosperity in Hollywood. The entertainment business had become increasingly well integrated, federal regulation (FCC, FTC, and Justice Department interference) had been all but eliminated, and everyone who could afford to make a product was making money. It is important, then, to look at the Time-Warner merger not as an isolated event, nor as a landmark deal later aped by other companies. Instead we should view the merger in light of the larger picture of this newest of new Hollywoods, in which Time Warner was a logical consequence.

In April 1989, while Time and Warner Communications, Inc. (WCI) were negotiating the details of their planned merger, the Gulf and Western Corporation, the parent company of Paramount studios, announced its decision to sell off its financial unit in order to consolidate its interests in the entertainment business. The announcement was newsworthy but hardly surprising. By 1989 the entertainment division, which just ten years earlier was hardly the conglomerate's most lucrative unit, accounted for over 50 percent of the company's revenue. Throughout the 1980s, Paramount Studios boasted the best average market share (16.2 percent), two of the best franchise properties (the *Raiders of the Lost Ark* and *Star Trek* films), and a lucrative television production unit.

Less than two months after its consolidation as an entertainment conglomerate, Gulf and Western CEO Martin Davis took out a full-page advertisement in *Variety* to announce the company's new name: Paramount Communications, Inc. (PCI).[52] The new studio/entertainment conglomerate was perfectly set up to do business in the nineties: its holdings crossed genres and industries, it had the ability to reproduce a single product in various forms and formats, and it had the distribution and exhibition network to exploit profits at every stage, in every market.

PCI's principal entertainment industry holdings in 1989 included Paramount Pictures, Paramount Television, Paramount Home Video, Famous Music, Madison Square Garden (which included the New York Knicks and Rangers, a cable television station, an attractive piece of New York real estate, and the Miss Universe Pageant), Simon and Schuster, Prentice Hall, Pocket Books, and majority interests in the TVX broadcasting group (including WTFX-TV in Philadelphia, WDCA-TV in Washington, D.C., and KTXA-TV in Dallas), two major theater chains (United Cinemas International and, in partnership with Warner Communications, Cineamerica Theaters with its subsidiaries Mann and Trans-Lux), and the USA cable television network.[53]

The restructuring of the company left Davis with a significant problem. PCI had little debt and the sale of its nonentertainment subsidiaries netted an overwhelming amount of cash that made the company attractive and vulnerable to a hostile takeover. The amount of cash in question was substantial by any standards: $3.5 billion. Industry experts speculated that PCI would use the money to go after MCA (which owned Universal). Subsequent rumors had PCI interested in acquiring the Chicago-based Tribune Company, ABC, NBC, CBS, and least likely (but most interestingly) Time, Inc. Also in the rumor mill was the possibility of a merger with Viacom, a company that owned a cable delivery system and a number of pay television stations that would provide PCI with access to and a profit stake in yet another media market.[54] Industry journalists assumed that PCI would move against another company in its sector, despite potential antitrust or free trade problems.

On June 6, 1989, Davis put an end to all the speculation and announced his decision to mount a hostile takeover of Time, Inc. From that date until September 20, 1989, the battle between WCI and PCI dominated the trades.[55] The resolution of the battle between these media giants struck many who closely follow the industry as somehow beside the point. That either company might be allowed (by the Justice Department, the FCC, or the FTC) to merge with Time prompted *Variety*'s Richard Gold to remark that in the future "all of show business [will be] controlled by two or three conglomerates."[56]

Paramount's bid to acquire Time—a hostile but astonishingly high $10.7 billion, $175/share offer—put the planned merger between Time and WCI on ice.[57] Speculation in the trades identified a number of possible scenarios, the most likely of which was that Time, in order to quash the PCI offer, would tap into its $5 billion line of credit and simply buy WCI outright. In doing so, the merger with WCI would ostensibly take (a somewhat altered) shape and Time would become far too debt-laden for PCI to buy. Moreover, the combined companies—Time Warner—would be in a strong position to take over PCI, itself vulnerable because of its enormous cash reserves and minimal debt load. Others guessed that Paramount would succeed in its hostile takeover of

Time, leaving WCI an attractive takeover target for another company in the sector.

Rumors then began to circulate that WCI chairman Steve Ross was negotiating the sale of his company to the French media giant Hachette. A deal with Hachette made sense and it caught Time's attention. If Time accepted the Paramount offer, Ross needed to prevent a hostile move on WCI, perhaps by PCI-Time. But it's certainly possible that Ross met with the executive team at Hachette in order to force Time's hand; given the astonishing stock bonus tied to the proposed Time-WCI merger, Ross had plenty of motivation to coerce Time into dealing with him.

Paramount's challenge to the Time-Warner merger prompted Gold, again writing in *Variety*, to wonder how much "Paramount's new acquisitive ferocity" might "escalate the traditional level of competition between the Hollywood majors and alter the gentlemen's rules by which the majors play the game." Hollywood insiders, none of whom would speak on the record to Gold, spoke anxiously about the evolving, less friendly, new Hollywood. "This is a major rift in what has become an extremely incestuous industry," one executive opined. "With corporate consolidation coming you have to wonder about how studio politics are going to settle." A second executive added, "Hollywood is a small town. Everyone is friendly . . . there hasn't been a war like this since the days of the moguls."[58]

On June 16, 1989, Time announced a significant restructuring of its proposed merger with WCI. In order to counter PCI's hostile bid, Time proposed to buy WCI outright for $14 billion. The plan did not require shareholder approval, which was a good thing, because after the new deal was announced in the press, Time's stock entered "free fall," dropping nine and a half points on June 16 and another six points the following day. Michael Price of Heine Securities, a mutual fund company that owned over one million shares of Time stock, spoke for the entire Wall Street community when he predicted, "if Time buys Warner at this price, the stock falls off a cliff."[59]

On June 26, Paramount sweetened its offer to $12.2 billion. The offer was summarily rejected. When news of the bid and its rejection was made public, Paramount's stock went up and Time's went down. For those who play the market, the message was clear. Investors were betting that Time would succeed in its efforts to buy WCI and as a result Paramount would become the target of a takeover.

When the second Paramount offer was rejected by the board, three of Time's biggest shareholders—Robert Bass, Jerry Perenchio, and

Cablevision, Inc.—filed suit in chancery court in Delaware. By early July, Paramount had filed a suit of its own, but the court rejected all attempts to block Time's acquisition of WCI. In a seventy-nine-page decision issued on July 14, 1989, Chancellor William Allen wrote, "There [is] no persuasive evidence that the board of Time has a corrupt or venal motivation in electing to continue with its long term plan even in the face of the cost that course will no doubt entail for the company's shareholders in the short run. In doing so, it is exercising perfectly conventional powers to cause the corporation to buy assets [in this case a major studio] for use in its business." The decision not only struck a blow to shareholders' rights (to influence corporate decisions, especially of the magnitude of Time's acquisition of WCI), it regarded competition and monopoly control in the film business in much the same terms as the Kerkorian decision had ten years earlier.[60]

When the chancery court decision was announced, Time's stock price again fell dramatically, another twelve dollars per share. But while stockholders failed to reap the benefits of the merger, the officers of the combined companies benefited from the moment the court decided in their favor: when the Time-Warner deal was finally signed, Steve Ross received a $200 million stock bonus.[61]

The new Time Warner formed in 1989 sported assets amounting to nearly $25 billion and annual revenues estimated at $7.6 billion.[62] Its holdings spanned a number of related entertainment industries, including film and television studios (involved in development, production, and distribution), movie theaters, magazine and book publishing, cable television delivery systems and pay television stations, recording industry operations, and theme parks. At the time of the merger, Time Warner's publishing division included book publishers Little, Brown and Company, Warner Books, and Time Life Books; comic book publisher DC Comics (which produces and distributes *Superman*, *Batman*, and *Wonder Woman*); and the mass market magazines *Time*, *Fortune*, *Sports Illustrated*, *Sunset*, and *Parenting*. Its publishing services division distributed books and magazines for other publishers and owned the Book of the Month Club. The company's music division was the most lucrative and extensive on the planet and included Warner Brothers Records (and its subsidiaries Reprise, Sire, and Paisley Park), the Atlantic Recording Group (and its subsidiaries Interscope and Rhino), Elektra Entertainment (and its subsidiaries Asylum and Nonesuch), and Warner Music International. Its wholly owned subsidiaries ATC and Warner Cable Communications made Time Warner the second largest cable provider in the nation (behind TCI) and its cable software division included two profitable premium channels: HBO and Cinemax. Also among the company's holdings were the Licensing Corporation of America (LCA), which managed and protected the copyright on all Warner Brothers characters (Batman, Bugs Bunny, etc.). Products bearing these trademarks are available for purchase all over the world at Warner Brothers retail stores.

In 1989, just before the merger was finalized, the Warner Brothers film division released *Batman*. The film grossed in excess of $250 million domestically. But for Time Warner, the domestic gross was a very small part of the film's overall worth to the company. Batman is a DC Comics character, licensed by LCA. The merchandising subsidiary has taken its cut from the profits of every T-shirt, cup, book, or action figure sold. The film has appeared on HBO and Cinemax and has been delivered into homes across the country via cable systems owned by Time Warner. When the film was released on video and laserdisk, it bore the Warner Home Video label and the popular soundtrack CD came out in two versions, both from companies owned by Time Warner. Coverage—constant reminders about the film (as an event, as a franchise)—appeared in Time Warner magazines like *Time, Life*, and in time for the first sequel, one of the company's newer and more successful magazine ventures, *Entertainment Weekly*.

TIME WARNER TURNER

Wall Street is betting the deal will be approved, albeit in a modified form. But what does the company really gain if it goes through in any form? A thumbs-up would add another $147 million to Time Warner's cash flow—but only at the price of making Ted Turner the company's largest shareholder, in possession of nearly a third of its stock. Imagine courting and marrying the prettiest girl in town and bringing her home only to discover that she's some hairy-legged dude named Ted who thinks he's the guy and you're the girl!

—Christopher Byron, *Esquire*, 1996

In 1995, in what would be the second largest takeover in United States business history, Disney purchased Capital Cities/ABC for $19 billion. The Disney acquisition was executed at the same time as another big deal, Edgar Bronfman Jr.'s (Seagram's) purchase of MCA from Matsushita. Both deals reveal the studios' growing reliance on market synergies and multinational capital and the government's unwillingness or inability to enforce antitrust regulations in Hollywood.

The Capital Cities/ABC acquisition gave Disney, in corporate president Michael Ovitz's own words, "amazing vertical clout." Disney became a company that not only manufactures a product (that is routinely reproduced in a variety of forms and formats) but also owns a network of venues into which to distribute that product, for example, ABC and the Disney Channel, the theme parks, and retail stores.

In many ways the acquisition was merely a sign of the times, a move Disney CEO Michael Eisner had to make in order to maintain the conglomerate's strong position in the evolving international marketplace. The deal not only gave Disney a television network (like Fox), but a second key cable television station, ESPN. The acquisition of ESPN was strategic—perhaps even the key to the entire deal—because it enabled Disney to package the sports station with its own Disney Channel. This promised to be very attractive to fledgling cable providers abroad, especially in Asia where fairly strict programming guidelines (regarding sexual and political content) have made it impossible for Time Warner (with its flagship cable station HBO) to participate.

The Disney-Capital Cities/ABC deal, much like Time's purchase of Warner Communications in 1989 and the Viacom acquisition of Paramount in 1993, was less a watershed moment than a symptom, a logical consequence of the industry's ongoing adjustment to the *Paramount* decision. Case in point: within weeks of Eisner's dramatic move, which briefly made Disney the largest media conglomerate, Time Warner chairman Gerald Levin announced the purchase of 82 percent of the outstanding shares in the Turner Broadcasting System, a stock deal worth roughly $7.5 billion.[63] With the purchase, Time Warner projected annual revenues for the combined companies in excess of $19.8 billion, surpassing the new Disney's $16.4 billion.[64]

The deal was held up initially by the FTC. Even a superficial survey of the acquisition reveals that Time Warner Turner is both a vertical and horizontal monopoly; the company has a stake in virtually every aspect of the production process and controls much of the hardware and software providing customers with access to that product. Federal regulations prohibit one company from owning cable systems that reach more than 30 percent of the nation's households.[65] The combination of Time Warner's and TCI's cable systems gave Time Warner Turner access to more than 50 percent.

Federal regulations are made to be broken, as long as you've got the cash and the contacts. Both Time Warner as a corporation and Turner shareholder, TCI chairman John Malone as an individual contribute strategically to political campaigns and for their time and money they expect something in return. In order to insure government approval, just as news of the deal was leaked to the press, Levin dispatched two teams of Time Warner attorneys to Washington—one to call in favors in Congress and another to negotiate a compromise with the FTC.

As the negotiations played out, it became apparent that the FTC's problems with the Time Warner–Turner deal had less to do with federal regulations than its distrust of John Malone. Malone owes this notoriety in large part to Vice President Al Gore.[66] In two speeches the vice president has called Malone "the Darth Vader of the cable industry" and "[the man who runs] the cable Cosa Nostra."[67]

On July 17, 1996, the FTC conditionally approved Time Warner's purchase of Turner Broadcasting. After lengthy negotiations between Time Warner attorney Robert Joffe and William Baer, the director of the Bureau of Competition at the FTC, Time Warner Turner agreed to comply with three fairly substantial changes in the deal as it was first set up by Levin and Turner: (1) in order to prevent Time Warner Turner's CNN (and CNN's sister stations CNN Headline News, CNN International, and CNNFN) from completely controlling cable television news (and public opinion), the cable systems owned and controlled by the combined companies had to carry an additional all-news station produced and distributed by someone other than Time Warner Turner (marking the first time the government has mandated what sort of programming a cable system must carry),[68] (2) because it so clearly disadvantaged competing cable systems and potentially destabilized pricing in the cable market, a sweetheart deal discounting Turner programming (TBS, TNT, Turner Classic Movies, the Cartoon Channel, CNN, and CNNFN) on John Malone's TCI systems was nixed, and (3) Time Warner Turner could not "bundle" or package its product: HBO, Cinemax, or any of the Turner-owned stations must be made available to all systems for a fair price whether or not the respective systems want all or just one of them.

FTC approval of Time Warner Turner was the biggest of three big media industry stories that broke within a few days of each other in the middle of July 1996.[69] The Tribune Company, which controls television stations and newspapers nationwide, announced a strategic alliance with the computer information service company America Online. The deal with America Online gives the Tribune Company a strategic ally should television cable systems be tied to home computer online services in the future, as many predict.

The other story—actually two related stories—far more closely paralleled Time Warner's blockbuster deal. On the very day the FTC–Time Warner accord was announced, Rupert Murdoch's News Corporation made two significant moves: (1) in order to expand its holdings in syndicated TV programming, Murdoch purchased New World Communications and its extensive television library from Ronald Perelman for $2.48 billion, and (2) Murdoch made official his intention to produce a twenty-four-hour news channel to compete with CNN. New World Communications gave Murdoch the most extensive television library in the industry. The cable news channel provided greater access to and potentially greater influence over public opinion.

At the time, Murdoch's all-news channel seemed certain to benefit from the FTC compromise compelling Time Warner Turner to carry an alternative news station on its cable systems. Murdoch's only competition for the slot at the time came from MSNBC, an all-news station launched earlier in 1996 by new partners NBC and Microsoft. In July, when the FTC agreement was first announced, the industry line was that despite Turner's problems with Murdoch (and with Murdoch's all-news channel director, Roger Ailes), Time Warner Turner chairman Gerald Levin would opt to carry the Fox News Channel. MSNBC had lobbied actively against the Turner acquisition. Industry insiders believed that Levin was anxious to send MSNBC a message.

But in September, the pundits were proven wrong; the combined Time Warner Turner cable systems signed with MSNBC. Murdoch was pretty much locked out of over 50 percent of the cable market.

After ten months of bitter fighting—in boardrooms, on the airwaves, in print—Levin and Murdoch reached a truce; beginning in July 1997 Time Warner's New York City cable system provided a slot for the Fox News Channel. The Levin-Murdoch alliance may not have pleased Turner, but it made good business sense. Turner's problems with Murdoch were hardly a secret. In a court deposition leaked to the press in October 1997, Turner called Murdoch "a joke," "a scumbag," "a pretty slimy character," and "a disgrace to journalism." In the *New York Post*, a tabloid owned by the News Corporation, Murdoch printed a cartoon depicting Turner in a straitjacket above a caption that read, "Is Ted Turner veering dangerously towards insanity—or has he come off the medication he takes to fight his manic depression?" When Turner got a look at the cartoon, he challenged Murdoch to a public boxing match.

Levin's decision to disregard Turner's feelings about Murdoch seemed at the time a reminder of who was in fact in charge at the combined companies. But the story is more complicated than that. When Time Warner first opted to exclude the Fox News Channel from its combined cable services (which included the lucrative New York City franchise), Murdoch threatened to move his city corporate headquarters (and some nine hundred jobs) across the river to New Jersey. New York City mayor Rudolph Giuliani interceded, publicly siding with Murdoch. In a move designed to irk Levin and Turner, Giuliani offered a city-run "public access" channel to Fox. The courts blocked the arrangement, prompting Giuliani to announce in the press his intention to cancel the city's cable deal with Time Warner. Recognizing that it was a fight Time Warner couldn't win, Levin made the deal with Murdoch.

When Levin announced the deal to the Time Warner board, Turner (who no doubt had been briefed if not consulted) remained uncharacteristically quiet. Wall Street experts, most of whom had been critical of Levin's management from the moment he took over after Ross's death, lauded the deal. And they couldn't help but appreciate the ways the deal helped Levin with Time Warner shareholders *and* helped the company in the larger entertainment marketplace.

It is important to note here that Levin solidified his position at Time Warner Turner not at the expense of a competitor (Murdoch) but rather as a consequence of a competitor's good fortune. While the New York City cable deal expanded the subscriber base for the Fox News Channel from twenty-two million to almost forty million, it supported at the same time a significant surge in the value of Time Warner stock. As former New York City Deputy Mayor (and Levin confidant) Richard Powers so aptly pointed out in the press, when the conglomerates get along, "It's win, win, win for everybody."[70]

3

What Everyone Should Know about the Motion Picture Code and Ratings

IN 1894, ABOUT a year before the Lumière brothers' first films were screened for paying audiences, police in Europe and the United States were already reacting to widespread public concern about the curious power and influence of the motion picture. *Dorolita's Passion Dance*, for example, just one in a series of "erotic dance" kinetoscopes, was pulled from circulation in 1894 in Atlantic City in response to public pressure.[1]

May Irwin and John Rice's clumsy, closed-mouthed kiss in 1896 was preserved for posterity on a roll of film that seems to the actors and the audience to last forever. It provided one of cinema's first erotic moments and was met immediately by calls for its and the medium's prohibition. As Herbert Stone, editor of the Chicago literary magazine *The Chap Book*, remarked at the time,

> When only life size [the kiss was featured in the stage drama, *The Widow Jones*, performed on Broadway in 1896 by Irwin and Rice] it was pronounced beastly. But that was nothing to the present sight. Manifested to Gargantuan proportions and repeated three times over it is absolutely disgusting. All delicacy or remnant of charm seems gone from Miss Irwin, and the performance comes near to being indecent in its emphasized vulgarity. Such things call for police interference.[2]

Short features depicting sporting events, especially boxing matches, hinted at cinema's promising future as a means of documenting important and interesting events. But however well or much these films seemed of historical importance or interest, the early boxing films struck would-be reformers as not only too violent (for children, for women, for the impressionable masses) but also too similar to the widely distributed circus-act kinetoscopes of bearded ladies, strongmen, and trapeze artists. Cinema seemed at the time firmly rooted in the carnival tradition, the low-culture entertainment that purported to exploit a sucker born every minute.

The first significant local government effort to regulate the exhibition of early cinema came on Christmas Eve 1908, when New York City mayor George McClellan closed all the nickelodeons in the metropolitan area. McClellan chose to close the theaters on Christmas Eve to make a statement. By instituting the ban on one of Christian America's most important holidays, he highlighted the fact that those most affected by the shutdown would be Jewish theater owners, men who were not celebrating Christmas.

New York City nickelodeon owners went to court and quickly reopened, thanks in large part to a sympathetic judge, William Gaynor. Judge Gaynor and McClellan soon became political rivals. Gaynor ran against McClellan for mayor of New York and won in part because of his campaign promise to protect the fledgling industry. Then as now, campaign financing played a significant role in the election as Gaynor's mayoral run was financed in large part by the motion picture companies and local exhibitors.

Less than a month after McClellan made his move against the Jewish theater owners, a meeting of Christian clergymen was held at the Marble Collegiate Church in order to develop a strategy to force theater owners to stop screening films on Sundays. Theater owners tried to improve their public relations by adding educational films and uplifting speakers to their Sunday progams. When it became clear that theater owners had little intention of shutting down on Sundays, some churches began screening uplifting movies as part of their morning service. These screenings soon rivaled the shows at the commercial venues, raising a very different sort of problem for Jewish theater owners.

In an attempt to reach a compromise between the various religious and political forces at play in film censorship at the time, in March 1909 the liberal-reformist People's Institute in New York City announced its intention to establish a censorship board. The People's Institute brought together Christian clergy (the Reverend Walter Laidlaw of the New York City Federation of Churches and the Reverend G. W. Knox of the Ethical Social League), local educators (Gustave Straubemiller and Evangeline Whitney, two members of the city board of education), leaders of women's groups (M. Serena Townsend of the Women's Municipal League), blue-collar labor leaders (Howard Bradstreet of the Neighborhood Workers Association), and nationally recognized artists and authors (the initial People's Institute group included Mark Twain).[3] Set up more like a think tank or book club than a bureaucracy for censoring movies, the People's Institute proposed a forum for discussion of film content. However promising such an institute board may have been, it never raised the level of public and state debate nor did it protect cinema from growing ethnocentric and state censorship pressure.

The Jewish exhibitors did not oppose censorship per se. They were all too practical and too careful for that. Instead, they supported federal, constitutional guidelines; from the start they were willing to put their faith in the federal judiciary. The Christian producers and distributors of the Motion Picture Patents Company opposed federal oversight and instead supported a national system of *self*-regulation. To that end, in 1909 the MPPC lent its support to the self-regulatory National Board of Censorship. All the members of the trust agreed to submit their films to the board and all agreed to make appropriate cuts in accordance with board decisions. Independent film companies were not required to submit their films to the board, but board approval significantly increased the number of theaters that were willing to screen their films.

The National Board of Censorship held its first meeting on March 25, 1909. At that meeting, the board viewed six hours of films and suggested a range of cuts in a number of them. In the first few years of its operation, the board had a reputation for reasonable administration of content censorship. But at the same time, so-called reformers focused much of their attention on the burgeoning medium with vastly increased political clout. Local law enforcement, at the behest of local reformers, terrorized exhibitors in defiance of the industry's self-regulatory apparatus.

As early as 1914 at a National Exhibitors' Convention held in New York City, local (as opposed to National Board) censorship was cited as the biggest problem faced by theater owners nationwide. Some cities were strict but consistent; others, like Chicago, were decidedly erratic. Major Funkhouser of the Chicago police banned films that included dancing, but licensed a film like *Henry Spenser's Confession*, which detailed the life and times of a notorious serial killer.

The mostly reasonable National Board of Censorship was too weak to stem the tide of grassroots reform. In an attempt to devise a system by which the industry might regulate its own product lines, in 1915 the National Board of Censorship revamped and renamed itself the National Board of Review. Consistent with the MPPC's claims in support of its industry trust, the new National Board of Review took as its primary objective the maintenance of quality production standards. The relevance of "quality production standards" to actual (moral/Christian) film content was left purposefully vague.

By 1922, censorship bills were under discussion in thirty-six states. There are a number of reasons moralists, reformers, uplifters, and legislators so quickly called for film censorship and/or prohibition.[4] The theatrical film experience was from the start intimate and immediate; recall all those early filmgoers hiding under their chairs as the train approached the station in the 1895 Lumière actuality *Arrivée d'un train en gare à La Ciotat*. The speed at which cinema's popularity grew as a leisure activity prompted would-be censors to fear the medium's persuasive, narcotic influence over its huge, loyal audience. The stylized depictions of violence and eroticism, essential elements early on, subtly combined antisocial behavior with commercial leisure.[5]

Concerns were raised about the uniquely social aspect of the theatrical film experience. The movie theater afforded the lower classes, which made up a significant portion of the early film audience, a safe place to express themselves physically and emotionally with laughter, tears, or sexual longing. Filmgoing quickly became something for single adults to do on dates and as a result Victorian moral codes were routinely defied on theater balconies nationwide. What could be done there in the dark (and ostensibly in public) seemed to suggest that the problem lay not only in film content but also in the theatrical experience itself.

Reformers also expressed health and safety concerns, some real and some imagined. Attempts to enjoin theatrical exhibition called attention to the real fire hazard posed by early film projection in what were in many cases unsafe buildings. Such legitimate safety concerns were accompanied by cockamamie theories contending that exposure to flickering cinema images might cause epilepsy.

THE *MUTUAL* CASE

It was often a case of inherited American standards—products of a Christian civilization—against alien customs variously described as "modern," "liberal," or "pagan." Hosts of Americans clung firmly to their own ideals and strongly resisted the invasion.

—Will Hays, first president of the MPPDA

In the first comprehensive history of U.S. cinema, *A Million and One Nights* (1926), Terry Ramsaye described the medium as primarily an entertainment business, which, like the circus, pandered to an undiscerning, uncultured clientele. The cinema, Ramsaye wrote in terms that hardly conceal his elitist disdain, was "definitely lowbrow, an entertainment for the great unwashed commonality."[6] Such a view was largely shared at the time by other art, theater, and film critics, reformers, legislators, and, most importantly, the courts.

As early as 1915, in its landmark decision in *Mutual Film Corporation v. Industrial Commission of Ohio*, the United States Supreme Court anticipated Ramsaye's elitist conclusions about motion pictures.[7] In the *Mutual* case, the Court drew a distinction between entertainment and art—as well as entertainment and information—and refused to grant cinema the same free speech protections afforded literature and the press. The *Mutual* case proved crucial. For almost half a century, movies were seen by the Court not as works of art but as industrial products of a business enterprise.

The *Mutual* case involved a conflict between a film production and distribution company, the Mutual Film Corporation, and the state motion picture censorship board in Ohio, which by 1915 had begun to prohibit the screening for profit of movies it found offensive and/or a threat to public safety and welfare. Mutual's attorneys claimed in the suit that the Ohio board's censorship and prohibition of certain motion pictures unfairly inhibited interstate commerce and violated free speech guarantees as elaborated in the Ohio and United States constitutions. The board's standards for censoring and/or prohibiting the screening of films, Mutual contended, were vague and inconsistent; the prohibition of certain films based on "overbroad criteria" amounted to an unlawful prior restraint of expression and trade.

In a unanimous decision, the Court found in favor of the Industrial Commission of Ohio and in doing so empowered other state boards of censorship nationwide. These boards would continue to have a significant impact on film content until the MPAA film rating system was adopted in 1968. Writing for the majority, Justice Joseph McKenna concluded that cinema must be treated differently from the press because it pandered to a very different audience. Movies, McKenna opined, appealed to and excited prurient interest in its mass audience, made up as it was "not of women alone nor of men alone, but together, not of adults only, but of children." McKenna also expressed concern that such a persuasive new medium might "be used for evil" and cautioned in general terms against the insidious "power of amusement." The *Mutual* case required the Court to weigh constitutional protections of free speech against the state and federal government's right and obligation to protect the public from harm. In the end, the Court's concern about the effects of cinema as "an unregulated social force" mitigated against the First Amendment and free and fair trade guarantees sought by the studios.

The unanimous decision in the *Mutual* case hinged on the Court's view of cinema as an entertainment business first and foremost and an art form secondarily, even incidentally:

> It cannot be put out of view that the exhibition of motion pictures is a business pure and simple, originated and conducted for profit, like other spectacles, not to be regarded, nor intended to be regarded by the Ohio constitution, we think, as part of the press of a country or as organs of public opinion. They are mere representations of events, of ideas and sentiments published and known, vivid, useful and entertaining no doubt, but, as we have said, capable of evil, having the power for it, the greater because of the attractiveness and manner of exhibition.

The hysterical rhetoric regarding cinema's potential for evil was rooted much more in the Court's fear, distrust, and distaste for the lower-class, immigrant film audience than in its earnest concern about the specific content of specific movies. The Court's view of cinema as primarily, even exclusively, a business formed the foundation for subsequent rulings: for example, the court's decision not to afford the industry an antitrust exemption in *Binderup v. Pathe Exchange* in 1923 and then again in its insistence on divestiture in *United States v. Paramount Pictures* in 1948. Between 1915 and 1948, the Court was consistent in its view of Hollywood as "a business pure and simple" and in its application of this view to cases concerning a variety of regulatory and censorship practices.

By the end of the Second World War, just as the Court was prepared to render its decision in the *Paramount* case, it was also ready to rethink the 1915 Court's decision to deny cinema free speech protections. Justice William O. Douglas's opinion in the *Paramount* case, which spoke directly to the issue of antitrust violations in the industry, explicitly argued that cinema, as *a business pure and simple*, should be afforded the same First Amendment protections already enjoyed by other parallel media businesses. "We have no doubt," Douglas concluded, "that moving pictures, like newspapers and radio, are included in the press whose freedom is guaranteed by the First Amendment."

SCANDALS, STARDOM, AND CENSORSHIP

> There were a lot of things the censors wouldn't let me do in the movies that I had done on stage. They wouldn't even let me sit on a guy's lap and I'd been on more laps than a napkin.
>
> —Mae West

As early as 1913, approximately a year before the first features were screened to paying audiences, a fan magazine subculture emerged attending the question, "What do movie stars do when they're not working?" As Richard deCordova argues, the discourse on the star at first focused on the "conventionality, stability and normalcy" of screen performers, despite all the temptations, despite all the money, despite all the adulation. [8]

These press releases about movie stars and the distribution of these stories via fan magazines were controlled completely by the studios. The narratives told in these fan magazines echoed the very sort of melodramatic scenarios that prevailed in studio films at the time. The world is fraught with temptation, or so these magazines contended, and only the stars' virtue, beauty, and talent could enable them to endure, to, as if on screen, triumph in the final reel. The studios used this formative star discourse as a means of regulating the industry's celebrity workforce and as a way of presenting an image of the film industry both on screen and off as conventional, stable, and normal.

Fan magazine stories in the early silent era, like the films that further mythologized the real lives of stars, attended contemporary tensions between Victorian codes of behavior and the temptations of a growing consumer culture. [9] Stars like Florence Hackett and Norma Talmadge—and not (just) the characters they played onscreen—were touted as models for how modest and responsible American women should behave and dress.

As the so-called roaring twenties took shape, the fan magazines increasingly celebrated postwar prosperity, occasionally even touting various stars' extravagance and conspicuous consumption.[10] This new star narrative was simply an effort on the part of the studios to keep up with the times. But it proved to be disastrous on the public relations front. It suggested the very skewed values reformers, up-lifters, and the like feared about the movie industry from the start: big images, big stars, big money, big problems. Stars, or so the new fan magazine mythology contended, lived better, freer lives than the rest of us. Such freedom, such prosperity, it seems, could not go wholly unregulated.

The private lives of movie stars were from the start produced in and by their relationship to the movies. Films, whether they really changed all that much or not after World War I, came to mean so much more, so much else, because they, like the fan magazines, were merely stories about, excuses to know more about, interesting, fabulous, probably li-centious movie stars. As the new postwar star discourse got too inter-esting for the fan magazines and the studios that ran the fan magazines to control, legitimate newspapers began to run gossip and news items attending the increasingly scandalous celebrity culture in Hollywood.

The three big scandals at the start of the 1920s—Roscoe "Fatty" Ar-buckle's alleged rape and murder of the starlet Virginia Rappe, the un-solved murder of the film director William Desmond Taylor, and the star actor Wallace Reid's death by drug overdose—were covered by newspapers nationwide.[11] So were somewhat smaller stories: the Mary Pickford–Owen Moore divorce, for example, was covered by the *New York Times*. The *Times* also weighed in on divorce "scandals" involving Conway Teale, Francis X. Bushman, and Pickford's next husband, Dou-glas Fairbanks.[12]

The self-regulatory apparatus fronted by the fan magazines proved wholly incapable of containing these stories. *Photoplay*, for example, de-cided to mostly ignore the Arbuckle scandal. Even after the news of Rappe's death had run in newspapers nationwide, *Photoplay* continued to feature stories on Arbuckle the dandy, the ladies' man, the fashion plate. Such an editorial strategy failed to help Arbuckle or the industry tainted by his scandalous behavior.[13]

At the very moment that the studios seemed to lose control of the star discourse, first to legitimate newspapers and then to popular mag-azines, and in the process abandoned their dependence on the fan mag-azines as a means of maintaining good public relations, film executives began to take more seriously public pressure to regulate film content. In doing so, the studios turned a potential public relations disaster (the

Fatty Arbuckle before the fall.

scandals) into an opportunity to consolidate their power and to establish new collusive guidelines to maintain industry profitability.

The star scandals suggested that Hollywood was somehow out of control; people in the movie business made too much money and had too much independence and power. The studios were able to exploit such an assumption to reign in their stars and reestablish complete control over their celebrity workforce. As early as 1922, the studios began insisting on morality clauses in their contracts with talent. While these clauses called further attention to the indistinguishability between stars' lives on and off screen, they functioned to protect the studios against having to pay out a star's contract even after a career-ending scandal (for example, Arbuckle, Mary Miles Minter, and Mabel Normand). These clauses also enabled the studios to more fully control the private and public lives of stars, regulate the star discourse, and if necessary discipline star talent should behavior or a sudden decline in popularity warrant it.

Immediately following the publication of newspaper stories about Arbuckle and Rappe, reformers across the nation organized a boycott of the comedian's films. In prompt response to the pressure, Paramount recalled all prints of Arbuckle's pictures and suspended the star indefinitely. Before 1921, Arbuckle was one of Paramount's biggest assets. But after the scandal broke he was a liability. Paramount executives were able to use their concession to public pressure to void a contract with an expensive star who was suddenly worth nothing to them in the marketplace. In the very process of enforcing the ban on Arbuckle's films, Paramount dramatized the extent of the industry's commitment to responsible self-regulation.

The MPPDA's first president, the former postmaster general Will Hays, had as his mandate a significant public relations job: to convince grassroots organizations and conservative legislators across the country that the industry wanted what they wanted, "to develop," as Hays described it, "the amazing possibilities for good in movies."[14] In a press release announcing the studio's decision to abandon its star (before his guilt or innocence was determined in court), Hays wrote,

After consultation at length with Mr. Nicholas Schenck, representing Joseph Schenck, the producers, and Mr. Adolph Zukor and Mr. Jesse Lasky, of Famous Players Corporation, the distributors, I will state that at my request they have canceled all showings and all bookings of the Arbuckle films. They do this that the whole matter may have the consideration that its importance warrants, and the action is taken notwithstanding the fact that they have nearly ten thousand contracts in force for the Arbuckle pictures.[15]

The industry's commitment to content regulation dates to the public relations flak mounted in response to the Arbuckle scandal. The

MPPDA, which managed this self-regulation, censored films solely to serve its studio members' corporate interests. When the Arbuckle scandal hit, thirty-six state legislatures were considering film censorship bills. The industry's swift action to ban Arbuckle's films, its success in preventing independent exhibitors from screening exploitative retrospectives of Virginia Rappe's films (an early example of industry regulation involving the complex relationship between the studios and theater owners), and its promise of responsible self-regulation under the auspices of Will Hays succeeded in diminishing the threat of widespread state regulation and censorship. By 1925, thirty-five of the thirty-six states contemplating film censorship abandoned their efforts, apparently deciding that the task was best left to Hays and the MPPDA.[16]

Because the hiring of Hays coincided with the first newspaper stories about the Arbuckle scandal and because, in his first weeks at the MPPDA, he was able to get Paramount to participate in the banning of the comedian's films, it was widely assumed that Hays was hired first and foremost as an industry policeman and censor. Hays's appointment seemed at the time akin to major league baseball's selection a few years earlier of Judge Kenesaw Mountain Landis as its first commissioner. Landis's appointment was the direct consequence of the infamous Black Sox scandal in which a number of Chicago White Sox players allegedly took money from gangsters in exchange for throwing the 1919 World Series. When scandals threatened the public image and profitability of the movie industry, the appointment of Hays seemed merely a reprise of a parallel entertainment industry strategy.

Hays's public image was used by the studios—much as Landis's sober, no-nonsense image was used by the baseball owners—to legitimate the entire industry. The industry mogul Carl Laemmle described Hays to a Detroit newspaper reporter as "a dictator of principles, a man whose reputation shall redound to the credit of the industry."[17] Hays was a Presbyterian elder, a popular member of Warren Harding's cabinet, what we would call today a political and social conservative. He was also an ugly little man with crooked teeth and huge ears, a man who looked nothing like a movie star. He was perfectly cast for the job at hand.

Because of his public image and his less than dashing profile, Hays was assumed to be a zealous reformer, a man, like the PCA chief Joseph Breen, bent on protecting the American public from the dangerous, persuasive power of motion pictures. Because his appointment was so closely tied to the Arbuckle scandal, Hays, like Breen, was widely viewed as an adversarial figure by directors, producers, writers, and actors. In his memoirs, Hays expresses regret that his arrival in Holly-wood was met with such suspicion and insists that his foremost goal at the time was to "convince the industry to work to common goals."[18]

A *New York Times* article chronicling Hays's first trip to Los Angeles includes a telling rumination. Though he had read all the scandalous stories in the newspapers, Hays insisted that he "failed to find the hor-rors of Hollywood." "Nothing is wrong with the moving pictures," Hays added, "except youth."[19]

Hays insists in his memoirs that the sole intent of this first trip to Los Angeles was not to clean house but rather to organize the West Coast division of the MPPDA. The newspapers of course characterized the trip as a moral crusade. That the two tasks—modernizing industry operations and self-regulating content—were somehow related, even indistinguishable, would become all too apparent in the years to come.

THE *MIRACLE* CASE

> As far as I am concerned, *The Miracle* is an absolutely Catholic work.
> —Roberto Rossellini, filmmaker

From the start, self-regulation was a balancing act. The studios rou-tinely submitted screenplays to state censorship boards and grassroots organizations like the Catholic Legion of Decency. It was hardly an ideal policy. But so long as their films made money, the studios were willing to play along. But when, after the Second World War, box office revenues declined, the studios began to question the practicality of al-lowing censorship activists so much power.

In 1952, the studios caught a break. In *Burstyn v. Wilson*, the so-called *Miracle* case, the Supreme Court significantly undermined the authority of state censorship boards. In doing so, the Court gave the stu-dios the chance they needed to establish a new self-regulatory policy.[20]

The Miracle, directed by Roberto Rossellini, the film at issue in *Burstyn v. Wilson*, was a particularly problematic picture for state and local censorship boards.[21] It told the story of a simpleminded peasant woman (played by Anna Magnani) who falls in love with a mysterious stranger (played by Federico Fellini), who claims as he seduces her that he is St. Joseph. The woman gets pregnant and after the stranger disappears she tells everyone in her town that her unborn child is the product of an immaculate, miraculous conception. For telling such a blasphemous story, she is ostracized by the community. Homeless, scared, and confused, she eventually gives birth in an abandoned church. The film ends as she holds the baby in her arms and is granted grace; whatever events led up to the birth of the child are unimportant in comparison to the love the baby brings to her life.

By the time *The Miracle* was imported to the United States it had already caused a great deal of controversy in its native Italy, where it was alternatively hailed and excoriated by critics and journalists, condemned by the Vatican, but never banned. In order to screen the film in New York City—and to fill out the bill, since *The Miracle* is barely an hour long—Joseph Burstyn, the film's U.S. distributor, ran the film along with Jean Renoir's *Day in the Country* and Marcel Pagnol's *Jofroi* under a single (albeit suggestive) title, *Ways of Love*.

Ways of Love opened at the Paris Theater in New York on December 12, 1950. In a press release made on Christmas Eve that same year, *The Miracle* (and thus *Ways of Love*) received a condemned rating from the Catholic censorship board, the Legion of Decency. The city's license commissioner, Edward T. McCaffrey (a former state officer in the Catholic War Veterans Association) attempted to enjoin the release of the film(s). McCaffrey had been successful in prohibiting the screening of other films in the past. But Burstyn was an able adversary, a veteran of censorship disputes; he had successfully fought with the Production Code Administration and various state boards in order to screen Vittorio De Sica's *The Bicycle Thief* two years earlier. When McCaffrey pressed for a statewide ban, Burstyn took the case to court and won a preliminary decision enabling him to show the film(s) at the Paris Theater.

On January 7, two days after Burstyn resumed screening the omnibus picture, Cardinal Francis Spellman, the nation's most famous and prominent Catholic clergy, publicly described *The Miracle* as "a subversion to the very inspired word of God" and "a vicious insult to Italian womanhood." Spellman remarked that the film should be retitled *Woman Further Defamed*, a thinly veiled reference to Rossellini's well-publicized relationship with Ingrid Bergman.[22]

Throughout the film's first run, picketers who objected to the film's seeming anti-Catholic content marched outside the Paris Theater and shouted slogans at ticket buyers like "This is a Communist picture!" and "Buy American!" Bomb threats were called in, prompting a city fire marshal's visit. A second visit got Burstyn a citation. Due to all the controversy, *Ways of Love* sold out the house; patrons were standing in the aisles and in the back, blocking fire exits at the rear of the theater.

Ways of Love received the New York film critics' annual award for best foreign film. Martin Quigley, a devout Catholic layman and censorship activist who edited the *Motion Picture Herald* at the time, called Radio City Music Hall, where the New York Film Critics Award ceremony was to be held, and threatened a future boycott of the theater. Radio City management decided to cancel its arrangement with the New York Film Critics Association and the award ceremony was moved to a smaller venue. When Joseph Burstyn accepted the award for *Ways of Love*, he apologized to the other award winners (who lost their evening of glory at Radio City thanks to him) and to Renoir and Pagnol, whose films would be forever linked to the controversy set in motion by the New York screening of *The Miracle*.[23]

A few days after the award ceremony the New York State Board of Regents, which presided over appeals in state censorship disputes, revoked the film's license in response to pressure from Spellman, Quigley, the Legion of Decency, and the Catholic War Veterans. Burstyn appealed the regents' decision, but the New York State Supreme Court upheld the ban.

The dispute put the MPAA in a difficult spot. *The Miracle* was not an MPAA film. Though Burstyn never submitted *The Miracle* to the PCA, it is safe to surmise that, given MPAA policy on content that could potentially offend a religious group, the film would not have been granted a production seal. Still, the New York State Regents decision to ban the film, which came at the behest of the various Catholic groups, was a potentially troublesome precedent. The last thing the studios wanted was a direct link between grassroots Catholic censorship boards and the New York State Regents.

The PCA's relationship with the Catholic Legion of Decency was complex. The two censorship boards cooperated with each other because it was to their mutual advantage to do so. Joseph Breen, the head censor at the PCA through most of its existence, was himself a Catholic procensorship activist. Though his primary commitment was to the safe passage of MPAA product lines into the marketplace, Breen was sensitive to the concerns of the Legion of Decency. Breen was anxious to do the legion's dirty work and he believed that in doing so he acquired a kind of moral authority for the PCA.

When Breen cautioned MPAA member producers that a certain scene risked problems with the legion, it behooved the studio to make the change.[24] Cautionary memos from the PCA to film producers were routinely phrased as "helpful advice," as was consistent with the PCA's function, as an organ of the MPAA, to help filmmakers overcome potential obstacles (like a legion ban or boycott) in the distribution and exhibition of a given film. Such helpful advice frequently called attention to subject matter that did not in itself run afoul of the PCA code. For example, in December 1940 Breen, after viewing a rough cut of *Heaven Can Wait*, warned Harry Cohn at Columbia about a potential problem with the legion: "certain religious groups will resent any expressed opinion on the controversial topic of predestination. . . . we recommend that any conversation about future life, recording angels etc. . . . be either omitted entirely or worded very carefully."[25]

The following year, Breen cautioned Universal about a scene that gently mocked the marriage ceremony in the W. C. Fields comedy *Never Give a Sucker an Even Break* and suggested that the producers recut the film and insert the "comedy *before* the ceremony begins." Breen reminded the filmmakers about the legion's directive that all religious ceremonies must be "played straight."[26]

Catholic activism on the censorship front emerged in concert with the growing influence of the church in the first two decades of the twentieth century, especially in the bigger cities. The concentration of the Catholic population in these urban areas made the church and the various clergy speaking out against certain films or the film industry in general a force to be reckoned with. Over 60 percent of the studios' first-run revenues came from their urban, showcase venues. When Catholic censorship activists threatened boycotts in response to a specific title, they targeted the initial run of the film as well as future screenings of other films from the same studio at key showcase theaters. Boycotts thus threatened not only box office revenues of specific controversial movies, but a studio's future slate of releases as well.

As Gregory Black and Frank Walsh argue in their works on Catholics and film censorship, church anti-Hollywood activism emerged in large part as an effort to counter appeals to the federal government made on behalf of the nation's Protestants. Protestant activists supported a Washington, D.C.-based national board of censorship.[27] These self-proclaimed reformers were motivated by a vision of a good society in which the federal government might apply their Protestant values to new social circumstances. According to the historian Frank Couvares, the call for a national system of film censorship managed by the government was "tinged with nativism and class prejudice"; it reflected growing disillusionment among the nation's Protestant majority with a seemingly immoral film industry that was run, so far as they could tell, by "un-Christian" Jews.

Catholics, Couvares contends, "were far more wary of the state" than the Protestant majority at the time, and for good reason. Like the urban Jews, who made up a much smaller percentage of the population, Catholics in the 1920s and 1930s suffered significant anti-immigrant prejudice. The call for local, grassroots regulation of film content by the church was a pragmatic decision based on a fear of Protestant theological and moral hegemony.[28]

Will Hays, American cinema's first censorship czar, was a Presbyterian elder, but because of his mandate, his responsibility to the membership of the MPPDA, he opted against federal regulation. Hays spent his first decade in charge of the MPPDA encouraging local, grassroots "movie betterment" committees as part of a larger public relations strategy to prevent federal, national regulation of film content and to maintain connection(s) with the various ethnic groups and religious organizations that had come to comprise the growingly diverse urban movie audience.[29]

The MPPDA's outreach to community groups was an inclusive public relations gimmick and an impractical long-term business strategy. Hays understood when he took the job that the Hollywood scandals of the 1920s were a symptom of a larger public relations problem.[30] The 1930 MPPDA production code implied the industry's willingness, even anxiousness, to self-regulate film content. But the public, at least at first, didn't buy it. Hays's decision to hire Breen, a well-connected Catholic activist, to preside over the PCA in 1934 established a balance of power between Jewish studio management, Protestant ownership (with its Presbyterian figurehead, Will Hays), and Catholic oversight/regulation.

The inclusion of the church in the operation of the cinematic enterprise was good public relations and it was also a business necessity. Bans and boycotts promised to unsettle especially the urban marketplace. Moreover, the church wielded significant power on Wall Street. Cardinal Mundelein, a close adviser and friend to President Roosevelt, had ties to the Wall Street firm of Halsey, Stuart and Company, which held the paper on several of the Hollywood studios. A. H. Giannini, the Catholic president of the Bank of America, provided financing for studio production. The Bank of America was also a major stockholder in a number of the studios and independent production companies.

Giannini's relationship with Archbishop Cantwell of Los Angeles, a procensorship, anti-Hollywood activist, made a studio deal with the nation's Catholics absolutely essential.[31]

When Burstyn took his case to the U.S. Supreme Court in May 1952, he was concerned primarily with a specific ban on a specific picture he had paid to distribute. But the case nonetheless proved pivotal to the larger history of film censorship. Writing for the majority, Justice Tom Clark overturned the New York State Board of Regents ban on *Ways of Love*. In doing so, Clark reversed a number of precedents dating back to the 1915 *Mutual* case. In perhaps the most important of these reversals, Clark elaborated on Justice Douglas's contention (in *U.S. v. Paramount Pictures*) that movies should be afforded the same First Amendment protections as other forms of art and the press. Clark described the cinema as "a significant medium for the communication of ideas" and concluded that "the importance of motion pictures as an organ of public opinion is not lessened by the fact that they are designed to entertain as well as inform." As to the Court's long-standing view of movie making as "a business pure and simple," Clark opined that films should not be subjected to censorship just because they are produced by an industry conducted for profit, "as such a category would also include the press." Finally, Clark addressed the specific censorship criteria used by the New York State Board of Regents. *The Miracle* was banned because it was sacrilegious. Clark argued that "sacrilege" was a vague term and moreover that it was not "the business of government in our nation to suppress real or imagined attacks upon a particular religious doctrine."[32]

The *Miracle* decision proved to be a watershed moment. In 1954 a New York City ban on *La Ronde*, a French import directed by Max Ophuls, was overturned because criteria like "immoral" and "tending to corrupt morals" were found to be "vague and over-broad." A Texas ban on Elia Kazan's *Pinky* (an MPAA-approved film that a Texas censorship board found "prejudicial to the best interests of the community") and an Ohio ban on *Native Son* (as "harmful" and "conducive to immorality or crime") were both overturned.[33] The decisions foregrounded the voiding of state censorship laws and the disbanding of a number of state censorship boards.[34]

Both *Pinky* and *Native Son* were politically sensitive pictures. *Pinky* is about a white nurse who returns to the South after discovering she is part African American. *Native Son* is based on Richard Wright's novel about a young black man's descent into criminality and racist hatred. That both films concerned race and racism high-lighted a number of larger jurisdictional, states' rights issues. The state board bans on *Pinky* and *Native Son*, which seemed at once racially and politically motivated, fueled a growing anti–states' rights sentiment at the Supreme Court. As the federal judiciary (the Court and the attorney general's office) geared up for a fight with the states on civil rights for people of color, film censorship became an impor-tant if unlikely parallel battleground.

From the very beginning of its role as industry censor, the PCA was sensitive to the fact that different state boards viewed films differently. Throughout the thirties and forties, the PCA recommended cuts to sat-isfy specific state boards and/or encouraged the production of alterna-tive versions of potentially censorable scenes. Since the production of multiple versions and prints was costly and confusing, studios rou-tinely took the safest route possible and produced films that would not offend even the most difficult state boards. For example, in response to a 1938 scenario of the film *Angels with Dirty Faces* sent by Jack Warner to the PCA, Breen wrote, as if he would have had it otherwise, "State boards will probably delete all suggestions of a strip poker game. We suggest that you change it."[35] The studio complied.

But however disingenuous, however ironic such warnings were at the time, filmmakers were invariably compelled to take the PCA's sug-gestions to heart. When Universal sent a rough cut of *The Bride of Frankenstein* to Breen in 1935, the PCA chief acknowledged that "in a story of this kind . . . a certain amount of gruesomeness is necessary." He nevertheless coolly warned Universal that in its present form, the film "will meet with considerable difficulty at the hands of state and local censor boards both in this country and abroad." Universal went ahead and released the film (with a PCA seal) the way the director James Whale cut it, but Breen's warnings proved prescient. A number of local boards and foreign markets banned it or called for significant and expensive cuts. The PCA, which often acted as a mediator in such disputes, turned its back on the film. When *The Bride of Frankenstein* was banned in Ohio, Universal asked Breen to intervene with the notori-ously troublesome board. Breen instead simply forwarded a copy of the state board's long list of problems with the film and told Universal pres-ident Carl Laemmle that so far as he was concerned Universal had "waved aside" the PCA's warnings and was getting pretty much what it deserved.[36]

■

While the Supreme Court's decision in *Burstyn v. Wilson* explicitly granted the studios First Amendment protections for their product, it did not completely free them to produce anything they wanted; obscenity was still not, in the Court's view, protected speech. It is important to note here that the Court's decision in *Burstyn v. Wilson* hinged not on obscenity or pornography but on prior restraint. At issue was not specific content but parallel concerns involving free and fair trade and due process. The way the decision was framed by the Court proved devastating to the various competing censorship boards across the nation because it rendered unconstitutional the very manner in which the local boards did their business.

It is ironic that it was Justice Douglas's opinion in *United States v. Paramount Pictures* that proved pivotal to victory in the industry's parallel struggle with state and grassroots regulatory boards and organizations.[37] Douglas's opinion in the *Paramount* case, which ostensibly supported the industrial regulation of cinema as "a business pure and simple," effectively outlawed the various collusive relationships between distributors and exhibitors and between exhibitors and other exhibitors. In doing so, it forced the studios to establish other sorts of alliances with each other. As a result, the MPAA became the site for another sort of industry collusion. The studios turned to the MPAA for a set of guidelines for competition in the revised marketplace, guidelines that might better exploit the free speech guarantees elaborated in Douglas's opinion in *United States v. Paramount Pictures* and Clark's opinion in the *Miracle* case.

As industry confidence in and dependence on the MPAA grew in the 1950s and 1960s, and as the MPAA's autonomy and authority over film production increased, the studios used what was at first a devastating blow to their business operations to gain more complex and complete control over their product. The *Paramount* and *Miracle* decisions proved pivotal in a larger industrial-corporate scheme: the development of a significantly revised classification (as opposed to censorship) system. This new system, adopted in the fall of 1968, enabled the studios to more fully exploit their newly found free speech protections to make more adult-oriented pictures and to more completely control participation in the exhibition market. Producers, distributors, exhibitors, and even importers (of American product abroad) quickly committed themselves to the new classification system that was developed, adopted, and enforced by the MPAA. In doing so, the MPAA established a network of collusive arrangements, all in the name of content regulation, that have come to characterize the so-called new Hollywood.

BREAKING DOWN THE CODE

Two goats, finishing up the contents of a film can. One says, "What 'ya think?" The other replies, "I prefer the book."
                                                        —an old Hollywood joke

The first successful challenge to the production code came when the independent producer/director Otto Preminger secured the screen rights to F. Hugh Herbert's play *The Moon Is Blue*, a moderately risqué Broadway farce about a young single woman and the two men who enter her life one fateful evening.[38] By the time Preminger purchased the option on the property, production executives at Paramount and Warner Brothers had already expressed interest in adapting the play, but decided against developing a screen version when Breen told them he would never approve it. Preminger's purchase of an option on the play and eventually United Artists' decision to develop the project in earnest revealed a willingness on their parts to invest in a film the PCA was certain to reject.

After optioning the property, Preminger, who directed *The Moon Is Blue* on Broadway, protected his investment cannily. He packaged the film in advance with "A" talent, signing stars William Holden and David Niven. With the two male stars committed to the project, Preminger got United Artists to finance the picture in exchange for domestic distribution rights. At the time, executives had to appreciate the problems the film would cause at the PCA. But they went ahead and financed the picture anyway.

It has always been hard to keep anything secret for long in Hollywood. Breen eventually got a look at a draft of the script and penned a memo renewing his objections to the project. On April 10, 1953, he refused to grant the film a seal of approval, though it is not clear whether anyone at UA ever officially submitted the picture for review. When news of the PCA's position reached Preminger, he refused to cut the film to suit the industry censors.

The standoff between Breen and Preminger put United Artists in a difficult spot. Preminger's contract prevented the studio from forcing him to cut the film (even to suit Breen). The studio's contract with the

William Holden (sporting a black eye), Maggie McNamara, and David Niven in Otto Preminger's film *The Moon Is Blue* (United Artists, 1953). The risqué dialogue made the film a box office sensation.

MPAA was clear as well; if it released the film without a seal of approval, it would be fined $25,000. The studio could afford the fine, but could it afford the risk of releasing a film the MPAA refused to accept or support? Since no major studio had ever defied the code with a big-budget, potentially big box office picture before, UA had no idea how many theaters might refuse to screen *The Moon Is Blue*. The studio also anticipated action from local and grassroots censorship groups emboldened by the MPAA's refusal to give the film its production seal. When the film came out, the Legion of Decency gave the film a condemned rating—as Breen had predicted—and, with other grassroots organizations, threatened a boycott not only of *The Moon Is Blue* but of other, less controversial UA films. The legion also threatened boycotts of local theaters screening the film.

UA's defiance of the PCA risked a breakdown of the collusive structure that worked to the advantage of all the MPAA studios. *The Moon Is Blue*, after all, was just one film. Was it worth the trouble? UA executives decided it was.

Less as a matter of principle than in acknowledgment of just how desperate things had gotten at the box office, UA quit the MPAA in order to release *The Moon Is Blue*. The publicity attending the film's problems with the PCA and the legion censors raised audience awareness of and interest in the picture. It was not the first, nor would it be the last time a PCA controversy sold a film to the public.

After UA resigned from the MPAA, the PCA washed its hands of the whole situation. In the newly deregulated theatrical marketplace, the absence of an MPAA seal proved surprisingly unimportant. Two big, newly independent theater circuits, United Paramount and Stanley Warner, picked up the film. After the circuits decided to defy the MPAA, smaller exhibitors followed suit.

The distribution and promotion of *The Moon Is Blue* more closely resembled a B movie roadshow than a studio release. After all, by the time it reached the marketplace, the film was the property of (technically speaking) an independent studio. The film's original trailer, which did not have a PCA seal, highlighted the picture's bawdy language, its (comic) examination of adult themes and situations. The trailer opens outside a theater screening the movie. A voice-over narrator intones, "For almost three years the stage play has delighted millions . . . now, with the same engaging characters, the same hilarious situations and the same provocative lines, *The Moon Is Blue* has finally hit the screen." We then cut to the ticket booth as an older woman gets a ticket and enters the theater. She walks in on the ending of the film: we see William Holden (sporting a black eye) kissing Maggie McNamara and then the lights come up. Seated next to the older woman is a big black bear. "You can't bring a bear to a movie," she tells the man seated next to the animal. "Why not," he replies, "he loved the play." We then see a series of scenes featuring some of the film's more risqué lines. We see Holden suggest to McNamara that their date end "with ham and eggs," then Niven wink at the audience as he ponders the inherent mysteries of a first date: "is she or isn't she? will she or won't she?" We then see McNamara (in character) quip, "Don't you think it's better for a girl to be preoccupied with sex than occupied?" Two subsequent shots show McNamara caught in the process of undressing by men who then wink knowingly at the camera.

The provocative trailer and the various news and feature stories chronicling Preminger and UA's decision to defy the code helped make the film a top twenty box office hit.[39] Even outright bans by local censorship boards failed to hurt the picture all that much. When, for example, the city of Memphis prohibited the screening of *The Moon Is Blue*, hundreds of interested filmgoers drove to see it at a theater some thirty miles away in Holly Springs, Mississippi.

The film's box office success gave Preminger access to news as well as entertainment reporters and he made the most of the opportunity. With the implied support of UA, Preminger called for a significantly revised production code, a classification system that would identify certain films as "adults only." Preminger and UA found support for such a proposition from film reviewers and newspaper columnists nationwide. W. R. Wilkinson, a columnist for the conservative trade journal the *Hollywood Reporter*, endorsed Preminger's proposal: "Anyone seeing *Moon Is Blue* can easily understand the Breen and Legion slaps. Still, the picture is carried on with such comedy there will be little objection on the part of adult audiences. And it's a good picture. However, if we had a theater and booked the picture, we would restrict its showing to 'adults only,' relieving our conscience—and jumping our ticket sales."[40]

The following year brought another controversial picture with big box office appeal, *The Wild One*, based in part on newspaper accounts of a motorcycle gang briefly taking over the town of Hollister, California. The film concerned Breen because its depiction of juvenile delinquency seemed at once too realistic *and* too attractive. Breen feared that especially the young and impressionable members of the audience might be inclined to enact offscreen the antisocial behavior represented onscreen. In a memo to the film's production team, Breen wrote,

> The callousness of the young hoodlums in upsetting the moral tenor of life in a small town, the manner in which they panic the citizens, the ineffectiveness of law and order for the majority of the script, the brawling, drunkenness, vandalism and irresponsibility of the young men are, in our opinion, all very dangerous elements. They cannot help but suggest to younger members of the audience, it seems to us, the possibilities that lie in their power to get away with hoodlumism, if they only organize into bands.[41]

Though they were cast (in the characteristic royal "we") as mere suggestions and subjective impressions, Breen's remarks about *The Wild One* alluded to specific code violations. According to the code, "the treatment of crimes against the law must not: (1) Teach methods of crime, (2) Inspire potential criminals with a desire for imitation, and (3) Make criminals seem heroic and justified."[42] After the initial

It is hard to imagine many young men who didn't identify with Marlon
Brando in the controversial biker-pic, *The Wild One* (Columbia, 1954).

screening for the PCA, Breen met with the film's influential producer,
Stanley Kramer, and the two hashed out a compromise that enabled
them to avoid a repeat of the problems caused by *The Moon Is Blue*.
Breen and the PCA allowed Kramer to retain intact much of the film's

realistic portrayal of the gang's crimes and most of the violence and rough language in exchange for a cautionary prologue (of the sort seen in a number of other crime dramas: Howard Hawks's *Scarface*, for example) and a speech added at the end of the film in which the county sheriff regards Johnny, the motorcycle outlaw played by Marlon Brando, with scorn: "I don't get you. I don't get your act at all. And I don't think you do, either. I don't think you know what you're trying to do or how to go about it. I think you're stupid, real stupid, and real lucky. Last night, you scraped by. . . . But a man's dead on account of something you let get started . . . I don't know if there's any good in you. I don't know if there's *anything* in you."[43]

Kramer's concessions to Breen and the PCA seemed even at the time absurd and irrelevant. When the sheriff ponders Johnny's potential for the future and "takes a chance" on that future by letting him go (though no crime has been committed, except maybe police brutality during the interrogation), by that point in the film most of the audience couldn't care less what the local authorities think or say. It is hard to watch *The Wild One* and not side with Johnny/Brando, not reject the sheriff as yet another symptom of a hypocritical and weak adult generation. The preamble and coda fitted onto the film by the PCA served only to highlight the film's essential ambiguity and irony. The PCA-approved version of *The Wild One* cautioned audiences about the alarming nature of mob violence and the lawlessness of real youth motorcycle gangs. But Brando's charismatic performance undermined whatever moral lesson Breen and the PCA had in mind. It's hard to imagine many young men who didn't want to be (like) Brando after seeing the picture.[44]

At the end of 1954 Breen retired and was replaced by Geoffrey Shurlock, his chief assistant for almost twenty years. The two men worked together amicably, but Shurlock, unlike Breen, had not joined the PCA as a censorship activist, nor did he have direct ties to the various Catholic censorship organizations. When he took the top post at the PCA, Shurlock immediately set a different tone: "There is no hard and fast rule about any script. . . . Each story has to be judged individually on the basis of morality and reasonable decency."[45] Shurlock's promise to evaluate each film on its own merits brought the MPAA/PCA in line with increasing industry interest in the production of more adult-oriented movies.

By the time Shurlock ascended to the top spot at the PCA, the box office slide was well under way. A number of films released between

1951 and 1953 that had run afoul of the old PCA code—*A Streetcar Named Desire, Born Yesterday, A Place in the Sun, The African Queen, From Here to Eternity,* and *The Moon Is Blue*—performed very well at the box office. Shurlock understood that a significant market awaited more adult-themed pictures and that the studios could not be expected to cooperate with a production code that prevented them from better exploiting the adult demographic.[46]

The PCA Shurlock inherited was in a bind. It was designed to protect industry product lines against outside censorship by anticipating problems with local and grassroots censors and making content changes before films got into the marketplace. But the PCA was also a subsidiary of the MPAA. That organization's primary objective was to support industry profitability.

By 1954 television had already cut into the theatrical market, making a bad situation at the box office even worse. The studios were licensing their films for small screen playdates but they longed for some sort of gimmick—3-D, Cinerama, Cinemascope—to define their product as somehow different and better than the shows and movies on television. A more liberal code promised to encourage the production of films that looked and sounded different from the strictly censored programming on television. But it also promised a showdown with the Legion of Decency and the various state and local censorship boards, the very sort of confrontation the PCA had endeavored to avoid.

Shurlock's commitment to view every film on its own merits was put to the test by a familiar team: Otto Preminger and United Artists. The project in question was a proposed adaptation of Nelson Algren's realist study of drug addiction and Hollywood ambition, *The Man with the Golden Arm.* Preminger and United Artists had already signed Frank Sinatra to play the lead, the luckless Frankie Machine, so it seemed likely that the studio would go ahead and produce the film without a PCA seal if it had to. Complicating the situation further for Shurlock was that Breen had read an early screenplay based on the novel some five years earlier and rejected the project: "We have read the script," Breen wrote in a memo to Preminger, "regarding your proposed production of *The Man With the Golden Arm* and regret to report that the basic story is unacceptable . . . and a motion picture based upon [it] cannot be approved."[47] Breen's objections to the project were predictable; the film transgressed against specific criteria laid out in the production code regarding the depiction of drug use and addiction.[48]

Subsequent efforts on the part of MGM to find a suitable screenplay

Frank Sinatra as the luckless Frankie Machine in *The Man with the Golden Arm* (United Artists, 1955). Otto Preminger's realistic treatment of drug addiction cost the film a PCA seal, but it did well at the box office anyway.

based on Algren's novel served only to make Breen impatient and angry. A third version met with as firm a rejection as the first: "I have read with extreme care the revised script for your proposed production *The Man with the Golden Arm* and it is our considered and unanimous opinion that this story is totally in violation of the Production Code."

When Preminger brought the project back to the board in 1955, Shurlock refused to contradict Breen. Shurlock wrote, "I regret to have to report your script for *The Man with the Golden Arm* is fundamentally in violation of the code clause which prohibits pictures dealing with drug addiction."[49]

Shurlock's terse memo to UA and Preminger seemed to suggest that the PCA had not changed much since Breen's retirement. But Shurlock was in a difficult spot. UA and Preminger were committed to producing the picture with or without his approval. Given the recent success of adult-themed films, PCA interference with the project was in direct conflict with the MPPA's larger effort to find a way to get people back into the habit of going to the movies. While *The Man with the Golden Arm* was in direct violation of explicit code criteria regarding the depiction of crime and drug use, Shurlock no doubt appreciated that it promised to be an important picture for its studio. And if the film did well with the critics, its success could well lend support to mounting pressure within the MPAA membership, the entertainment press, and the filmgoing public to update the production code.

In December 1955 Preminger delivered a cut of the film to Shurlock. Under pressure from the U.S. narcotics commissioner Harry Anslinger, Shurlock denied the picture a PCA seal. Strangely enough, the Legion of Decency did not give the film its condemned rating. *The Man with the Golden Arm* received a B rating from the Catholic censorship body. The B classification identified the picture as "morally objectionable in part for all," but did not prohibit adult Catholics from viewing the movie if they still wanted to see it.

Shurlock's official memo to UA was curt: "We have reviewed your picture *The Man with the Golden Arm*. As we advised you, the picture is basically in violation of the Production Code." Though it was released without a PCA seal of approval, *The Man with the Golden Arm* got a wide enough theatrical release to tie *The Man in the Grey Flannel Suit* as the thirteenth-highest grossing film of 1956. UA's problems with the PCA and the MPAA seemed a distant memory when Frank Sinatra received an Academy Award nomination for best actor for his performance in the film.

The possibility that Sinatra might win (he didn't; Ernest Borgnine won for *Marty*) had much the same effect on the industry as the 1969 best picture Oscar for UA's *Midnight Cowboy*, an X-rated film released without an MPAA rating system seal. The nomination suggested not only that there was considerable audience interest in pictures that did not conform to MPAA content guidelines, but also that MPAA leadership was out of step with its own membership.

In 1956, with the support of MPAA president Eric Johnston, Shurlock made the first of what would become a series of changes in the old code. Responsible depictions of crime, to be judged on a case-by-case basis, could be approved. "Hell" and "damn," when used in context (and not excessively) could also survive PCA scrutiny. But these minor changes served only to highlight the code's obsolescence.

Much as Valenti would argue in the fall of 1968, the studios' desire to revise or rewrite the code in the mid-fifties had little to do with free speech or anticensorship politics. Instead, the studios' serial nudging of the code with adult-themed productions was simply a response to a market trend. The filmgoing audience had dwindled significantly in the early 1950s. Adult-themed pictures made money and helped maintain studio and industry recognition in the growingly competitive pop culture marketplace. Mores were changing in the United States in the 1950s. But social change was relevant to the studios only insofar as that change could be empirically measured in terms of box office grosses. The zeitgeist, such as it was, was there to be exploited.

Box office revenues were of paramount importance, but after the war the studios began to look at the mass audience as something too diverse to satisfy with any single product. One lesson executives learned from television and other parallel pop culture media like feature magazines, comic books, music (on radio and on record), and advertising was that money could be made by focusing on specific audience demographics. By 1956 the mass audience quite suddenly had a number of choices, not only between specific movies (from specific studios) but between media, some of which (like radio and TV) were ostensibly free. Market research suggested that a targetable sector of the mid-1950s movie audience—those people still interested in spending their entertainment dollars at the box office—were interested in adult-themed material. Once studio executives accepted the fact that they were no longer making movies for everyone, the development of a system to classify rather than censor movies was inevitable.

The highly subjective practice of judging films on a case-by-case basis proved to be a significant problem for Shurlock and the PCA. The 1934 code, which was still in effect in 1956, was objective by design. PCA criteria and production standards were designed to be applied uniformly to adaptations of serious stage plays, historical melodramas,

westerns, horror pictures, and comedies. Films of vastly different quality (as works of art, as industrial pop culture products) were equal in the
eyes of the PCA. That certain films might be given preferential treatment under a new rating system—that certain films might defy specific
code criteria and still merit a seal and nationwide distribution/exhibi-
tion—enabled and encouraged studios to define their products as wor-
thy of special consideration from the PCA in advance of production and
release. A cursory look at studio production in the mid-fifties reveals a
pattern of "prestige" adults-only production: *A Streetcar Named Desire*,
Death of a Salesman, *The Red Badge of Courage*, *The Browning Version*, *From
Here to Eternity*, *The Man with a Golden Arm*, and *East of Eden*.

Two of the most difficult projects brought to the PCA in 1956 were
Tea and Sympathy and *27 Wagons Full of Cotton* (later retitled *Baby Doll*).
Both were based on serious, controversial stage plays and both were
products developed well in advance of their arrival on Shurlock's desk.
Moreover, the two projects had a cultural currency; the mass audience
knew a lot about them well in advance of their release. The PCA needed
to consider its treatment of the projects carefully. Changes from stage to
screen would be recognized and most likely examined in the trades and
the national press.

Tea and Sympathy opened on Broadway in September 1953.[50] The
play tells the story of Tom, a boy at a posh prep school who is perse-
cuted by his classmates, who circulate a rumor that he is gay. Tom begins to doubt his masculinity and tries a variety of things, including an
encounter with a prostitute, to prove them wrong. Tom's classmates
find support from the residence housemaster, a macho thug, and the
torture escalates, prompting the boy to contemplate suicide. The housemaster's wife, at once attracted to Tom—he is, unlike the rest of the men
in the story, sensitive and sweet—and exasperated at her husband, decides to seduce and in doing so, rescue the boy. The play ends as she
undresses and utters the classic line, "Years from now . . . when you talk
about this . . . and you will . . . be kind."

In October 1953, in response to a tip from Martin Quigley, the editor of the *Motion Picture Herald*, Breen dispatched Shurlock and another
PCA executive, Jack Vizzard, to New York to see *Tea and Sympathy*
and meet with the playwright, Richard Anderson, and the director,
Elia Kazan. Anderson at the time boldly maintained that he would
not allow a studio to option the play unless (1) the seduction ending
was left intact, (2) the body of the play still concerned accusations of

"Years from now, when you talk about this . . . and you will . . . be kind."
Housemistress Deborah Kerr begins to realize what she must do to save a tor-
mented schoolboy in *Tea and Sympathy* (MGM, 1956).

homosexuality (Anderson was no doubt familiar with *These Three*, the
1935 film adaptation of Lillian Hellman's play *The Children's Hour*, in
which the plot concerning a rumored lesbian affair was replaced by a
story line about a student falsely accusing her teachers of heterosexual
infidelity), and (3) the boy, in desperation to prove his masculinity and
heterosexuality, visits a prostitute.[51]

Anderson's refusal to budge on what were, of course, three important plot points in the play made the film impossible to make under
1953 PCA guidelines. Warner Brothers negotiated the purchase of the
rights to the property anyway and, as UA had done with *The Moon Is
Blue*, announced its intention to produce the picture without PCA participation. Rumor had it at the time that Milton Sperling, the Warner
Brothers executive in charge of the project, was looking into the possibility of producing and distributing the picture under an independent
company banner. In doing so, Warner Brothers, which owned the inde-

pendent company, would still directly profit from the picture's release but would not have to quit the MPAA.

When Warner Brothers, on Breen's and Johnston's urging, shelved its plan to independently produce the movie and decided against renewing its option, first Paramount and then Columbia showed interest in the play. But when Anderson continued to refuse to budge, both studios backed down.[52]

Two years later, Dore Schary and MGM stepped in with an astonishingly lucrative offer to develop a film based on the play. The deal included a $100,000 "pay or play" option on the property, which guaranteed Anderson $100,000 whether or not MGM ever made the film and a lump sum payment of $300,000 should the studio exercise its option to actually make the movie.[53] In exchange for the cash up front and the guarantee of more upon completion of the picture, Anderson backed off on his insistence that the film be faithful to the letter and spirit of the play. In March 1955 MGM submitted a script to Shurlock for PCA perusal. In the revised screenplay, Tom's "problem" is an apparent effeminacy. Tom still seeks solace from a local woman (an undiscriminating waitress) but does so not on the urging of classmates, whom we gather have preceded him in her bed. He instead overhears local townspeople talking about her and foolishly assumes that she has the solution to his apparent problem. The housemaster's wife still delivers the cure at the end, but does so only after Tom, whose failed suicide attempt has brought him to her attention, talks about making good on a second try.

Shurlock, who supported Breen's stand on the film, acknowledged the studio's efforts to "change and improve" the play, but continued to point out the three significant code violations that persisted (albeit less explicitly depicted) in the script. MGM was already $100,000 in the hole to Anderson and thus inclined to produce the film anyway. Anderson, who stood to make another $300,000 should the production get the green light, was inclined to compromise even more in order to see a big payday. The studio was anxious to get the film into the marketplace while the public was still keen to see it.

In the "good old days" of MPAA unity and PCA authority, Anderson could well have expected the studio to bully him into revising his play. After all, the studio had too much money invested in the project not to make the film. But after UA's success with *The Moon Is Blue*, MGM executives appreciated the fact that they did not need to deal with the PCA if they didn't want to. The reasonable assumption that the film, with or without a PCA seal, would make money emboldened MGM in its negotiations with the PCA.

But censorship in the 1950s involved more than just the PCA and more than just the task of securing playdates from independent exhibitors for a controversial film. Ignoring the PCA was one thing; risking a ban or boycott from the Legion of Decency was another. When the studio's plan to produce the film without a PCA seal became public, Loew's, which owned MGM at the time, received a disturbing note from Monsignor Little on behalf of the legion. Little wrote that while he routinely waited to see a final cut of a film before conferring a rating or classification, he was alarmed at MGM's apparent disregard of the PCA. *Tea and Sympathy*, Monsignor Little opined, was "gravely offensive to American Catholics."[54]

The threat of a legion-organized ban or boycott coupled with its pay-or-play option on the property encouraged MGM to renegotiate with Anderson. With $300,000 on the line, Anderson eventually gave in to studio pressure to soften all three of the significant plot points. As it was screened upon its release in 1956, the film was framed by material not included in (or consistent with the narrative or themes of) the play. The film opens with Tom, now grown up, returning to his old school, the site of his long past adolescent turmoil. Tom's story, then, is told in flashback, and its impact is blunted. We see from the very start that Tom did not commit suicide, that he grew up more or less okay. The original play, in slightly altered form, is told entirely in flashback. In the film, the mean-spirited teasing never explicitly refers to homosexuality: Tom likes folk music and doesn't much like sports, but that's as far as it goes. The curtain line from the play is left intact, but the film does not end there. Instead, we return to the present tense, and see the man who was once a tortured adolescent by chance meet his old nemesis, now an old, bitter man. The housemaster hands him a letter his wife wrote but never sent. It is read in voice-over to close out the film:

> As you must know, I couldn't go back to Bill after that afternoon with you and pretend that nothing had happened. And my not going back ruined his life—both of you, in a sense, were crying out to be saved from what you thought you wanted. In answering your cry, I took the easier way, and unhappily, the wrong way—These are terrible things to write to you, Tom, about sin and guilt, but you are old enough now to know that when you drop a pebble in the water, there are ever-widening circles of ripples—ripples that may carry afar a burden of

good or of evil. Anyway, Tom, I have come to realize that I showed a lack of faith in you, in your ability to meet a crisis by yourself and come through it manfully alone.

After the film was released, Anderson confessed regret that he changed the play to suit the PCA and the Legion of Decency. He vowed that he would never again give in to pressure to censor his art. The critics were divided about the changes made in the film adaptation of the play. One critic suggested that filmgoers leave the theater before the last scene (the reading of the letter); others applauded the PCA for enabling the production of even a watered-down version of such adult-themed material. Bosley Crowther, the influential reviewer for the *New York Times*, used his review of *Tea and Sympathy* to call for changes in the old code: "That long-time formidable obstruction to morally controversial material in American films—we speak of the operation of the industry's own Production Code—is slowly and quietly being loosened to accord with what is obviously a change in social attitudes. And the industry is much better for it, as is certainly the medium of films." Crowther's contention that the old code somehow stood in the way of industry profitability *and* the production of better movies was something few industry executives in 1956 could afford to ignore.

Baby Doll, perhaps the fifties' most controversial picture, was based on *27 Wagons Full of Cotton*, Tennessee Williams's notorious one-act play about a teenage bride and her hapless husband. The screenplay first submitted for PCA approval posed a number of problems for Shurlock, not the least of which was Williams's gothic depiction of the reconstructed American South, which promised to raise the ire of regional censorship boards. (Congressman John Rankin's anti-Semitic screed on the floor of the House in 1947 after the first round of hearings conducted by the House Committee on Un-American Activities highlighted the very sort of regionalist sensitivity the PCA endeavored to respect.)[55] The play's plot concerns a sexually ambiguous, perhaps even ambivalent child-bride who exchanges her vows of marriage for her husband's promise not to have sex with her until she turns twenty. Her virginity as much as her budding sexuality becomes the focus of the play's action: she sleeps in a crib and sucks on her thumb, both childlike activities made adult and carnal by the way they are viewed by the husband, who watches her through a hole drilled through the bedroom wall. (By implication, the audience shares his view.)

As Shurlock dutifully pointed out, the play violated several specific code criteria. The proposed film promised a significant amount of "partial nudity, undue exposure and suggestive costumes." (In the film, Baby Doll spends virtually the entire movie in a two-piece shortie nightgown, which, much as the PCA code was designed to prevent, swept the nation as a fashion for young women after the first run of the film.)[56] The husband's tendency to deal with his sexual frustration by spying on his young wife and the plotline concerning Silva, the vengeful immigrant who ruins the husband's business and most likely seduces his wife, violated code criteria concerning the depiction of "low forms of sex relationship" and its insistence that films respect the "sanctity of the institution of marriage and the home."[57]

The moral ambiguity inherent in Williams's larger vision of the rural South may well have worked well on the New York stage, but the PCA code was designed to maintain very different standards for motion pictures. Breen and Shurlock were both anxious to view Williams's adult dramas as art, which explains why they were so anxious to censor them on film. Much as Justice Joseph McKenna wrote in his opinion in the *Mutual* case in 1915, the PCA held that movies should be treated differently from other art forms because they appealed primarily to the baser concerns of its mass audience.

Under the heading "Reasons Supporting Preamble of Code," the PCA maintained that "theatrical motion pictures . . . are primarily to be regarded as entertainment." Thus, "the latitude given to film material cannot, in consequence, be as wide as the latitude given to book material." Books, after all, depend "largely on the keenness of the reader's imagination." Films instead depend on "the vividness of presentation" and on viewers who are not so keen or sophisticated as the readers of books. As to the differences between stage and screen, the code maintained that "the screen story is brought closer to the audience than the play" and that, in an argument that reveals the code's roots in the star scandals, "the [movie] audience is more ready to confuse actor and actress and the characters they portray" and thus "more receptive of the emotions and ideals presented by their favorite stars." In order to appear not as censors but as intermediaries in a larger economic endeavor in which immoral films were bad for business, Breen and then Shurlock affirmed the artistic value of Williams's work on paper and on the stage while at the same time insisting that "Everything in a play is not possible in a film."[58]

By the time the producer-director Elia Kazan and the distributor, Warner Brothers, began to develop a film version of the play, Williams, who was retained by the studio to write the screenplay, was already a veteran of PCA controversy. The production of the film version of *A Streetcar Named Desire* in 1951 resulted in a bitterly negotiated four minutes' worth of cuts for a PCA seal.[59] The agreed-upon cuts in *A Streetcar Named Desire* were comically arbitrary, especially since the plot and theme of the play and film in themselves violated a number of code criteria. The PCA, for example, insisted on the excision of the last three words of the line. "I would like to kiss you softly and sweetly on the mouth," but left intact dialogue suggesting Blanche's nymphomania. The climactic scene in which Stanley rapes Blanche (shot in tasteful low contrast) remained in the picture, as Williams insisted it must from the outset. In exchange for its inclusion, Williams agreed to change the ending of the play.[60] As Blanche is carted off to the lunatic asylum, Stella, who in the play accepts the rape as wholly consistent with her husband's nature, which she, alas, can't resist, decides in the film version to leave Stanley. Such is his punishment for his crime and betrayal.[61]

In defense of the *27 Wagons Full of Cotton* script submitted to the PCA, Williams tried to explain to Breen and then Shurlock that the characters in the play are all pretty awful people and thus act in self-interest. Filmgoers would not be inclined, or so Williams argued, to identify with any of the characters in the scenario.

The notion that a play featuring immoral characters behaving immorally might make for a moral film was predictably an argument lost on the two PCA managers. Breen, for example, expressed concern about "the low and sordid tone of the story as a whole." "As far as the three principals are concerned," he argued, "this story seems mainly interested in crime, sex, murder and revenge." Breen suggested to Williams that he might frame the picture with some voice-over narration provided by the one seemingly decent character in the script, the affable African American, Charlie.[62] By contemporary standards, Breen's suggestion seems all too neat and politically correct. But in the early 1950s, Breen's desire to give audiences "somebody to cheer for" in this case promised to antagonize grassroots religious groups and censorship boards in the South, which at the time routinely called for bans on films that featured positive depictions of African Americans. With or without such a positive depiction of an African American character, virtually any adaptation of the play promised to offend audiences in the South. In the end, the regional/political problems posed by *Baby Doll* outweighed its more openly discussed sex and costuming code violations.

What made the *Baby Doll* situation unmanageable for Breen and

Shurlock were the specific conditions of its production. Elia Kazan was the project's producer-director. He was at the time a powerful industry player. His adaptation of *A Streetcar Named Desire* was the fifth highest-grossing film of 1951 and won Academy Awards for Vivien Leigh, Kim Hunter, and Karl Malden. (Kazan lost to George Stevens, the director of *A Place in the Sun*; Brando lost to Humphrey Bogart for his performance in *The African Queen*.) Three years later, Kazan, Brando, Eva Marie Saint, and the screenwriter Budd Schulberg all won for *On the Waterfront*, which placed fifteenth on the box office list in 1954. While *A Streetcar Named Desire* highlighted Kazan's reputation as a stage and film director of difficult and provocative material, *On the Waterfront*, a film that demonizes unions and glorifies snitching on one's peers, offered a reminder to MPAA management of Kazan's "friendly" testimony before the House Committee on Un-American Activities. Kazan (who named eleven names), like screenwriter Budd Schulberg (who named fifteen) and the film's costar Lee J. Cobb (who named twenty), was a high-profile cooperative witness for the MPAA in its complicity with the various congressional inquisitions.[63] By the time he proposed an adaptation of *27 Wagons Full of Cotton*, Kazan was important to the MPAA because he was a bankable auteur *and* because his testimony before HUAC had made for good public relations. He was thus a player with whom the MPAA was inclined to cooperate.

When Kazan first optioned *27 Wagons Full of Cotton*, his agents were able to secure a contract with Warner Brothers that gave him final cut on the film. Kazan was to be both director and producer of the picture, a hefty load that suggested the shifting power relations in the post–contract-era marketplace. The *Baby Doll* contract forced the PCA to deal directly with Kazan. But Kazan was under no obligation to comply with code guidelines. By the time Kazan was ready to start shooting the film, Warner Brothers had invested so much money in the project that it was committed to completing it with or without a code seal. Shurlock, who inherited the Kazan/*Baby Doll* headache after Breen retired, was charged less with regulating the film's production than with negotiating some sort of compromise (as he had brokered in the *Tea and Sympathy* controversy) that might allow the PCA to offer a seal of approval for a film based on a property his predecessor had deemed unfilmable from the outset.

Warner Brothers executives did the only thing they could to influence the development of the project: they kept out of the fray as Kazan and Williams negotiated directly with the PCA. From 1952 to 1955, as part of the negotiation process, Williams experimented with a variety of changes in the plot and structure of the play. In one version, Archie kills Silva and then is carted off to jail; in another, a cyclone rolls into town and kills off pretty much everyone.[64] Both revisions seem satirical in retrospect, mere parodies of the PCA's penchant for "compensating values," for sinners to be punished, if necessary in arbitrary and absurd plot twists or tacked-on voice-overs, as used in *Tea and Sympathy*, which contradict the plot and themes of the rest of the film.

When Williams submitted a final draft of the script to the PCA in 1955, the Warner Brothers story executive Finlay McDermid cannily described the scenario as an "ironic comedy."[65] Comedies, after all, were often afforded more latitude than dramas. Williams's gothic sensibility evidenced in the play's ambiguous depiction of larger-than-life sinners, all of whom seemed to be asking for a cyclone to spirit them off into oblivion, was a kind of joke lost on Breen and Shurlock. The notion that Archie, Silva, and Baby Doll might be caricatures, like those naughty Connecticut residents in some thirties screwball comedy, was a stretch. But McDermid was playing the hand he was dealt, as a drama, even the revised script seemed destined for problems with the PCA.

In 1955 Shurlock understood that after three years of buzz in the popular press, Kazan and Warner Brothers were finally going to make the film. Shurlock decided to try to influence the production as much as possible even though he and the PCA would most likely never grant the film a production seal. Kazan seemed aware of Shurlock's strategy and wisely opted to shoot the picture in Mississippi, far from the PCA offices and the entertainment press in Los Angeles.

When Kazan delivered his final cut to the PCA, Shurlock complained about the apparent adulterous relationship between Silva and Baby Doll, which is implied twice in the film: first when the two touch each other on the swing (eventually prompting Baby Doll's apparent ecstasy) and then when Silva joins her in the crib and the camera cuts away.[66] Williams's final draft included a gesture on the young woman's part that suggests that intercourse, at least, was not involved. But Kazan cut the gesture and added a scene in which Silva promises to return the following day, implying that it was. Kazan argued that the swing scene was mostly talk and little action and that the crib was too small for intercourse. He then took the PCA censor Jack Vizzard and Shurlock through the film frame by frame, defying the censors to show him when and where Baby Doll and Silva consummate their affair. It was a deft strategy; of course, no such explicit scene was in the film. The frame-by-frame analysis deflected attention away from the film's larger thematic defiance of the code. It was not so much what *happened* onscreen as what the entire picture was about.

Astonishingly, *Baby Doll* was awarded a PCA seal. The Legion of Decency, more predictably, gave the film a condemned rating. The legion maintained that the subject matter of the film was "grievously offensive to Christian and traditional standards of morality and decency," and that its production and release were in "open disregard of the Code." The legion was of course right on both counts; Williams intended the film as an affront to traditional moral standards and Kazan and Warner Brothers made the film in open disregard and defiance of the PCA.

In response to pressure from the Legion of Decency and the journalist-activist Martin Quigley, a group of MPAA executives took a look at *Baby Doll*. After the screening, they confessed that they too were bewildered by the PCA's decision to grant the film its seal of approval. In a memoir on his life as a movie censor, Vizzard put the situation in context. The PCA's decision to grant *Baby Doll* a code seal resulted from a three-year process during which the project was revised significantly in accordance with PCA memoranda. The legion's condemnation of the picture resulted from the fact that the Catholic group was not in on the development process. Its first contact with the material was at the screening of Kazan's release print of the film.[67]

The MPAA's attempt to satisfy the Legion of Decency was undermined by Warner Brothers' advertising campaign for the film. The trailer ads distributed by United Artists that featured the most risqué lines from *The Moon Is Blue* (which, after all, did not receive a PCA seal) hardly prepared anyone in the industry for the sort of provocative imagery employed in the print advertising and lobby posters and cards supporting *Baby Doll*.

A promotion department's job is always a difficult one; it must define a picture it did not develop, produce, or edit in such a way as to convince audiences to buy tickets for something they have not yet seen. The Warner Brothers promotion department downplayed *Baby Doll*'s pedigree; though it was adapted from a stage play like *The Moon Is Blue* and *Tea and Sympathy*, the advertising campaign seemed more like something from the grindhouse exploitation circuit. Many of the ads featured Carroll Baker as Baby Doll, characteristically sucking her thumb, supine in her nightgown peering out through the bars of her crib. The decision to promote the film's erotic, kinky appeal was not only an obvious marketing strategy, it was an arrogant position to take vis-à-vis the PCA. The PCA's only viable defense of its decision to grant the film a seal of approval was the project's high art pedigree. The Warner Brothers advertising scheme seemed designed to render such a characterization of the film irrelevant and absurd.

Immediately following its premiere, Cardinal Spellman took to the pulpit to attack the picture, calling on "every loyal citizen" to boycott the film.[68] He reminded his parishioners of their pledge, as elaborated in the amended 1934 Legion of Decency charter: "I condemn indecent and immoral pictures, and those which glorify crime or criminals. I promise to do all that I can to strengthen public opinion against the production of indecent and immoral films, and to unite with all who protest against them. I acknowledge my obligation to my moral life. As a member of the Legion of Decency, I pledge myself to remain away from them. I promise, further, to stay away altogether from places of amusement which show them as a matter of policy."[69]

Baby Doll opened big, then died. Its failure at the box office resulted in part from poor word of mouth; the film is awfully dark and almost camp in its caricature of southern white trash. Its sensational, risqué depiction of the child-bride was less explicit than the public was led to expect by the posters, ads, and all the attention the production had received from the mainstream and Catholic press.

Baby Doll was never really a bankable project. It was based on a serious, complex, and rarely seen one-act play performed by mostly little known New York stage actors and Hollywood character players. *Baby Doll* did not have a Brando or even a Vivien Leigh and its release did not immediately follow a successful run on Broadway. The film was too complex and its tone too strange for the mass audience. Controversy in itself was not enough to sell the picture.

Marketing executives at Warner Brothers tried to exploit the PCA/Legion of Decency controversy. But the strategy backfired. When the film performed disappointingly at the box office, the Legion of Decency, whose opposition to the picture was explicitly mentioned in the studio's advertising scheme, took credit for its failure. To an extent it was justified in doing so. The legion successfully disrupted the release of the film by targeting theater owners, many of whom were faced for the first time with a film that had received a PCA seal but nevertheless was the target of significant local censorship activity.

Theater owners who opted to show the film risked a six-month boycott. Parishioners attending screenings of the film risked the ire of their priests, many of whom lurked in theater lobbies, pad and pen in hand, taking down names. The bad publicity and economic pressure exerted by the Legion of Decency, Quigley, and Cardinal Spellman prevented the wide release/quick payoff strategy indicated by the film's high-profile development, slick ad campaign, and poor word of mouth. From the start, Warner Brothers struggled to get the film into theaters. Positive word of mouth might have saved the picture, but when the film failed to hit the way *The Moon Is Blue* or *A Streetcar Named Desire* did, many exhibitors declined to book *Baby Doll*. It just wasn't interesting enough, nor was it making enough money to justify taking on the legion.

Though *Baby Doll* did poorly at the box office, after 1956 the studios continued to defy the MPAA/PCA in order to get their adult-themed films into the marketplace. One ironic effect of the *Paramount* decision was that, in the process of diminishing MPAA control over or influence with exhibitors, the court created a niche for films released without a PCA seal; it afforded theater owners the opportunity to screen such films without industry penalty. But such a freedom came at a price. When the studios failed to police the industry themselves, the Legion of Decency and other censorship bodies condemned the MPAA. But unlike the old PCA, these extra-industry organizations had no power on their own to meaningfully alter the product itself. Instead, these organizations took to terrorizing theater owners, who, after divestiture, were no longer protected by their major suppliers and were vulnerable not only to boycott but also to arrest.

Baby Doll was a particularly difficult picture for theater owners. First, there was the legion and the very real possibility of a boycott. Business was bad enough without picketers and priests on the sidewalk in front of the theater. And then there were the regional/local censorship boards. Booking the film in the South, for example, was a bold political act, and given the film's poor performance nationwide, it was unnecessary. The *Paramount* decision enabled theater owners to book films in an open and competitive free market. It also isolated them from a studio industry no longer inclined or able to defend them.

As the PCA increasingly lost its ability to control the studio product, censorship of film content was left to grassroots organizations and local censorship boards. These organizations and boards knew that taking on the studios was a difficult and expensive project. But taking on a local, independent theater owner was another matter entirely. The shift in public pressure from production to exhibition was good news for the studios. They produced more and more adult-themed pictures and then stood by as restrictive actions against exhibitors escalated. From 1962 to 1965, censorial action—including prosecutions, arrests, confiscations, license revocations, and local boycotts—increased tenfold. By 1965 roughly 60 percent of the films in general release were met by some sort of local censorship action, all of it targeted at the nation's exhibitors.[70] Three years later, when the MPAA offered a classification system that might protect exhibitors against such action, the National Association of Theater Owners (NATO) was anxious to cooperate, even though the new MPAA system made enforcement of its age-based code their problem. The conflict between NATO and the MPAA, between exhibitors and distributors, set in motion by the *Paramount* decision was resolved once and for all not as an antitrust matter per se, but as an ancillary consequence of the parallel regulatory process attending film content.

JACOBELLIS v. OHIO

The "contemporary community standards" by which the issue of obscenity is to be determined are not those of the particular local community from which the case arises, but those of the Nation as a whole.
—Justice William Brennan, *Jacobellis v. Ohio*

The controversies attending *The Moon Is Blue, Tea and Sympathy*, and *Baby Doll* signaled a decline in PCA influence over film production. Supreme Court reversals on state board prohibitions and bans— *Burstyn v. Wilson, Gelling v. Texas*, and *Superior Films v. Department of Education of Ohio*—rendered *state* censorship impractical if not impossible. The apparent ineffectiveness of formal, industrial, and state censorship apparatuses led to a marked increase in grassroots activism.

For the nation's theater owners, the reemergence of local censorship was particularly bad news. Grassroots regulation was unpredictable, extralegal, and highly effective. Organizations with colorful names like Combat (a church-based group in Wisconsin) and the Mothers of Minnesota were established with the express purpose of regulating the local exhibition of motion pictures. But much of the burden of local activism fell to already established organizations that branched out into censorship. Local chapters of the PTA, NAACP, Catholic War Veterans, and even the International Longshoreman Association pressured local law enforcement, which in turn pressured theater owners.

Police and district attorneys employed a variety of methods to regulate the sort of product screened at local theaters. Prints of controversial films were occasionally seized and theater owners and managers fined or incarcerated for violations of (mostly unconstitutional) local obscenity statutes. Uncooperative exhibitors were often denied renewals on their business licenses. To prevent theaters from moving into certain neighborhoods, city governments exploited obscure zoning ordinances or refused to grant building permits. The zoning/building permit strategy was routinely employed when drive-in theaters were involved. Censorship activists, with some justification, tended to associate outdoor venues with exploitation pictures that targeted the burgeoning, "impressionable" teen audience, the very group they sought to protect.

The primary difference between the PCA's formal regulation of film content and informal censorship originating on the local level was that the industry censors viewed the movies (often several times at various stages of development), while local organizations directed their efforts at movies they seldom bothered to see.[71] The PCA endeavored to apply industry standards to each version of each film submitted for review. Local censors rarely possessed such a comparative frame of reference; they often disliked cinema in general and their complaints about specific films were generally based on movie reviews in newspapers and articles in magazines published by their local diocese or church.

The police units charged with responding to citizen complaints about specific motion pictures were often staffed with officers who shared local activists' concern about film content. Police censors had little (and really didn't need any) perspective on the medium or the movie business as a whole. For example, in the mid-fifties the police inspector charged with responding to and evaluating local obscenity complaints in Madison, Wisconsin, freely admitted that he never went to the movies or watched television, except for football games.[72]

While the PCA had a number of appeal mechanisms in place and often engaged in dialogue with filmmakers in order to bring certain films into compliance with the code, such procedural safeguards were nonexistent at the local level. Theater owners were subjected to prior restraint without any opportunity to mount a defense or engage in a dialogue with the citizens who precipitated the action against them. Unlike the studios, which responded only to organizations with national clout, local theaters were extremely vulnerable to even the most narrowly focused groups and individual local activists, many of whom attained some authority and/or official capacity in censorship disputes simply because they had the time and desire to get involved.

Local bans rarely took into account the binding financial arrangements involved in booking films. Once a booking agreement is made, exhibitors are under contractual obligation to screen the film. When theater owners pulled certain films as a consequence of local censorship, they had to pay a fee to the distributor as compensation for holding up the print that might otherwise have been booked and screened at another venue.[73]

Theater managers were particularly vulnerable to local authorities. Fines for screening films deemed obscene were most often imposed not on theater owners, but on their employees who presided over the projection of the film in question. Unlike their bosses, theater managers seldom booked movies and rarely if ever had a financial interest in a given film's success or failure at the theater.

The legal appeal process was an available but expensive alternative for theater owners and managers. And as things played out after the war, it was an expensive alternative they had to finance entirely by themselves. Because they no longer had a direct financial interest in the success or even survival of the newly independent theater owners, the MPAA studios held fast to a policy not to intervene in local censorship cases.

In addition to the cost of fighting each local censorship action, theater owners had to consider the possibility that a victory in court might simply raise the stakes the next time a controversial picture hit town. Local movie houses, like all local businesses, depend on community relations. Fighting local activists to make a constitutional point was hardly a good strategy for establishing an endearing local reputation.

In the absence of financial or public relations support from the MPAA, exhibitors and their managers and projectionists routinely capitulated to local activists. This pattern of compliance was broken, or at least interrupted, on November 13, 1959, when Nico Jacobellis, the manager and projectionist at the (Cleveland) Heights Art Theater, defied a local police order and screened Louis Malle's non-MPAA, foreign-made picture *Les Amants* (*The Lovers*).[74]

The screening proved to be a turning point in the history of American film censorship. As the film unspooled on opening night, Jacobellis was arrested by local law enforcement. He was taken to the police station, fingerprinted, booked on charges of possessing and exhibiting an obscene motion picture, and released on a $100 personal bond. The following morning, the arrest was the lead story in the *Cleveland Plain Dealer*. The little suburban theater and its eclectic programming of foreign and American independent art films was suddenly front-page news and its Italian immigrant manager, himself not yet an American citizen, became the most controversial man in Ohio.

The Heights Art Theater first opened in 1954, the very year the Supreme Court dismantled the Ohio state censorship apparatus (*Superior Films v. Department of Education of Ohio*). From the day it first opened, the Heights Art Theater annoyed local residents, many of whom had fled Cleveland's declining downtown to get away from neighborhoods poisoned by so-called art theaters. Local opposition to the theater, which was expressed primarily in persistent censorship activity, had more to do with property values and suburban aesthetics (such as they are) than with specific film content.

Local law enforcement had been called to the theater a number of times between 1954 and 1959 to respond to citizen complaints about specific movies. When they got to the theater to investigate these complaints, local authorities did not always find management anxious or even willing to cooperate. For example, after a preview screening of the Swedish picture *The Snow Is Black*, local police insisted on an adults-only admissions policy for the film. The police provided Jacobellis with a sign to be posted on the box office window. The theater manager refused to display it. Police preceded Jacobellis to the theater the following day and taped a sign on the outside of the box office window. Jacobellis took it down.

After Jacobellis's arrest and conviction for screening *Les Amants* in 1959, the theater owner, Louis Sher, and Zenith International Films president Daniel Frankel (the distributor of the Malle film) decided to contest the local obscenity ruling. The suit took five years to make its way through the courts and proved to be one of the key cases in the history of not only film content regulation but state censorship in general.

Sher's decision to take on local activists in Cleveland was at once an expression of his exasperation at informal censorship and an acute appreciation of certain changes in the film marketplace. Over the years, Sher had so annoyed local residents that he reasonably assumed that things could not get much worse for him in Cleveland Heights. Unlike first-run commercial movie exhibitors, Sher depended on a small but loyal clientele with a vested interest in his survival. This audience was hardly sympathetic with local efforts to censor scenes in or enjoin screenings of art movies. (The local censorship of specific scenes in con-

Jeanne Moreau as the unhappy wife in Louis Malle's *Les Amants (The Lovers)* (Zenith International, 1958), the film at issue in *Jacobellis v. Ohio.*

troversial films was a routine practice in the 1950s, especially with regard to non-MPAA, non-PCA pictures. Preview screenings were standard operating procedure: local police and/or clergy would view the film in question and on occasion urge the excision of entire scenes as a condition of their approval. Theater owners and managers would then cut the positive print to suit the local censors. Exhibitors who refused to comply risked arrest, fine, boycott, and unfriendly visits from the board of health, the fire department, and the IRS.)[75]

Like Sher, Frankel had little to lose and perhaps a lot to gain by challenging the Cleveland Heights ban on his film. *Les Amants* was a foreign art picture with very limited box office potential in the United States. It stood to benefit from the notoriety a controversial court challenge might provide. Moreover, by almost any measure even at the time, *Les Amants* was clearly not obscene and the local prohibition on its exhibition was at once unconstitutional and a little ridiculous.[76]

Unlike *Burstyn v. Wilson*, which was a controversial case because the film at issue, *The Miracle*, was itself controversial and offensive to a particularly powerful religious/political organization, *Jacobellis v. Ohio* was a much less complex, much less politicized obscenity case. *Les Amants* featured partial nudity and closed with a fairly long (and thus uncuttable) romantic sequence during which a young, unhappily married woman meets a young man, falls in love, and (we are led to understand) has sex with him and decides to leave her husband. The film would not have received a PCA seal had Frankel submitted it for review. But Jacobellis's case hinged not on industry production standards but on constitutional criteria concerning obscenity.

Though Sher and Frankel financed the court battle, Jacobellis got most of the publicity. The notoriety brought him nothing but trouble, an object lesson for theater employees nationwide. The police searched his house on a number of occasions, hoping to find obscene materials. Once, on a warrant prompted by a tip from an anonymous source, the police came up with a record album titled *The People, Yes*. They assumed it was Communist Party propaganda but were disappointed when they discovered that it was just a recording of poetry written and read by Carl Sandburg. Phone calls and visits at all hours from folks posing as deliverymen, repairmen, salesmen, and taxi drivers were accompanied by all sorts of threatening letters, many of which were anti-Semitic. Jacobellis was not Jewish, but Roman Catholic, a piece of information that, once made public, brought the theater manager yet another headache. When local church officials were informed that Jacobellis was a Catholic, they pressured federal authorities to have him deported.[77]

The case proceeded slowly—so slowly that by the time the Supreme Court rendered its decision in 1964, *Les Amants* was hardly risqué and no longer marketable. Jacobellis was finally exonerated; his conviction for possessing and exhibiting an obscene film was overturned. The $2,500 fine was rescinded and all but his six days in county jail were forgotten. The cost of defending Jacobellis was $70,000, a bargain by today's standards but a whole lot of money for a theater manager or even a theater owner and an indie distributor in 1964.[78]

The Supreme Court's six-to-three decision to overturn Jacobellis's conviction was based in large part on the view (of the majority at least) that, with regard to community standards, *Les Amants* was not obscene. The term "community standards" as applied to obscenity dates to 1913 and *United States v. Kennerly*.[79] In his opinion in the *Kennerly* case, Judge Learned Hand wrote, "If there be no abstract definition . . . should not the word 'obscene' be allowed to indicate the present critical point in the compromise between candor and shame at which the community may have arrived here and now." "Community," Hand contended, referred not to local jurisdictions, but to "the society at large . . . the public, or people in general." In his opinion for the majority in *Jacobellis v. Ohio*, Justice William Brennan, following Hand's reasoning, contended that while obscenity might have "a varying meaning from time to time," it should not vary "from town to town or county to county."

Brennan did not believe in absolute First Amendment protection for literature or film. Instead, he supported the institution of age-based criteria as elaborated by the Court in a 1957 case, *Butler v. Michigan*.[80] In that case, the Court held that literary material could not be banned solely on the grounds that it might incite minors to violent or immoral acts. Putting aside the thorny issue of whether or not literary material *incites* action of any type in anyone, the Court cautioned against statutes that "reduce[d] the adult population . . . to reading only what is fit for children."

In his opinion for the majority in *Jacobellis v. Ohio*, Brennan applied the criteria established for literature in *Butler v. Michigan* to film: "We recognize the legitimate and indeed exigent interest of States and localities throughout the Nation in preventing the dissemination of material deemed harmful to children. . . . state and local authorities would be better served by laws aimed specifically at preventing distribution of objectionable material to children, rather than at totally prohibiting its dissemination."

The film industry had long embraced standards by which it might protect, to quote Will Hays, "that sacred thing, the mind of a child . . . that clean, virgin thing, that unmarked slate," and might show "the same responsibility, the same care about the impressions made upon it, that the best clergyman or the most inspired teacher would have."[81] The production code that took shape in the early 1930s was designed to make every film suitable for every age.

In the 1930s the studios could afford to make one product for everyone. But as the leisure/entertainment industry changed in the 1950s, the studios began to appreciate that certain films could be profitably marketed to specific segments of the audience. The increasingly well educated adult audience as well as the burgeoning adolescent rock and roll demographic were easy markets to identify but difficult to serve under the strict guidelines of the PCA code. Too much money was at stake for the studios to abide by production guidelines that pre-vented them from exploiting such potentially lucrative target markets.

The Court's systematic undermining of local censorship—*Burstyn v. Wilson, Gelling v. Texas, Superior Films v. Department of Education of Ohio, Butler v. Michigan,* and *Jacobellis v. Ohio*—further encouraged the MPAA to develop a national system consistent with an evolving fed-eral, legal standard of obscenity. Such a revised code promised to sup-port studio investment in pictures that better reflected the diversity of the filmgoing public, which was at once multiethnic, multiregional, and multigenerational.

4

Hollywood v. Soft Core

ON OCTOBER 7, 1968, MPAA president Jack Valenti, a former Houston adman and LBJ administration insider, issued a press release to the
trades outlining a radically new motion picture production code/
movie rating system. The rating system went into effect just a few
weeks later and has remained in force ever since.

The rating system was adopted at a crucial moment in Hollywood
history. Box office revenues were stuck in a two-decade-long decline.
Studio executives, who had learned to work together to establish a new
working relationship with exhibitors after the *Paramount* decision and
reestablish control over the Hollywood workforce during the blacklist
era, broke ranks and began to explore short-term solutions to their box
office problems.

Some of these short-term strategies worked; certain films got released and screened because the studios were willing to ignore long-
standing codes of industry conduct. But the abandonment of the
gentleman's rules that had prevailed in Hollywood for almost half a
century threatened the long-term stability of the industry. A new production code became necessary because the studios had given up adhering to the old one. *The Moon Is Blue, Tea and Sympathy, Baby Doll,
Room at the Top, Never on Sunday, Lolita, Kiss Me Stupid, The Pawnbroker,*
and *Blow-Up,* all mature-content films that did well in an otherwise
dead box office, reached America's screens only after their studio distributors circumvented the letter and spirit of the PCA code.

Valenti, ever the adman, sold the new code to the public with continued reference to the changing times. But first and foremost the rating
system was a business proposition. The studios needed to update their
product lines and the new rating system was a means toward that end.
The new film classification system supported a product overhaul.
American movies after the fall of 1968 look and sound different from
those produced before then. Valenti's rating system also promised to

better insulate the studios against local efforts to interfere with the production, distribution, and exhibition of their product.

Though the code was announced and summarily adopted in the fall
of 1968, it was the product of a long-term MPAA strategy. As early as
1963, the MPAA began courting one of John F. Kennedy's key advisers,
Louis Nizer, to preside over the development and implementation of a
new production code. Universal Studios president Lew Wasserman
eventually backburnered Nizer (an attorney) in favor of Valenti because
the latter was an advertising man. When Valenti was named president
of the MPAA in 1966, Nizer was installed as the organization's special
counsel.

The studios had a test case—a serious, important, potentially very
popular movie—waiting for Valenti and Nizer: Warner Brothers' *Who's
Afraid of Virginia Woolf.* The screenplay for the film, based on a serious
and notorious stage play, was denied code approval. The film went into
production anyway, in anticipation of a change. Valenti tells the story
about the development and production of *Who's Afraid of Virginia Woolf*
in a 1996 MPAA Web page document titled "The Voluntary Movie Rating System":

> within weeks in my new duties, I was confronted with controversy,
> neither amiable nor fixable. The first issue was the film *Who's Afraid of
> Virginia Woolf,* in which, for the first time on the screen, the word
> "screw" and the phrase "hump the hostess" were heard. In company
> with the MPAA's general counsel, Louis Nizer, I met with Jack Warner,
> the legendary chieftain of Warner Bros., and his top aide, Ben Kalmen-
> son. We talked for three hours, and the result was the deletion of the
> word "screw" and retention of "hump the hostess," but I was uneasy
> over the meeting. It seemed wrong that grown men should be sitting
> around discussing such matters."[1]

Valenti understood from the start that content regulation had less
to do with specific scenes in specific movies than with a complex set
of industrial and political relationships. "When I became president of
the Motion Picture Association of America (MPAA) in May 1966," he
wrote, "the slippage of Hollywood studio authority over the content
of films collided with an avalanching revision of American mores and
customs." Late sixties culture, Valenti reminds us, was characterized
by "insurrection on the campus, riots in the streets, rise in women's

Elizabeth Taylor and Richard Burton in *Who's Afraid of Virginia Woolf* (Warner
Brothers, 1966). Jack Valenti took over the MPAA just in time to preside over
the censorship of the film.

liberation, protest of the young, doubts about the institution of marriage, abandonment of old guiding slogans, and the crumbling of social traditions."

In acknowledging the tumultuous cultural politics of the late sixties and its seeming effect on the studios' ability to maintain authority
over the industry and marketplace, Valenti suggests (misleadingly I
think) that in the film business demand drives supply, an argument
the MPAA has steadfastly maintained in response to criticism regarding the content of so many of its movies. "It would have been foolish
to believe," Valenti argues, "that movies, that most creative of art
forms, could have remained unaffected by the change and torment in
our society."[2]

Valenti's reflection that "It seemed wrong that grown men should
be sitting around discussing" the excision of harsh language in a proposed film adaptation of a stage play reveals just how different he
was from his predecessors, Hays, Breen, and Shurlock. But Valenti
still finds himself sitting in a room with "grown men" and women

"discussing such matters." The primary difference between 1966 and 2000 is that films are now *classified*, which is to say that they are more subtly regulated.

The MPAA no longer enforces a strict production code. Unlike the "Formula" (a list of suggested regulations instituted in 1924 by Will Hays but never really enforced), the 1927 List of Don'ts and Be Carefuls (a list of eleven subjects that could never appear in films and twenty-five themes that should be handled with care, also implemented by Hays through the MPPDA), or the 1930 production code (administered by Breen from 1934 to 1954, and then Shurlock from 1954 to 1968), the rating system developed by Valenti and Nizer ostensibly licenses a far wider range of movie themes and images.

But it is important to understand that the rating system functions much like the earlier codes. It is, first and foremost, a studio-managed entryway into the marketplace. Though filmmakers need to "be careful" about fewer things these days, decisions made by grown men and women in a room discussing such matters still govern the way films are defined before they are screened in theaters. The rating system's mode of identifying products in advance of consumption is essential to the ways movies move into and through the marketplace.

Valenti writes in "The Voluntary Movie Rating System" that when he first took control of the MPAA he was "uncomfortable with the thought that [*Who's Afraid of Virginia Woolf*] was just the beginning of an unsettling new era in film, in which [the PCA] would lurch from crisis to crisis, without any suitable solution in sight."[3] Valenti understood that it was not so much *Who's Afraid of Virginia Woolf* but the old code itself that was at issue at that 1966 meeting at Warners. And by the time the confab was over, Valenti realized that a new production code, even a significantly more modern or permissive one, was not the answer. It was his job instead to figure out a way, in the name of self-regulation, to enable the production of mature-themed movies.

The meeting convened to hear Warner Brothers' appeal of the PCA's preliminary ruling to deny *Who's Afraid of Virginia Woolf* an MPAA seal was a brilliantly orchestrated public relations event, the first of many for Valenti. The film, which was seen as important for a number of reasons, was eventually granted an exemption, but only after a protracted and well-publicized fight, and only after reconsideration of Shurlock's stated objections to the project were reviewed by Valenti and Nizer, the vaunted new breed at the MPAA. Valenti was aware that the exemption (an inappropriate term since the film was technically granted code approval) might encourage other studios to make films that defied the code. He was careful to describe *Who's Afraid of Virginia Woolf* in the press as an exceptional movie, one "not designed to be prurient," but instead a faithful adaptation of an award-winning stage play steeped in "tragic realism."[4] How many other projects submitted for PCA approval could be described in such lofty terms?

As part of the deal to secure an MPAA-sanctioned release, Warner Brothers agreed to label the film "for adults only," and then left the task of enforcing the agreement to the nation's exhibitors. In doing so, the studio appeared responsible. But more important for Warners, and for the industry as a whole, the code exemption offered an opportunity to see how an age-based, exhibitor-enforced system might work and whether a film targeted at such a narrow demographic could still make money. The answer to the latter question was a resounding yes. *Who's Afraid of Virginia Woolf* ranked third on the box office list in 1966 behind two other mature-themed pictures, *Thunderball* and *Dr. Zhivago*. By the end of 1966, *Who's Afraid of Virginia Woolf* sported over $10 million in box office revenues, an astonishing figure for an adults-only film.

After the release of *Who's Afraid of Virginia Woolf*, Valenti went on record: the exemption for the film did "not mean that the floodgates are open."[5] But the picture's success suggested that, once and forever, they were. Under a revealing December 21, 1966, front-page headline, "A Topless Liz [Taylor] 'Promised' by WB," *Variety* reported: "Warner Bros., which dared the censors with its current *Who's Afraid of Virginia Woolf*, disclosed last week that it may try again. In two separate statements, the company declared that it was in the process of shooting nude scenes, one presumably involving what Msgr. Thomas F. Little used to call 'bare breasted nudity,' and another involving what the former Catholic film office chief referred to as 'derriere nudity.'"[6]

Reflections in a Golden Eye, the film at issue in the *Variety* piece, was a troubled big-budget project in production at Warner Brothers when *Who's Afraid of Virginia Woolf* took off at the box office. To curry prerelease buzz for the picture, the studio supplied *Variety* with the story about the nude scenes and then used the *Variety* piece in two clever ways: (1) to lobby the PCA for the inclusion of the scenes in the picture, and (2) since the PCA would likely decide not to allow them, to create the impression that *Reflections in a Golden Eye* was somehow a landmark film anyway, a film so daring and risqué the PCA *had* to censor it.

∎

Ginsberg v. New York and *Interstate Circuit v. Dallas*, two Supreme Court decisions announced on April 12, 1968, offered considerable encouragement to Valenti as he put the finishing touches on the new MPAA production code.[7] Like *Butler v. Michigan*, the *Ginsberg* case hinged on the concept of *variable obscenity*, the notion that a book or film might be made available to adults that would and should otherwise be banned for minors.[8]

Valenti is not a lawyer, so he used legal precedent as merely one of several not altogether consistent ingredients to promote the new code. Selective references to legal precedent in the many press releases hawking the new code were routinely accompanied and thus partly undercut by moral platitudes of the sort the MPAA might well have embraced some thirty years earlier. For example, in a press release published in *Variety* on October 9, 1968, Valenti elaborated moral criteria that might be used in the future. Films that "respected" or "upheld" "the basic dignity and value of human life," he maintained, could be rated less harshly than those films that exploited "evil, sin, crime, wrongdoing, sex aberrations, excessive cruelty and illicit sex relationships."[9]

In another autumn 1968 press release, Valenti supported nearly absolute First Amendment protection for feature films: "we believe the screen must be as free for filmmakers as it is for those who write books." At the same time, however, he endorsed the MPAA's mission to develop a "moral apparatus" that might regulate the screening of certain films to certain audiences (under the age of sixteen or seventeen). Valenti insisted at one point in the press release that "censorship and classification by law are wrong . . . we [at the MPAA] believe the screen should be free for filmmakers." Then, later in the same document, Valenti urged directors and producers to remember that "freedom without discipline is license, and that's wrong too."[10]

Acknowledging Justice William Brennan's opinion in *Ginsberg v. New York*, Valenti wrote, "We must never make motion pictures for just one audience . . . that would be, as one Supreme Court Justice put it, inane." After all, Valenti continued, there is "no valid evidence . . . that movies have anything to do with anti-social behavior." But while Valenti appreciated the importance to the studios of a system that might enable them to distribute a variety of different products to different demographic groups, he nevertheless understood that the MPAA had to maintain the appearance of responsibility: "We" must (still) be "concerned about children." Such a concern for children, he wrote by way of conclusion, was no less than the "primary objective" of the new classification system.[11]

The new rating system so valued "parental guidance"—a term lifted from Justice Abe Fortas's opinion in the *Ginsberg* case—that the phrase was eventually used in two of the code's descriptive categories, PG and PG-13. Valenti's initial reluctance to have an MPAA designation harsher than the R or "restricted" rating (barring persons under sixteen from admission to certain films unless accompanied by a parent or guardian) had little to do with any personal or official industry position on soft- or hard-core pornography. Instead, it signaled his high regard for parental guidance and responsibility. As Valenti explains in "The Voluntary Movie Rating System," "Our original plan had been to use only three rating categories. It was my view that parents ought to be able to accompany their children to any movie the parents choose, without the movie industry or the government or self-appointed groups interfering with their rights."[12]

However much Valenti supported free speech and parental rights, he understood that any rating system that left enforcement to parents effectively distanced filmmakers and the studios distributing films into the marketplace from the site of regulation and censorship. The MPAA's stated mission was "to educate and inform," not regulate. Such a policy underscored a larger and more crucial industrial objective to reconnect adult filmgoers to film culture. In a press release titled "What Everyone Should Know about the Motion Picture Code and Ratings," Valenti encouraged parents not only to consider a film's MPAA rating, but also to carefully read reviews in local newspapers, pay attention to discussions of new releases in family-oriented and popular magazines, and access detailed production information made available in a new serial, *MPAA Film Reports*, which was distributed by the MPAA to local theaters and public libraries. Valenti encouraged responsible parents to take a more active interest in new releases, to preview promotional material in advance of a film's arrival in town, and, when concerned about content, to pay admission and preview certain films on their own.

The immediate industrial effect of the new rating system was that it encouraged the production of a more diverse range of movie products. The studios used the new rating system to differentiate between these products, to better advertise their pictures, and to more precisely target audiences. The system may well have been designed to educate and inform. But it was adopted by the MPAA, the National Association of Theater Owners (NATO), and the International Film Importers and Distributors of America (IFIDA) to get people back into the habit of going to the movies.

Interstate Circuit v. Dallas, like the *Ginsberg* case, concerned the imposition of variable obscenity regulations. But unlike *Ginsberg*, the principals in the *Interstate* case were all major industry players. The stakes were higher and as a result erstwhile adversaries—the theater chains and the studios—found themselves on the same side in a fight that could only be won if they cooperated with each other.

The Interstate theater chain, the largest circuit in Texas, had a history of motion picture exhibition dating back to 1905. It was formerly owned by Paramount, then, after divorcement, by the national theater chain United Paramount. Also named in the suit were COMPO (an organization formed by twelve exhibition companies operating thirty-three theaters in the Dallas area) and United Artists (the U.S. distributor for the film in question, the controversial 1965 Brigitte Bardot vehicle, *Viva Maria*, directed, as was *Les Amants*, by Louis Malle).

The MPAA chief counsel Louis Nizer represented Interstate. His participation at once affirmed the MPAA's interest in defending a member distributor (UA) in a local censorship dispute and held promise for some sort of détente between the embattled exhibitors of NATO and the MPAA studios.[13]

In 1965, as part of an effort to prohibit the screening of certain films to minors, the city of Dallas instituted an age-based, variable obscenity statute. Soon after the ordinance went into effect, *Viva Maria* received an N/S (Not Suitable for young people) rating. But the Interstate theater slated to screen the picture refused to post or enforce the restriction. In doing so, it set in motion a constitutional challenge to the local censorship board's authority.[14]

In an eight-to-one ruling citing the ordinance's "vagueness" and "attendant evils," the Supreme Court voided the Dallas law. Writing for the majority, Justice Thurgood Marshall contended that the problem with the Dallas ordinance was that it inhibited free expression and free trade. Studios concerned about potential bans in various markets—as big as the one in Dallas, for example—might opt to produce only those sorts of films that might safely be screened everywhere and anywhere. State and local regulatory boards such as the one in Dallas, Justice Marshall warned, promised to turn the film market into "a vast wasteland."[15]

The decision in *Interstate Circuit v. Dallas* revealed the growing complexity of obscenity law, especially when cases highlighted states' rights issues. Since the Court had already come out in support of variable obscenity statutes, its decision to overturn the Dallas ban came as something of a surprise. In retrospect, it is fair to conclude that the justices' decision had less to do with obscenity than with their growing distaste for persistent city and state refusals to administer and enforce federal civil rights laws, especially in the South. When states and cities refused to comply with federal civil rights laws, the justices found cause to distrust local jurisdictions in other matters, like obscenity.

In an opinion circulated in support of the majority decision in a 1967 case, *Redrup v. New York*, Justice William O. Douglas explicitly acknowledged the state rights/obscenity connection. Douglas quoted the Reverend Howard Moody to make explicit his growing reluctance to leave much of anything of importance up to the states: "The dirtiest word in the English language is not 'fuck' or 'shit' in the mouth of a tragic shaman, but the word 'nigger' from the sneering lips of a Bull Connor."[16]

1968: A NEW HOLLYWOOD

When you're in power, everyone wants to know you and spend time with you.

—Jack Valenti, MPAA president

In 1966 the MPAA annual report revealed a number of significant industrial shifts.[17] The Production Code Administration approved 168 feature films. Of the 149 features released by members of the MPAA, only thirty-eight were produced by the major studios. While the number of independently produced films far exceeded those made at or by the studios, only nineteen films that got screened nationwide were distributed by a non-MPAA company.

Six films released in 1966 received the "suggested for mature audiences" designation: *Deadlier Than the Male, A Funny Thing Happened on the Way to the Forum, Georgy Girl, Long Ride Home, Rage,* and *Welcome to Hard Times.* Three of the six—*Deadlier Than the Male, Georgy Girl,* and *Rage*—were foreign-made. *Who's Afraid of Virginia Woolf* got its own designation: on all advertising for the picture, an MPAA legend read (all in capital letters), NO PERSON UNDER 18 ADMITTED UNLESS ACCOMPANIED BY A PARENT. The data published in the MPAA report reveal a dramatic decrease in studio production, but no significant increase in the number of mature-themed films that reached the marketplace, especially among the features made in the United States. But the number of films, scenarios, and treatments that led to negotiations between the MPAA censors and filmmakers in 1966 tells a slightly different story. "Unacceptable elements" were found in twenty-nine rough cuts screened by the censors, including (in addition to the mature-tagged films) *Alfie, Cast a Giant Shadow, The Chase, Dead Heat on a Merry-Go-Round, A Fine Madness, How to Succeed in Business without Really Trying, Murderers' Row, The Professionals, Sand Pebbles,* and *Torn Curtain.* An additional list of projects in development deemed unacceptable by the PCA included *Blow-Up, Bonnie and Clyde, Candy, Cool Hand Luke, Ice Station Zebra,* and *Little Big Man*—all films that eventually made it into general release and despite or because of mature themes or elements did well at the box office.

The annual report for 1967 further revealed the extent of the shift away from studio production and the growing studio reliance on distribution. Just 43 out of 206 films submitted to the PCA were produced by MPAA members. Only 9 of the 206 were distributed independently. Popular titles such as *Casino Royale, The Dirty Dozen, Doctor Dolittle, For a Few Dollars More, The Good, the Bad and the Ugly, A Man and a Woman, The Night of the Generals,* and *You Only Live Twice* were all produced overseas, then picked up for distribution in the United States by a major studio.

The studios' arrangement with foreign production companies worked to both parties' advantage. The studios needed product; they were producing less and less on their own and the majority of the independently produced American films they picked up for distribution foundered in the marketplace. Foreign producers needed the studios to get their films into American theaters; moreover, they needed the MPAA member studios to protect their product against the PCA. The top four films for 1967—*The Dirty Dozen, You Only Live Twice, Casino Royale,* and *A Man for All Seasons* (which won Academy Awards for best picture, best director, and best actor in 1966)—were all produced overseas. Two more British imports, *Georgy Girl* and *To Sir With Love,* were listed among the year's ten best box office performers. Of the six hit films, only one—the prestige title *A Man for All Seasons*—had an easy time with the PCA. Adult or mature content, which seemed responsible for success at the box office for a number of films in 1967, became increasingly associated in filmgoers' minds with foreign-made pictures.

The growing reliance on foreign-made product in the late 1960s at least partly explains the studios' embrace of auteurism in the early 1970s. Studio investment in auteurism was the direct consequence of the failure of industry executives to produce or select for distribution profitable movies. Trusting the likes of Francis Coppola, Martin Scorsese, and Robert Altman was a logical, practical response to a trend that suggested that European-style films made money.

In an interview published in the September 18, 1968, issue of *Variety*, less than two months before the new system was slated to take effect, Valenti expressed concern about the growing value of foreign-made pictures in the American film industry. Unwilling to blame filmmakers or the studios, Valenti instead reproached American film reviewers, who, he opined, seemed suddenly "hung up on [foreign] film directors whose names end with 'o' or 'i.'" Valenti reminded reviewers that foreign auteurs had an unfair advantage because they produced their films without significant regulatory pressure. The new classification system, Valenti promised, would make for freer and fairer competition in the U.S. market. The reviewers would soon need to see past their prejudice against the domestic product or risk being left behind by the popular audience.

A persistent question in 1968 was, who at the studios was prepared to make films that might exploit the freedom provided by the rating system and capture the interest of the educated-adult and teenage demographics? Valenti knew that old-school Hollywood filmmakers might have problems making the transition(s) and boldly announced to the trades that "the future of the film business lies on the campus." Ironically, Valenti's prediction (which proved prescient) called attention to a new generation of film school–educated would-be auteurs, themselves enamored with the films of foreign directors whose names ended in *o* or *i*.[18]

The number of films designated for "mature audiences only" in 1967 rose dramatically from the previous year, from six to forty-four. Included among those restricted pictures are such familiar titles as *A Man and a Woman, In Cold Blood, Point Blank, The Valley of the Dolls, The Good, the Bad and the Ugly, In the Heat of the Night* (which won the Oscar for best picture), *Marat/Sade*, and *Reflections in a Golden Eye*. A number of films, including *Belle de Jour, I Love You Alice B. Toklas, Petulia, Rosemary's Baby,* and *The Fixer,* were deemed unacceptable. In anticipation of the new code, their producers did not resubmit them.

In the twelve months preceding the adoption of the 1968 MPAA rating system—from November 1967 to November 1968—roughly 60 percent of the films released by the studios carried the "suggested for mature audiences" tag. But even with the newly available and newly popular "mature audiences" designation, some key studio films were denied a production seal. The most problematic of these films proved to be Michelangelo Antonioni's *Blow-Up,* a foreign-made production contracted for release in the United States by MGM. When MGM submitted *Blow-Up* to the industry's censorship board, it was denied a seal. The controversy that followed spelled the end for the PCA.

In a January 11, 1967, front-page story in *Variety,* under the headline "Valenti Won't 'Blow-Up' Prod. Code for Status Films; No Church Push," the MPAA chairman remarked that while he agreed with most critics that *Blow-Up* was well worth seeing, he still supported PCA chief Geoffrey Shurlock's decision to deny the picture a production seal.[19] The problem with the film, Valenti pointed out, was not its overall quality but rather a single nonnarrative/nonessential sequence that featured female nudity.

So far as Shurlock and Valenti were concerned, the only satisfactory solution to the problem was to cut the scene. But Antonioni's contract was such that, without his permission, MGM could not cut the film to suit the PCA or the National Catholic Office of Motion Pictures (NCOMP), which had, predictably, issued *Blow-Up* its condemned rating.

Blow-Up was made in England and by the time MGM submitted it for PCA review it had already been released to box office and critical success in Europe. It was Great Britain's official entry at Cannes and won the festival's grand prix. It is difficult to believe that studio executives were taken by surprise when the PCA refused to grant the picture a production seal. And it is equally difficult to believe that they contracted to release the film, which they knew they couldn't cut, without a strategy for defying or subverting the PCA.

When Shurlock refused to grant the picture a PCA seal and Valenti backed him up, MGM made its move. In order to avoid an MPAA fine and possible sanction—in order to get the picture out without quitting the MPAA—the studio distributed *Blow-Up* under the banner of its wholly owned and operated non-MPAA subsidiary Premier Films.

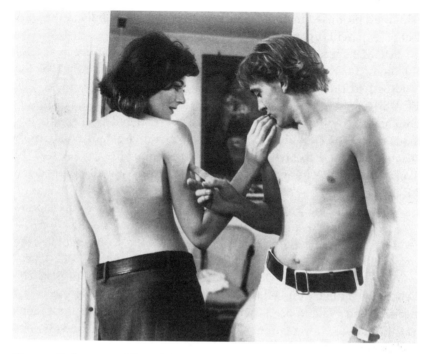

Vanessa Redgrave and David Hemmings in just one of several controversial scenes in Michelangelo Antonioni's *Blow-Up* (MGM, 1967). Though the *Variety* headline claimed that "Valenti Won't 'Blow-Up' Prod. Code for Status Films," MGM's success with the film (touted in a subsequent headline, "'Blow-Up B.O. Comforts Metro") forced his hand.

MGM's release strategy was a calculated gamble. Executives at MGM did not know how the other studios would react to their decision to subvert MPAA authority, or how future MGM films might be received by the PCA board. Distribution executives at the studio also appreciated how difficult it would be to contract venues to exhibit *Blow-Up*, especially if it did not perform well in its initial urban run. But after its first week in release, it was clear that the studio's gamble had paid off. *Blow-Up* opened to terrific reviews. The opening-week numbers were strong and the film eventually grossed seven times the studio's investment.

Under the headline "'Blow-Up' B.O. Comforts Metro," *Variety* staff writers speculated that other studios with adult-oriented films would soon follow MGM's strategy.[20] The possibility that non-MPAA subsidiary releases of controversial studio titles might become something of a trend promised to undermine the effectiveness not only of the PCA but of its parent organization, the MPAA, as well.

MGM's success with *Blow-Up* exposed the growing irrelevance of the old code. The PCA was set up to regulate production. By 1967 the studios had pretty much gotten out of the production business. The PCA advised studios about potential problems with regional censorship boards. By 1967 the Supreme Court had rendered local board decisions moot. The PCA and NATO had a cooperative arrangement; most theaters declined to book films released without the MPAA seal. In 1967, when *Blow-Up* opened strong, theaters nationwide ignored the MPAA/PCA and booked the film anyway.

One of the first press releases announcing the MPAA's decision to test the feasibility of an age-based, exhibitor-enforced classification system appeared in the March 22, 1967, issue of *Variety*. Coincidentally, the press release was laid out directly above an article touting MGM's decision to publicly acknowledge its role in the distribution of *Blow-Up*. Few in the industry missed the relationship between the two pieces, especially since Valenti used the press release to focus on the limitations of the "mature" designation, which at the time was applied to all films that posed problems for the PCA.

In order to better differentiate between product lines—for example, prestige/art films and soft-core exploitation pictures, two genres that routinely raised problems for the PCA—Valenti proposed the creation of "other qualifying lines," other designations that might "genuinely inform parents about the content of films."[21] In the spring of 1967, executives in the industry closely watched a curious censorship case in Chicago that turned out to be quite significant. The case involved three very different, non-MPAA films—Joseph Strick's adaptation of James Joyce's *Ulysses* and two soft-core exploitation pictures, *Rent-a-Girl* and *Body of a Female*—all of which were banned in Chicago by the city's persistent and still remarkably effective censorship board.[22] In order to screen *Ulysses*, the theater circuit owner Walter Reade obtained a temporary injunction from an Illinois state court that allowed him to show the film for three days without a city permit.[23] The city censorship board decided not to contest the state court ruling. A spokesman for the board acknowledged that the film in question was, after all, based on a famous (albeit controversial) novel, that three days was not very long, and, perhaps most importantly, that Reade owned a lot of theaters and had the resources to mount an expensive appeal. What was not said was of at least equal importance: Reade had the money to support opposition candidates in upcoming elections.

At the same time, the Chicago board took a far firmer stand against the two exploitation features. *Rent-a-Girl* and *Body of a Female* were slated to be screened in Chicago by Chuck Teitel, who was also both films' local distributor. When the city board decided not to contest the three-day exemption for *Ulysses*, Elmer Gertz, Teitel's attorney, filed a brief arguing that his client's films should be afforded the same consideration. All three films had been found obscene by the local censorship board, Gertz argued, but Reade, a more mainstream and wealthy player, received preferential treatment. Gertz strategically ignored the difference between the Strick film and the soft-core pictures distributed by his client; at stake, he argued, was an unfair and unconstitutional restraint of trade. *Ulysses*, *Rent-a-Girl*, and *Body of a Female* were all movies. As products ("pure and simple"), Gertz contended, all three films should be afforded the opportunity to freely compete in the marketplace. While the situation did not directly concern an MPAA product, the local skirmish in Chicago highlighted the sheer absurdity of any rigid code—such as the one employed by the Chicago censorship board—that equated *Ulysses* with *Rent-a-Girl* and *Body of a Female*.

The MPAA rating system that went into effect in 1968—G, M, R, and X—did not provide (as Valenti had promised it would) "other qualifying lines" to differentiate between such films. It featured only four categories, only three of which (G, M, and R) were eligible for a Code and Rating Administration production seal. The descriptive language accompanying the rating symbols featured in all advertising and on all prints exhibited to paying audiences was from the start uniform and brief:

> G (Suggested for *General* audiences), M (Suggested for *Mature* audiences [parental discretion advised]), R (*Restricted*—Persons under 16 not admitted, unless accompanied by parent or adult guardian) and X (*Persons under 16 not admitted*. This age restriction may be slightly higher in some areas. Check theater or advertising).

Absent specific designations to accurately classify and describe the films submitted to the MPAA, Valenti instructed the Code and Rating Administration to consider each film on its own merits and to view identical content as different in different (sorts of) films. Qualitative differences between films are a matter of objective as well as subjective criteria. The Code and Rating Administration board—those *everyday* citizens who watch and classify films for the MPAA—is encouraged to make objective as well as subjective distinctions.[24] Under such a system, more ambitious, better-produced, better-*looking* studio films routinely receive preferential treatment from the board.

The rating system was the turning point in the new Hollywood not so much or not only because it so affected the look and sound of the films produced there, but because it reestablished a system by which the studios might continue to produce and distribute films under a set of mutually agreed-upon guidelines. When Valenti formally announced the new MPAA rating system, he had the support of the nine member companies of the MPAA, as well as NATO and IFIDA (the International Film Importers and Distributors of America). As Valenti put it in an October 7, 1968, "personal statement" issued to the press, "for the first time all essential elements of the industry (producers, distributors and exhibitors) are in agreement."[25]

In order to preclude alternative local or state codes, Valenti got the various organizations to agree to adopt and adhere to the new rating system within weeks of the first press release heralding the change.[26] Left out of the agreement, significantly, were the smaller American independent producers and distributors (who, Valenti contended in a September 1968 interview, "will have to accept our classification as they must get booking for their films and exhibitors will demand that they be classified"),[27] theater owners who were not members of NATO (which represented approximately 15 percent of the nation's theaters but accounted for barely 5 percent of the domestic box office), and the producers, distributors, and exhibitors of hard-core pornography.

The 1968 motion picture rating system successfully established a national film censorship standard but, more importantly, it gave the studios control over entry into the entertainment marketplace. You can't make much money on a film without an MPAA rating. And you can't get an MPAA rating without first paying a fee to the studio-run organization and then submitting your film to the CARA board.

The 1968 rating system allows for a wide range of product lines. The studios have gotten back into the exhibition business (with theaters as well as pay TV) and conglomerates like Time Warner Turner and Disney/Capital Cities/ABC exert monopoly control over the business to an extent the old studio trusts could never have achieved.[28] That said, the MPAA rating system is still a subtle but nonetheless effective form of regulation, not of film content but of participation in the marketplace. At issue, then, is not whether the film business is regulated, but who gets to make the regulations and who gets to benefit from them.

As I mentioned in the book's introduction, the MPAA rating system did not save Hollywood, at least not all on its own and not right away. The new code enabled the production and distribution of some noteworthy and profitable adult titles: *Midnight Cowboy, Goodbye Columbus, MASH,* and *Bob and Carol and Ted and Alice.* But the transition from old to new Hollywood proved slow, and the box office slide continued.

In March 1970 *Variety* revealed the extent of the damage: Hollywood unemployment had reached 42.8 percent, an all-time high.[29] Less than a month later, information was leaked to the trades that Paramount, a company with a rich and long history, was on the verge of collapse.

The rumors about Paramount, like most rumors in the trades, turned out to be true. On April 8, 1970, *Variety* published details of an attempt by studio parent Gulf and Western to sell the legendary Melrose Avenue studio lot for real estate development. The complex deal had local developers paying somewhere between $29 and $32 million for the production facility and an adjacent property. The possibility that Paramount might go out of business, that the studio lot might be razed and in its place some office building or condo might be erected, revealed the extent of the desperation felt not only at Paramount but at all the studios and their parent companies. This desperation increased the pressure on the MPAA and its new rating system to hurry up and save Hollywood.

The deal never went through, but not because Gulf and Western got cold feet. Local bureaucrats refused to rezone the adjacent property, a cemetery, and the developers found themselves another site.[30] When the sale fell through, Gulf and Western CEO Charles Bluhdorn staked the studio's future on three men: a respected albeit low-profile Hollywood veteran, Stanley Jaffe (who exited quietly after about a year); a young and ambitious studio advertising man, Frank Yablans; and a former actor and neophyte fashion industry executive, Robert Evans.

Bluhdorn was a notoriously impulsive and unpredictable CEO, so the shakeup at Paramount seemed more an act of impatience than a strategy for turning things around at the studio. But history is often a process of lucky accidents. With the 1971 release of *Love Story,* a film developed by Evans and Yablans, Paramount was the first of the studios to break out of the box office slump. The following year Paramount was the first to enjoy blockbuster-era profits with *The Godfather*, another project developed by the two young executives.

The top two box office films for 1969—the first full year after the new rating system was adopted—were *The Love Bug* and *Funny Girl*; the former a lighthearted comedy from Disney, the latter a big-budget musical in the tradition of such sixties blockbusters as *The Sound of Music* and *My Fair Lady*. *The Love Bug* was a modest hit and gave Disney a recyclable and profitable film franchise. But *Funny Girl* seemed only a reminder of how things were changing in the marketplace; unlike *The Sound of Music* and *My Fair Lady*, *Funny Girl* cost so much to make it barely broke even.

Funny Girl came at the end of a cycle that the *New Yorker* critic Pauline Kael called "super-gigantic blockbuster musicals," a genre that included such late-sixties films as *Camelot* (which cost $15 million), *Sweet Charity* ($8 million), *Star!* ($14 million), *Doctor Dolittle* ($18 million), and *Paint Your Wagon* ($20 million).[31] The desperate search for the next *Sound of Music* revealed just how out of step the studios had become, how little studio executives seemed to understand or appreciate the marketplace. *Paint Your Wagon*, a musical improbably cast with Lee Marvin, Clint Eastwood, and Jean Seberg, none of whom could sing, was the worst of the lot, a quintessential late-sixties Hollywood product, a symptom of an industry run by businessmen (as opposed to movie men) trying too hard to find, as Kael put it, "the secret of someone else's success." "The major studios are collapsing," Kael observed, "but they're not being toppled by competitors; they're so enervated that they're sinking of their own budgetary weight."[32]

Neither *Funny Girl* nor *The Love Bug* seemed to benefit much from the revised production standards introduced in November 1968. And neither did nearly so well at the box office as the top films of the previous year, films made under the old code but that anticipated, indeed exploited, new generic formations and new audience demographics. *The Love Bug* grossed a respectable $17 million in 1969; *Funny Girl*, a comparatively disappointing $16.5 million. *The Graduate*, the number one film released in the last year before the rating system was adopted, grossed $39 million. The number three film in 1968 (behind *The Graduate* and *Gone with the Wind* in reissue) was *The Valley of the Dolls*, a trashy, adult-themed melodrama that, at $20 million, outgrossed *Funny Girl*.

Though the top twenty box office films for 1969 were headed by two family pictures, they also included four adult titles: a studio film with a self-imposed X (*Midnight Cowboy*, the number seven film for the year), two films released by non-MPAA members (*I Am Curious Yellow* at number twelve and *Three in the Attic*, which ranked eighteenth), and an independently financed and produced film eventually picked up for distribution by Columbia (the AIP-style exploitation biker film *Easy Rider*, which ranked eleventh).

The release of *Midnight Cowboy* called into question the industrial utility of the X rating. The film did well enough at the box office ($11 million domestic) and won the best picture Oscar for its studio, United Artists. (It also won a best director Oscar for John Schlesinger, best screenplay for former blacklistee Waldo Salt, and best actor nominations for Dustin Hoffman and Jon Voight, both of whom lost to John Wayne in *True Grit*.) But its success at the various awards ceremonies and at the box office ultimately did not support a trend in X-rated film-making industry-wide. *Midnight Cowboy* was more of a prestige than an adults-only film and the studios were anxious to believe that its success had more in common with other successful auteur films like Arthur Penn's *Bonnie and Clyde* than with X-rated soft- and hard-core porn.

By 1969 standards, *Midnight Cowboy* was an adults-only film. (My guess is that the CARA board would have given it an X, but we will never know for sure—it never got to classify it.) But it was clearly not porn. The self-imposed X rating attracted an adults-only audience, a demographic United Artists wanted desperately to reach in 1969. But it also confused the film with other "dirty movies" in circulation at the time, like Russ Meyer's soft-core exploitation picture *Vixen* and the explicit foreign art film *I Am Curious Yellow*, both of which were also rated X in 1969.

The primary goal of the rating system was to differentiate between product lines, to inform parents about film content and more importantly to better describe and promote in advance of release films with erotic, violent, and/or controversial content. That *Midnight Cowboy* and *Vixen* might be in some way the same sort of picture was worrisome for the studios, especially since they could not fully control the X rating.

In 1968 Jack Valenti decided against obtaining a copyright for the X designation. He did so for a variety of reasons, not the least of which was to keep the studios out of the dirty movie business. At first, the strategy proved problematic. The new rating system was designed to protect studio products against local censorship and to force independents to submit their films to the MPAA/CARA for classification before gaining entry into the legit marketplace.

Independent distributors could not release a picture with a G, M, or R rating without first submitting their film to the MPAA/CARA board. But nothing stopped independent, even hard-core distributors from applying the X rating to their films. Independently made and released (mostly soft-core) X-rated films were made somehow legitimate because they shared a rating designation with a studio prestige picture like *Midnight Cowboy*. While the indie titles seemed to gain respectability by association, the Schlesinger film suffered by comparison. It, like all those awful indie soft-core pictures rated X in 1969, was, for some filmgoers at least, just another dirty picture.

The end-of-the-year box office tally for 1970 proved almost as unpromising as 1969. The top film for the year, *Airport*, earned almost as much as *The Graduate* had two years earlier, but did so at several times the cost. *Airport* did not exploit the new code, but it proved to be a significant film, first as a moneymaker and then as a reminder of the importance of targeting audiences in the postwar entertainment marketplace. The disaster film provided a formula that was easily reproducible and briefly bankable: *The Poseidon Adventure* was the number one film in 1973; *Airport 1975*, a simply dreadful sequel, earned over $12 million and ranked twelfth in 1974; and *The Towering Inferno* weighed in at number two in 1975. Though all four films placed in the top twenty for their year of release, they did so by successfully targeting older adults, the least lucrative of the age-based demographics.[33] Older adults, market research at the time indicated, seldom went to the movies. Their brief interest in the disaster picture cycle in the early seventies served as a reminder to the studios that they were somehow still tied to the past.

Once the disaster picture cycle ran its course, Hollywood pretty much abandoned the older adult audience and focused primarily, at times even exclusively, on the expanding "youth" audience (aged fifteen to thirty-four). In doing so the studios moved into direct competition with exploitation and hard-core filmmakers—producers, directors, and executives with a whole lot more experience exploiting the youth demographic.

Several successful films released in 1970 revealed the studios' growing interest in the youth market: *MASH* (at number two), *Bob and Carol and Ted and Alice* (number four), *Woodstock* (number five), and *Catch-22* (number eight). But while these films hit their mark, so to speak, each was unique in ways that troubled studio executives. *MASH* was an auteur (and antiwar) picture. *Woodstock* was a documentary of a landmark event in American teen culture. *Catch-22* was an adaptation of a popular and topical (antiwar/anti-establishment) novel, and *Bob and Carol and Ted and Alice* was a timely and sexy parody. Unlike *Airport*, which was a formula picture the studios quickly remade, these films were difficult to reproduce.

The studios employed a number of strategies to attract the youth audience. One such strategy was set in motion in November 1969, when Warner Brothers advanced Francis Coppola $600,000 to develop films under the American Zoetrope banner. Warners' strategy was simple: *Easy Rider*, an independent film produced for the youth market, had just made a lot of money (over $40 million in its initial release) and had cost relatively little to produce (approximately $500,000). Coppola and his creative colleagues at American Zoetrope (George Lucas, Jim McBride, Carroll Ballard, Walter Murch, Gloria Katz, Willard Huyck, John Korty, Robert Dalva, Matt Robbins, and Hal Barwood) were all young, they all had long hair, and they all seemed a part of the very youth subculture depicted in *Easy Rider*. For what amounted to petty cash for a studio of Warner Brothers' size and wealth, the executives hoped American Zoetrope would produce a product line of films in tune with the times.

Unfortunately for the executives at Warners, Coppola et al. had loftier things in mind, and the arrangement soured after just over a year. American Zoetrope failed to develop a single property that interested the studio. But the deal was historically significant for two reasons. First, it revealed the extent of studio desperation at the time: Coppola was hardly a bankable director in 1969; he had directed just four films, none of which made any money at the box office. Second, the deal fore-grounded the studios' eventual acquiescence to the cult of the auteur and the so-called Hollywood renaissance set in motion two years later by Coppola's auteur classic, *The Godfather*.[34]

At the end of the 1960s, studio executives seemed to have two choices, neither of them any good. They would either have to trust young, maverick directors whom they could not fully understand or control, or resign themselves to a dwindling market share and an in-creasing identification with the very sorts of films, like *Funny Girl* and *The Love Bug*, that had lost them the movie audience in the postwar box office slide.

One of the immediate effects of the new rating system was not so much the production of more explicit movies but the reluctant and brief adoption, industry-wide, of a new system of production. That new system—which fostered the auteur renaissance—saved Hollywood.

THE CRITICS

It is now no longer possible to tell whether, if there is a twenty-first century, there will be a Twenty-First Century Fox.
—Stefan Kanfer, *Time*, 1969

After examining the end-of-the-year box office numbers, the *Time* magazine film reviewer Stefan Kanfer wrote, "1969 may have been to the movies what 1955 was to Detroit."[35] Kanfer was hardly the only major critic to point out that studio product lines had gone hopelessly out of date. Pauline Kael, writing for the *New Yorker*, made similar use of an auto industry metaphor to issue a call for a new American cinema. "The movie companies keep bringing out these Edsels, Kael declared, all in service of "a rotting system in which mediocrity and skyrocketing costs work together to turn out films that would have had a hard time making money even if they were good."[36] The rest of the world was up to something different, Kanfer and Kael pointed out, something leaner, smarter, more youth-oriented . . . better.

End-of-the-year retrospectives penned by several of the better-known members of the National Society of Film Critics struck a single, ominous note: notwithstanding the new rating system, Hollywood had finally come to the end of the road. Four of the six studios (Paramount, Universal, MGM, and United Artists) were in serious trouble. The two that were not were Warner Brothers, which sported record revenues from its music division and had received an enormous cash boost in a merger with Kinney National Service (which made its money not in the film business, but in funeral parlors and parking lots), and Columbia. Columbia, the one studio that turned a real profit making and distributing movies between 1968 and 1969, could draw little practical encouragement from its success. A significant percentage of Columbia's profits at the box office could be attributed to a single film: the last fully successful roadshow musical, *Oliver!* (which won the best picture Oscar in 1968). But as *Newsweek*'s Joseph Morgenstern pointed out at the time, *Oliver!* was a success not because it was a musical but because it was a terrific movie "made by uncommonly gifted artists." "The lesson would seem clear," Morgenstern mused. "To succeed, a studio need only make good movies. That, however, is just what the studios can't do with any consistency."[37] As Morgenstern predicted, Columbia was unable to stay in the black very long. The profits earned in 1968–69 were quickly lost and forgotten after the 1970 release of a big-budget turkey, *MacKenna's Gold*.

Valenti's cockeyed optimism about the industry at the end of the 1960s seemed at the time the stuff feature films are made of. "What's cheering me up is that the new leadership coming up recognizes the problems," Valenti said. "I can't tell you when these dinosauric vestiges of the old Hollywood are going to disappear, but I know it's going to happen." Valenti's good cheer may not have been just public relations, and in retrospect we can see that he was right, the studios did turn things around in the early seventies and the rating system had a lot to do with that. But it is worth wondering even now who exactly Valenti had in mind when he waxed optimistic about "new leadership coming up." As Morgenstern observed in his dire account of the industry at the end of 1969, exactly who was running the studios at the time was a complex and difficult question: "Because of the conglomerates, no one knows who controls Hollywood. No one is what he's supposed to be."[38]

What attracted the conglomerates to Hollywood had nothing to do with the movies made there. The studios' principal asset in the 1960s was not their annual slate of films but real estate. Fox owned over 2,700 acres (74 of which adjoined Beverly Hills), MGM 1,850, Universal 420 (including a mountain).[39] Bluhdorn's move to sell the Paramount lot to developers in the spring of 1970 was little more than a routine move on the part of a huge company to jettison a failing subsidiary. The value of the Paramount lot had nothing to do with the filmmaking facilities; the developers interested in the property planned to raze the soundstages and office blocks. They just wanted the land.

The consensus among the nation's top film reviewers was that Hollywood (as we knew it then) was dead, that something or maybe nothing might emerge in its place. A quick survey of the National Society of Film Critics Awards for 1969 reveals a pervasive anti-Hollywood sentiment. The critics' selection for best picture, Constantin Costa-Gavras's *Z*, was a foreign-made political thriller. The two runners-up were both made in France: *Stolen Kisses*, directed by François Truffaut, and *La Femme Infidel*, directed by another New Wave auteur, Claude Chabrol. Only one American-born director got mentioned at all by any of the critics: Sam Peckinpah for *The Wild Bunch*.

Americans did a little better in some of the second-tier categories: Paul Mazursky and Larry Tucker won best screenplay for *Bob and Carol and Ted and Alice*, Jon Voight won best actor for *Midnight Cowboy*, and Jack Nicholson won best supporting actor for *Easy Rider*. The only American-made films mentioned on any of the individual critics' ballots for best picture—*Medium Cool* (rated X), *They Shoot Horses Don't They* (rated R), and *The Sterile Cuckoo* (rated R)—along with the three American-made award winners mentioned above, were all of a kind. They were all thematically anti-establishment (as the term was used back then) not only with regard to the culture they reproduced but also with regard to the Hollywood moviemaking culture they seemed to repudiate.

The two most talked about films of the year were the X-rated Swedish import *I Am Curious Yellow* and the low-budget youth-culture picture *Easy Rider*. *I Am Curious Yellow* proved to be an important if not really interesting film, the first foreign-language picture ever to top the *Variety* top grossing films chart, a distinction it held for the week ending on November 26, 1969. The film focused on a free spirit named Lena whose political and sexual curiosity form the reason if not the basis for the fragmentary narrative told in the film. *I Am Curious Yellow* took itself far too seriously to be (just) pornographic and it was frankly far too boring to be erotic. But there were scenes of fairly explicit (simulated) sex, scenes that went further than even the most lurid American-made pictures in release at the time.

The film's success at the box office was not really a matter of content. In fact, audiences seemed anxious to ignore content—the incessant political chatter, the film within a film premise (which by 1969 had become an all too familiar art movie trope), and the unattractive performers. Audiences just wanted to see the film everyone was talking about. They just wanted to see *what* everyone was talking about.

I Am Curious Yellow got some help at the box office from the most unlikely of sources: the United States Customs Service.[40] In 1969 Grove Press, a book publisher just getting its feet wet in film distribution, contracted to release the film in the United States. When it tried to import *I Am Curious Yellow* into the country, the film was found to be obscene and the print was seized by customs. The seizure could not have come as much of a surprise.

Though Grove Press was just starting out in the film business, its publishing division had a lot of experience in court with First Amendment cases. Grove fought the film's seizure by customs and

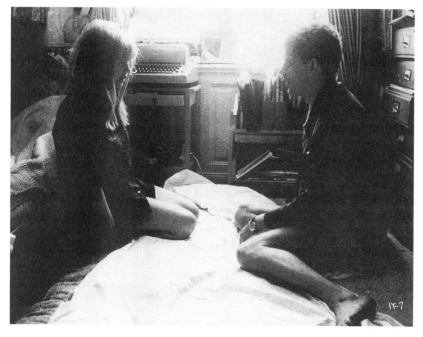

The first and one of the most successful explicit foreign imports: *I Am Curious Yellow* (Grove, 1969).

the obscenity ruling that supported that seizure and won, and then did well to exploit the controversy in its initial, limited release of the film. The New York opening of *I Am Curious Yellow* was quite successful: $91,785 while playing at just two small theaters. Within its first six months in release, the film grossed more than $4 million on just twenty-five screens.[41]

The critics were for the most part split; some found the film thoughtful while others found it pretentious and unerotic. John Simon, who hated almost every film he saw that year, liked *I Am Curious Yellow* enough to testify in support of its release before the circuit court of appeals.[42] *Look* magazine provided the film with its best notice by affirming its similarity to other foreign-made art films.[43] Penelope Gilliatt of the *New Yorker* hated the picture. She described *I Am Curious Yellow* as "puny-hearted . . . you have the strong impression that sex is on its last legs and will soon die out, like crochet work."[44] Stefan Kanfer was similarly unimpressed: "If it were not for the sex scenes, [*I Am Curious*] *Yellow* would probably never have been imported. It is simply too interminably boring, too determinedly insular, and, like the sex scenes themselves, finally and fatally passionless."[45]

Hollis Alpert, writing for the *Saturday Review*, suggested that the relative quality of the picture was somehow beside the point. After all, on a screen-by-screen basis, *I Am Curious Yellow* outearned *The Sound of Music* (in rerelease). The film's success, Alpert concluded, was just a matter of Grove "giving the public what it wants."

Alpert's review was the most apt if the least descriptive. The appeal of *I Am Curious Yellow* was simple. People were paying to see the nudity, the frank talk about sex, which in itself was so unusual, so different that the rest of the film hardly mattered at all.

Grove Press appreciated from the start that *I Am Curious Yellow* was less a film than a phenomenon, and it exploited that phenomenon to the best of its capabilities. In support of the release, the publisher rushed into press *I Was Curious: Diary of the Making of a Film*, complete with explicit stills from the picture.[46] The cross-industry promotion proved a deft strategy.

Grove's success with the film in its initial, limited urban run hardly prepared the publisher for what happened when it took the film on the road. The playoff in smaller markets was met with a seemingly endless series of expensive legal hassles that put Grove out of the film business forever. That Grove ran into problems in the South and the heartland revealed a trenchant geographic divide in the U.S. market. It also offered yet another reminder that film distribution is an expensive, economically perilous job best left to those with the money to do it right.

There is little evidence that any of the studios ever seriously contemplated making a film like *I Am Curious Yellow*. But *Easy Rider* was another matter entirely; it seemed like something they not only could but should reproduce. Kanfer's *Time* review of the film suggested that the studios might someday have to make a lot of *Easy Riders*, and argued that despite its low budget and its exploitation-film roots, *Easy Rider* was "a major film," perhaps the most important release of the season.

Kanfer traced the development of the film to a 1967 speech given by Valenti to the MPAA membership in which the association president stated that he had grown weary of "drug and motorcycle films" (which were mostly produced and distributed by non-MPAA independents at the time). Valenti said he looked forward to a day in the near future when theaters might be full of *Doctor Dolittles*—ironically, a 1967 big-budget studio release that, soon after Valenti's speech, un-

Perhaps Peter Fonda and Dennis Hopper did look "like refugees from some gorilla love-in," but their film *Easy Rider* (Columbia, 1969) nonetheless proved to be something of a turning point for the new American cinema.

derperformed at the box office. An unidentified respondent to Valenti's speech challenged the MPAA membership to develop projects for the youth market, to produce "a good movie about motorcycles." Legend has it that Peter Fonda, whose money and celebrity got *Easy Rider* made, was in attendance and took the challenge seriously. In the amusing conclusion to his review, Kanfer commented on the ironic turn of events: "There are only two courses open to the Motion Picture Association: prohibition of drug and motorcycle pictures—or of speeches by Jack Valenti."[47]

Kanfer didn't much like *Easy Rider*, especially when Dennis Hopper or Fonda was onscreen. But he was aware that his was a minority opinion, even among his fellow film reviewers. Indeed, many of the New York critics as well as festival juries loved the film: Jack Nicholson was the only unanimous selection for a National Film Critics Association Award (for best supporting actor) that year and the jury at the Cannes Film Festival gave Hopper an award for best first film.

The award for *Easy Rider* at Cannes and then its two Academy Award nominations—Nicholson for best supporting actor; Terry Southern, Hopper, and Fonda for best screenplay—revealed growing international, critical, and even intra-industry support for a new American style, one closely tied to a creative freedom made possible by the new production code. *Easy Rider* was a quintessentially American film, a road picture in a long line of road pictures dating back at least as far as *It Happened One Night*. But the search, the road, in *Easy Rider* led not to true love—as absurd as that notion is in *It Happened One Night*—but to a seeming truth about an America divided generationally and politically.

Today *Easy Rider* seems hopelessly dated; as much as any film ever released in the United States, it seems forever of its time. But in its time, the film was original, even insightful. True to its theme and narrative, the film's style *feels* free-form. Though Hopper, a veteran actor but inexperienced director, had little formal education in film history or theory, his film was rooted in the French New Wave and the American Direct Cinema movement, the two most popular genres with the growing film culture on university campuses at the time. Scenes set in various rural outposts, especially in the South, were shot in documentary style. In one particularly disturbing scene, two white truck drivers observe Fonda and Hopper (in costume, thus in character, I guess) and remark that they "look like refugees from some gorilla love-in . . . we ought to mate them up with black wenches . . . that's as low as you can git."

The clever use of documentary-style camera work, unprofessional actors, and unscripted dialogue—the conflation of fiction film and documentary codes—revealed a truth about that other America. As Penelope Gilliatt remarked in her review of the film for the *New Yorker*,

> *Easy Rider* is the real thing. Ninety-four minutes of the reason why so many Americans trust film fiction more than wrapped up actuality reports. Ninety-four minutes of the connective tissue binding Americans to a continent that, to go by those actuality reports, they would be entitled to loathe. Ninety-four minutes of what it would be like to swing, to watch, to be fond, to hold opinions, and get killed in America at this moment.[48]

The 1969 New York Film Festival opened with a very un–festival-like feature: *Bob and Carol and Ted and Alice*. As many critics pointed out, the timely (but mostly tame and light) comedy was not too controversial, but too popular, too American, and too Hollywood to headline a festival that was scheduled to screen the likes of Robert Bresson's *Un Femme*

Douce, Jean-Luc Godard's *Le Gai Savoir*, Eric Rohmer's *My Night at Maud's*, Agnes Varda's *Lion's Love*, Paolo Pier Pasolini's *Pigpen*, and Bo Widenberg's *Adalen '31*. The flap over the festival screening of *Bob and Carol and Ted and Alice* seemed to support Valenti's suspicion about American critics and their misguided affection for things foreign. At the same time, it seemed to offer promise that a new American cinema, in the very process of exploiting the new rating system, might begin to compete successfully at festivals worldwide.

Before 1969, European filmmakers dominated the New York Film Festival program. These filmmakers enjoyed greater creative freedom and significantly less regulatory pressure than their Hollywood peers. Beginning in 1969 and the controversial inclusion of *Bob and Carol and Ted and Alice*, studio-made American films began to appear with regularity on festival programs not only in New York but worldwide. This was as Valenti had always predicted. Only two American films appeared on the New York Film Festival program in 1968: Norman Mailer's *Beyond the Law* and John Cassavetes' *Faces*—the former a low-budget film by a famous and controversial novelist, the latter an independent picture made by the best-known independent American filmmaker at the time. A third film by an American-born director, Orson Welles, was screened as well. But his *Histoire Immortelle*, produced overseas, was not in any way an American film and its very existence seemed to speak to the failure of Hollywood to accommodate—to provide enough creative freedom to support—a talent as large as Welles's.

Beginning in 1970 some familiar new Hollywood directors began to place their films on the festival program. After 1970 new films by Martin Scorsese, Peter Bogdanovich, Robert Altman, Robert Benton, and Bob Rafelson were featured along with work by the usual slate of European cineastes: Bernardo Bertolucci, Luis Bunuel, Godard, Truffaut, Bresson, and Chabrol.

In 1970 Robert Altman's *MASH* won the grand prix at Cannes. American films won at Cannes again in 1973 (Jerry Schatzberg's long-forgotten *Scarecrow*), in 1974 (Coppola's *The Conversation*), and then again in 1976 (Scorsese's *Taxi Driver*). In the very process of attaining a respectability worldwide, these auteur directors solved, at least temporarily, the studios' two-decade-long problem at the box office. As Morgenstern had predicted in his end-of-the-year obituary on the film business in 1969, the answer to the studios' box office problem was simple: they needed to make better movies.[49] In the first few years of the 1970s, the studios did just that.

RATED X

Love Doctors Changes Nothing, but X Now an R.
—*Variety* headline, 1970

Less than a month after the rating system took effect, the Code and Rating Administration faced its first appeal on an X rating. The appeal was filed by Sigma III, a tiny non-MPAA company. It concerned a low-budget, satirical antiwar film, *Greetings*, directed by a then unknown filmmaker, Brian De Palma. CARA responded to the appeal by formally explaining why it had rated the film X. At issue, for CARA at least, was just a single scene in which the film characters watch, from a point of view we occasionally share, a hard-core stag reel. Implied in the CARA explanation was that cuts and/or strategic changes in the offending scene would merit review and most likely an R rating.

For reasons that are still not altogether clear, Sigma III declined to respond to the specific suggestions elaborated in the CARA memo and instead used the appeal process to call attention to a larger problem concerning the very structure of the new rating system. Sigma III argued simply that its film had been evaluated unfairly, that CARA would have given *Greetings* an R if it had been a studio film.[50]

The executives at Sigma III had a point, but their argument fell on deaf ears. Their appeal was heard by an "all-industry committee" consisting entirely of MPAA member executives—hardly a sympathetic bunch. The controversy attending *Greetings* disappeared from the trades quickly; it was, in the end, just a story about a little film distributed by a little independent outfit.

A year later, two additional appeals gained a significantly wider industry forum for the same argument: the MPAA, or so the independent distributors claimed, had begun using the X rating as a means of regulating not only the onscreen content but the theatrical release of non-MPAA product lines. The two appeals were filed separately on behalf of two very good movies: *If*, which received an X for a scene that included full frontal female nudity, and *The Killing of Sister George*, also a British import, which received an X for its frank depiction of a destructive lesbian relationship. *If* director Lindsay Anderson negotiated an R from the CARA board after agreeing to cut some footage. But Robert Aldrich, the director of *The Killing of Sister George*, was stuck with his X; he could not appease CARA without significantly changing the content, indeed the subject, of his film.

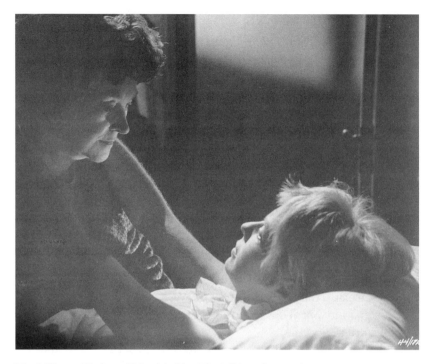

The killing of Robert Aldrich's film *The Killing of Sister George* (ABC, 1968) revealed how easily the MPAA rating system could be used to handicap independent films in the marketplace.

After losing his CARA appeal, Aldrich sent a letter to Jack Valenti, a portion of which was leaked to *Variety*. In the letter, Aldrich complained that the X rating was not only too severe for his film, it unfairly "created the impression" that his film was "a dirty picture not fit for viewing by anyone." Aldrich's letter highlighted two distinct problems with the new rating system: (1) the X rating as a descriptive designation was too broad: it equated controversial content (as featured in his film) with prurient content (which ranged from soft-core simulation to hard-core live action), and (2) the marketplace was such that an X rating effectively killed a film's chances at the general adult audience, which unfortunately assumed (in part because the MPAA refused to grant such films a production seal) that all X-rated films were pornographic.

The NATO membership and a number of influential industry journalists were inclined to agree. As Robert Landry wrote in a March 1970

Variety article on the controversy attending *The Killing of Sister George*, "The X rating has become the shorthand of moral accusation . . . the key to snap judgments against unseen films or against theaters that starve with family films."[51]

Aldrich's letter to Valenti called specific attention to the MPAA's continued reluctance to support adults-only entertainment. The "barrage of propaganda" preceding the adoption of the rating system, Aldrich contended, had led him and other filmmakers to assume that the primary function of the X rating was to *facilitate* the production of new, more adult product lines and to protect from local censorship and prosecution those endeavoring to exhibit adults-only films. Nowhere in the press releases, Aldrich argued, does one find so much as an implication that the X rating would be used to denote "a dirty picture." Aldrich did not argue that his film was suitable for—or even that it would be interesting to—children. Instead, he maintained that nonpornographic adult-themed films like *The Killing of Sister George*—like the 1966 release *Who's Afraid of Virginia Woolf*—might be better served by a designation that at once identified the picture as adults-only *and* as a serious dramatic work.

Valenti could not afford to agree with Aldrich because he could not control the X rating. Unlike the G, M, PG, PG-13, and R ratings, Valenti did not hold the copyright on the X rating. As a result, MPAA and independent film companies were well within their rights to rate their own pictures X and gain by implication the impression that their film was reviewed by CARA, even if it wasn't.[52]

Regional theater owners in West Virginia, Kentucky, Ohio, and western Pennsylvania sympathetic to Aldrich's battle with the MPAA proposed the adoption of an AO (adults only) rating. The new rating would help audiences (and local censors) discern serious, adult-themed films "from those with the X-rating which are of far lesser quality and moral values."[53] The proposal had the support of NATO membership nationwide, but Valenti was determined not to change the system. From the very beginning of his tenure, Valenti actively discouraged the studios from producing soft- or hard-core features and opposed the adoption of any designation that might make it easier to make those sorts of films.

The killing of *The Killing of Sister George* was particularly irksome for Aldrich because it smelled of collusion and emphasized his powerlessness in the larger scheme of things. The X rating kept *The Killing of Sister George* out of showcase theaters. It also kept ads for the film out of newspapers, many of which refused to carry advertisements for movies rated X.

NATO addressed the advertising problem in an April 1970 press release in *Variety*. A spokesman for the exhibitors' organization highlighted the free speech problems posed by the advertising ban and argued that "daily newspapers around the country more and more are taking on the role of censor of motion pictures."[54]

When the appeal to CARA to reclassify *The Killing of Sister George* failed, ABC tried to back out of its contract to release the film in the United States. Aldrich ultimately prevailed upon ABC to at least try to make some money with the picture. But he could not force theater owners to book his film.

The problem promoting and distributing *The Killing of Sister George* got so acute that Aldrich sought help from the ACLU. On the advice of his ACLU attorneys, Aldrich filed a complaint with the FCC, calling into question certain antitrust issues. Then in a well-publicized lawsuit, Aldrich targeted the Times-Mirror Corporation (which owned the *Los Angeles Times*) and endeavored to force the syndicate to accept ads for his film.[55] At stake were fair access to advertising—for X-rated films, for independent filmmakers and distributors who were responsible for the lion's share of X-rated product—and by extension fair access to a free(r) entertainment marketplace.

While the MPAA behaved as if it were uninterested in Aldrich's suit, NATO publicly expressed its support.[56] After all, the advertising ban significantly undermined the theater owners' autonomy, their freedom to screen non-MPAA motion pictures.

Aldrich and his ACLU legal team alleged that the newspaper syndicates, mass-market magazines, and TV and radio networks operated in collusion with the film studios to make it difficult for independents to market their X-rated product lines. They made their point but lost the case. Today the studios are well diversified into parallel media: the News Corporation, for example, which owns Fox, owns a number of big market newspapers (like the *New York Post*); Viacom/Paramount, Time Warner, and Disney own TV stations and mass-market magazines. Collusion has become standard operating procedure.

The newspaper advertising ban in the late sixties and early seventies, whether it was the result of collusion or not, exerted a significant regulatory effect on film content. When Aldrich's case was lost, the net effect was the elimination of a studio product line the MPAA actively and consistently discouraged.

WHAT TO DO ABOUT SOFT AND HARD CORE

N.Y. Rivals Frisco's Beavers: Female and Male Nudes Alongside on
Separate Screens at Mermaid.
                                                —*Variety* headline, 1970

The advertising ban all but killed the serious, adults-only picture. But it
did little to impede the success of soft- and hard-core sex films. On February 25, 1970, in a front-page article under the title "Trade Ponders: X
the Key to B.O.?" the editors at *Variety* pondered whether "stimulation
[had finally become] the name of the game" in the otherwise "depressed state of first run business," that while "it cannot be said with
authority that an X can make a picture and a G break it . . . it is known
that some non-major distributors plant an X on their pictures on their
own and view this as a move toward profitability."[57]

X-rated exploitation films were at the time making a lot of
money—on a screen-by-screen basis, more money than some very big
studio releases. Case in point: the soft-core feature *Without a Stitch*, a
Danish film distributed by VIP (a non-MPAA independent) with very
little going for it except simulated sex and onscreen nudity. *Without a
Stitch* earned $30,000 in each of its first five weeks in release at a single New York City theater, Loew's flagship venue on Broadway. By
the time Loews had "come off" *Without a Stitch*, the new Cinerama
theater down the street had begun screening the soft-core comedy
How to Succeed with Sex. The message was clear: even the biggest and
best theaters were willing to book soft-core titles so long as they made
money. While the MPAA refused to acknowledge X-rated films, the
nation's exhibitors were anxious to view all films as somehow the
same. A good picture was one that made them money. And they were
in the business of making money.

In a January 1971 interview in *Variety*, Valenti discussed the problem posed by soft- and hard-core movies. In a thinly veiled warning to
exhibitors, Valenti said, "If there is a proliferation of the quasi-porno
film in first class houses at the exclusion of product of a wider appeal,
we [meaning the entire legit industry] are in deep trouble . . . if other
large, responsible theater operators decide to play this kind of film, then
we are going to witness the death of quality exhibition in this country."[58] In a free market in which exhibitors are free to choose and contract for the sorts of products they want to exhibit, Valenti concluded,
the only way to maintain quality onscreen was for theater owners to

care a little less about quick payoffs and a lot more about their customers, the communities in which they operated, and the larger film
business they otherwise undermined every time they screened a (foreign) "sexploiter" like *Without a Stitch* or *I Am Curious Yellow*.

In the spring of 1970 *Variety* reported that over six hundred theaters
in New York City alone—many of them formerly legit houses—had
begun booking what the trade journal described as "exploitation spe-
cials (skin flicks)."[59] While Valenti continued to insist that the mainstream industry needed to play it safe, that dirty movies were little
more than a novelty, that their appeal was short-term and their production, distribution, and especially exhibition were financially risky, *Variety* staff writers like Addison Verrill began to report on hard- and soft-
core porn as if they might someday soon be writing about such films as
often and as earnestly as they presently reported on studio pictures.

In an April 1970 article, for example, Verrill wrote about Rex and
Chelly Wilson, a husband-and-wife team who, after fifty years in the exhibition business, opted to abandon legit studio pictures in favor of sexploitation at their seventeen New York sites. Verrill was inclined to read
the market shift as a larger sign of the times and as a harbinger of things
to come: "Today's Nixon-celebrated silent majority [may] be caught out
at first base . . . fact is a substantial segment of the general public is buying screen sex in all its variations."

Whether or not, as Verrill suggested, it was indeed "the age of
Aquarius" was far less important to the Wilsons than how soft core
seemed to afford them a chance at a quick payoff in the last years before
their retirement. The Wilsons had been in the business a long time. If
their brief run with soft core came at the studios' expense, as Valenti had
suggested it might, it did not weigh much on their conscience. "You
have to look at it like the business it is," Rex Wilson told Verrill. "If I
didn't do it, someone else would because it's what the public is buying.
Sure I'd love to go back to the old style, in fact I'd change my policy
overnight if I thought I could make any money that way. But with the
rates the major companies are charging, it's impossible. . . . No one is
holding a gun on people and ordering them into [our] theaters."[60]

The controversy over adults-only movies dominated Valenti's
early tenure at the MPAA, so much so that in January 1971, the MPAA
chief turned to *Variety* to vent his frustration. Through an unnamed
MPAA source, Valenti acknowledged that neither the studio organization "nor any other aligned group [was] particularly happy with
the X rating of films."[61]

Valenti's call for patience from the studios hinged on a deft public relations strategy. The rating system was designed to sell the image of a responsible and responsive industry. Valenti believed that such an image was necessary for the studios' long-term success. He also foresaw a second wave of local censorship disputes and he appreciated the importance of keeping the studio membership of the MPAA out of court. The logical extension of such a strategy was that if the exhibitors continued to screen X-rated films, they would soon enough find themselves in court. That bit of bad news for the nation's exhibitors promised to be good news for the MPAA membership.

In the spring of 1970, alongside articles in *Variety* heralding the astonishing box office performance of soft-core films like *Without a Stitch*, Valenti could not help but notice a second set of articles chronicling local efforts to censor, ban, or tax X-rated screenings. The threat of a return to the unpredictable, unconstitutional world of local censorship, Valenti reminded his membership, was bad news only for those in the business of making and exhibiting X-rated films.[62] Exhibitors not up for a fight over local taxation and content prohibitions, Valenti cannily predicted, would be compelled to remain loyal to the studios. Theater owners would soon screen only films with the MPAA seal because it would be less risky to do so. For these theater owners, it would be just like the old days, only different.

The attempt to tax X-rated film admissions ultimately failed, but it proved nevertheless to be a significant regulatory threat. In April 1970 the New Hampshire state legislature voted to impose a $500 per screening tax on theaters exhibiting X-rated features.[63] By the time the New Hampshire law went into effect, thirty-nine other states were in the process of developing some sort of taxation mechanism to make it more expensive and thus less attractive for exhibitors to book X-rated movies. Several states planned to adopt a graduated tax structure based in part on the MPAA rating system: a five-cent tax would be added onto each ticket sold for a G-rated film, ten cents for GP, twenty-five cents for R, and as much as fifty cents for X-rated movies.[64]

The graduated tax system was a win-win strategy for state and city legislatures. The increased cost of tickets promised to decrease admissions for X-rated films. But even if the increased cost of going to such films failed to discourage admissions, the states and cities stood to gain significant revenue from the fifty-cent tax it collected per ticket.[65]

Certain cities and states doled out stiff fines when spot checks of X-rated movie houses found theater patrons under the age of eighteen. In Maine, for example, theater owners were subject to fines up to $1,000 and incarceration for as long as eleven months if they failed to enforce age-based restrictions on X-rated movies.[66] Of course no fines were imposed and no spot checks were ever undertaken to enforce the mainstream industry's rating system, as compliance with its guidelines was voluntary and tied to business arrangements as opposed to legal criteria.

Local, informal censorship exclusively targeted theater owners. Even when virtually all local tax and/or fine statutes were found to be unconstitutional, local efforts proved to be enough of a nuisance to keep many exhibitors loyal to the safer if less immediately profitable studio product.[67]

INDEPENDENTS AND INDEPENDENCE

I have little interest in hard-core porn, because it always looks like open-heart surgery to me. And I wouldn't care to see a real snuff movie. I don't think that would be especially interesting. Unless it was, maybe, someone famous.

—John Waters, director

On my very first picture, *Last House on the Left*, Sean Cunningham was the producer, I was the writer/director/editor. . . . we discovered at the very end that we had to submit the picture to this weird group out in Hollywood called the MPAA. Off the picture went and soon it came back with an "X." This process repeated itself for a week until the film was 75 minutes long and made absolutely no sense anymore. Finally Sean just swore under his breath, went down the hall to someone who'd made an "R" film and got their "This Film is Rated R" banner and spliced it onto the head of our totally restored, original cut, sent it across the street to the optical house for blow-up (we were in our 16mm days), and released it that way.

—Wes Craven, filmmaker

For non-MPAA filmmakers and distributors, the most disconcerting problem with the rating system is CARA's variable criteria. When the MPAA was in the process of developing the new rating system, Valenti argued in favor of more flexible criteria as adopted by the Supreme Court in 1967 in its decision in *Redrup v. New York*.[68] While

CARA seldom used such variable criteria to discern between different sorts of potentially obscene materials—obscene, at least in the legal sense—rating board members were encouraged to consider a film's overall quality and the context of potentially objectionable material when distinguishing between R-rated films, which were released with an MPAA seal of approval, and (mostly not obscene) X-rated films, which were not.

Just three weeks after the rating system took effect, *Variety* examined the ratings of two films, *The Fox*, based on the D. H. Lawrence novella, which received an R, and *Birds in Peru*, an erotic drama starring the once famous Jean Seberg, which received an X. *The Fox* featured extensive above-the-waist nudity and a female masturbation scene. The film was beautifully produced; the erotic content was presented in the context of what looked and sounded like a quality production. *Birds of Peru* was a low(er)-budget picture with significantly less professional production values. The film was about sex, or at least about people who have sex, but there was little onscreen nudity. *Variety* remarked that "many in the N.Y. trade simply cannot understand the criteria employed for these two pix."[69] But considering the variable criteria systematically employed by CARA, the apparent rating inconsistency is hardly mysterious. *The Fox* fared better with CARA because it looked more like a studio film than *Birds of Peru*. Specific content, the CARA board was encouraged to believe, was less important than the larger context, the measurable quality of the film itself, the overall look and sound of a picture—the sort of stuff only money could buy.

The variable censorship guidelines employed by CARA are complicated by its various relationships and/or conflicts of interest within the larger industry. CARA is a subsidiary of the MPAA, and appeals of its decisions are overseen by a board composed of MPAA executives. In the process of ensuring widespread adoption of the new rating system, in 1968 the MPAA entered into formal, strategic agreements with NATO member exhibitors and IFIDA, agreements that worked to the studios' collective advantage. Independent filmmakers and distributors have to go through CARA to get into the legit marketplace and do not benefit from any significant vertical or horizontal corporate arrangement. The vague and variable nature of code designations enable CARA to be far more permissive in its ratings of studio films, most of which are better written, better acted, and most important, better looking than the indie product. These films are distributed into NATO theaters by companies that control the MPAA and are licensed into foreign markets through

IFIDA. Inequities are inevitable as these fundamental conflicts of interest undermine the objectivity and autonomy of the rating system.

In a particularly revealing "open letter to the industry," published in the
April 6, 1970, issue of *Variety*, the indie distributor Alfred Nichtenhauser called attention to the ways the X rating was being used by
CARA in the early seventies to ghettoize independently produced and
distributed films. The letter called on the MPAA to make the system
more fair to independents and suggested that an appropriate first gesture might be to revise the classification system at the adult end of the
rating scale.

The solution to the local censorship problem in 1970, Nichtenhauser suggested, was twofold. Independents had to stop grousing
about the MPAA/CARA: "Every effort should be made by the entire industry to promote [a] spirit of constructive cooperation." To solidify
such a "constructive cooperation" between the powerful studios and
the small independent distributors, Nichtenhauser proposed a new "binary system" in which films would be rated either for all audiences or
for adults only. Under such a system, children and teenagers under the
age of seventeen could be admitted to any all-audience film at any time
as well as any adults-only film so long as they were accompanied by a
parent. The binary system, Nichtenhauser pointed out, was consistent
with Valenti's early press releases that explored the possibility of leaving content regulation entirely up to parents.[70]

The proposal held little in the way of advantages for the studios.
Nichtenhauser no doubt appreciated that his open letter had little hope
of success with Valenti and the MPAA. Like a lot of press releases, advertisements, and so-called open letters published in the trades, Nichtenhauser's missive was largely symbolic, a safe means by which an independent distributor might call attention to an inequity without naming names and without making any powerful enemies.

Nichtenhauser's proposal of "a more constructive method of identifying adult-oriented films" called attention to a specific inequity in the
film rating process, an inequity encouraged by the MPAA. As Valenti
had hoped it would, the new system effectively conflated distinct and
diverse indie adult product lines, rendering a wide variety of X-rated
films "dirty" in the public's view. Nichtenhauser's letter unintentionally revealed just how well the system was working to protect legit studio product lines and to render independent adult films vulnerable to
local censorship. The movies targeted by local censors and activists

were mostly rated X, mostly produced and distributed by independents. X-rated films were targeted, Nichtenhauser alleged, because they reached the marketplace without an MPAA seal. Valenti was inclined to agree and endeavored to make sure the situation did not change.

The initial if not principal motivation behind Nichtenhauser's missive was a specific CARA decision involving a soft-core feature, *Daddy Darling*, produced and distributed by his company, Cinelex. *Daddy Darling* received an X rating, which by the standards of the day was perfectly understandable. In a letter addressed to Nichtenhauser dated February 24, 1970 (and reprinted in the "open letter" in *Variety*), CARA spokesman James Bouras wrote, "in its present form, *Daddy Darling* could only be rated X. Moreover, it is our judgment that the modifications necessary to bring this picture into the R category would do serious harm to what is now a very fine adult film."

Bouras's note to Nichtenhauser reveals how CARA downplays its adversarial relationship to filmmakers and distributors. After generously affirming the "very fine" quality of *Daddy Darling*—an absurd but polite remark exploited by Nichtenhauser in the open letter—Bouras outlined the various large-scale changes that would be necessary before the indie distributor might resubmit the film for a possible R rating.[71] Bouras's letter recalled the sort of polite rhetoric routinely employed by Joseph Breen, who, on behalf of the PCA decades earlier, censored movies by offering "advice" and "suggestions" that filmmakers dared not ignore. Whether a filmmaker was dealing with the PCA or CARA, a decision not to follow code suggestions promised to create significant problems with local censors and less adventurous exhibitors.

The content at issue in *Daddy Darling*, the specific changes deemed necessary to bring the film in line with the 1968 code, were of a sort Breen could hardly have ever imagined:

(1) the scene in which Katja lies awake while her girlfriend and a boy engage in nude lovemaking in an adjacent bed will have to be reduced substantially, (2) The scene in which Katja surrenders her virginity will have to be reduced considerably, including elimination of the sound effects and close-ups which clearly indicate defloration, (3) The sound effects which accompany the lovemaking of Katja's father and her stepmother must be toned down considerably and should be eliminated in part, (4) The scene in which Katja is seduced by two lesbians will have to be eliminated almost entirely. This must include the more

blunt dialogue, (5) The scene in which Katja seduces her stepmother must be reduced considerably, including the repeated shots of the two women engaged in nude lovemaking."[72]

Nichtenhauser and Cinelex were hardly household names, even on the indie circuit in the early 1970s. But the distributor's open letter to the industry spoke for all independent filmmakers whether they made porn or not. Even such legendary figures on the indie circuit as Russ Meyer, John Waters, and Wes Craven attest to the anti-indie prejudice of the CARA board.

Whatever we make of his films today—and the films date badly, I think—Russ Meyer is a significant independent American filmmaker as well as a key player in the history of postwar content regulation. His breakthrough film, *The Immoral Mr. Teas*, went a long way toward shattering the nudity taboo onscreen. His later work, much of it successful on the indie circuit, was perhaps less revolutionary. But it was so eccentric and unique it met with considerable resistance from the CARA board. Most of Meyer's films—*Vixen*, *Cherry, Harry and Raquel*; *Super-Vixens*; *Up!*; *Beneath the Valley of the UltraVixens*; and *Mud Honey*—were rated X upon release.[73] Meyer's camp/trash-style B pictures were seldom any more explicit or violent than a number of the R-rated studio films in general release at the same time. But the cheesy camera work, the dreadful acting, the absurd female caricatures, the obsessive attention paid to big breasts were precisely the sort of stuff CARA dismissed as lowbrow, filthy, and X-rated.

Meyer's box office success in the late sixties brought him to the attention of the studios and in 1970 he was offered a contract to direct *Beyond the Valley of the Dolls* for Twentieth Century Fox. Initially, Meyer seemed the perfect man for the job. But he wasn't. *The Valley of the Dolls* was one of the last mature-themed films released under the old code restrictions. It was based on a popular, trashy adult novel and as such seemed very much the sort of project the studio might use to tap into the adults-only market. It also seemed to be a project well suited to Meyer's trash sensibility and his reputation for over-the-top soft-core imagery.

After signing with Fox, Meyer went about putting his peculiar auteur signature on the project. But as soon as the studio brass got a look at some of the early footage, they panicked and began to pressure Meyer to make the film less dirty, less trashy, less funny, less like the films Meyer had made on the cheap and on his own. "[Richard

Zanuck] was very concerned about his own image," Meyer reflected in a *Film Comment* interview in 1980. "I later learned that [he] was telling people that he hated *Beyond the Valley of the Dolls*, [that] he wished it were never made, that he was embarrassed and so on."[74]

When Fox submitted Meyer's cut of *Beyond the Valley of the Dolls* to CARA for review, it received an X rating. Even by 1970 standards, the rating was harsh. Still, Meyer was not surprised. He had expected CARA to be ungenerous; as an independent he had already experienced such treatment from the rating board. Zanuck, on the other hand, was used to the ways variable criteria favored studio pictures, so he appealed the decision.

When the CARA appeal failed, Meyer offered to reedit *Beyond the Valley of the Dolls* in order to make it a "legitimate" X-rated picture. Zanuck balked, citing the studio's cash flow problems at the time.[75] The fiscal problems at Fox in 1970 were real enough; all the studios were suffering to one extent or another. But Zanuck's decision to kill the film betrayed a larger discomfort with Meyer and the sorts of films he made. The CARA board worked for and represented Zanuck and his studio. Meyer was an outsider best left to make his films on the margins of Hollywood.

Much like Meyer, the Baltimore-based independent John Waters made his reputation with camp comedy films in the adults-only range. But while Meyer's films were rooted in the Playboy mystique and thus appealed to a middle-aged audience, Waters embraced and satirized the emerging sixties and seventies youth culture. *Pink Flamingos, Female Trouble,* and *Desperate Living,* three of Waters's early X-rated comedies, introduced hard-core footage—blow jobs, artificial insemination, beaver-shots, even sex with chickens—to young audiences. These audiences were only just getting their first taste of more explicit post–rating system teenpics: soft-core R- and X-rated youth-oriented films like *The Swingin' Stewardesses, The Swingin' Cheerleaders, The Naughty Cheerleaders, Revenge of the Cheerleaders, Cheerleaders' Beach Party, Fugitive Girls, Reform School Girls, Slammer Girls, Wild in the Streets, Three in the Attic,* and *The Hot Box.* Waters's "mondo trasho" pictures offered a deft satire of an absurd and obscene pop culture.

While Waters's films featured hard-core imagery and content, they were far more obscene than erotic. The primary venue for Waters's films was thus not the urban porn theater, but the midnight movie slot at legit-mainstream and so-called art theaters. *Pink Flamingos, Female Trouble,* and *Desperate Living* had less in common with hard-core films than

Divine *über alles*: the three-hundred-pound drag queen plots to take over the world in John Waters's hilarious X-rated satire *Pink Flamingos* (Saliva, 1971).

with cult-pics like *The Rocky Horror Picture Show* and Robert Downey's X-rated black comedies *Putney Swope* and *Greaser's Palace*.

Pink Flamingos was a frequent target of local censorship activists. But even where local censors appreciated the difference between hard-core sex pictures like *Deep Throat* and graphic parodies like *Pink Flamingos*, bans and prohibitions were seldom reconsidered. To a large extent, local attacks on X-rated midnight movies were based on the very generation gap lampooned in the films themselves.

Waters now makes fairly sweet parodies like *Polyester, Cry Baby, Serial Mom*, and *Pecker*, films that seldom push the barriers of the R rating. But in the early seventies his unrated or X-rated films met with significant local censorship. *Pink Flamingos'* first run in Waters's hometown of Baltimore, for example, was held up until the director made specific cuts in the film. The cuts were arbitrary and strange. They made the film no less obscene and served only to highlight the subjective and arbitrary nature of content censorship. "We had a horrible censor board in Baltimore," Waters reminisced in a recent interview,

> one of the only states to have one, and it was headed by this woman who had a fourth grade education and used to say things on national television like: "Don't tell me about sex, I was married to an Italian." . . . she watched *Pink Flamingos* and she only cut two scenes from the movie—she cut the artificial insemination, which is correctly the most repulsive scene in the movie, and she cut the blow job. She left in eating shit because there were just no laws against it.[76]

In what could well have been a scene in one of his movies, Waters recounts his day in court on Long Island:

> When *Pink Flamingos* came out in Hicksville, New York, which is on Long Island, we discovered that it was cheaper to plead guilty and just pay the $5000 fine. Because the film *is* obscene, but in a joyous way, which is very hard to prove legally. And when you show these films in a courtroom at 10 AM to a jury who have never met . . . believe me it's frightening. They see it completely out of context. When audiences go to see that movie, they know what they're getting—they go to laugh, they go to be outraged. But with the jury, they don't know if they're getting a burglary case or what, and then they suddenly get *Pink Flamingos*. And it looks *really* weird in a courtroom."[77]

Both Meyer and Waters are for the most part directors of camp entertainment and audiences assembled in a public theater to watch their films are encouraged to have fun. The CARA board screens films in private and thus has no way to appreciate or anticipate the ways these

films might be used by certain audiences. The teen horror films produced and/or directed by Wes Craven—*A Nightmare on Elm Street*, for
example—are hardly camp in the traditional sense. But they too depend
on public presentation, on audience interaction. Weird as it may seem
to most adults, teenagers find Craven's more recent films amusing as
well as, if not instead of, frightening. The films are mostly about
teenagers, of course—about terrible things happening to teenagers, especially those who engage in the sorts of behaviors most teenagers either engage in or wish they did.

Teenagers and young adults account for the vast majority of ticket
sales and video rentals for these films.[78] It is their reading of content that
seems relevant here, but the rating system is such that public presentation and reception are never considered in the classification process.
The middle-aged members of the CARA board view Craven's films in a
private screening room where, as Waters suggests, cult films look *really
weird*. Instead of considering the films in the context of their intended
use, CARA board members recognize the markers of low-budget entertainment and treat Craven's films more harshly than similar but more
polished movies released by the studios.

Like *Pink Flamingos*, teen horror films like *A Nightmare on Elm Street*
are socially and politically relevant for teenagers. That CARA makes it
difficult or impossible for teenagers to see these films amounts to a form
of political censorship, a problem acknowledged by Craven in interviews. "I believe we are at a fairly frightening, transitional stage in history," Craven mused in 1990.

> We tried the Ozzie and Harriet thing in the 50's, and that didn't work.
> We tried the hippie peace-and-love-thing, and that didn't work. We
> tried the yuppie thing and the world got worse. So what's next? Today,
> there is no clear way for teenagers to go. All they have are politicians,
> TV preachers, and cynical heavy metal musicians telling them things
> they sense are lies. No one is offering them the truth they crave so
> deeply. I make horror movies in which a character comes out of peo-
> ple's dreams and slashes away at anything that's bullshit. All I can tell
> you, I guess, is that I'm not surprised that Freddy Krueger [the maniac
> who haunts the dreamscape in Craven's *Nightmare on Elm Street*] is a
> teen hero.[79]

Craven's harder-edged, less well known early work is chronicled at
length by Robin Wood in *Hollywood from Vietnam to Reagan*. The Hills

When the MPAA tried to force director Wes Craven to cut sixteen minutes out of *Last House on the Left* (AIP, 1973), the director "borrowed" a "This Film Is Rated R" banner from someone else's film and attached it to his own.

Have Eyes and especially Craven's debut film, *The Last House on the Left,* Wood argues, are profoundly political films in which audience members often find it difficult to establish any sort of critical distance, let alone the sort of ironic distance essential for fans of comedy-horror films like *A Nightmare on Elm Street* or *Scream.* "The reason people find the violence in *Last House* so disturbing is not simply that there is so much of it," Wood writes, it is that the violence in the film so unflinchingly reflects and resonates with a violence "powerfully and obstinately inherent in human relationships as we know them," a violence we recognize as not limited to just a movie.[80]

In the harsh treatment Craven's early films received from CARA we find an example of a potentially larger problem with the industry's system of censorship: that the MPAA or local jurisdictions might someday use—might already be using—content regulation as an excuse for suppressing politically unpleasant or unpopular speech. Craven himself is anxious to make just such an argument: "Salman Rushdie commented that the reason the State frequently wars with its artists is because the two represent two conflicting versions of the truth. . . . We of course do not have government censors—that would be totalitarian. It would also be unnecessary. What we do have is the MPAA." The manner in which political speech is suppressed, restricted, or labeled by the MPAA can only be understood, Craven argues, once one considers the complex and contradictory relationship between art and business in Hollywood: "Art/Business is even more oxymoronic than State/Art. At least the latter is a marriage visible and viable enough to remain in the public eye . . . global, transnational corporations [like the ones that own and control the studios these days] are much more secretive entities, forces unto themselves increasingly operating outside the borders of public checks and balances."[81]

In the process of cutting films to suit CARA, filmmakers are forced to sacrifice potentially revelatory or radical political messages. "Increasingly, the tactic used by the MPAA that really can devastate your film is judgment not against specific content (blood, whatever)," Craven says, "but against intensity itself." When filmmakers negotiate with CARA to secure an R rating for a controversial film, they are often encouraged to cut back on the volume of the music accompanying a scene, to remove sound effects, to shorten or lengthen sequences, to cut out certain frames, "to make it not so darned intense." The end result, Craven aptly points out, are movies that occupy a safe middle ground. These movies earn their MPAA seal, their R rating, and are released in profoundly diminished form and have a diminished effect on the audience. Again, as Craven describes it, "The very thing you've struggled all those months to attain is dismissed as too much to be tolerated. Tone it down. Round it off. Pull it back. . . . A general sick feeling creeps into your work."[82]

ZABRISKIE POINT

PLAYBOY: "Was it intentional, in the scene [in *Blow-Up*] where the photographer has an orgy with the two girls . . . that pubic hair appear visible?"
ANTONIONI: "I didn't notice. If you can tell me where, I'll go look."

The PCA regulated erotic, violent, *and* political content in films. For the most part, the studios cooperated with the industry censors because it was in their best interests to do so. Erotic and/or violent imagery risked problems with rival, local censorship boards and activist organizations.

Controversial political content in films diminished foreign revenues, promoted a poor image of the United States abroad, and, especially in the first few years after the Second World War, tempted fate with the House Committee on Un-American Activities as well as the MPEA, the one government agency anxious to do business with the studios.

The 1968 rating system promised to support films featuring a far wider range of erotic and violent imagery. But controversial political content was another matter entirely. CARA could not explicitly discourage the production of politically sensitive films. Nor could it establish punitive rating criteria that might inhibit such films at the box office. As a result, the self-regulation of political content was left largely to the studios themselves. It has proved to be a responsibility they have handled all too well.

Movie executives cling to the old saw about politics onscreen: "If you want to send a message, call Western Union." Political films—especially those that focus on narrow or peculiarly American issues—pose short-term box office and long-term public relations problems in the international market. The studios reach that international market through IFIDA, one of their principal partners in the development and implementation of the new rating system. The MPAA has a vested interest in keeping IFIDA happy. And IFIDA is kept happy only so long as the studios continue to make films that can be safely and successfully screened worldwide.

Films with controversial political content pose problems at home as well. Though signature studio styles went out with the contract system in the 1940s, studio trademarks remain important, so much so that they are run at the head of virtually every film screened in the United States and abroad. To protect the integrity of these trademarks, the studios have historically discouraged the production of X- or NC-17–rated films *and* they have avoided controversial political material.

Studio self-regulation of politically sensitive material was significantly put to the test in October 1968, when MGM entered into a contract with Michelangelo Antonioni, the director of the controversial pre–rating system hit *Blow-Up*. MGM no doubt entered into the contract with the expectation that Antonioni would produce another erotic thriller. He didn't.

The contract between MGM and Antonioni was unique at the time. In its haste and panic to sign the Italian cineaste, MGM gave Antonioni nearly complete creative autonomy. When he decided to make a film openly critical of the police and the government, a film eventually titled *Zabriskie Point*, the studio found itself in a bind. The film promised to embarrass the studio at a particularly sensitive political moment and there was no efficient in-house mechanism to influence the film's production.

In some important ways, MGM's problems with Antonioni paralleled Fox's problems with Russ Meyer. Antonioni and Meyer are of course very different filmmakers. But the distinction between them in 1968 was perhaps not so obvious to executives at MGM. Antonioni came to MGM's attention not because he made great, important movies. Indeed, I doubt that many American studio executives had even heard of let alone seen *L'Avventura*, the film that made the director notorious and famous in Europe and popular with film students in the United States in the early sixties.[83] When they hired Antonioni in 1968, MGM executives were interested in exploiting his notoriety as the director of *Blow-Up*, which had earned a whole lot of money in a faltering American marketplace by, so far as MGM executives were concerned, showing a flash of pubic hair during a three-way sex scene. By the time Antonioni had signed with MGM to direct *Zabriskie Point*, industry estimates had *Blow-Up* grossing as much as $20 million, an astonishing sum given that the film cost less than $2 million to produce.

But even before principal photography on *Zabriskie Point* commenced, the project was beset by rumors, most of which concerned the director's radical politics and the possibility that he might exploit his contract with the studio to make an anti-American film.[84] At the time, all the studio had to go on was the playwright Sam Shephard's outline about wilderness exploitation by real estate developers in the desert Southwest. But early in the fall of 1968 information was leaked to the trades that Antonioni had little intention of sticking to the outline and instead intended to focus on another story about two young lovers caught in the maelstrom of student activism on college campuses at the time. The rumors were by and large accurate. Antonioni was fascinated with student activism. In the process of developing the shooting script for the film, he conducted a series of interviews with radicals on campuses on the West Coast. When news of these interviews reached executives at MGM, they panicked.

The production proved a ceaseless headache for MGM. For example, the shooting script called for a scene in which hundreds of couples are shown making love in the sandy dunes of Death Valley. What came to be referred to as the "love-in" scene, complete with full nudity and simulated sex, raised the ire of the National Park Service in

Director Michelangelo Antonioni offers some last-minute advice to Daria Halprin and Mark Frechette during the production of the X-rated *Zabriskie Point* (MGM, 1970).

Death Valley. Upon hearing about the scene, Park Service officials refused to grant Antonioni permission to film any scene at all in Death Valley. Environmental activists, who were sympathetic to the production because it promised to present an unflattering story about real estate developers in the area, subsequently persuaded Park Service officials in Washington, D.C., to allow Antonioni to shoot his film. But conservative park rangers at the site opposed the official Park Service decision and sent letters of complaint to MGM and to law enforcement agencies in Washington. The confrontation between Antonioni and the park rangers brought the project even more bad publicity. And, rumor has it, the letters written by the park rangers resulted in a sudden interest in the picture at the FBI.

Antonioni's production methods, grounded as they were in the far more autonomous auteur system in Europe, made matters worse. For example, he insisted on casting unknown, inexperienced actors in the principal roles in order to present an authentic, neo-neorealist picture of American youth. The female lead was a dancer named Daria Halprin; the male lead, Mark Frechette, a former mental patient with a history of violence and ties to a radical, anarchist commune. Neither had any acting experience. Early rushes suggested that neither had any talent either.

Antonioni's politics and rumors about the political themes in the script (which was kept secret from the studio through much of the production) led to problems with the mostly conservative craftsmen hired by MGM to work on the film. Most of the crew members had never heard of Antonioni and those who did knew only that he had directed *Blow-Up*, a notoriously "dirty movie." According to Beverly Walker, a publicist hired by "Antonioni's people" to do damage control during the production of the film, the crew commonly referred to the director as "a pinko dago pornographer." Their reaction was a sign of the times, perhaps. It was 1968, after all: the Chicago convention was a recent memory and Richard Nixon was about to be elected president.

The crew was uncooperative, unresponsive, and downright subversive during the production of the film. They reported each little violation of union and industry rules in order to hold up production and inflate the picture's already bloated budget. A series of anonymous phone calls, which Walker blames on the unruly crew, alerted union reps at various locations and warned them that their work would facilitate the production of an anti-American film. As a result of these calls, Antonioni suffered through a series of union slowdowns or sick-outs. Production at various sites was often delayed or canceled altogether.

It is hard to dismiss the conspiracy theories that have come to accompany the strange history of the film. Antonioni's interviews with student radicals, the letters from forest rangers to National Park Service headquarters in Washington, D.C., and the presence on the set of Kathleen Cleaver (whose husband, Eldridge Cleaver, was one of the nation's ten most wanted fugitives at the time) as an unofficial adviser to the film made the production interesting to the FBI. Antonioni was convinced that the phones on location were tapped and that some of the extras hanging around the location site were undercover agents. On both counts he was right.

Less than a month after principal photography was completed in April 1969, several of the major players in the production company were named in a bizarre criminal action. The U.S. attorney's office alleged that the extras who were bused in to appear in the love-in scene were ostensibly transported across state lines for immoral purposes, in direct violation of the Mann Act. When several members of the crew came forward as friendly witnesses to testify against Antonioni, things began to take on much the same tenor as the political inquisition in Hollywood in the late forties. Even the *Hollywood Reporter*, a politically conservative trade journal, called the U.S. attorney's investigation "politically inspired" and condemned the government's "attempt to thwart the release of the picture, which is said to be anti-American."[85]

Most of the film was shot on location, an expensive proposition in even the best of circumstances. "[MGM] asks me why the film is so expensive," Antonioni remarked at the time, "but that's what I'm going to ask them. I'm seeing such a waste of money. It seems almost immoral. . . . They are consumers. They are used to wasting."[86] But some of the budget problems were the director's fault, or at least certain scenes cost a lot because of the way Antonioni wanted to shoot them. The love-in on the dunes proved costly because Antonioni had to bring in smoother sand so the actors could roll around in less abrasive conditions. The explosion that caps the film was slated to be shot in miniature, but the production designer Dean Tavoularis (who, not incidentally, would be the designer of both *Apocalypse Now* and *One from the Heart*, two other gorgeous films that went way over budget) insisted that the developer's house had to be erected in life-size.

By the time it was ready for release, *Zabriskie Point* was a significant embarrassment to MGM. The studio had given carte blanche to Antonioni and what it got for its money—for a whole lot of its money—was a Marxist, neorealist film without a coherent plot or professional performances. More problematic still was the fact that MGM had virtually nothing else in production at the time and its new corporate owner, Kirk Kerkorian, and the company's new cost-conscious chief executive, James Aubrey, were intent on significantly cutting back on spending at the studio. If Antonioni's big-budget American debut was as dangerous or as bad as studio executives believed it was, Kerkorian and Aubrey seemed poised to shut the studio down altogether.

When *Zabriskie Point* was finally released in the United States in 1970, it was excoriated by the same reviewers who had celebrated Antonioni and *Blow-Up* just two years earlier. The film did nothing at the box office and its political impact was hardly felt.

Zabriskie Point is a strange film to sit through today; it's dated and pretentious and gorgeous. It is also wholly unflinching in its depiction of the very sort of disturbingly divided America captured in *Easy Rider*, a film MGM would have wanted Antonioni to remake. But while the box office success of *Easy Rider* encouraged the studios to target younger audiences, *Zabriskie Point* served to remind them that the success of *Easy Rider* was more mysterious than they at first suspected; that *political* films in America—the new production code notwithstanding—were still risky to make.

DEMOGRAPHICS AND THE BIRTH OF A NEW AMERICAN CINEMA

Everything is just addition or subtraction—the rest is just conversation.
—Abraham Polonsky, screenplay for *Body and Soul*

The first hint that the postwar box office slide might finally abate came in 1972 when *The Godfather* single-handedly turned fortunes around at Paramount. A more complete, industry-wide turnaround seemed fully under way by 1975. Between 1968 and 1975—the period between the adoption of the new rating system and the release of *Jaws*—the studios mostly shied away from X-rated films.

Valenti lobbied strongly against tinkering with the code at the adult end of the rating scale and continued to defend the new rating system as the best means of regulating the industry into prosperity. Valenti's refusal to expand the CARA system was founded on his belief that studio participation in the soft- and/or hard-core business was tantamount to surrender. He maintained that the studio feature was the most attractive and viable entertainment package and that diversifying into dirty movies would signal the end of a form and formula for entertainment that had sustained the studios through most of the century.

In the late sixties and early seventies, the trades were openly critical of Valenti's steadfast refusal to adopt an alternative adults-only classification. The AO classification proposed by NATO, for example, had considerable support industry-wide but was never taken seriously by Valenti, even during uncertain years at the box office.

In 1990 Valenti added the NC-17 designation to facilitate the release of Universal's *Henry and June*, a Philip Kaufman film that had received an X rating from the CARA board. But when public pressure (demonstrations, threatened boycotts) successfully interfered with the film's initial run, the studios quickly realized that the new classification, which had been copyrighted by Valenti, did not protect their products in the marketplace. The studios today are decidedly *not* in the NC-17 business. Because the MPAA and the studios have abandoned the NC-17 designation, the clamor for a change at the adult end of the rating scale persists. In the summer of 1999, the New York Film Critics Circle, *Variety*'s editor Peter Bart, the popular film reviewer/TV personality Roger Ebert, and a host of high-profile filmmakers all called on the MPAA to adopt an A (adult) rating to finally distinguish adult-content films from porn. Valenti dismissed the suggestion as bad for the industry and added a new, as in new Hollywood, spin to the old argument: "If we institute an A rating, we'll be forcing the board to make qualitative judgments—in other words, be critics. The A rating would be for 'quality,' and the NC-17 would be for 'sub-quality.' The producer of an NC-17 film could sue [the MPAA] for damages." Later in the same interview, Valenti vented his frustration at Ebert in particular: "If Mr. Ebert's employers would legally indemnify the ratings system, then I'd seriously consider an A rating in a week."[87] However serious Valenti is about making such a deal, it is worth pointing out here that Ebert's employer is the Disney Corporation, one of the heavyweight members of the MPAA.

Though Valenti has never supported an alternative studio X designation—he added the NC-17 reluctantly in response to considerable studio pressure—he has serially tweaked the lower end of the range: M became GP in 1970, then PG in 1972, then PG and PG-13 in 1984. More important, Valenti has encouraged CARA to make the R designation increasingly inclusive. Of the 165 films rated from November 1968 through February 1969, sixty-three (38.2 percent) were rated G, sixty-three (38.2 percent) were rated M, thirty-three (20 percent) were rated R and only six (3.6 percent) were rated X.[88] Starting at the end of 1969, the percentage of films rated R began to increase significantly. For the fiscal year 1969–70, 37 percent of the films submitted to CARA received an R rating; four years later, R-rated films accounted for 48 percent, a plateau more or less maintained from 1975 to 1999.[89]

By expanding the range and number of films granted an R rating, the studios further identified X as a designation reserved for non-MPAA films. In doing so, they further emphasized the very outlaw status of what were presumed to be "dirty pictures." Valenti's reluctance to expand the code proved to be an effective long-term strategy. As more and more films that would have been rated X in 1968 were rated R in and after 1970, the MPAA used the X rating to effectively marginalize foreign art as well as American independent, underground, and experimental films.

The studios' reluctance to make or release films rated X empowered CARA; indeed, by 1973 CARA functioned much like the old PCA. Films rated X were released without a production seal, much as certain mature-themed films were in the fifties. Distributors of X-rated films were forced to seek a payoff on a parallel, limited theatrical circuit. Non-MPAA members hoping to participate in the legit market had to submit their films to CARA in order to get a G, PG, PG-13, or R code designation. If CARA returned their print with an X rating, even non-MPAA distributors were compelled to alter their product to suit an anonymous ratings board appointed and supervised by their competition, the MPAA studios.

In 1969 Valenti enlisted the help of the Opinion Research Corporation to give the MPAA membership, in his words, "a reliable portrait of the American moviegoing public." At first the surveys served only to remind everyone in the MPAA that business was bad. Surveys conducted in 1969, 1970, and 1971 confirmed industry estimates concerning declining admissions and declining studio revenues but failed to identify any useful market or audience trends. Then finally in 1972 a sudden improvement at the box office produced some very useful data. The blockbuster success of *The Godfather* not only saved Paramount, it signaled, perhaps even captured on its own, growing interest from a key moviegoing demographic: the twelve- to twenty-nine-year-old age group. This age group represented only 40 percent of the twelve and over population in 1972 but accounted for 73 percent of total theater admissions. A more exacting profile of the eighteen and over moviegoer revealed a surprising connection between higher education and film culture: approximately 80 percent of those surveyed with some college education frequently went to the movies. Approximately half of those without college experience identified themselves as infrequent filmgoers. The vast majority of those with less than a high school education claimed that they rarely if ever went to the movies.[90]

The education-based demographic at first supported the auteur renaissance at the studios and it indicated that the narrow target audience for these films (the young and the well-educated) was indeed being hit. At the same time, however, the numbers revealed that a significant portion of the eighteen and over audience was put off by these more ambitious, more difficult films.

In 1973 Valenti remarked to the trades that the "major attendance problems are in the older generation," but he knew better.[91] Since the advent of the new Hollywood, the studios have made little effort to meet the needs of this older demographic.[92] The studios' key task in 1973, or so the market research suggested, was to figure out a way to meet the needs of the still disinterested, less-educated younger audience. By the end of the 1970s the studios succeeded in dramatic fashion in meeting those needs as mostly FX-driven high-concept/blockbuster entertainment pictures captured the youth audience in record numbers.[93]

Valenti's steadfast resistance to the industry-wide clamor for an alternative adults-only classification and his efforts instead to expand the parameters of the R designation and to encourage the development of product lines to better attract a wide range of young American moviegoers proved deft in the long term. In retrospect, we must appreciate Valenti's savvy understanding of the American mass culture at the time and his prescient fear of a conservative backlash, the seeds of which were already sown in 1968. Valenti developed and sustained the new rating system in full acknowledgment of the slow swell of the vaunted silent majority. By the time Nixon was elected for a second term and four conservative Nixon appointees sat on the Supreme Court poised to revise liberal obscenity rulings dating back to the mid-fifties, studio product lines were, at least by widely held community standards, safely ensconced in the legitimate range.

Between 1966 and 1968 Valenti's many connections in Washington, D.C., proved useful as he mapped out the industry's future. His continued close relationship with President Lyndon Johnson kept him in the political loop. By the time Johnson declined to seek a final term and the Democratic Party imploded in Chicago in the late summer of 1968, Valenti was already committed to a rating system that anticipated the very winds of change signaled by the election of Richard Nixon.

The political situation in the late fall of 1968 seemed at first glance bad news for everyone concerned. How, after all, could a Nixon presidency be good for Hollywood? There was, at least at first, considerable anxiety throughout the membership of the MPAA over a possible return to stricter censorship and workforce regulation. But the Nixon election proved to be good news for the studios because stricter censorship and workforce regulation were exactly what the industry needed at the time. The lesson learned by the studios in the first few years under the new rating system was that a completely free and deregulated marketplace was the last thing they wanted or needed to get back on track.

5

Hollywood v. Hard Core

THE FIRST SPATE of G, M, R, and X studio pictures performed disappointingly at the box office. At the same time, features produced and distributed by the burgeoning hard-core porn movie industry recorded astonishing box office revenues. The competition from hard core reached its zenith when, from June 1972 to June 1973, *Deep Throat*, *The Devil in Miss Jones*, and *Behind the Green Door* outearned—on a screen-by-screen basis and in terms of total revenues—all but a handful of the major studios' legit releases.

In the late sixties, as the first wave of hard-core films reached urban theaters nationwide, *Variety* began to write about porn movies as if someday hard core might evolve into a rival entertainment industry, like television. As porn titles began to earn more and more money, articles and reviews of hard-core films appeared alongside legit features, as if the only distinction between the two product lines was a rating designation. By the early seventies, hard-core features routinely appeared on *Variety*'s weekly top fifty box office list, the most widely consulted page in the magazine. Under the freer production standards ushered in by the rating system, boundaries between legitimate moviemaking and hard-core pornography became simply a matter of taste.

The PCA was developed and adopted in the early 1930s to short-circuit local, informal censorship. It worked only so long as the box office remained receptive to such a rigid code. CARA was designed primarily as a port of entry into the legit film market and its success hinged rather tenuously on a number of complex intra- and interindustry relationships. The 1968 MPAA rating system at once regulated film content and maintained professional relationships between "rival" studios. It also regulated dealings between the studios and the National Association of Theater Owners (NATO), foreign distributors who marketed American films abroad, and the American distributors handling foreign films for screening in the United States.

Jack Valenti and his fellow MPAA executives initially underesti- mated the extent to which the new rating system might open things up for non-MPAA filmmakers, especially hard-core producers and distributors with little or no interest in running their films by the CARA board. The X rating, which the MPAA failed to copyright, was there for the taking. A whole lot of independent filmmakers and dis- tributors took advantage of the X rating to successfully market their films first at non-NATO theaters and then at the growing number of member theaters—many of them with long histories of screening legit pictures—willing to exploit the burgeoning market for soft and hard core.

In the late sixties and early seventies, most Americans were not aware that the vast majority of X ratings and virtually all the XXX rat- ings were self-imposed. These films reached a parallel marketplace without so much as a token fee paid to the CARA board.[1] This parallel marketplace exploited and exacerbated long-standing rivalries and grudges dating back to the government's first filing of the *Paramount* case in 1938.

The fragile relationship between exhibitors, many of them disgrun- tled with the seeming inequities of the CARA system (its variable ob- scenity guidelines, the burden it placed on theater owners to enforce in- equitable, unpredictable rating designations), threatened to short-cir- cuit the new rating system before it had the chance to fully resurrect studio product lines. After a generation's worth of bad films and bad times at the box office, the lure of a quick payoff led a number of theater owners to alter their programming format in order to screen non- MPAA, soft- and hard-core titles.

The hard-core industry had no self-regulatory apparatus and thus no screening guidelines to impose on theater owners. The XXX rating was self-imposed, arbitrary. It was more a come-on to adult au- diences and a guarantee of a certain kind of entertainment than a warning to parents about a given movie's suitability for kids. All XXX-rated films were unsuitable for children. No one making or screening the films argued otherwise. Between 1968 and 1973 local theater owners had only to concern themselves with local censorship activists and government officials, most of whom were rendered powerless by the Supreme Court's decisions in *Ginsberg v. New York* and *Interstate Circuit v. Dallas*.[2]

Widespread exhibitor disloyalty to studio product lines seemed at first glance the very sort of short-term thinking Valenti had cautioned industry players against. As mentioned in the previous chapter, Valenti had ample market research and insider information from inside the Beltway in Washington, D.C. Valenti was convinced that the "anything goes" mindset of the late sixties and early seventies would be short-lived. He refused to add an AO (adults only) rating for certain studio films because he foresaw a turn to more conservative American values of the sort that would eventually fuel Nixon's silent majority and the so-called Reagan revolution.

The year 1972 proved to be pivotal for the studios. But at the time the signs of change were difficult to read. It is only in retrospect that we can see 1972 as the beginning of a dramatic box office turnaround, which took shape more fully in the summer of 1975. In 1972, studio executives were not so confident or encouraged by the end-of-the-year box office figures. The overall box office numbers were up. But even a cursory look revealed that one film, *The Godfather*, not only carried the day, its record-breaking revenues skewed upwards the overall industry statistics. Things were indeed better at the box office, but mostly for one studio, Paramount, and at that studio things were better because of just one film.

In 1972 industry players had every reason to believe that the block-buster success of *The Godfather* was something of a fluke or something at the very least difficult to reproduce anytime soon. *The Godfather* was an R-rated film. But its exploitation of the new code—its R rating—seemed to have little to do with its success. The film features a brief and partial nude scene and a reasonable but wholly appropriate amount of graphic violence (given the new code, given that the film updates the gangster genre). The formula for success initiated by *The Godfather* was at once simple and daunting. Studios could get people back into theaters if they only made better movies. People went to see *The Godfather* in record numbers because it is a terrific film.

By the end of 1972 *The Godfather* became the highest-grossing picture in history. But if the studios turned to it for some sort of sign, they had to also take a close look at *Deep Throat*, which at the same time set box office records for hard core. Which film was easier to reproduce? The answer was at once obvious and disconcerting.

The effect on the studio industry of *The Godfather* and *Deep Throat*—two films seldom linked in film history, I know—was immediate. When the studios accepted Valenti's argument that the hard-core business was best left to smaller, sleazier entrepreneurs, they began courting directors who seemed capable of producing quality pictures. The studios put these directors' names above the titles of their films and began exploiting a sort of auteur marketing theory. In doing so, the studios began to accept or believe the notion that good directors mostly made good movies and that good movies, whatever they are, made more money than bad ones.

The top twenty box office list for 1972 revealed the wisdom of such a strategy. The end-of-the-year list included no fewer than nine auteur pictures: *The Godfather* (at number one), Peter Bogdanovich's *What's Up Doc?* (number four) and *The Last Picture Show* (number six), Stanley Kubrick's *A Clockwork Orange* (number seven) and *2001: A Space Odyssey* (in reissue at number twenty), Woody Allen's *Everything You Wanted to Know about Sex* (number ten), Franklin J. Schaffner's *Nicholas and Alexandra* (a three-hour prestige picture at number thirteen), and Alfred Hitchcock's last relevant feature, *Frenzy* (number fourteen). *Deliverance* (John Boorman), *The Getaway* (Sam Peckinpah), *Paper Moon* (Bogdanovich), *Last Tango in Paris* (Bernardo Bertolucci), and *American Graffiti* (George Lucas) hit the top twenty in 1973. By the end of the summer of 1975, Coppola's *The Godfather Part II* and Steven Spielberg's *Jaws* provided no less than a model for a new new American cinema that merged the prestige auteur picture with familiar and bankable genre formulas.

This sudden cine-renaissance had, alas, little to do with executives finally coming to their senses. Instead, the roots of this auteur renaissance lay in the studios' desperation to combat America's befuddling affection for hard core.

EXPLOITATION PICTURES

Sign of the Gladiator is a crudely made spectacle. The deepest thing about it is Anita Ekberg's cleavage.

—*Variety*, 1959

Dirty movies have had a long history in the United States. They date back to pre-cinema "motion photography" experiments like the so-called series photographs first exhibited by Eadweard Muybridge in 1877. A number of Muybridge's series photographs—his sequential still pictures shot by a battery of strategically placed cameras in order to simulate movement—featured naked women performing simple household tasks and leisure-time activities. These crude "motion pictures," with titles like *Woman Walking Down Stairs* and *Woman Setting Down Jug*, were essentially cast as figure studies, along the lines of high art nudes in pencil sketches and paintings.

But while *Woman Walking Downstairs* and *Woman Setting Down Jug* seem at least superficially rooted in museum culture, series studies like *Woman Throwing Baseball* and *Woman Jumping from Rock to Rock* were more clearly rooted in the carny peep show. The models in the latter two titles smile, even laugh, as they look back at Muybridge's camera, at once acknowledging the act of voyeurism (that all of these series photographs attend) and apparently taking an exhibitionist delight in being seen. Like a lot of cinema's so-called pioneers, Muybridge was primarily an entrepreneur and only secondarily, even incidentally, an artist. His series photographs reveal a keen sense of his audience as well as a prescient understanding of the ways motion pictures might someday conflate and confuse the very different worlds of the museum and the midway.[3]

In an interview published in *Film Comment*, the B movie impresario David F. Friedman reflected, "After Mr. Edison made those tintypes gallop, it wasn't but two days later that some enterprising guy had his girlfriend take her clothes off for the camera."[4] Histories of stag and exploitation films bear Friedman out. In an essay on hard-core films, Joseph Slade dates scenes featuring full frontal female nudity in publicly exhibited films to 1899. Scenes of sexual intercourse can be found in films as early as 1902.[5]

The earliest stag films preserved at the Kinsey Institute were made between 1907 and 1915: *Am Abend* (Germany, circa 1910), *El Satario* (Argentina, circa 1907–15), and the oldest extant American stag film, *A Free Ride* (alternatively titled *A Grass Sandwich*, circa 1915–17).[6] All three films open with rudimentary narrative frames and, after a brief gesture to a more conventional cinema, segue into considerable, fragmentary hard-core imagery. *Am Abend* begins—as so many of these films do—with an act of voyeurism: a man looking through a keyhole, in this case at a woman masturbating alone in her bedroom. The man then enters the room and the two engage in a variety of acts in a variety of positions, shown in a series of discontinuous master (full-figure) shots and inserts (of genitalia, penetration, etc.).

El Satario features a slightly more extended narrative hook. We see a group of naked women bathing in a river. They exit the river and dance, but their idyll is interrupted by someone (else, besides *us*) watching them: a devil, complete with horns and tail. The women run; the devil gives chase. Eventually he catches one of the women and the crudely but conventionally shot narrative sequence gives way to fragmented hard-core action, punctuated by what would eventually become one of the distinguishing factors between hard-core XXX features and studio X (and NC-17) pictures, the money or come shot.

A Free Ride sets up the hard-core action with a simple and brief narrative gesture: a man picks up two women for a drive in the country, they see him naked, he sees them, action ensues. Though the fragmented and fragmentary hard-core action included in the Kinsey print is purported to be from another film, one can safely argue that, except for historical or ethnographic specificity, it doesn't really matter.[7]

In her critical history of the hard-core film, Linda Williams offers extensive evidence of the repeated figure of voyeurism in these early stag films. One such film, *A Country Stud Horse* (from 1920 or so), sets up its action with a scene of a man peering into a mutoscope, an early cinema viewing device. A second shot reveals what he is looking at, an early film, which appears at first to be much like *Dorolita's Passion Dance* or Edison's *Serpentine Dance* series, erotic shorts featuring fully clad women dancing with veils, simulating a striptease or belly dance. The third shot reveals that the man is masturbating; the fourth, that the dancer is up to something a whole lot more revealing than Edison cameraman William Heise ever got from Fatima or Little Egypt. The sequence continues to get more graphic in both the film of the man masturbating and the film within a film of the woman "dancing." The second section of the film takes the man away from the solitary act at the mutoscope and introduces a woman named Mary, with whom he engages in the usual fragmentary hard-core action. The film ends with someone offscreen tossing a towel onscreen, suggesting that this second sequence, much like the film within a film in the opening sequence, was just a performance for the camera.

The Pirandellian allusions notwithstanding, *A Country Stud Horse* cleverly examines the phenomenon of prurient looking. But it does so by evoking the commonplace imagery of *The Serpentine Dance* and the (at the time) equally commonplace act of cranking the mutoscope, itself a gesture, so the film reveals, that mimics the act of a man pleasuring himself. The film then follows the usual trajectory of the stag film—

from narrative hook to explicit, fragmentary action—but does so only after reminding the viewer that film viewership in itself is sexually charged. Ironically, reformers and advocates of film censorship at the time shared such a view, not only of surreptitiously distributed and exhibited stag films, but of all kinetoscopes and early motion pictures.

These early stag films were released outside conventional channels and were exhibited, as the term "stag film" suggests, exclusively for men, primarily at whorehouses and private parties. What we now call "exploitation films" first reached theaters in the early 1920s.[8] These films were from the start distinct from stag films in several key respects. Stag films were rarely much more than ten minutes long, seldom told much of a story, were screened clandestinely, and were strictly illegal. Exploitation films were mostly feature-length generic narratives screened in public theaters. They were defined to a large extent by their (claims of) defiance of PCA guidelines. Though exploitation industry distributors and promoters occasionally ran into problems with local authorities, it was never illegal to produce, distribute, or exhibit exploitation movies.

Exploitation distributors operated outside MPPDA/MPAA guidelines. They maintained, and at times exploited, a contentious relationship with local censorship boards and grassroots groups like the Catholic Legion of Decency. The PCA's mission to communicate with state boards and the legion and to anticipate their reaction to certain films was part of a larger effort to maintain the image of a responsible Hollywood. The institutional practice of self-censorship was designed to insulate the studios against surprises at the local level. Exploitation film distributors, many of whom traveled a common circuit with their product, had no such image to protect. These film distributors did not fear bad press; indeed, they curried controversy in order to promote their product.

Theater owners screening exploitation fare avoided confrontations with local authorities by contracting their venues to the various distributors in a practice called four-walling. These four-wall contracts enabled the distributors to rent out theaters for a flat fee and to run their show(s) as they saw fit within the leased four walls. The four-wall arrangement allowed exploitation promoters to come into town, like the carny or the circus, quickly showcase their product, and then, before local authorities wised up to the game, move on to the next town, the next four-wall gig, the next group of angry parishioners and parents.

According to Eric Schaefer, the history of the exploitation film roughly parallels the history of the classical American cinema. This shadow industry persisted, not incidentally, throughout the duration of strict content self-regulation in the mainstream industry. As Schaefer points out, the exploitation film was defined to a large extent by an apparent disregard for mainstream production standards. But exploitation filmmakers were forced to develop new product lines when PCA authority was challenged by 1950s films like *The Moon Is Blue, Tea and Sympathy, The Man with a Golden Arm,* and *Baby Doll* and early 1960s titles like *The Apartment* (which, though it treaded carefully on the subject, chronicled an affair between a married man and a much younger unmarried woman), *Butterfield 8* (which dealt, kind of tastefully, with the subject of promiscuity if not nymphomania), *Walk on the Wild Side* (which featured a prostitute heroine), and *The Pawnbroker* (a studio prestige picture with two scenes of female nudity).

Schaefer argues that the exploitation film changed significantly and all at once in 1959 with the release of Russ Meyer's soft-core feature *The Immoral Mr. Teas.* For Schaefer, Meyer's film marks the end point of "classical exploitation"—an apt if oxymoronic term. *The Immoral Mr. Teas* tells the story of a man who mentally undresses many of the women he meets. It strayed from classical exploitation in that it fully and unapologetically followed through on the promoters' promise. Unlike the nudist colony films, which date to the early thirties (*This Nude World* and *This Naked Age*) and more or less persisted on through to the release of Meyer's film (see *Elysia,* a.k.a. *Valley of the Nudes, The Unashamed, Nudist Recruits, World without Shame, As Nature Intended,* and *Garden of Eden*), *The Immoral Mr. Teas* was not framed, even disingenuously, as an advertisement for a certain lifestyle. Meyer's film was clearly, unashamedly about naked women. As Meyer's biographer David K. Frasier writes, "in content and theme *Teas* is a literal translation of what [Meyer] had been doing for *Playboy* [as a centerfold photographer], a movie version of a girlie magazine."[9]

The nudity for nudity's sake in Meyer's film had been made possible by a 1957 New York State Court of Appeals decision in what turned out to be a landmark case: *Excelsior Pictures v. New York Board of Regents.* The decision in the case hinged on whether or not onscreen nudity in *Garden of Eden,* a ludicrous nudist colony picture, was legally obscene.[10] *Garden of Eden* was distributed by Excelsior Pictures, a New York–based exploitation outfit specializing in burlesque short subjects. The film was not the studio's first prurient title, nor was it the first nudist camp film to show onscreen nudity.

The narrative in *Garden of Eden* is set up by a fairly pat postwar morality tale: an aggrieved father has become cold with the death of his son in the war and takes it out on his daughter-in-law and her daughter, his only grandchild. Things get so bad, mother and child exit his unhappy home for Florida. En route to Miami they take a detour, then a wrong turn, have car trouble, and find themselves alone on an isolated rural road miles from anywhere. They are rescued by a good samaritan who takes them to his home at a bungalow park called the Garden of Eden. The Garden, alas, is a nudist camp, and mother and daughter are left to wait inside its gates for a mechanic to take care of their car, which, given the rural location, takes several days. The rest of the film has the family reconciling, all the while trying out and ultimately converting to the nudist lifestyle. The "story" is accompanied by images of nude volleyball, sunbathing, water-skiing, and so on. In approximately sixty minutes of running time, about twenty minutes depict nudists enjoying their alternative lifestyle.[11]

The New York State Board of Regents, which supervised film censorship throughout the state at the time, prohibited the exhibition of the film.[12] Excelsior challenged the state ban and the case eventually made its way to the New York State Court of Appeals, where Judge Charles Desmond found in favor of the exploitation distributor, ruling that nudity onscreen, per se, was not obscene: "There is nothing sexy or suggestive about [*Garden of Eden*] . . . nudists are shown as wholesome, happy people in family groups practicing their sincere but misguided theory that clothing, when climate does not require it, is deleterious to mental health, by promoting an attitude of shame with regard to the natural attributes and functions of the human body."

While Judge Desmond hardly endorsed nudism as a way of life, he maintained that nudity per se was not obscene. The ruling proved significant to the exploitation industry, which moved quickly to feature nudity onscreen in nudist camp films and a variety of other genres. It was also significant to studio directors and producers, who appreciated the fact that in light of the *Excelsior* decision, PCA prohibitions on nude scenes were unconstitutional if not unenforceable.

The Immoral Mr. Teas—a film made very much with the *Excelsior* decision in mind—spawned a brief second wave of exploitation pictures. These more frank and explicit films included a variety of colorful(ly termed) new genres: nudie cuties (suggestive, often light comedy pictures with nudity but no touching: *Adam Lost His Apple, Mr. Peter's Pets,* the Francis Coppola–directed *Tonight for Sure*), roughies (which depicted shocking antisocial behavior as well as nudity: *The Defilers, The Debauchers, The Degenerates*), kinkies (with appropriate and revealing titles like *Olga's House of Shame, The Twisted Sex, Love Camp 7*), and ghoulies (merging kink with gruesome horror: *Satan's Bed, Mantis in Lace*).[13] The common element in all these films was onscreen nudity.

By the early 1960s, exploitation film distributors used onscreen nudity to promote an additional product line: the foreign art film. William Mishkin and Radley Metzger, to name just two art-porn entrepreneurs, not only showcased risqué foreign art titles, mostly uncut, but occasionally inserted nude (stock) footage into otherwise tame foreign-made films, hawking the augmented versions "for American audiences only."[14] These enhanced versions of foreign art films proved successful at the box office and more importantly saved Mishkin and Metzger the headache of getting controversial foreign films past U.S. Customs.

The exploitation/foreign art film connection dates as far as back as 1934, when Samuel Cummins (for Eureka Films) arranged an American release for the notorious Czech film *Extase* (*Ecstasy*).[15] The 1933 melodrama depicted an unhappy marriage between a young, beautiful woman (played by Hedwig Kiesler, later and better known in Hollywood as Hedy Lamarr) and a much older, impotent man. Early on in the film, the woman leaves her husband for the family farm, but she finds no peace there either. In a scene fraught with symbolism, she runs naked through the woods and is reborn after taking a nude swim. She then meets a handsome young engineer with whom she takes refuge from a driving rainstorm. The two young lovers have sex, but then the husband arrives to take her back with him. He is told about the affair and kills himself. The young woman deserts her new lover and the film ends.

From its first sensational screening at the Venice Film Festival, where *Ecstasy* played only after being granted an exemption from Italy's censorship laws, Kiesler's nude scene fueled a wealth of publicity worldwide. Rumors circulated that Kiesler's then husband, Fritz Mandl, had attempted to buy the negative and all the positive prints of the film. The rumor was exploited—and perhaps invented—to promote the picture. The European promotion and distribution of *Ecstasy* seemed to mirror an American exploitation release.

When Cummins first attempted to bring *Ecstasy* into the United

States, the film was seized by customs, marking the first time obscenity laws were used to keep a film out of the country. As Cummins awaited a court date to appeal a federal district court decision supporting the customs ban, the print was mysteriously burned by an anxious federal marshal. In 1936 an alternative print—a less sensational version made for release in Germany—passed customs. This second version was significantly different from the first: the nude romp through the forest from farm to lake was preceded by a narrative insert (courtesy of Cummins) of a typewriter and a voice-over informing the woman (and the audience) that a final decree of divorce had been granted. The film's signature scene was in the augmented version mostly obscured by bushes—it was an alternative take made in anticipation of censorship problems—and the film's ending was changed to suggest that the woman's relationship with the engineer begins only after she is divorced. We never see the first husband after the woman returns to the farm, so no suicide is mentioned. In the end, the woman marries the engineer and has a baby.

Despite such significant changes in the film's imagery and narrative, Cummins ably promoted the picture as if he was distributing the far more frank original. Audiences and local censors alike were attracted by the come-on and even in its watered-down state *Ecstasy* did well at the box office.

Censorship activists targeted the film in New York, Baltimore, and other cities around the United States. Several of the local censorship prohibitions and bans could be attributed to the film's foreignness, the notion that art films in general were seen as dangerous because they were foreign.[16] A *Look* magazine story with the clever title *"Ecstasy:* The Movie That Caused a War" characterized the film as exotic. The article maintained that the film was, as rumored, obscene, but nevertheless provided its readers with a two-page spread of suggestive stills from the picture.[17] A review in the *New York Post* used the foreign angle to make another point, a subtle criticism of the PCA and of Hollywood filmmaking in general: "the picture is un-Americanly frank, yet typical of those ventures of certain foreign studios to which cinema is a true art itself."[18]

A little over a decade later, Italian neo-realist films like *Paisan, Open City, Bitter Rice,* and *The Bicycle Thief* were distributed in the United States by independents. Several of these films ran afoul of the PCA and local censors but, like *Ecstasy,* they did relatively well at the box office. As the distributor Arthur Mayer candidly reflected in 1953, "The only sensational successes scored by [my partner, Joseph] Burstyn and myself in the fifteen years in which we were engaged in business were the pictures whose artistic and ideological merits were aided and abetted at the box office by their frank content."

Taking their cue from exploitation distributors, Mayer and Burstyn highlighted the at times surprisingly rough PCA treatment of European art films after the war. In support of the first run of *Open City*, Mayer jumbled phrases from a *Life* magazine review and produced the following ridiculous tag line for the film: "Sexier than Hollywood ever dared to be." The poster ad for *Paisan*, a documentary-style film about the Italian resistance, depicted a young woman undressing while a male, seated on a couch, watched.[19]

Under a typically colorful headline, "Sexacious Sellin' Best B.O. Slant for Foreign Language Films in U.S.," *Variety* acknowledged how well exploitation tactics worked in the theatrical runs of certain foreign art films. But while the tactics and sometimes the players behind exploitation cheapies and foreign art pictures were the same, the audiences attracted to the two genres were markedly different. The typical foreign-made art picture grossed 60 percent of its revenues in New York City. Exploitation films grossed only 25 percent in the city and, as *Variety* put it, "the balance in the hinterlands."[20] The bottom line in the *Variety* piece was that "sexacious" fare could attract two distinct and eminently targetable demographics, characterized by the exploitation impresario David F. Friedman as "the sophisticated white-wine-and-canapes crowd" in New York and the "cold beer and greaseburger gang" elsewhere.[21]

The single product/multiple market formula has a long history on the exploitation circuit. One of the first to employ the formula was the legendary exploitation producer-distributor Kroger (Howard W.) Babb. In the forties, Babb made his mark with so-called sex-hygiene films like *Mom and Dad*, leaden melodramas about teen pregnancy and VD.[22] Babb's films were often remakes of or slight variations on familiar themes staged in equally clunky thirties exploiters. *Mom and Dad*, for example, reprised *High School Girl*, a 1935 melodrama. But specific content on the exploitation circuit was mostly beside the point. For Babb and other exploiters of his generation, the key to success was in the presentation, in the transformation of a film into an event.

The promotion and presentation of *Mom and Dad* was expert. The poster hawking the film was all carny come-on:

Once in a lifetime comes a presentation that truly pulls no punches! Now you can see the motion picture that dares discuss and explain sex as never before seen and heard! the one, the only, the original: *Mom and Dad*. Truly the world's most amazing attraction! No one under high school age admitted unless accompanied by parents! Everything shown! Everything explained![23]

For shows in towns where local censorship was a particular problem, Babb hired a so-called sexpert, Elliot Forbes, the supposed author of *The Secrets of Sensible Sex*, to answer questions after the screenings. Forbes never really existed; he was a character invented by Babb and was played by several actors all on Babb's payroll. That Forbes was a phony and that the film failed miserably to deliver on its promise were of little concern to Babb, who was in and out of town with the picture before word of mouth could do him much harm.

Mom and Dad is an awful film. But Babb understood something the studios would discover some three decades later: in the film business, it is the package—the spectacle of promotion and exhibition—and not the film itself that matters.

Babb's expertise as a film promoter was in evidence once again, in the 1950s, when he added foreign art films to his slate of exploitation melodramas. The single product/multiple market formula came into play in Babb's expert distribution of the legendary Swedish cineaste Ingmar Bergman's *Summer with Monika*, a 1953 import that featured a nude bathing scene. To exploit the film's prurient content in New York *and* in the "hinterlands," Babb promoted two simultaneous runs of two versions of the picture. A sixty-two-minute version dubbed in English and renamed *Monika, the Story of a Bad Girl* was distributed on the exploitation circuit. *Summer with Monika*, more or less in its original ninety-five-minute form, was released to urban art film theaters. Both versions, of course, featured the nude bathing scene.

Roger Vadim's *And God Created Woman*, released in the United States in 1957 by Kingsley International, played simultaneously in an awful dubbed English-language version on the exploitation *and* art theater circuits. The promotional campaign for the film focused on its star, Brigitte Bardot. The lobby poster for the film was a classic example of the exploitation come-on: "*and God created woman . . .* but the devil invented Brigitte Bardot." The blurbs featured on the poster (from the *New York Times*: "a phenomenon you have to see to believe," and *Life* magazine: "much more than American audiences are used to seeing of what 23 year old girls are made of") similarly regarded both the film and its star as equal (prurient) attractions.

Subsequent Bardot features sported the same exploitation promotion strategy. *Female and the Flesh* promised "sex, violence, eroticism all in a single package"; *Mademoiselle Striptease*, a film "witty, wicked, wonderful as only the French can dare!" Bardot became an iconic figure, at once the quintessential foreign sex symbol and an exploitation trademark promising a certain form, a certain type of adult entertainment.

Foreign art films—even ones as ridiculous and awful as *And God Created Woman* or as wonderful but falsely advertised as *Bitter Rice, Open City*, or *Summer with Monika*—went a long way toward legitimating nudity and frank erotic and/or political content on American screens. The various soft-core genres that came to dominate the exploitation circuit in the fifties and sixties—the nudie cuties, roughies, kinkies, and ghoulies—accommodated the more controversial and more explicit material of the European pictures, albeit without the foreign films' narrative or stylistic sophistication. The hard-core films of the late sixties and early seventies took the explicit imagery of the second-generation exploiters to another level and in doing so found (an albeit brief) success never before achieved in the exploitation market.

When hard core was pushed out of the theatrical marketplace in 1973, the studios did little to fill the void in the adults-only market. As a result of the studios' continued efforts to play it safe and in the absence of an adults-only XXX circuit, soft-core films that pushed, defied, and/or exceeded MPAA guidelines once again became the stuff of the urban art theater.

Urban art theaters are seldom affiliated with NATO and thus are free to book unrated, X, or NC-17 features. Art theaters pride themselves—or at least define themselves—in their presentation of alternative product lines. Sexually explicit independent and/or foreign-made cinema has come to fill, at least in part, one of the few niches the studios continue to express no real interest in filling.

For example, consider the recent spate of North American–made independent lesbian-themed pictures like *Desert Hearts, Go Fish, The Incredible Adventures of Two Girls in Love, High Art, When Night Is Falling*, and *Better Than Chocolate*. These lesbian-themed pictures—none of which could be described as hard-core, but most of which feature normalized, unfetishized same-sex sex scenes—earn modest profits by serving a target audience too small to show up on the studios' radar. In the practical business of relegating specialty product lines to the art house circuit, the industry marginalizes already marginalized audiences.

Art theaters continue to make money with serious and sometimes fairly graphic heterosexual sex-themed pictures that, for a number of reasons, do not play at the local multiplex. In 1986, for example, there was the surprising success (with the "sophisticated white wine and canapes crowd") of Marco Bellochio's *The Devil in the Flesh*. Bellochio was at the time an Italian auteur familiar only to film professors and avid cinephiles. But a brief albeit graphic oral sex sequence caused a minor sensation and got the film booked at art theaters nationwide. The scene could easily have been cut to suit CARA had the film's distributor needed an MPAA rating.

Catherine Breillat's 1999 release, the ironically titled *Romance*, is only the most recent example. The film is sequentially graphic, which is to say that unlike *Devil in the Flesh*, it features not just one glimpse of forbidden, graphic imagery but a series of images and scenes that made the film, by today's industry standards at least, hard-core or pornographic. The film, which tells the story of a bored young woman who finds little joy or even relief in a series of sexual encounters, was a hit in the relative terms of the art house world. The lobby poster reveals all too clearly why. It features a graphic color photo of Caroline Ducey, the film's star, cut off at the upper thigh and the belly, her hand only partly concealing her genital area. The film's title, in white, crosses her upper thighs and highlights a glimpse of her pubic hair. Between the white title and the woman's flesh, in blood red, is an X—the film's self-imposed classification as a film released in defiance of the MPAA code. The blurbs on the poster further highlight the film's prurient appeal: "possibly the sexiest picture ever made" (*Gear*), "The most sexually audacious movie since *Last Tango in Paris*" (*Newsweek*), "Sizzling . . . pushes the envelope as far as possible" (*New York Post*).

While *Romance* had a spirited run on the art house circuit, the film was met with a significant critical backlash. This attack focused less on the picture's graphic content than on the way the promotion of the film exploited that content to reach the ever hungry art house audience. Several critics described an uncomfortable feeling of having been had—by the film's director, by its indie distributor, Trimark, by the French. At a time when the studios have steered clear of even simulated soft-core action, the critics suggested that audiences may be all too apt to mistake the audacity of graphic imagery for provocative, controversial art. The problem may not have been the film itself, but

The provocative lobby poster for Catherine Breillat's X-rated *Romance* (Trimark, 1999).

rather a film market that has made *Romance* possible, necessary, alternative, important.

In a particularly nasty capsule review for the *New Yorker*, David Denby put the film and its foreign pedigree in context:

> The great advantage of growing up French is that you can be absurd without ever knowing it. In Catherine Breillat's sexually explicit drama, Marie (Caroline Ducey), a dark teardrop of a girl spurned by

her live-in boyfriend, drags herself without apparent pleasure through one sordid sex situation after another while intoning such thoughts to herself as: "I like it to be anonymous. It's my purity—more metaphysical." Only in a French movie would a woman embrace sexual experimentation merely to attain an enormous *pensée*. Pornographic but unarousing, the movie feels like a third-rate Left bank novel from fifty years ago.[24]

Despite its graphic content and contemporary *ennui, Romance* is a throwback. As such, it at once harks back to those adult-themed foreign films released to art houses in the fifties and sixties and reminds us that such films—which mostly disconnected the explicit from the erotic—were, for U.S. audiences at least, popular only because the PCA prevented the studios from making any real adult-themed, adult-content films of their own. It is daunting, then, to find a film like *Romance* in theaters thirty-one years after the rating system was first adopted—daunting to discover that after so long, a film like *Romance* is still necessary, still "alternative," still decidedly "foreign."

DEEP THROAT AND THE DEVIL IN MISS JONES

Heterosexual intercourse, group sex, explicit penetration, fellatio, cunnilingus, female masturbation and sodomy, seminal ejaculation, sex scenes with only minor interruption.
—Description of *Deep Throat*, from the majority opinion in
State v. American Theater Corp.

The June 28, 1972, *Variety* review of *Deep Throat* began with the following summary headline: "Hardcore Hetero Sex Feature with Humor a Plus. Tops in the Current Market."[25] Much to the astonishment and chagrin of virtually everyone in the mainstream industry, the "current market" for *Deep Throat* turned out to be a whole lot bigger than the *Variety* reviewer could ever have imagined. In 1972 *Deep Throat* became the first crossover adults-only hit, a film that piqued the interest of audiences previously disinclined to patronize hard core.

Like all *Variety* reviews, this one was preceded by summary production information. But unlike the reviews of more mainstream films, only minimal production credits were provided: "Aquarius release of

Vanguard (Lou Perry) production. Directed, written and edited by Jerry Gerard. Camera (color), Harry Flecks; sound, Morris Gottlieb; set decoration Len Camp. (No other credits)." The conspicuous absence of a cast list seemed to support popular assumptions about hard core—that performers who work in porn court anonymity (who wouldn't, given the content?) or hide behind catchy pseudonyms (like the film's redoubtable star, Linda Lovelace, a.k.a. Linda Marchiano, and the film's writer/director/producer Jerry Gerard, a.k.a. Gerard Damiano).

Both Lovelace and Gerard soon reclaimed their birth names, she to allege, in her memoir *Ordeal*, that she was hypnotized and drugged into performing in hard core, he to lay claim to auteur status in the industry, to take credit under his real name for *The Devil in Miss Jones* and *The Memories within Miss Aggie*.[26] Like the emerging directors in the mainstream industry at the time—Francis Coppola, Martin Scorsese, Robert Altman, Peter Bogdanovich, and later Steven Spielberg and George Lucas—Damiano became a trademark of sorts for a certain quality of filmmaking, a certain product for which his name was something of a guarantee.

In 1972 porn films were not routinely made available to reviewers in press-only screenings. Few if any titles were reviewed or even mentioned in legit newspapers or in pop culture magazines at the time. The *Variety* reviewer assigned to cover *Deep Throat* attended a packed lunchtime screening of the film on the first day of its first and exclusive run at the New World Theater in New York City. That the reviewer first saw the film with its intended clientele in a public theater with a paying audience—a fundamentally different experience from seeing it in a lonely press screening—played to the picture's advantage. The reviewer could not help but be influenced by the event as much as the film itself; he had fun at the screening and found the audience's appreciation of the film's humor contagious and appropriate. "Pre-opening word on this latest hard-core feature was hot enough to pack the lunchtime show on opening day at N.Y.'s New World Theater," the reviewer wrote. "While *Deep Throat* fails to live up to its advance reputation as the *Ben Hur* of porno pix, it is a superior piece which stands a head above the current competition."

In his brief synopsis of the film, the reviewer offered two allusions to mainstream films. The first, to *Ben Hur*, regarded box office potential rather than specific film content and proved to be less ridiculous than the film's distributors and marketers could ever have imagined at the time. The second allusion, one more directly tied to content, proved to be at once ironic and appropriate. So much as propriety allowed at the time, the reviewer described the film's "climax" with a reference to a similar scene in Alfred Hitchcock's *To Catch a Thief*. Though the comparison between *Deep Throat* and the Hitchcock suspense-comedy was no doubt meant by the reviewer to be absurd and funny, the allusion made by Damiano to Hitchcock was clearly intentional. Pivotal sex scenes in both films are punctuated by a cutaway to fireworks exploding in the sky. It's a corny little device played for laughs in both films.

The *Variety* review, which poked fun at the film and the adult/hardcore genre as a whole, neatly fit the tone and intent of the picture itself. *Fun*, after all, was what *Deep Throat* was all about. The film made light of the conventions of stag and hard-core films yet did not stint on the extent, duration, or clinical specificity of the requisite hard-core action. True to its roots in the much-publicized sexual revolution, the film maintained that sex and by extension sex onscreen need not be taken so seriously. Its closing sequence affirms, "diff'rent strokes for diff'rent folks." So long as nobody gets hurt, go for it.

Deep Throat had an astonishing nationwide notoriety. It is hard to imagine another 1972 release besides *The Godfather* that had wider name recognition. The opening-week run of *Deep Throat* at the New World Theater in New York—renamed the New Mature World Theater as its playlist changed—pulled in $30,033, a record at the time for a porn title playing on a single screen.[27] *Deep Throat* was subsequently platformed in extended runs on a handful of screens in selected big cities and eclipsed the $1 million mark by the end of seven weeks. End-of-the-year figures for 1972 were astonishing: reported grosses for *Deep Throat* exceeded $3 million (after just six months in limited release), another record at the time for a hard-core title.[28]

After forty-eight weeks in release, *Deep Throat* was still ranked as high as tenth in box office revenues. For that same week in May 1973, *Last Tango in Paris* weighed in at number one; *Billy Jack*, Tom Laughlin's independently distributed youth-culture feature, number three, and *Mary Poppins* number six.[29] For studio executives trying to get a handle on this new American cinema, it was a difficult pattern to read.

The *Variety* review of writer/director/producer Gerard Damiano's follow-up feature, *The Devil in Miss Jones*, appeared seven months after the tongue-in-cheek review of *Deep Throat*. The differences between the two reviews were obvious and significant. The review of *The Devil in*

Miss Jones included a full production credit and cast list. Jerry Gerard was now Gerard Damiano, auteur of the notorious *Deep Throat*. *The Devil in Miss Jones* was unironically regarded as the product of a director with something approximating an artistic signature.[30]

The review opened ominously for those still inclined to dismiss hard core: "With *The Devil in Miss Jones*, the hard-core porno feature approaches an art form, one that critics may have a tough time ignoring in the future." To describe the plot of the film, the reviewer referred to Jean-Paul Sartre's play *No Exit*, which similarly attends the respite between life and whatever comes afterwards. In an assessment of Georgina Spelvin's acting in the film, the reviewer posed a comparison to legit cinema's most famous if not best actor: "if Marlon Brando can be praised for giving his almost all in *Last Tango in Paris*, one wonders what the reaction will be to *Miss Jones'* lead Georgina Spelvin . . . her performance is so naked it seems a massive invasion of privacy." Throughout the review the film is taken seriously, as if its hard-core content were less the point of the film as a whole than an element intrinsic to the genre the film happened to evince.

The reviewer further asserted that *The Devil in Miss Jones* might well compete head to head with the (more) legit studio product: "Steering away from the fraternity-boy comedy approach taken by so many recent hard-core directors, Damiano has expertly fashioned a bizarre melodrama. . . . Anyone who doubts that Damiano can handle straighter material need look no further than pic's opener, a sequence so effective it would stand out in any legit theatrical feature." Having already witnessed the successful first run of *Deep Throat*, the reviewer predicted very big things at the box office for *The Devil in Miss Jones*. By way of conclusion, the reviewer offered the following advice to the film's distributor: "Booking a film of this technical quality into a standard sex house is tantamount to throwing it on the trash heap of most current hard-core fare."[31]

The Devil in Miss Jones was the most successful of the three most successful hard-core films released between 1972 and 1973: *Deep Throat* was a distant second, the Mitchell Brothers' *Behind the Green Door* an even more distant third. The *Variety* review suggested that it was less the quantity or even quality of the sex onscreen that accounted for this success. Instead it was the professional production standards maintained by the sound engineer Bill Rich and (former *Deep Throat*) cinematographer Harry Flecks, Damiano's "canny direction," the "sensual score" composed by Alden Shuman, and the compelling performances by

Spelvin and such "familiar porno vets" as Harry Reems.[32] In other words, what made *The Devil in Miss Jones* in particular so successful at the box office was the very sort of stuff that distinguished a good legit movie from the trash heap of most studio films in release at the time.

The possibility that more and more porn titles might cross over into legit theaters and render the distinction between legit and hard core unimportant (at least in certain key markets and with certain key audience demographics) no doubt worried executives at the major studios. The bottom line in the film industry has always been box office. As hard-core movies began to sport impressive box office revenues, porn movie producers and distributors and, in a less enthusiastic way, the mainstream trades were inclined to argue that legitimacy was less a matter of content than audience share. Films like *Deep Throat* and *The Devil in Miss Jones* competed successfully against mainstream films, most of which benefited from wider and more professionally executed release strategies.

Variety's end-of-the-year review for 1973 came after the Supreme Court had eliminated hard core from most communities nationwide. But the end-of-the-year numbers were nevertheless interesting, especially if one took into account the fact that the top hard-core titles were outlawed almost everywhere for the last six months of the year. *The Devil in Miss Jones* grossed $7.7 million and ranked seventh overall in 1973, just below the James Bond film *Live and Let Die* and the Academy Award–nominated comedy *Paper Moon*. *Deep Throat* grossed $4.6 million and ranked eleventh, sandwiched between the controversial studio film *Deliverance* and the Broadway-play adaptation *Sleuth*.[33]

In 1968 a group of farsighted porn movie producers and distributors established the Adult Film Association of America (AFAA), an organization patterned after the parallel if not truly rival MPAA. Much like the MPAA, the AFAA was primarily a public relations organization. Its goal at the time was to establish a larger audience base for adults-only films and to clean up the image of the hard-core industry. At the time, of course, the AFAA was far less interested than the MPAA in regulating content.[34] Though the AFAA made an effort to encourage adults-only filmmakers to diminish the sexual violence in their films and to develop product lines more attractive to women, it appreciated the fact that the come-on for hard core was the absence of lim-itations, the guarantee that the action onscreen was at once real and unexpurgated.

Public relations—especially if we are talking about the general public—was at once more important and more difficult to finesse for the executives in the AFAA than it was for those in charge at the MPAA. One of the AFAA's first moves was to develop a new language to classify the genre. The AFAA insisted that its members substitute the term "sexually explicit" for "hard-core" and established the catchall "adult entertainment" to describe the entire range of porno films. However minor or even silly these changes appear in retrospect, they reveal at the very least a sensitivity to public relations. The AFAA's attempt to refigure if not actually regulate content evolved in concert with a larger project to sanitize the porn industry's image, which continued to be complicated by rumors about white slavery, child prostitution, and ties between the makers and distributors of adult entertainment and organized crime.[35]

The AFAA leadership did not always get much help from the rank-and-file membership, which consisted, in large part, of exploitation circuit veterans. This was especially evident in the print ad campaigns supporting hard-core releases, which were purposefully provocative. Between 1968 and 1973, porn distributors and exhibitors tended to run exploitation-style ads in newspapers and weeklies highlighting their films' explicit content, the opportunity to see "more and more than ever before."

These AFAA distributors felt that they could not afford to appear "soft" in newspaper ad copy and lobby posters, but the positioning of their films in the trades often betrayed the continued appeal and lure of legitimacy. Indeed, it suggested that much as legitimacy was important to them, it was primarily an internal, industry matter. Hard-core action got the public to buy tickets to their films. Respect was something they needed or wanted to gain from legit filmmakers, distributors, and most of all exhibitors. Legitimacy was a matter for the readers of *Variety* and the *Hollywood Reporter* to ponder.

Whenever a hard-core title did well at the box office, adults-only filmmakers and distributors purchased ad space in the trades to tout the at times astonishing per-screen performance of their films. These ads were patterned after those taken out in support of successful studio films. They featured simple graphics and bold headlines touting box office figures. In these ads box office success was figured as a mark of legitimacy and quality.

The full-page ad in *Variety* for *Deep Throat*, for example, featured the bold-print headline "Book Like a Winner . . . and Be a Winner." At the center of the ad was a crude line drawing of Linda Lovelace in her nurse's outfit. The crude drawing does not look a whole lot like the film's star, nor was it meant to call attention to her contribution to the film's success. (That came later.) The ad made no mention of any of the film's stars or the film's director, and instead highlighted box office grosses ("30,033—1st 7 days)," a blurb from a good review (Al Goldstein of *Screw* magazine calling *Deep Throat* "the very best porn film ever made"), a copy of a letter from Terry Levine of Aquarius Releasing to the New World Theater congratulating it on its "showmanship" in presenting the film, and an excerpt from a *Variety* news article dated June 21, 1972, which acknowledged the film's legit-like first-week grosses: "Five exclusive newcomers bowed and one of the hottest was a hardcore feature, *Deep Throat*, that amazed even porno vets by hitting $30,000 on opener at the World, a house record."[36]

The ad's overall design was amateurish; its messy, unprofessional graphic design betrayed Aquarius Releasing's inexperience. But its message was clear. What made *Deep Throat* a sensation was not the sex or its soon to be legendary star, but, in and of itself, its popularity. The film's success was something one could measure empirically and in much the same terms routinely applied to more mainstream pictures.

Man and Wife, another popular title at the time, touted its success as part of a larger "boxoffice sexplosion," the logical consequence of something that got started by *Deep Throat*. The ad design for *Man and Wife* was similarly spartan: there was the headline about the box office "sexplosion," the film's title in fairly small print, a simple logo (the symbols for male and female intersecting suggestively) and, in huge print, box office numbers that were indeed impressive: $1,434,526 in just eight first-run urban engagements.[37]

The revenues generated by certain hard-core and explicit softcore features in the late sixties and early seventies encouraged adultsonly filmmakers and distributors to invest more money in their films. The result was a visible improvement in product. More money could buy better technicians, better equipment, better sets, better labwork. Access to the sort of capital necessary to finance these better adult entertainment pictures depended, as the AFAA maintained from the start, on public relations, on getting more and better theaters to screen their films. Attracting quality theater owners was the adult industry's primary goal at the time. If they were to achieve that goal, their product had to be regarded as somehow legitimate, within the industry at least.

Legitimacy in hard core had less to do with subjective issues regarding quality or even obscenity than with the objective, pragmatic utility of dollars and cents. As the exploitation film producer David F. Friedman bluntly contends, legitimacy was and is just a matter of money; if you've got it you can get more of it and if you can get more of it you become legitimate: "The old-time image of the porn broker as a guy in a derby hat selling Tijuana bibles to kids is a thing of the past. Look: the business is booming, and inevitably, with money, comes a certain standing in the community. The bank never asks you where you got the money, they only ask *if* you've got it."[38]

The push to improve the cinematic quality of hard core came very much at the AFAA's urging. At the very moment the mainstream industry began exploiting the director's name above the title of certain films, AFAA distributors briefly indulged their own auteur renaissance: Damiano, the Mitchell brothers, Radley Metzger (an ambitious cineaste with a thing for Antonioni-like composition and ennui and terrifically well lit and well shot hard-core sequences). The result was a marked improvement in porn production values.

The struggle for legitimacy was lost in June 1973; the decision in *Miller v. California* saw to that. Still, some AFAA distributors soldiered on, at times with only a slim grasp on reality, for example: porn distributor Inish Kae's ridiculous 1975 Oscar-ad campaign. For the studios, 1975 was a particularly good year. *One Flew over the Cuckoo's Nest*, *Barry Lyndon*, *Dog Day Afternoon*, *Jaws*, and *Nashville* were nominated for the best picture Oscar; Milos Forman, Robert Altman, Federico Fellini, Stanley Kubrick, and Sidney Lumet vied for best director, and Louise Fletcher, Isabelle Adjani, Ann-Margret, Glenda Jackson, and Carol Kane competed for best actress. That same year, Inish Kae took out a full-page advertisement in *Variety* for its feature *Memories within Miss Aggie*. The ad carried the following message: "We are proud to be participating for the Academy Award nominations: Best Picture of the Year, Best Achievement in Direction (Gerard Damiano) and Best Performance by an Actress (Deborah Ashira).[39]

READING HARD CORE, TAKE ONE

If people are worried about aggression, then we shouldn't live in a capitalist society. Capitalism is based on aggression, and violence against women has to do with that aggression. . . . I don't particularly want to chop up women but it seems to work.

—Brian De Palma, filmmaker

Censorship, as I have contended from the start of this book, is not about texts per se but rather state and, by extension and/or collusion, industrial power. We come to read pornography in terms of what gets censored. Content censorship must be read not in terms of objective criteria or empirical studies but rather in the subjective and temporary terms of morality, ideology, and politics that govern regulation at a given point in time. And since we are talking about movies here, morality, ideology, and politics often serve a distinctly economic motive.[40]

If pornography is indeed something we *know when we see it*, as Justice Potter Stewart so famously remarked, how precisely do we recognize it? Is porn, like the more mainstream genres of comedy or horror, defined by its effect on audiences? And how is that effect the result of reading porn in a larger cultural context? How is the act of reading porn culturally determined by standards of morality, ideology, politics, and economics? How much of how we read pornography is temporary, subjective, and approximate, as the Supreme Court came to recognize with regard to obscenity after World War II?

In *Bound and Gagged: Pornography and the Politics of Fantasy in America*, Laura Kipnis argues convincingly for a cultural reading of porn that accounts for the ways the genre is "defined less by its content than the efforts of those in power to eliminate it."[41] Kipnis suggests that "the endless attention that porn commands" in contemporary society has less to do with specific content issues—how much or how little is left to the imagination onscreen or in a photo spread in a magazine—than with a larger fascination with "mass cultural spectacles" like the O. J. Simpson trial on TV.[42] In such a pornographic culture, she asks, what might porn—and the efforts to regulate or ban porn—tell us about ourselves?

If we focus first on porn in the context of the various regulations and proscriptions in place at a given point in time, we find "a very precise map of that culture's borders."[43] Censorship and prohibition establish the boundaries of mass cultural decorum, the realm of the polite, the socially acceptable. Porn by definition resides someplace outside those boundaries, outside traditional systems of regulation and censorship. Hard core comes under regulation not because of its specific content but instead as a consequence of mostly unscientific assumptions regarding what porn film audiences might *do* with the content up there on screen.

The contemporary effort to regulate porn reveals a parallel history in the legit industry dating back over half a century. The regulations enforced by the PCA were from the start based on assumptions made not about film content per se but about the American film audience. These assumptions were at once ethnocentric and elitist. Hays and Breen, studio ownership, local reformers, and even the Supreme Court regulated cinema in order to protect the movie audience from potentially persuasive, antisocial film content.[44] The *hoi polloi* were thus protected against their own worst impulses. And the larger American population was thus protected against what those worst impulses might lead *them* to do to *us*.

Assumptions made about the effect of pornographic content—that prolonged or repeated contact with such material leads to sexual violence and/or deviance—reveal a similar ethnocentrism and elitism. As Kipnis explains,

> The argument that pornography causes violent behavior in male consumers relies on a theory of the porn consumer as devoid of rationality, contemplation, or intelligence, prone instead to witless brainwashing, to monkey-see, monkey-do reenactments of the pornographic scene. This would be a porn spectator who inherently *has* a propensity to become violent (not presumably the Meese Commission, who spent years viewing pornography without violent consequences). It becomes clearer how fantastical this argument is when you consider how eagerly we accept the premise that pornography causes violence—and are so keen to regulate it—compared to the massive social disinclination to accept that handguns cause violence . . . and it's certainly more probable that they do. Guns, without the same connotation of lowness [assumptions that only lower-class types buy guns], don't seem to invite the same regulatory zeal, despite a completely demonstrable causal relation to violence."[45]

Kipnis suggests that despite the state's efforts to identify it with lowbrow culture(s), pornography has "what might be called [a] political philosophy." Porn, Kipnis posits, offers a deft cultural critique of mainstream, mid-cult America.[46] It "refuses to let us so easily off the hook for our hypocrisies." Its denial of propriety offers "a form of cultural critique."[47]

The political philosophy of porn is a product of its cultural function and has little to do with intent. Making pornography is a business and the bottom line for those who produce porn is to make money. That their product courts state regulation bestows a subversive function and thus meaning to porn that is at once unintended and readily exploitable. If making dirty movies is a counterculture enterprise, filmmakers discovered in the late sixties it was a moneymaking one as well.

Porn movies from 1968 to 1973 self-consciously courted the vaunted youth-oriented counterculture. "Diff'rent strokes for diff'rent folks," the one line of dialogue people were likely to remember from *Deep Throat*, spoke specifically to the anatomy lesson presented in the movie. But it also spoke, perhaps unintentionally, to and for a number of late-sixties/early-seventies phenomena ranging from the sexual revolution to women's lib and the civil rights movement.[48]

The youth orientation of porn movies between 1968 and 1973 took the studios by surprise. The studios had similarly identified the youth demographic (aged eighteen to thirty-five) as a primary target, but with the exceptions of *The Graduate* and a few other films, they had little success in making movies young people paid to see. That porn movies captured this audience's interest so keenly and so quickly was a major concern for the studios at the time. It also concerned the more conservative members of Congress and the Supreme Court who began to target porn for regulation or elimination in the early seventies.

Youth culture at the time seemed bent on transgressing the very cultural norms, the very decorum satirized or undermined in porn. The state eventually succeeded in reestablishing decorum by more efficiently and completely regulating pornography. In the act of censoring porn, the state short-circuited the counterculture that had so embraced the genre.

However revolutionary or even subversive films like *Deep Throat* might have seemed or been at the time, it is important to note that the so-called porn renaissance was brief. It ended not because audiences got tired of seeing the films—*The Devil in Miss Jones*, the last big porn title released before the summer of 1973, broke box office records for the genre—but because a realigned judiciary, a culturally conservative Supreme Court stacked by the godfather of the silent majority, Richard Nixon, engineered its demise.

If porn is defined by the nature and efficiency of state censorship, the message one might take from this little cultural history is that the liberalism embraced and evinced in porn movies during their brief theatrical heyday was what Nixon and the Supreme Court were really after from the start. The criminalization of porn was only one aspect of a larger endeavor to combat liberalism, an endeavor picked up by Reagan and Bush in the 1980s and 1990s, two decades in which the conservative moral majority waged a cultural war on pornography.

READING HARD CORE, TAKE TWO

I've heard a lot of talk . . . the time has come to put your mouth where the money is.
— Richard Fish, a character on the TV show *Ally McBeal*

In *Hard Core: Power, Pleasure and the Frenzy of the Visible*, Linda Williams identifies two different ways we might begin to read the texts that constitute hard core.[49] The first regards the ontology of the hard-core image, the genre's stake in *the real*; the second, the curious formal and ideological parallels between hard core and the Hollywood musical.

True to its roots in the early stag reels, and in at least passing reference to the then popular documentary genre of direct cinema, feature-length porn effaced traditional fiction-film boundaries of artistic performance. As Al DiLauro and Gerald Rabkin write in *Dirty Movies: An Illustrated History of the Stag Film*,

> The stag film or dirty movie was, and is, the *cinema verite* of the forbidden, an invaluable record of the images of openly unacknowledged feelings about sex assume. In a time when verbal and visual images of sex were suppressed, when open art could only euphemize, the stags documented those isolated and unmentionable private experiences which were nonetheless in some form universal. . . . The films proved that a world of sexuality existed outside one's limited individual experiences. Here were real people and real sexual activity made all the more real because the aesthetic embodiment was so weak, the "performers" so clearly not actors."[50]

For DiLauro and Rabkin, the stag reel and its offspring, the feature-length porn movie, served an ethnographic function. The markers of realism—handheld camera work, unprofessional actors, a seeming absence of narrative—prompted certain responses from audiences that exceeded the films' immediate and undeniable erotic effect. We take what we see onscreen in hard core as true and thus read these films much as we might read a documentary, a travelogue, an ethnographic film about tribesmen living in the depths of the Amazon jungle.

Williams's take on the reality effect of seventies porn begins and ends with the *come* or *money shot*, that moment in hard core when a sex number is punctuated by visible evidence of male ejaculation. Images depicting penetration—vaginal, oral, and anal—additionally insist that what we see is real. The various inserts of genitals in contact and the master shots of full-figure performers performing sex onscreen simply give us a variety of ways of seeing the same thing, the same act. Duration—the length of screen time and real time given to the scene—offers additional documentary proof. The come shot, which we take as something impossible to fake onscreen—an interesting notion given how easily blood spurting from a wound in a studio war or crime film is rigged and staged—punctuates the scene if only to remind us that what we have seen *ain't* Hollywood.

The come shot is the sine qua non of porn, as Stephen Ziplow contends in his glib primer, *The Film-Maker's Guide to Pornography*: "There are those who believe that the come shot, or, as some refer to it, 'the money shot,' is the most important element in the movie and that everything else (if necessary) should be sacrificed at its expense. Of course, this depends on the outlook of the producer, but one thing is for sure: if you don't have come shots, you don't have a porno picture."[51]

It is at once ironic and indicative that people in the hard-core industry have come to use the terms "come shot" and "money shot" interchangeably. In porn, as in the legit cinema, it is difficult to distinguish between the formal and the financial, between entertainment value and the larger economy of exploitation and/or commercialization. As Williams writes, "The money shot most perfectly embodies the profound alienation of contemporary consumer society." The money shot, Williams asserts, is simply a matter of "delivering the goods" both onscreen and at the box office.[52] It is the moment at which the film becomes hard-core and real—real and marketable as porn. It is like that moment attorneys talk about when certain testimony turns a trial in their favor: "I hear the angels sing and the cash register ring."[53]

The money shot attends that moment in a porn film when the male performer's performance is complete. But such completion, such closure, is only temporary. The trajectory of feature-length porn is not only toward the bigger and better (in all the ways one might imagine) but toward a kind of endless, albeit formally refigured repetition. Like other more traditional genres, the porn film takes shape according to certain fundamental conventions. The pleasure of viewing porn, much like the pleasure in viewing other more traditional genres, is generated in the playing out of expectation; viewers are satisfied by the fulfillment of desire.

That one come shot only suggests the next come shot reminds viewers that even in such a utopian sexual scenario one spends only to spend again and again. Each purchase involves something spent and something acquired. But the satisfaction in acquisition is fleeting—the thing acquired only temporarily satisfying. As Williams writes, "In the money shot's repeatedly inflated, 'spending' penis we can see condensed all the principles of late capitalism's pleasure-oriented consumer society: pleasure figured as an orgasm of spending: the fetish not simply as a commodity but as the surplus value of orgasm."[54]

In porn, we are invited to dismiss the superfluous and superficial narrative sequences; the actors can't act, the dialogue is clunky, the story ludicrous and pointless. What we've come to see—what are important—are the sex scenes, most of which are punctuated by come shots. In such a system of (re)presentation, as Williams asserts, we find a deft albeit unintended parody of the very consumer society in which porn plays a part. In the narrative economy of the money shot, we find the performers buying, wasting, or losing, then buying more, again and again forever.

Deep Throat, Behind the Green Door, and *The Devil in Miss Jones,* which presented graphic sexual content in more or less dramatic, narrative contexts, reached audiences about two years after a series of Danish-made sex work documentaries: *Sexual Freedom in Denmark, Pornography in Denmark,* and *Pornography: Copenhagen 1970.* These nonfiction films exploited the "redeeming social importance" exception in federal obscenity criteria (as first elaborated in the Supreme Court's 1957 opinion in *Roth v. United States* and then again in *Jacobellis v. Ohio* in 1964) to present for the first time in more or less legit theaters graphic, hard-core content.[55]

Under the pretense of sex education, these films encouraged the sexual frankness that later characterized the narratives as well as the imagery of early-seventies porn, much of which similarly regarded the sexual revolution as something of a quest for knowledge and experience. How much these sex documentaries educated Americans about sex is difficult to assess. But they were briefly popular and their claims to clinical, scientific realism at once satisfied the Supreme Court's criteria and established a form and formula for extending the stag reel into feature length and then into public theaters. *Deep Throat,* with its laughable "medical discourse" but graphic, clinical realism, repackaged the documentary effect of the stags and the Danish imports in a far more entertaining, almost-Hollywood package.

The recent popularity of homemade porn—independently distributed amateur videos of "real people" having sex on camera—seems a big step back into the past for the genre. Homemade porn videos recall in both form and function the early stag reels. Both genres exploit dreadful production values in an affirmation of realism inherent in all amateur production: the artless appears real because of an inherent lack of artifice; it lacks the technique to appear otherwise.

Hollywood never had to assimilate or in the final analysis accommodate porn. Hard core's brief renaissance went by fast enough for the studios to do nothing and still end up all right. But porn by necessity had to assimilate and accommodate Hollywood. As Williams points out, hard-core moviemakers made reference to and assimilated conventions inherent in a number of popular narrative film forms: horror (*Sexorcist Devil*), teen (*Beach Blanket Bango*), sci-fi (*Flesh Gordon*), and high concept (*Urban Cowgirls*). These films used mainstream genres as a means to narrativize the sex numbers (which of course define the porn film) in order to achieve feature length. But, like exploitation pictures, they did so by gently parodying the very films they borrow from. The end result of such an assimilation was a genre of films that was at once strangely familiar and funny. People went to see porn films to see the sex. But what they got, in addition to all that sex, was a satire of Hollywood that cleverly revealed the banality of the generic narrative form. Indeed, the sex scenes, which are connected by the stuff of conventional Hollywood narrative, rendered ridiculous the expository devices routinely employed in more mainstream films.

Williams's discussion of the structural similarity between feature-length hard core and Hollywood musicals highlights this subversive/satiric effect. Both genres, Williams contends, negotiate an imaginative (and imaginary) relationship between dramatic or comic narrative and the numbers (sexual or musical) that define the genre. This is not to say that porn films developed plot, theme, or character all that much or well, but then again neither do musicals.[56]

Williams's reading of *The Opening of Misty Beethoven* and *Deep Throat* as musicals, for example, reveals not only interesting structural similarities between the mainstream Hollywood genre and early seventies porn, but important thematic similarities as well.[57] Musicals routinely offer (heterosexual) love and sex as problems to be solved, problems that despite class or age or ethnic differences can be solved. The various numbers—musical or sexual—offer attempts at solving the problems at hand, problems that can be solved fairly easily once the characters lighten up a little and begin to appreciate the nature, the absurdity, the comedy of their situation. The trajectory of these two film forms is toward the bigger and better, toward inclusion and acceptance. In the musical, couples learn to live with or look past their differences. In the porn film, they learn to find fulfillment in the daunting sexual wilderness. Both genres are utopian and often parodic. Viewers are encouraged to read from a comic and critical distance. Such a spectatorial distance, given the social upheaval in America between 1968 and 1972, provided a wide range of individuals in America an escape from turbulent, troubling times.

The cultural politics of the musical, with its mostly buoyant confidence in the mythos of romance and success in America, seems a curiously snug fit for feature-length porn, which seems similarly optimistic and happy, at least between 1968 and 1973 (with a few notable exceptions like *The Devil in Miss Jones*). The same might be said for independently produced soft-core films but most certainly not about the R- and the rare X-rated Hollywood feature. For the most part, the more explicit the presentation in a Hollywood film, the more pessimistic the mindset.

LAST TANGO IN PARIS AND *EMMANUELLE*

The Dance of the Seven Scott Tissues Award (to the most lewd and completely unwarranted dancing scene): Marlon Brando, *Last Tango in Paris.*

—*Harvard Lampoon* Movie Worst Awards, 1972

The studios never attempted to assimilate hard core, despite its considerable market share in the early seventies. No studio ever tried to distribute a film in which hard-core imagery (a money or come shot, an erect penis, penetration) was featured. And no studio ever seriously considered purchasing an adults-only production or distribution company, even solely to diversify its entertainment industry portfolios.

The studios' tentative forays into X-rated distribution reveal the importance of legitimacy to them. Case in point: two early seventies X-rated titles, Bernardo Bertolucci's *Last Tango in Paris* (distributed by

United Artists, the studio distributor of *Midnight Cowboy*) and Just Jaeckin's *Emmanuelle* (a French film picked up for North American release by Columbia). Both were rated X and deserved it. Yet both were platformed successfully by their studio distributor as prestige pictures, as somehow a legitimate or at least quality adult product. The former title banked on the status and reputation of its auteur and even more so on its star; the latter on the continued appeal of things French.

Last Tango in Paris was released eight months after *Deep Throat* and two months before *The Devil in Miss Jones*. While it was produced overseas (for PEA Artistes Associates by the Italian producer Antonio Grimaldi) and helmed by a foreign-born director known mostly if not only to serious filmgoers, *Last Tango in Paris* received a first-rate mainstream studio release. It was reviewed favorably by critics and well received by other filmmakers and actors in the legit industry (Bertolucci received an Oscar nomination for best director; Brando received a nomination for best actor). Moreover, the film did well at the box office, earning over $12 million and ranking sixth, just above *The Sound of Music* in rerelease in 1973). This success seemed to suggest that X-rated titles, albeit of a distinctly art house style, might be something the studios might pick up more and more in the future.[58]

The negative pickup (the purchase of already produced films for distribution) became increasingly important to studio release slates after 1968. Pickup deals for all sorts of films provided inventory without committing future resources to the production of more, similar products. If a trend played itself out—teen films, for example, or science fiction or even soft-core art films—the studio could simply opt not to purchase any more films in the line. If a film paid off, the studio could pick up a similar title and have it in theaters a whole lot faster and cheaper than if it had tried to produce a sequel or similar picture itself.

Distribution contracts on these negative pickups allowed studios to license and release films nationwide within a matter of weeks. And the film was only nominally theirs; when it made money or received awards, the studio could take credit for the film's success and quality. If it bombed, or worse offended a whole lot of people, studio investment in the project was limited to a distribution licensing fee and whatever it invested in advance advertising for the picture. Simply pulling the film from distribution, preferably before much money was spent on ad space and promotional campaigns, effectively made the film disappear and minimized negative public relations exposure. By purchasing their

Marlon Brando and Maria Schneider star in "a different breed of adult film":
Bernardo Bertolucci's *Last Tango in Paris* (United Artists, 1973).

soft core fully shot, the studios stayed completely out of the soft- and
hard-core development and production business.

United Artists handled *Last Tango* very well. For one of the first
times in Hollywood history, the studio prepared a release strategy that
hinged on a debut screening at the New York Film Festival. Initial advertisements for *Last Tango* highlighted the film's art house/festival
pedigree and promised "a different breed of adult film," a film, despite
its X rating, that was "more than just the sum of its sex scenes."[59] Moreover, Brando's presence in the film seemed to speak convincingly to the
legitimacy question, as noted in the *Variety* review of the film dated October 18, 1972: "Bold subject matter, and even bolder treatment, the
Bertolucci reputation and an extraordinary post-*Godfather* Brando
should give the United Artists release solid openings in the U.S."[60]

Local censors, flexing their muscles in anticipation of a significant
retrenchment at the Supreme Court, attempted to enjoin screenings of
the film. United Artists proved up to the challenge. Its willingness to
fight was something of a surprise. In Atlanta, Toledo, Cincinnati, and

virtually everywhere else the film faced local opposition, UA attorneys fought injunctions and seizures in court and prevailed.[61]

The controversy contributed significantly to the film's box office success. *Last Tango* is a ponderous and pretentious film; slow moving even by foreign art film standards in 1972. But the legal battles chronicled in newspapers nationwide allowed UA to exploit the film's controversial content while at the same time insisting in its own print ads that *Last Tango* was first and foremost just an art film.[62]

The platforming of *Last Tango* was ably forecast in the *Variety* review of the film:

Pic is graphic but hardly pornographic by domestic standards. A lengthy sodomy sequence, frequent full-frontal female nudity, probably the roughest dialog heard in a film from a major distributor and one grotesque scene involving Brando and Ms. Schneider that can't be described here at all will probably result in an X-rating from the Motion Picture Association, if submitted sans cuts. In any event, U.S. preem will certainly provoke critical and public controversy, at least equal to that surrounding *A Clockwork Orange*."[63]

The comparison to *A Clockwork Orange* was apt. Though the films are quite different, they were promoted in much the same way. UA used the X rating on *Last Tango* to classify the film as somehow unique, as a departure from the usual studio fare. Much the same strategy was employed in support of the release of *A Clockwork Orange*, another prestige picture that took audiences someplace they'd never been and showed them some things they'd never seen before.

Studio distribution of a limited number of X-rated titles was consistent with the objectives of the rating system as it was developed and adopted in 1968. The studios all supported the criteria that classified *Last Tango* as an X-rated film, even though such a rating significantly inhibited its promotion and reduced the number of screens nationwide that might be booked to screen the film. Back in the final days under PCA guidelines, films that defied the code were sometimes released over the expressed displeasure of the MPAA and its censorship body. The films came and went fast enough, but the studios' increasing willingness to ignore or defy the PCA undermined the larger cooperative and collusive agreements that made the industry work. After 1968, studio pictures rated X were denied a production seal but were nonetheless, even in the eyes of the MPAA, perfectly legitimate enterprises. Stu-

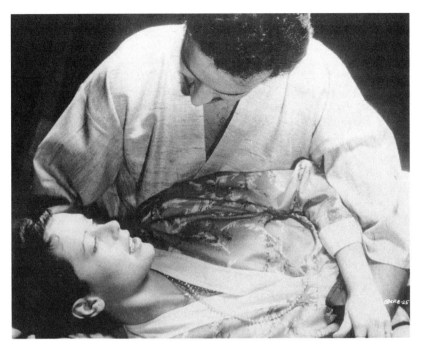

"X was never like this!" Hollywood goes soft-core with *Emmanuelle* (Columbia, 1975).

dios did not use the X rating to avoid censorship or to defy the MPAA. Instead, studios used the X rating to classify and advertise an alternative, albeit limited, product line, one that the MPAA did not endorse but at the same time did not regulate or condemn.

An interesting highlight of—and an appropriate end point to—this studio strategy was *Emmanuelle*, released in the United States in 1974 by Columbia Pictures. Though the film is essentially a soft-core travelogue, more or less attending the sexual education of a very pretty young woman (played by Sylvia Kristel), the film was platformed as somehow like, as somehow in the same tradition as a studio X art film like *Last Tango in Paris*. Like *Last Tango*, *Emmanuelle* was foreign; it was developed, produced, and released initially in France. It sported excellent production values (the locations, the lighting, the sound were all first-rate) of the sort American audiences routinely associated with studio films. And though *Emmanuelle* was little more than the sum of its sex scenes, the sex in the film was attractively rendered—indeed, the sex itself was significantly less troubled, less pathological, more *fun* than in the Bertolucci film. As a result, Columbia was able to take advantage of the film's supposed foreign art film pedigree and its uncomplicated eroticism.

Though hardly as explicit as *Deep Throat*, *Emmanuelle* maintained that sex could and should be free and fun. It is interesting and perhaps culturally significant to note that explicit sex scenes in mainstream films of the sort likely to merit an X rating routinely involve some sort of pathology: rape/coercion, guilt, ulterior motives. In *Emmanuelle* as in a number of other hard- and soft-core X-rated films in the early seventies, characters have sex because they want to and they want to have sex because it's fun.

Columbia promoted *Emmanuelle* with a simple and effective slogan: "X was never like this." The slogan was consistent with ongoing studio efforts to maintain an association between the X rating and unique products like *Last Tango in Paris* and *Midnight Cowboy*. By the time *Emmanuelle* reached American screens, the Supreme Court had all but outlawed the exhibition of hard core. In the absence of a more explicit alternative, *Emmanuelle* filled the adults-only niche, a demographic the studios had been too cautious to fully exploit before 1973.

The tag line supporting *Emmanuelle* was deceptive and ambiguous. "X was never like this" because before the spring of 1973 hard-core X-rated films were a whole lot more explicit. Given the stricter state and local regulation in place after the summer of 1973, a more accurate tag line might have been "X has to be like this." *Emmanuelle* was released at the precise moment the studios no longer had to concern themselves with hard core. Its success was a matter of timing and expert promotion and a whole lot of luck.

In an interview with *Variety* in May 1975, Columbia president David Begelman claimed that he was first attracted to *Emmanuelle* when he noticed that the lines outside theaters showing the film in Paris "were comprised of 75 to 80% women." "We would have had no interest in the film if its appeal was totally to men," mused Begelman. "Then it could be taken as pornographic."[64] Begelman's efforts to distinguish *Emmanuelle* from the hard-core films that came to characterize adult entertainment in the early seventies were bound by necessity. At the time, local exhibitors formerly screening hard-core films were in desperate need of product. Theater owners who had made a lot of money in the sexploitation boom found in *Emmanuelle* a happy albeit temporary transition: an erotic film that had studio money and attorneys behind it should local authorities seize the print or worse, take theater owners to court.

The press kit distributed in support of *Emmanuelle* emphasized the ways the film was at once unique, safe, and most of all fun for men *and* women: "*X* has never been known for its elegance. Or for its beautiful people. Or for its intelligent story line. *X* has been known for other things. At Columbia Pictures we're proud to bring you a movie that will change the meaning of *X*. A movie that begins with the sensual and takes it places *X* has never been before."

Columbia's advertising of *Emmanuelle* introduced design elements that proved useful in the release of a new line of high-concept block-busters beginning with *Jaws* and *Saturday Night Fever*. As Justin Wyatt points out, the lobby poster for *Emmanuelle* was a blueprint of sorts. It featured a simple and graphically bold design: the film's title, for ex-ample, was laid out to move the eye to a familiar graphic metaphor con-flating the image of an apple and a woman's face. The ad campaign hinged almost entirely on a simple, memorable, and ambiguous slogan ("*X* was never like this"). The summary of a film in a single tag line soon became the hallmark of studio advertising for all high-end products.[65]

But despite an apparent knack for releasing soft core, Columbia and the rest of the industry steered clear of X-rated products after *Em-manuelle*. Valenti's cautious attitude toward X-rated films and the *Miller* decision no doubt played a part. But more important was the sudden success of high-concept blockbusters like *Jaws* and *Star Wars*, films that ably targeted huge, multiple demographics. This decision coincided with and likely precipitated a diminished interest in *all* foreign art films. As the market became more and more dominated by blockbuster-style entertainment packages like *Jaws*, *Star Wars*, and *Raiders of the Lost Ark*, auteur films, like Coppola's *The Conversation* as well as ambitious and controversial films made by lesser known directors (like Haskell Wexler's *Medium Cool*) became a thing of the past as well.

The ironic fallout of the studio's brief skirmish with hard core was an industry-wide abandonment of the sorts of films that made the sev-enties so wonderful for filmgoers (studio-released adult titles like *A Clockwork Orange*, *Last Tango in Paris*, Haskell Wexler's *Medium Cool*, and serious auteur pictures like *The Godfather*, Robert Altman's *McCabe and Mrs. Miller*, and Peter Bogdanovich's *The Last Picture Show*). For a brief time, hard core proved good for American cinema, even though it was not particularly good for Hollywood.

6

Movies and the First Amendment

Congress shall make no law respecting the establishment of religion, or prohibiting the free exercise thereof; or abridging the freedom of speech, or of the press; or the right of the people peaceably to assemble, and to petition the government for a redress of grievances.

—First Amendment to the Constitution of
the United States of America

THE FIRST AMENDMENT was added to the U.S. Constitution in 1791. While the amendment says nothing about pornography or obscenity per se, notions of what the framers might have had to say on the subject continue to dominate and at the same time cloud the public and legal debate.[1] Exactly what were the framers thinking when they weren't really thinking about pornography?

The framers had only two precedents to draw from here in the New World and neither was worth remembering, let alone assimilating. Only one colony, Massachusetts, enacted an anti-obscenity statute. The Massachusetts statute, a draconian measure betraying the colony's Puritanism, focused mostly on "blasphemy," which was punishable by death until 1697, by boring through the tongue with a hot iron thereafter.[2] A second colonial statute enacted in 1711 targeted the importation of pornography from England and France. Given the various tensions in play at the time, it is safe to argue that this statute was less about artistic content than complex trade issues with the Old World.[3]

The first state statute written after the signing of the Constitution and the Bill of Rights was enacted in Vermont in 1821.[4] The first federal law was enacted twenty-one years later. Both focused on the importation of pictorial obscene matter, once again betraying larger political tensions between the Old and New World.[5]

A second federal statute was not enacted until 1865. It too focused on the traffic in as opposed to the production or possession of pornographic material.[6] There is little evidence that pornography or obscenity was of much interest to lawmakers in the last years of the eighteenth century through the first half of the nineteenth century even though there was plenty of material, some of it fairly hard-core, in circulation at the time.

Censorship in England dates to 1538 and the licensing system created and overseen by King Henry VIII. Like most early modes of content censorship, the licensing system was designed to regulate heretical and politically seditious speech. Sexual and/or erotic material was regulated only when it crossed over into the political or religious or when it was libelous. Even after Parliament allowed the Licensing Act to lapse in 1695, the basic parameters of King Henry's licensing system remained in force. For example, in 1708 an author named Read, who wrote a book titled *The Fifteen Plagues of a Maidenhead*, was brought up on charges but eventually acquitted because the court held that while the work was "bawdy stuff" it "libeled no one [and] did not reflect upon the government or attack religion." In conclusion, the court found that Read's transgression was "punishable only in the spiritual court."[7]

Twelve years later a writer named Curl, the author of *Venus in the Cloister or The Nun in Her Smock*, was brought before the court. This second case took seven years to adjudicate, but when the court finally reached a decision, it found against the author. There was no evidence that Curl's "dirty book" breached the peace or that it was libelous. But because, as the title of the book suggests, religion was the target of Curl's naughty satire, he was held accountable and his work banned. According to a curious logic, the court found that since "religion was part of the common law . . . whatever is an offense against [religion] is evidently an offense against the common law."[8]

In 1853, for economic and ethnocentric as opposed to moral or legal reasons, Parliament enacted a law restricting the traffic in naughty French postcards, few if any of which were blasphemous or politically seditious.[9] Then in 1857 Parliament signed Lord Campbell's Act, which most legal and literary historians regard as the first modern obscenity statute.[10] Lord Campbell's Act authorized English magistrates to seize "works written for the single purpose of corrupting the morals of youth and of a nature calculated to shock the common feelings of decency in a well managed mind."[11] The act was put to the test for the first time in 1868, eleven years after it was first enacted, in a landmark court case, *Queen v. Hicklin*.[12] The *Hicklin* case involved an antireligious pamphlet with considerable sexual content entitled *The Confessional Unmasked*.

The pamphlet alleged widespread depravity among the Roman Catholic priesthood and suggested that priests hearing parishioners' confessions had a more than passing interest in the gory details of human sexuality. The pamphlet would have been found obscene under virtually any of the regulations that had been on the books since 1538. Using Lord Campbell's Act to ban the pamphlet was thus easy enough. Speaking for the court, Chief Justice Alexander Cockburn wrote, "I think the test of obscenity is this: whether the tendency of the matter charged as obscenity is to deprave and corrupt those whose minds are open to such immoral influences, and into whose hands a publication of this sort might fall."

Encouraged by the success of antipornography forces in Great Britain, U.S. activists lobbied Congress to pass legislation that might be used by our courts much as Lord Campbell's Act and the so-called *Hicklin* standard were used across the Atlantic. Enter Anthony Comstock, a Civil War veteran working at the time as a clerk in a dry goods store. In his hours off the job, Comstock headed the New York Society for the Suppression of Vice.[13] With the help of YMCA president Morris K. Jessup, Comstock began an antiporn crusade that would make him one of the most famous and influential men in America in the second half of the nineteenth century.

To draft an antipornography bill that might stand the test of constitutional inquiry, Comstock and Jessup enlisted the help of U.S. Supreme Court justice William Strong. The bill, written by Strong, specifically prohibited the use of the U.S. mail to distribute literature "promoting" abortion as well as materials of an "obscene, lewd or lascivious" nature and/or "of an indecent character." The bill, widely known as the Comstock Act, was passed in 1873.

The first obscenity case to reach the U.S. Supreme Court was *Rosen v. United States* in 1896.[14] Lew Rosen was a New York publisher who had used the U.S. mail to distribute "indecent" pictures. A lower court had found him in violation of the Comstock Act and the Supreme Court upheld the conviction. Writing for the majority, Justice John Marshall Harlan established the *Hicklin* standard as the Court's principal definition of obscenity.[15]

A second 1896 case, *Swearingen v. United States*, offered further clarification on the subject of obscenity.[16] Dan K. Swearingen, a newspaperman in Kansas, used the U.S. mail to distribute a newspaper that contained a scathing personal attack on another citizen (whose name was never used, but was nonetheless identifiable to most of the newspaperman's readers).[17] Because the U.S. mails were involved, free press guarantees were held (at least by local authorities) to be irrelevant and Swearingen was arrested, tried, and found guilty of violating the Comstock Act.

While it concurred with the lower court's conclusion that Swearingen's article was outrageous and potentially libelous, the U.S. Supreme Court reversed the Kansas judgment against Swearingen. "Coarse and vulgar language" was not, the justices concluded, in itself obscene. In what would be a precedent-setting interpretation of the *Hicklin* standard, the Court held that foul language alone could not be obscene unless it was that "form of immorality which has relation to sexual impurity." Whatever might constitute "sexual impurity" was left unsaid, but the Court maintained that material could be deemed obscene only if it had a specific *effect*—to *sexually* deprave or corrupt a segment of its potential audience.[18]

Much the same elitist argument supports the first important censorship case involving motion pictures: *Mutual Film Corporation v. Industrial Commission of Ohio* in 1915.[19] Writing for the majority in the *Mutual* case, Justice Joseph McKenna concluded that cinema was not necessarily guaranteed First Amendment protection because, unlike serious literature or newspapers, it appealed to a mass audience, and like pornography, it exploited the audience's prurient interests. McKenna believed that this mass audience—consisting "not of women alone nor of men alone, but together, not of adults only, but of children"—had to be protected from their own worst impulses. He also believed that the rest of society had to be protected from this mostly lower-class, urban, immigrant audience.

McKenna pointedly warned against the "insidious power of amusement." Amusement, McKenna believed, was an industrial product as much as an activity of leisure. And it was potentially dangerous because those with the capital to amuse (all those first-generation American Jews in the film business) often behaved irresponsibly.

The *Hicklin* standard, which defined obscenity less as a matter of specific content than apparent or potential effect ("to deprave and corrupt" minds "most open to corrupt influences"), governed obscenity decisions from 1878 to 1933—forty-five years spanning the development of the technology that made cinema possible, the first public exhibition of movies in France and the United States, the entire silent era, and the first years of sound film up to and including the emergence of the MPPDA and its implementation of content censorship through its first production code. For almost fifty years, courts and local boards endeavored to ban material if, in their subjective opinion, it *might* tend to deprave or corrupt audiences consisting of adult couples (together!) or their children.

The film industry found in *Hicklin* not only workable guidelines but a measure of respectability. By employing standards wholly consistent with those used by the courts and local boards with whom the industry eagerly complied, the MPPDA established the responsible public image it needed in order to avert federal and local interference in the production, distribution, and exhibition of its product. In doing so, the studios also established a network of relationships with these groups that would persist for half a century.

THE RULES FOR LITERATURE ARE NOT (NECESSARILY) THE SAME AS THEY ARE FOR FILM

Ravished over her I lay full lips full open kissed her mouth. Yum.
—James Joyce, *Ulysses*

The first real challenge to the *Hicklin* standard came in 1913 with *United States v. Kennerly*.[20] In his opinion in the case, Judge Learned Hand suggested that the *Hicklin* standard had finally outlived its utility.[21] "However consistent it may be with mid-Victorian morals," Hand wrote, "[the *Hicklin* standard] does not answer to the understanding and morality of the present time."

Hand's opinion in *Kennerly* was eloquent as it introduced the notion that community standards must change along with the culture, that obscenity criteria, especially those based on assumptions about the mass audience, must be revised in concert with shifts in the American zeitgeist. It also introduced the notion that obscenity criteria had to be variable enough to enable the free flow of ideas, even unpopular ideas. Moreover, such criteria should not be used to deny adults access to materials that are suitable for them but unsuitable for children. "I question whether in the end men will regard that as obscene which is honestly relevant to the adequate expression of innocent ideas," Hand wrote,

> and whether they will not believe that truth and beauty are too precious to society at large to be mutilated in the interest of those most likely to pervert them to base uses. Indeed, it seems hardly that we are

even to-day so lukewarm in our interest in letters or serious discussion as to be content to reduce our treatment of sex to the standard of a child's library in the supposed interest of a salacious few, or that shame will for long prevent us from adequate portrayal of some of the most serious and beautiful sides of human nature.

Hand was right about the relationship between the *Hicklin* standard and "mid-Victorian morals," but he was wrong about the time(s). A major break with *Hicklin* did not come until 1933, when the courts examined a case involving the publication and sale of James Joyce's controversial modernist novel *Ulysses*.[22] Under the *Hicklin* standard, *Ulysses* was unquestionably obscene. But in 1933 district court judge John M. Woolsey suggested that another standard should be applied to serious works of literature, one that took into account the dominant effect of a book, taken as a whole, on a more or less typical reader, one not necessarily inclined to be unduly depraved by erotic or controversial content.

Woolsey did not argue against an effects-based standard per se; he maintained only that the *Hicklin* standard was too strict and rigid. But he did suggest that the courts should evaluate works on a case-by-case basis. Additionally, Woolsey held that questionable content must be viewed in the context of the work as a whole.[23]

The district court ruling was upheld on appeal by Judge Augustus Hand: "that numerous long passages in *Ulysses* contain matter that is obscene under any fair definition of the word cannot be gainsaid; yet they are relevant to the purpose of depicting the thoughts of the characters and are introduced to give meaning to the whole, rather than to promote lust or portray filth for its own sake."[24] Hand's opinion proved crucial to the development of the notion of "redeeming social importance," eventually elaborated in Justice William Brennan's opinion for the majority in *Roth v. United States* in 1957.[25]

The *Hicklin* standard took another significant hit in 1936, when, in *United States v. Levine*, Judge Learned Hand wrote,

This earlier doctrine [the *Hicklin* standard] necessarily presupposed that the evil against which a statute is directed so much outweighs all interests of art, letters or science, that they must yield to the mere possibility that some prurient person may get a sensual gratification from reading or seeing what to most people is innocent and may be delightful or enlightening. No civilized community not fanatically puritanical would tolerate such an imposition.[26]

Learned Hand, like his cousin Augustus, did well to identify the *Hicklin* standard as a vestige of Victorianism. But neither jurist fully rejected the effects-based definition first established in *Queen v. Hicklin*. Both judges argued that material should be judged according to its effect on a *normal or average person*, but in doing so only replaced one effects-based standard with another.

The constitutionality of any effects-based standard was for the first time significantly questioned by Judge Curtis Bok in *Commonwealth v. Gordon*, a 1949 case.[27] Bok argued that a work could be found legally obscene only if a "causal connection" could be drawn between a specific book and criminal behavior and moreover, that the causal connection must "appear beyond a reasonable doubt." In doing so, Bok effectively placed the burden of proof on the state; if obscenity was a criminal matter that involved conspiratorial intent to commit a crime, the state would have to present proof much as it did in other criminal proceedings.

In *Pornography and the Justices: The Supreme Court and the Intractable Obscenity Problem*, Richard Hixson links *Commonwealth v. Gordon* with another 1948 case, *People v. Doubleday*.[28] The *Doubleday* case concerned *Memoirs of Hecate County*, a fictional work by the legendary literary critic Edmund Wilson that contained graphic sexual descriptions.[29]

By the time Wilson's book reached stores nationwide, it was already notorious and local censors were lying in wait for its arrival. In New York, at the behest of the New York Society for the Suppression of Vice (the organization formerly headed by Anthony Comstock), well over a hundred copies of *Memoirs of Hecate County* were seized from four bookstores all owned by Wilson's publisher, Doubleday. The book was also pulled from the shelves of the New York Public Library. Doubleday challenged the New York injunction against selling the book, but a three-judge panel upheld the ban by a vote of two to one.[30]

According to Hixson, what makes the *Doubleday* case so significant has nothing to do with its outcome. (When the case went to the U.S. Supreme Court in 1948, the New York conviction was upheld.)[31] Instead, the case is important because it set in motion a dialogue on obscenity that focused on two new, intersecting issues: (1) the need to establish formal, legal criteria defining obscene content, and (2) the need to establish content criteria that might somehow distinguish between obscenity in serious works of fiction (like *Memoirs of Hecate County* or Joyce's *Ulysses*), in which controversial content served a larger intellectual/artistic purpose, and works that appealed primarily, even solely, to readers' prurient interests.[32]

A 1957 case, *Butler v. Michigan,* concerned a less lofty title, John Griffin's novel *The Devil Rides Outside.*[33] A Michigan court banned the novel because it "tended to the corruption of the morals of youth." The U.S. Supreme Court overturned the Michigan ban and in doing so expressed a willingness to supplant the *Hicklin* standard with a more variable, more content-based test. Writing for the majority, Justice Felix Frankfurter opined, "quarantining the general reading public against books not too rugged for grown men and women in order to shield juvenile innocence. . . . Surely this is to burn the house to roast the pig."[34]

ROTH v. UNITED STATES

All ideas having even the slightest redeeming social importance—unorthodox ideas, even ideas hateful to the prevailing climate of opinion—have the full protection [of this Court].

—Justice William Brennan, *Roth v. United States*

In his opinion for the majority in *Interstate Circuit v. Dallas* (1968), Justice John Harlan concluded that "the obscenity problem" was essentially "intractable."[35] "The subject of obscenity," he wrote, "has produced a number of views among the members of the court unmatched in any other course of constitutional adjudication." Harlan observed that all too often decisions in obscenity cases were based on subjective criteria wholly contingent on the politics and personal tastes of the individual justices. In the absence of consistent, objective criteria there was idiosyncrasy, emotion, politics.[36]

In thirteen decisions in obscenity cases heard by the Supreme Court between 1957 and 1967—dates coinciding with the release of Kazan's *Baby Doll* and Antonioni's *Blow-Up*—the nine justices filed fifty-five separate opinions. Careful review of the opinions in these cases reveals little about what legally defines a work as obscene. Instead, such a review discloses a larger political history, one in which the Court's problems with obscenity were complicated, at times even obfuscated, by parallel civil libertarian concerns regarding privacy and states' rights.

Roth v. United States, a 1957 case in which the Supreme Court upheld the conviction of a well-known pornographer, was in many ways the key case in the evolution of a modern obscenity standard. Samuel Roth was a sixty-five-year-old self-described poet, publisher, and bookseller specializing in erotica.[37] He was indicted in 1955 on twenty-six counts of violating and conspiring to violate the 1873 Comstock Act by mailing an obscene advertisement for the magazines *Photo and Body*, *Good Times*, and *American Aphrodite*. Roth became the first in a series of interesting if not unlikely players (now including *Penthouse* publisher Bob Guccione and *Hustler* publisher Larry Flynt) charged with the task of fighting to uphold our First Amendment rights and protections.[38]

When Roth was tried in a U.S. district court in New York, the judge allowed him to present as evidence works of contemporary fiction that, unlike the magazines advertised in his circular, had some redeeming literary, social, or cultural value. In his instructions to the jury, the New York trial judge tweaked the *Hicklin* standard. Per *United States v. Levine* and in apparent anticipation of *Butler v. Michigan*, the judge told the jury that they would have to find that the material Roth sent to his customers was "calculated to corrupt and debauch the mind and morals of those into whose hands it may fall."

The instructions seemed to tip the scales for an acquittal, since it was hard to imagine how Roth's mailer might offend *his* customers. But the jury found Roth guilty on four counts. Roth was sentenced to five years in prison and fined five thousand dollars. The conviction was subsequently upheld on appeal. Though he upheld the conviction, Judge Jerome Frank wrote convincingly in favor of developing a new national standard by which in the future the likes of Roth might be left to sell his books and magazines to his clientele. "Obscenity dissemination, a ridiculously vague crime, punishes people for selling books or pictures which may only 'evoke thoughts' and nothing more," Frank wrote. "This is carrying government suppression too far. Just as with soapbox political zealots, so with 'publishers' like Roth: let them alone as the price we pay for freedom, unless and until we can show that they have produced some tangible danger to society, a danger more 'clear' and more 'present' than mere stimulation of 'lustful thoughts.'"[39]

The *Roth* case was granted a limited writ of certiorari by the U.S. Supreme Court in 1957. Though Roth was just a dirty bookseller and the case concerned work hardly in the class of *Ulysses* or even *The Devil Rides Outside*, the Court was inclined to agree with Judge Frank's opinion that the case presented an opportunity to elaborate a more modern, objective standard for obscenity. Such a new standard considered content in context and rendered obsolete the nineteenth-century effects-based standard that had dominated obscenity law for almost ninety years.

Before it was heard by the nation's highest court, *Roth* was consolidated with another, similar case, *Alberts v. California*. This second case also concerned the use of the mails to circulate a bookstore advertisement (in the *Alberts* case, it was a mailer touting *Sword of Desire, She Made It Pay*, and *The Business Side of the Oldest Business*). David S. Alberts, a Beverly Hills–based purveyor of erotica, was, like Roth, a small-time player and the work he sold was hardly the sort of stuff the Court endeavored to protect in *United States v. One Book Called* Ulysses *by James Joyce*. Nonetheless, *amicus curiae* (friend of the court) briefs were filed by the American Civil Liberties Union and the American Book Publishers Council.[40]

Writing for a seven-to-two majority upholding the *Roth* and *Alberts* convictions, Justice William Brennan argued that a work could be found obscene only if "to the average person, applying contemporary community standards, the dominant theme of the material taken as a whole appeals to prurient interest." Brennan expressed a desire to establish a distinction between serious works of fiction and visual art that depicted nudity and/or sex and "material which deals with sex in a manner appealing to prurient interest—i.e., material having a tendency to excite lustful thoughts."

Brennan argued that "all ideas having even the slightest redeeming social importance—unorthodox ideas, even ideas hateful to the prevailing climate of opinion—have the full protection" of the Court. But for Brennan, obscenity fell outside the realm of ideas. It was thus "utterly without social importance." Any potential "benefit that might be derived" from the free flow of such material was "clearly outweighed by the social interest in order and morality." Brennan maintained that obscenity was not nor was it ever intended to be "within the area of constitutionally protected speech or press."

In a dissenting opinion written by Justice William O. Douglas and signed by Justice Hugo Black, the Court's two strict civil libertarians elaborated the first of what would become a series of objections to any attempt to deny First Amendment protection to so-called obscene speech. Douglas highlighted the absurdity of the California statute in particular (as applied in the *Alberts* case), which held that a work could be deemed obscene if it had "a substantive tendency to deprave or corrupt its readers by exciting lascivious thoughts or arousing lustful desire."[41] "By these standards," Douglas wrote, "punishment is inflicted for thoughts provoked, not for overt acts nor anti-social conduct." Such a statute, Douglas maintained, amounted to a mode of thought control and moreover could be extended to acts not traditionally viewed as speech:

> The tests by which these convictions were obtained require only the arousing of sexual thoughts. Yet the arousing of sexual thoughts and desires happens every day in normal life in dozens of ways. Nearly thirty years ago [1927], a questionnaire sent to college and normal school women graduates asked what things were most stimulating sexually. Of 409 replies, 9 said "music," 18 said "pictures," 29 said "dancing," 40 said "drama," 95 said "books," and 218 said "man."

In a deft challenge to the constitutionality of effects-based standards, Douglas cited studies that concluded that written or pictorial material had little or no role in the lives of the antisocial and young, the very group censorship laws protected "us" against. A number of recent studies, Douglas argued, revealed that "delinquents read very little" and what they read "has so little effect upon their conduct that it is not worth investigating." In the absence of scientific proof of a criminal or antisocial effect, "there is good reason for serious doubt concerning the basic hypothesis on which censorship is defended."

Douglas concluded that throughout modern history censorship has proven to be "both irrational and indiscriminate." In articulate defense of the First Amendment, Douglas wrote,

> Any test that turns on what is offensive to the community's standards is too loose, too capricious, too destructive of freedom of expression to be squared with the First Amendment. Under that test, juries can censor, suppress, and punish what they don't like, provided the matter relates to "sexual impurity" or has a tendency "to excite lustful thoughts." This is community censorship in one of its worst forms. It creates a regime where, in the battle between the literati and the Philistines, the Philistines are certain to win.

Douglas and Black were not alone in their opposition to the imposition of national obscenity criteria. The conservative Justice John Harlan opposed Brennan's quest for federal guidelines in order to preserve the autonomy of the states. Like Brennan, Harlan was troubled by the Court's inability to adequately define obscenity. But his reasons for sustaining the *Roth* and *Alberts* convictions differed dramatically from Brennan's because he had no interest in using the case to introduce new and improved obscenity criteria. In a long, complex, at times contradictory opinion, Harlan focused only briefly on the notion of redeeming social importance. Though he valued literature that might run afoul of state censorship guidelines, Harlan was a rigid states' rights conservative committed to protecting regional diversity. He insisted on the right of the states "to differ on their ideas of morality" at the expense of even the loftiest and most artful of unorthodox or controversial speech: "The fact that the people of one State cannot read some of the works of D. H. Lawrence seems to me, if not wise or desirable, at least acceptable. But that no person in the United States should be allowed to do so seems to me to be intolerable, and violative of both the letter and spirit of the First Amendment." The result of any federal or national standard, Harlan concluded, would be a "deadening uniformity," a world much like the one projected in George Orwell's *1984*.[42]

JACOBELLIS v. OHIO

> I shall not today attempt further to define the kinds of material I understand to be embraced within [the] shorthand description [of hardcore pornography]; and perhaps I shall never succeed in intelligibly doing so. . . . But I know it when I see it.
> —Justice Potter Stewart, *Jacobellis v. Ohio*

As discussed at length in chapter 3, *Jacobellis v. Ohio* (1964) was a pivotal case in the history of film exhibition. Following on the heels of a series of successful court challenges to local censorship activity—*Burstyn v. Wilson, Gelling v. Texas, Superior Films v. Department of Education of Ohio*—it seemed finally to provide exhibitors with the freedom to screen controversial films.[43] The opinion explicitly mentioned motion pictures and laid out a standard or test that could not be abridged or circumvented by state or local censorship activists or boards.

In an opinion for the majority reversing the Ohio judgment against the theater manager Nico Jacobellis, Justice Brennan further refined the national standard previously elaborated in the *Roth* case. In his majority opinion in the *Jacobellis* case, Brennan wrote, "The test for obscenity is whether to the average person, applying contemporary community standards, the dominant theme of the material, taken as a whole, appeals to prurient interest." Brennan added four significant clarifications to the *Roth* standard: (1) a work cannot be proscribed unless it is *utterly without redeeming social importance*, "and hence material that deals with sex in a manner that advocates ideas, or has literary or scientific or artistic value or any other form of social importance, may not be held obscene and denied constitutional protection"; (2) "the constitutional status of allegedly obscene material does not turn on a 'weighing' of its social importance against its prurient appeal, for a work may not be proscribed unless it is 'utterly' without social importance"; (3) "Before material can be proscribed as obscene under this test, it must be found to go substantially beyond customary limits of candor in description or representation"; and (4) "The 'contemporary community standards' by which obscenity is to be determined are not those of the particular local community from which the case arises, but those of the Nation as a whole."

Brennan's use of the term "community standards" was imaginative and extremely controversial. The term dates to an opinion written by Learned Hand in *United States v. Kennerly* in 1913. As Brennan read Hand's opinion, "community standards" referred to "the society at large . . . the public, or people in general." After all, Brennan contended, Hand was "referring not to state or local communities, but rather to 'the [national, American] community.'" Brennan's desire to formulate a flexible national standard that would have "a varying meaning from time to time—not from county to county, or town to town" jibed with a larger ideological or political agenda concerning states' rights.[44]

Brennan's national community standard protected theater owners from local bans and film seizures. The MPAA, which hardly operated in concert with the National Association of Theater Owners at the time, no doubt appreciated how significantly the *Jacobellis* decision served its interests as well. Brennan's opinion temporarily assured the studios that so long as a film did not run afoul of the (still evolving) national legal criteria, local censorship decisions would be summarily reversed by the Supreme Court. In promotional material circulated in support of his new film rating system, Jack Valenti took specific account of the third aspect of the *Roth/Jacobellis* test, appreciating the fact that under virtually any new set of production guidelines, there was little likelihood that studio films would ever "go substantially beyond customary limits of candor."

However much Valenti wanted to use Brennan's national standard, he could not help but notice a growing volatility at the Supreme Court.

Perhaps this worried him. Perhaps this is why the CARA system was designed to be so responsive to cultural change and community standards as they evolve over time.

Jacobellis produced seven separate opinions, no more than two justices signed on to any one of them. Black and Douglas warned that Brennan's proposed national standard put the Court "on the dangerous road [to] censorship." Stewart's concurring opinion was unintentionally comical. Like Brennan, Stewart wanted to proscribe hard-core pornography. But unlike Brennan, he resisted any federal legal test that went much further than recognizing porn when he (and the rest of the justices) saw it.

The concurring opinion written by Justice Arthur Goldberg seemed to suggest a growing impatience with obscenity cases in general. Goldberg resigned from the Court soon after the *Jacobellis* decision to become U.S. ambassador to the United Nations, so his views on the subject were soon to become moot, but at the time, his reading of the First and Fourteenth Amendments seemed even more conservative than Brennan's: "To hold that liberty of expression by means of motion pictures is guaranteed by the First and Fourteenth Amendments, is not the end of our problem. It does not follow that the constitution requires absolute freedom to exhibit every motion picture of every kind at all times and all places."

Chief Justice Earl Warren and Justice Tom Clark, centrists when it came to social and civil libertarian issues, dissented. Warren (with Clark concurring) opposed Brennan's larger efforts to establish a national, federal, judicial standard on states' rights grounds. Challenging Brennan's imaginative reading of Hand's community standards argument, Warren wrote,

> It is my belief that, when the Court said in *Roth* that obscenity is to be defined by reference to "community standards," it meant community standards—not a national standard. . . . I believe that there is no provable national standard and perhaps there should be none. . . . communities throughout the Nation are, in fact, diverse, and it must be remembered that, in cases such as this one, the Court is confronted with the task of reconciling conflicting rights of diverse communities within our society and of individuals.

In a separate dissent, Harlan called for "a sensible accommodation between the public interest sought to be served by obscenity laws . . . and protection of genuine rights of free expression." Such an accommodation, Harlan concluded, could work only if the problem of obscenity was returned to the states, which, he argued, "were constitutionally permitted greater latitude in determining what is bannable." Harlan disregarded the *Roth* test in favor of a purposefully vague "federal test of rationality." So long as it seemed rational for the state of Ohio to ban screenings of films like *The Lovers*, whether or not he or the other justices found the film in question offensive or obscene was beside the point.

A BOOK NAMED JOHN CLELAND'S MEMOIRS OF A WOMAN OF PLEASURE v. ATTORNEY GENERAL OF MASSACHUSETTS

Every time an obscenity case is to be argued here, my office is flooded with letters and postal cards urging me to protect the community or the Nation by striking down the publication. The messages are often identical even down to commas and semi-colons. The inference is that they were all copied from a school or church blackboard. Dozens of postal cards often are mailed from the same precinct. The drives are incessant, and the pressures are great. Happily, we do not bow to them. I mention them only to emphasize the lack of popular understanding of our constitutional system. Publications and utterances were made immune from majoritarian control by the First Amendment, applicable to the states by the Fourteenth. No exceptions were made, not even for obscenity. The Court's contrary conclusion in *Roth*, where obscenity was found to be "outside" the First Amendment, is without justification.

—Justice William O. Douglas, *A Book Named John Cleland's Memoirs of a Woman of Pleasure v. Attorney General of Massachusetts*

John Cleland's *Memoirs of a Woman of Pleasure*, more commonly known as *Fanny Hill* (the name of its adventuresome heroine), was first published in England in two volumes: the first in 1748, the second in 1749. The novel tells the story of a penniless orphan, Fanny Hill, who at fifteen travels to London and accepts a job at a bordello. Fanny takes the job fully intending to stay out of the sex trade, but soon gets curious enough to give it a try. A first and aborted experience involves some coercion and violence but it is followed by a more consensual and satisfying encounter with a man named Charles, with whom Fanny falls in love and subsequently marries. The marriage starts off happily enough until it is subverted by Charles's father, who arranges to have his son sent to sea. In Charles's absence, Fanny makes ends meet by turning tricks at an upscale bordello and then by taking up with an older gentleman, who teaches her about life and love. He then dies, leaving her all his money.

I offer this little synopsis for a reason: to assert that *Memoirs of a Woman of Pleasure* does indeed have a plot—a key issue with regard to obscenity law in 1966. The book is otherwise "comprised of minutely described sexual episodes," as Justice Tom Clark wrote in his dissenting opinion. But the episodes do have a narrative context, and as my summary suggests, that narrative context is familiar to anyone who has read *Clarissa* or *Moll Flanders*, canonical (though less graphic) texts.

When *Memoirs of a Woman of Pleasure* was reissued by G. P. Putnam and Sons in 1963, it immediately and predictably caused a sensation. Public and private libraries, including the Library of Congress, placed orders for the book. After all, it had been out of print for over 140 years. But local censorship authorities were less impressed by the reissue, and moved quickly to prohibit the sale of the book. Bans in New York, New Jersey, and Massachusetts were met with court challenges financed by Putnam and engineered by Charles Rembar, a legendary figure in obscenity cases.[45]

Rembar's strategy in the New York, New Jersey, and Massachusetts cases was simple. At all three venues, Rembar attempted to focus attention away from the specific content of the book, which was fairly shocking when read out of context. Instead he insisted that the only issue of relevance was whether or not, according to the *Roth* standard, the book as a whole could be considered obscene. Of specific relevance, Rembar maintained, was the section of the *Roth* standard that held that "a book cannot be proscribed as obscene unless found to be utterly without redeeming social value." At the heart of this defense strategy was the testimony of expert witnesses, literary critics, and historians like Harvard's John Bullitt, Norman Holland from MIT, and Rutgers's Paul Fussell Jr. and David Burrows, all of whom affirmed the literary and historical importance of Cleland's book. The strategy brought mixed results: after two years of litigation, eight judges in three states ruled against the book, seven ruled for it.

Three years after the first ban was imposed against Putnam's reissued edition of the book, the Supreme Court agreed to hear Rembar's appeal of the Massachusetts ban. In his opening remarks to the Court, Rembar again highlighted the testimony of his expert witnesses:

> Where you have highly qualified witnesses who come to court and stake their professional reputations on their analysis of the book and its values—where you have published reviews and critical essays, by people [including V. S. Pritchett and Bridget Brophy] who have no interest in the outcome of the litigation, which establish that value—then, on the record, the book is entitled to the protection of the First Amendment.[46]

A Book Named John Cleland's Memoirs of a Woman of Pleasure v. Attorney General of Massachusetts generated five separate opinions: two in support of the majority decision, three (one each by Clark, Harlan, and White) in dissent.[47] The six-to-three decision overturning the state court verdict in the case continued a trend at the Court of reversing state and local bans on literature and films if censors did not adhere to the *Roth* and *Jacobellis* standards. But the opinions suggested that the Court was growing further from a consensus on the subject with every significant case.

Brennan wrote the opinion for the majority, joined by Justice Abe Fortas (who replaced Goldberg) and Chief Justice Warren. In the opinion, Brennan took the opportunity to once again call for a national obscenity standard that could combine aspects of both the *Roth* and *Jacobellis* tests.[48] The *Memoirs* standard stipulated that all three elements mentioned in the previous tests "must coalesce." For a book or film to be found obscene, Brennan wrote, the work *taken as a whole* must appeal to a prurient interest in sex, the material must be "patently offensive because it affronts contemporary community standards," *and* the material must be *utterly* without "redeeming social value." Whatever one made of *Memoirs of a Woman of Pleasure* with regard to the first two criteria, given the testimony of the literary experts, it was, as Rembar had hoped, difficult to argue that the book had *no* literary and/or literary-historical value.[49]

Douglas's concurring opinion predictably invoked the argument that "the First Amendment leaves no power in government over expression of ideas." Returning to the question of what the framers of the First Amendment were thinking when they weren't really thinking about obscenity, Douglas reminded his fellow justices that the framers designed the U.S. Constitution to free Americans from the repressive laws of the Old World. The roots of U.S. obscenity law, Douglas argued, still lay in an Old World case, *Queen v. Hicklin*. *Hicklin* restricted freedom of speech with regard not only or even primarily to sex, but to politics and religion as well. "To assume that English common law in this field became ours, " Douglas bristled, "is to deny the generally accepted historical belief that [per the Court's majority opinion in *Bridges v. California*][50] one of the objects of the Revolution was to get rid of the English common law on liberty of speech and of the press."

Douglas continued to resist Brennan's efforts to develop a compromise national standard: "Judges cannot gear the literary diet of an entire nation to whatever tepid stuff is incapable of triggering the most demented mind. The First Amendment demands more than a horrible example or two of the perpetrator of a crime of sexual violence, in whose pocket is found a pornographic book, before it allows a Nation to be saddled with a regime of censorship." Lampooning the whole notion of literary or historical value as a measure of obscenity, Douglas sarcastically cast Cleland's book against a very popular text (at the time) that also chronicled "the human quest for what is moral," Norman Vincent Peale's *Sin, Sex and Self-Control*. "These two books are not very important in themselves," Douglas wrote. "They may not be great literature. Whether or not they will survive through the centuries to come is a question, although John Cleland has an historical edge on Norman Vincent Peale."

As to the effect of pornography on the general public and the rationality of the government's attempts to censor on our behalf, Douglas offered two telling case studies:

Heinrich Pommerenke, who was a rapist, abuser, and mass slayer of women in Germany, was prompted to his ghastly deeds by Cecil B. DeMille's *The Ten Commandments*. During the scene of the Jewish women dancing about the golden calf, all the doubts of his life came clear: Women were the source of the world's trouble, and it was his mission to both punish them for this and to execute them. Leaving the theater, he slew his first victim in a park nearby. John George Haigh, the British vampire who sucked his victim's blood through soda straws and dissolved their drained bodies in acid baths, first had his murder-inciting dreams and vampire longings from watching the "voluptuous" procedure of—an Anglican High Church Service!

While the steady stream of obscenity cases led Douglas to sarcasm, it led Justice Clark to exasperation. "I have stomached past cases for almost ten years without much outcry," Clark wrote in his dissenting opinion. Dumbfounded by the majority's insistence that *Memoirs of a Woman of Pleasure* was not obscene, Clark offered the following clever and fairly accurate summary of Cleland's book:

> The book starts with Fanny Hill, a young 15-year-old girl, arriving in London to seek household work. She goes to an employment office where, through happenstance, she meets the mistress of a bawdy house. This takes ten pages. The remaining 200 pages of the book detail her initiation into various sexual experiences, from a lesbian encounter with a sister prostitute to all sorts and types of sexual debauchery in bawdy houses and as the mistress of a variety of men. . . . In each of the sexual scenes, the exposed bodies of the participants are described in minute and individual detail. The pubic hair is often used for a background to the most vivid and precise descriptions of response, condition, size, shape and color of the sexual organs before, during and after orgasms. There are some short transitory passages between the various sexual episodes, but, for the most part, they only set the scene and identify the participants for the next orgy, or make smutty reference and comparison to past episodes.

My guess is that Douglas would not have taken issue with Clark's account of the novel's narrative content. But the larger debate over censorship and obscenity has seldom regarded content independent of its supposed effect. And on that issue, Clark and Douglas could not have been further apart. Countering Douglas's claim that no causal link had or could ever be established between pornography and criminal conduct, Clark offered evidence to the contrary. Clark's expert witnesses on the causal link between obscenity and criminality included George W. Henry, a Cornell professor who expressed the opinion that "obscenity, with its exaggerated and morbid emphasis on sex, particularly abnormal and perverted practices . . . may induce antisocial conduct in the average person"; Detroit police inspector Herbert Case, who argued that "sex murder cases are invariably tied to some form of obscene literature"; FBI director J. Edgar Hoover, who emphasized that "pornography is associated with an overwhelmingly large number of sex crimes"; and Cardinal Spellman, who shared Hoover's fears regarding "the direct influence obscenity has on immature persons."

Harlan's dissent was the least colorful of the opinions and it was utterly predictable. Reiterating his argument that federal authorities should only concern themselves with material that was hard-core, Harlan continued to insist that the states should be left on their own to regulate or censor outright material they deemed to be obscene. So long as the state employed rational criteria, Harlan maintained, the Fourteenth Amendment assured them jurisdiction in the matter.[51]

REDRUP v. NEW YORK: MOVIE DAY AT THE COURT

Well Harry, I didn't learn anything, did you?
—Justice Thurgood Marshall to Justice Harry Blackmun during
a reel change in a Supreme Court screening of
Sexual Freedom in Denmark

Redrup v. New York presented a number of problems for the Supreme Court, not the least of which was that it provided a number of rationales for reversal. Robert Redrup was a clerk at a New York City newsstand. He was arrested after selling two paperbacks, *Lust Pool* and *Shame Agent*, to an undercover policeman for $1.65. The majority at the Court concerned itself not with whether the New York judgment against the newsstand clerk should stand, but rather why it shouldn't.

Justice Abe Fortas circulated two opinions, both of which made some of his brethren a little nervous. In the first draft, Fortas wrote that "any civil action [of this sort] would be invalid"; in the second draft he went even further, describing the confiscation of literary materials as tantamount to book burning.[52] While Fortas failed to obtain a majority for either draft, it seemed as if, in frustration, he had finally joined William O. Douglas and Hugo Black at the far end of the debate.

Black and Douglas went about restating their positions for the record in two very different drafts. Black stated simply that obscenity was protected speech and left it at that. In support of a larger argument eliding the distinctions between censorship and other forms of social regulation, Douglas attached to his opinion an article written by the Reverend Howard Moody. One sentence in particular proved especially provocative, an effect Douglas no doubt desired: "The dirtiest word in the English language is not 'fuck' or 'shit' in the mouth of a tragic shaman, but the word 'nigger' from the sneering lips of a Bull Connor."

John Harlan, who found himself once again in the minority in his steadfast support of the states' right to censor material so long as they went about it in a fair and rational manner, circulated an opinion that focused on the issue of prior restraint. In doing so, he seemed to express sympathy for those who intended to reverse on *Redrup*, if only to establish a precedent that might make things clearer for the states. Harlan argued convincingly that the states should have to prove that a defendant actually knew that what he was selling was (legally) obscene. The *Redrup* case was such a mess, Harlan implied that he was willing to join the majority so long as the decision was not used to further define and refine Brennan's evolving national standard. It was and Harlan dissented.

In the opinion finally offered by the Court, Potter Stewart affirmed that *Redrup* could have been reversed on any number of counts: "Whichever of these constitutional views [Black's, Douglas's, Brennan's, Fortas's, even Harlan's] is brought to bear . . . it is clear that the judgment cannot stand." Stewart endorsed Brennan's evolving three-part test, then added two more criteria. The first proscribed hard core (which, he again maintained, was something one can readily recognize); the second adopted the suggestively termed "variable yardstick" and affirmed the states' right to enforce statutes protecting minors against certain material and protecting the privacy of "unwilling individuals" from "assault" by panderers.

Redrup proved to be a pivotal case, but not necessarily for the expected reasons. The case brought some common sense to the subject at hand: it made obscenity a matter of specific content viewed in context. It once and for all did away with the *Hicklin* standard and promised to give producers and exhibitors their day in court. In the first eighteen months after the *Redrup* decision, the Court reversed thirty-five state and federal convictions.[53]

But however fair the painstaking task of due process may have been, the justices found the new *Redrup* guidelines impractical and ultimately intolerable. As the constitutional law historians James Foster and Susan Leeson contend,

> By 1967, the Justices could do no more than declare that a finding of obscenity would depend on the independent determination of each Justice employing his own theory of what constituted obscenity. The Court subsequently heard and decided thirty-one cases in this manner. If the *Roth* decision created uncertainty for state and lower federal courts, the *Redrup* approach created virtual chaos.[54]

Redrup put the Court in the unhappy position of evaluating each obscenity ban on an individual basis. This required the justices to view a wealth of exhibits—films, books, and photographs—a task that struck at least three members of the Court, despite *Redrup*, as irrelevant and/or repugnant. These three justices steadfastly refused to attend films or review pictorial or printed material. Chief Justice Warren Burger, who joined the Court in 1968, a year after *Redrup*, declined to view exhibits for personal reasons. He just didn't like pornography. Justices Douglas and Black refused to view exhibits because they believed that nothing should be banned. "If I want to see [a] film," Justice Black bristled, "I should pay my money." Black wondered aloud how nine men, many in their seventies, could make relevant judgments about sexuality. In the process of attempting to clarify the obscenity question, the Court was acting, Black wrote, "as a Supreme Board of Censors."[55]

The other six justices dutifully screened materials as they arrived at the Court. According to Bob Woodward and Scott Armstrong in *The Brethren*, their insightful account of the Court from 1969 to 1975, the screening of relevant exhibits in film obscenity cases (collectively referred to as "movie day" at the Court) offered the jurists a strange, sometimes surreal diversion. Convened in a basement storeroom, seated on folding chairs in the dark, six Supreme Court justices and all the clerks did their civic duty and watched dirty movies. By the late sixties, Justice Harlan had such bad eyesight he had to sit just a few feet from the screen. Even up so close to the action, Harlan could only make out shadows and outlines. Inevitably, a fellow justice or clerk would sit next to him in order to provide a running commentary. Prompted during appropriate scenes, Harlan was reputed to exclaim, "By Jove" or "Extraordinary."

The accounts of movie day in *The Brethren* suggest a boys' or men's club atmosphere, characterized by a camaraderie and good-natured ribbing that were otherwise absent, and by custom inappropriate, elsewhere in the building. For example, clerks openly made light of Stewart's infamously naive remark in *Jacobellis v. Ohio*: "I shall not today attempt to further define the kind of materials I understand to be embraced within [the] shorthand definition [of hard-core]; and perhaps I shall never succeed in intelligibly doing so. . . . But I know it when I see it." At appropriate and sometimes inappropriate points in a given film, under cover of darkness, clerks were wont to call out, "That's it. That's it! I know it when I see it!"

Justice Thurgood Marshall's quips were often more entertaining than the film under review. During the screening of a picture in a 1970 case, one of a number of hard-core films framed by pseudoscientific discourse so as not to appear "*utterly* without redeeming social importance," an actor posing as a psychologist concluded the hard-core action by observing, "And so our nymphomaniac subject was never cured." To which Marshall added, "Yeah, but I am." During the last few minutes of a screening of Russ Meyer's *Vixen*, a soft-core feature that ends as an Irish-communist-terrorist-hijacker bound for Cuba offers a treatise on the relative merits of communist and capitalist societies, Marshall ironically quipped, "Ah the redeeming social value."

RICHARD NIXON SAVES HOLLYWOOD

I'm going fishing. You kids [clerks] can fight the battles. What difference does it make? Why fight when you can just dissent.
—Justice Thurgood Marshall after four Nixon nominees
were appointed to the Court

When Richard Nixon ascended to the presidency in 1968, the studios had every reason to expect the worst. Nixon, after all, was a major player on HUAC. He had gotten to Congress by Red-baiting Helen Gahagan Douglas, the spouse of the liberal Jewish actor Melvyn Douglas, whose real name was Melvyn Hesselberg, as John Rankin pointed out in his terrifying anti-Semitic speech on the floor of Congress in 1947. But what began as altogether bad news ended quite happily for the studios. By the time he was forced to resign, Nixon appointed four new Supreme Court justices who together engineered an end to almost all theatrical exhibition of hard core. In doing so, they inadvertently saved Hollywood.

It is hard these days to view Nixon independently of the events that led to his resignation in 1973. He is now less a character than a caricature, his rise to power a kind of mystery: how could we have been so stupid? so blind? But such is the stuff of hindsight. Nixon was, if nothing else, a savvy political player. From those early days during the Red Scare—the high-profile public performance on HUAC, the evisceration of Alger Hiss—on through to his complicity in the Watergate Hotel break-in, Nixon clung to a rigidly conservative domestic social agenda. Success was an end that routinely justified whatever means proved or seemed necessary.

In 1968 Nixon inherited former president Lyndon Johnson's Commission on Obscenity and Pornography. Nixon recognized that Johnson, also a tough political player, had stacked the commission with civil libertarians.[56] In an attempt to subvert the proceedings, in 1969 Nixon appointed commission member Kenneth Keating ambassador to India and then replaced Kenneth Keating with Charles H. Keating Jr., an antiporn activist.[57] Charles Keating expressed his (and Nixon's) opposition to the committee's mostly liberal/libertarian/anti-alarmist conclusions by writing a lengthy formal rebuttal.[58]

Charles Keating Jr., of course, would continue his antiporn crusade through the seventies and eighties, including a well-publicized appearance in support of Jerry Falwell in his court tussle with *Hustler* publisher Larry Flynt. Keating's vigilance for the public good, alas, did not extend to his financial wheeling and dealing as he was a principal player in the savings and loan scandal that rocked the Bush administration and cost American taxpayers an astronomical amount of money.

But while Keating has been discredited, the interests he served in 1970 have won out, thanks in no small part to Ronald Reagan. One need only take a quick look at the so-called Meese Report, published as *The Final Report of the Attorney General's Commission on Pornography* in 1986, to see Nixon's agenda finally served by Reagan. While Johnson's commission found no link between pornography and antisocial behavior, the Meese Commission alleged a conspiratorial relationship between the porn industry and organized crime. It incorporated anecdotal testimony by self-proclaimed "victims" of porn and it showcased so-called expert witnesses like the antiporn feminist Andrea Dworkin. The study highlighted anecdotal testimony that some producers in the industry abuse underage performers and participate in the concurrent trafficking of kiddie porn nationwide.[59] To be in favor of First Amendment protection for pornography, or so the study implied, was to be in favor of the sexual exploitation of children.

Nixon's eventual victory in what we now term "the culture wars" began with his brilliant if not altogether subtle realignment of the Supreme Court after the 1968 election. When the MPAA first developed its new rating system, the Court sported a liberal majority: Chief Justice Earl Warren, along with Justices Abe Fortas, Thurgood Marshall, William Brennan, and William O. Douglas. Only Potter Stewart and John Harlan were dependable conservatives; Byron White and Hugo Black were liberal on certain issues and conservative on others.[60] Under Chief Justice Warren—a Republican, but of the Wendell Willkie and significantly anti-Nixon stripe—the Court had found in favor (but had failed to fully enforce) school desegregation, it had banned prayer in public schools, and it extended constitutional protections in criminal cases to the poor and indigent.[61] The Court's various attempts at establishing federal guidelines for obscenity had largely failed, but it had succeeded in rendering local censorship obsolete.[62]

Warren appreciated the significance a Nixon presidency might have on the Court. When Johnson announced his decision not to run for reelection, Warren submitted his resignation in order to allow Johnson, instead of Nixon, to replace him. But, uncharacteristically, Johnson failed to take advantage of the situation. First he nominated the insupportable associate justice Abe Fortas to replace Warren as chief justice. After wasting time on the Fortas appointment, Johnson failed to get a nominee to replace Warren before the Senate in time.

By the time Nixon took office, he had the opportunity not only to select Warren's replacement but to weigh in on the selection of a chief justice as well. Nixon appreciated the importance of selecting the right jurist. His former running mate and boss, President Dwight D. Eisenhower, had selected Warren without adequately researching or even fully considering his public record.[63] When Warren began to impose his politics on the Court, Eisenhower came to regret the choice, so much so that he later remarked that the appointment of Warren was "the biggest damned-fool mistake I ever made."[64]

When Nixon chose the U.S. District Court of Appeals judge Warren E. Burger to replace Chief Justice Warren, he set in motion a political shift to the Right at the Court. From the start, Burger was Nixon's man in every sense of the term. Burger was a strict law-and-order Republican, a former deputy attorney general under Eisenhower. Burger had the support of Nixon's top aide at the time, John Erlichman, and Nixon's legal adviser, attorney general John Mitchell.[65]

Impatient to make good on his campaign promise to realign the Court, Nixon targeted two of the more liberal Supreme Court justices—Fortas and Douglas—and wasted little time in getting his "dirty tricks" squad on the case.[66] The first stop was the IRS, which began an audit of Justice Douglas's tax return five days after the inauguration. At Nixon's behest, the FBI began looking into Douglas's relationship with the Las Vegas casino owner Albert Parvin, an alleged mob player. The advantage of going after Douglas was obvious: he was a liberal on race issues, a civil libertarian with regard to law enforcement and obscenity, and hardly a friend to big business.[67] The downside of courting a confrontation with Douglas was that he seemed to care little about his public image. Even in the face of the sort of adversity Nixon hoped to manufacture, Douglas was not apt to go quietly.

Fortas was significantly more vulnerable than Douglas for a number of reasons. The confirmation process in the Senate after President Johnson nominated Fortas for chief justice exposed his vulnerabilities to Nixon and his aides. According to the investigative journalists Bob Woodward and Scott Armstrong, the Justice Department quickly exploited Fortas's weakness and engineered his ouster. Under the direction of John Mitchell, the attorney general's office began leaking information to William Lambert, a writer at *Life* magazine, alleging a criminal conspiracy involving payoffs to Fortas from Louis Wolfson, a millionaire industrialist under investigation at the time by the SEC. When the investigation of Wolfson heated up, the industrialist boasted to friends, or so Mitchell told Lambert, that he had Fortas on his payroll, that he had nothing to fear from the SEC.[68]

As things played out, Wolfson had plenty to worry about (he was eventually convicted of securities violations), and so did Fortas. Though Fortas returned the twenty thousand dollars Wolfson had given him (which Fortas claimed was a onetime payment), the *Life* article, titled "Fortas and the Supreme Court: A Matter of Ethics," took the jurist to task in precisely the ways Nixon and Mitchell had hoped it would.

Four days after advance copies of the *Life* article circulated at the White House, Wolfson turned himself over to the police. In his hand was a document that seemed to prove that the twenty thousand dollars he had paid Fortas was not, as Fortas had claimed, a onetime consulting payment, but instead the first installment in what promised to be a yearly stipend, payable until the justice's death.[69]

Mitchell then went to Warren and brokered a deal. In exchange for Fortas's resignation, Mitchell promised that the criminal investigation, to be led by future Chief Justice Rehnquist, would "die of its own weight."[70] On May 14, 1969, less than two weeks after the *Life* article first exposed his relationship with Wolfson, Fortas submitted his resignation.

On June 3, three weeks after Fortas's resignation, Burger went before the Senate Judiciary Committee expecting a bloody battle. Burger had the support of the American Bar Association, the Federal Bar Association, and the District of Columbia Bar Association. But he had every reason to fear a payback for Nixon's part in the ouster of Fortas. The committee member he most feared was Senator Edward Kennedy, whom Burger believed had been prepped by Justice Brennan and a longtime adversary, the liberal appeals court judge David L. Bazelon. But Kennedy declined to ask so much as a single question during the speedy and uneventful confirmation hearing, and when Burger's name went before the full Senate, he was confirmed by a vote of seventy-four to three.

Securing confirmation for a nominee to replace Fortas proved to be a significantly stickier task. Nixon's first choice to replace Fortas was an antiunion, segregationist southerner, Judge Clement Haynsworth Jr. of the Fourth Circuit Court of Appeals.[71] The Democratic majority in the Senate opposed Haynsworth on ideological grounds. But they could not reject the nominee simply because they did not like his politics. Instead, they found an old case involving a company in which Haynsworth held stock and challenged the judge's decision not to recuse himself. The conflict of interest accusation held up and by a vote of fifty-five to forty-five, the Senate rejected the Haynsworth nomination.[72]

Nixon's second choice to replace Fortas was Judge G. Harrold Carswell. Like Haynsworth, Carswell was an outspoken opponent of school desegregation. When Carswell was brought before the Judiciary Committee, Senate Democrats highlighted a 1948 speech in which the nominee remarked that "Segregation of the races is proper and the only practical and correct way of life in our states. I have always so believed and I shall always so act."[73] In the end, Carswell proved easier to reject than Haynsworth.

Nixon's third choice was from well north of the Mason-Dixon: the Minnesotan Harry Blackmun, a judge on the Eighth Circuit Court of Appeals. Blackmun was a far less outspoken and far more politically moderate jurist than Haynsworth and Carswell. His curriculum vitae—Phi Beta Kappa at Harvard, then Harvard Law School, a clerkship at the Eighth Circuit, sixteen years in private practice, ten of which were spent as general counsel to the Mayo Clinic—was unassailable.[74] Blackmun was the best man at Burger's wedding in 1933, and his personal ties to the chief justice may well have worried some of those on the Left. But Blackmun was clearly a compromise, albeit one who could be depended on to share Burger's and Nixon's views regarding civil rights as they pertained to race, capital punishment, due process, and obscenity.[75]

Before he was forced out of office, Nixon got to appoint two more justices. In August 1971 Hugo Black, who was then eighty-four years old, tendered his resignation. Harlan, who was just seventy-one but could no longer see well enough to read on his own, handed in his resignation six days later.[76]

Finding replacements for Black and Harlan again proved difficult. Nixon wanted to nominate Democratic senator Robert Byrd from West Virginia (again in an effort to pay back the South), then Herschel Friday, a New York bond lawyer (recommended by the attorney general John Mitchell), then a top woman candidate, California Court of Appeals judge Mildred Little. The White House attorney John Dean interviewed the candidates and found fault with all three of them.[77] Rehnquist did not much like any of them either and recommended a compromise candidate, American Bar Association president Lewis Powell, a political moderate but still a southerner.[78] Nixon selected Powell and then in something of a surprise nominated Rehnquist to fill the Harlan vacancy.

While Powell seemed a lock for confirmation, Rehnquist posed problems. He, like Burger, was a law-and-order conservative in favor of questionable civil rights tactics like wiretapping antiwar activists. And like Haynsworth and Carswell, both of whom Rehnquist had supported, Rehnquist had publicly spoken in favor of limitations on school desegregation. In what can only be characterized as a major victory for Nixon, both men were confirmed: Powell by a vote of eighty-nine to one, Rehnquist by a vote of sixty-eight to twenty-six.[79] By the end of 1971, the Court sported four Nixon appointees and the stage was set for yet another stab at the intractable obscenity problem.

STANLEY v. GEORGIA

Pornography is to freedom of expression what anarchy is to liberty.
—President Richard Nixon

The first significant obscenity case after *Redrup v. New York* came in 1969: *Stanley v. Georgia*.[80] At first glance, *Stanley* seemed a landmark case: a rare unanimous decision supporting an individual's right to possess and use pornography in their own home. The case involved a Georgia court judgment against a man named Robert Stanley in whose home, on a warrant that permitted them to search for gambling paraphernalia, authorities found obscene movies. In his opinion for the Court (which by then included the first two Nixon appointees, Warren Burger and

Harry Blackmun), Justice Thurgood Marshall maintained that "The First Amendment as made applicable to the States by the Fourteenth prohibits making mere private possession of obscene material a crime." Later in the same opinion, Marshall added, "If the First Amendment means anything, it means that a State has no business telling a man, sitting alone in his own house, what books he may read or what films he may watch."

At long last there seemed to be a consensus at the Court that extended free speech protection to private use of pornography and moreover protected users or owners of pornographic materials from "unwarranted government intrusions into [their] privacy." Marshall's critique of the state of Georgia's principal argument—its "right to protect the individual's mind from obscenity"—was made in terms impossible to misconstrue: "We are not certain that this argument amounts to anything more than the assertion that the State has the right to control the moral content of a person's thoughts."

In a concurring opinion, Hugo Black reiterated his belief that "mere possession of reading matter or movies, whether labeled obscene or not, cannot be made a crime by a State without violating the First Amendment." But Potter Stewart, in an opinion joined by William Brennan and Byron White, decided not to mention the First Amendment at all. Instead, they focused on the Fourth Amendment, ostensibly throwing out the conviction on what was clearly a "bad search": the police weren't looking for films, after all, and the fifty minutes they spent watching dirty movies in Stanley's house was hard to justify in connection to the warrant.

The unanimous decision in the *Stanley* case proved misleading. In a case heard the following year, *Cain v. Kentucky* (1970), Burger wrote in support of the state's attempts to ban a screening of the soft-core feature *I, a Woman*. Burger supported the autonomy of the states and the consequent irrelevance of the First Amendment when he wrote, "[the Court] should not inflexibly deny to each of the States the power to adopt and enforce its own standards as to obscenity and pornographic materials."[81] In *Walker v. Ohio* (1970), Burger targeted *Redrup*, challenging the Court's justification in "assuming the role of a supreme and unreviewable board of censorship for the 50 States, subjectively judging each piece of material brought before it without regard to the findings or conclusions of other courts, state or federal."[82] Nixon's second appointee, Blackmun, similarly attacked Brennan's national criteria. In *Hoyt v. Minnesota* (1970), Blackmun wrote, "I am not persuaded that the First or Fourteenth necessarily prescribe a national and uniform measure—rather than one capable of some flexibility and [per Harlan] resting on concepts of reasonableness—of what each of our several States constitutionally may do to regulate obscene products within its borders."[83]

In three 1971 cases, *United States v. Reidel, United States v. Thirty-seven Photographs,* and *Grove Press v. Maryland State Board of Censors* (a case concerning the seizure and ban of *I Am Curious Yellow*), the Court held against an individual's right to import, transport, or sell obscene materials. Though the court held that mere possession of obscene material was not a crime, distribution was another matter.[84]

Stanley proved to be a misleading but important case. In the very act of protecting private ownership and viewership, the Burger/Nixon Court made its first move toward outlawing the public exhibition of so-called obscene material nationwide.

Obscenity decisions tend to be intensely personal, subjective, idiosyncratic. As the makeup of the Supreme Court changed, findings in obscenity cases reflected those changes. Case in point: between 1957 and 1969 William Brennan, the Court's great compromiser on the subject, wrote seven majority opinions in obscenity cases and only one dissent. In the 1970s he wrote only two for the majority and eleven personal dissents. He also signed on to several dissents in concurrence with Black and Douglas, with whom, in his later years, he seemed to agree more and more.[85] By then, the conservative majority on the Court was poised to reverse all of his hard work and there was nothing he could do about it.

MILLER v. CALIFORNIA

The danger [of pornography] lies in the half-way house of the weak, the indeterminate and uncultured who will be toppled into corruption by the powerful influence of what is read and seen.
                    —Frances Cowper, reporting on a British pornography
                        commissioner's visit to a sex show in Denmark

The decisions in *Miller v. California, Paris Adult Theater I v. Slaton, United States v. 12 200' Reels of Super 8 mm Film, United States v. Orito,* and *Kaplan v. California* were reported in a front-page article in the June 27, 1973, issue of *Variety*.[86] Under the headline "Show Biz's Fig-Leaf Crisis,"

Variety blithely acknowledged the decisions'significance to the hard-core industry and, less directly, to the studio industry as well: "The impact of the new rulings will have to be assessed in the months ahead, but the market for pornography should be effectively reduced almost at once. In some respects, the proclaimed standards are similar to anti-obscenity provisions that President Nixon has asked Congress to adopt in revising the U.S. criminal codes."[87]

For a variety of reasons, *Miller v. California* was the most important of the five cases. It concerned the mass mailing of an advertisement circular by Marvin Miller, a seller of erotic books. The circular touted four books, *Intercourse, Man-Woman, Sex Orgies Illustrated*, and *An Illustrated History of Pornography*, and one film, *Marital Intercourse*. When the circular arrived, unsolicited, at a Newport Beach restaurant, the manager and his mother promptly called the police. They filed a complaint and Miller was arrested for violating the California state criminal obscenity statute. At the time, the statute elaborated the following test, in part based on the *Roth* and *Memoirs* standards:

> Obscene means that to the average person, applying contemporary standards, the predominant appeal of the matter, taken as a whole, is to prurient interest, i.e. shameful or morbid interest in nudity, sex, or excretion, which goes substantially beyond customary limits of candor in description or representation of such matters and is matter which is utterly without redeeming social importance.

Miller was tried and convicted and his appeals were all denied. The series of decisions upholding the conviction seemed in line with the California standard. By the time the U.S. Supreme Court agreed to hear the case, at stake was not only or not really the fate of one pornographer but instead the state's right to adopt and enforce an obscenity statute stricter than the one elaborated by the federal judiciary. The American Civil Liberties Union filed an amicus brief in Miller's defense. The brief contended that the California state courts had based their decisions on a local or regional as opposed to national community standard—a potentially crucial new interpretation of a key aspect of the *Roth* and *Memoirs* tests.[88]

Justice Byron White and all four Nixon appointees voted to vacate the judgment and return the case to the California state courts with a new set of prosecutorial guidelines that virtually guaranteed yet another conviction. Writing for the five-to-four majority, Chief

Justice Warren Burger used the *Miller* case to establish a new standard as well as a new procedure strictly limiting federal oversight (per *Redrup v. New York*).

The new standard explicitly targeted hard core—which again was assumed to be something prosecutors would *know when they saw it*— and effectively returned content regulation to the states. "State statutes designed to regulate materials must be carefully limited," Burger wrote, but later in the same opinion he added that so long as local jurisdictions operated in a reasonable manner, it was not in the Court's "function to propose regulatory schemes for the states."

As the ACLU attorneys had feared he would, Burger used the *Miller* case to revise the *Roth* standard: "We [Burger, Blackmun, Rehnquist, White, and Powell] do not adopt as a constitutional standard the '*utterly* without redeeming social value [test].'"[89] That aspect of the test, Burger argued, never had the support of more than three justices at any one time and thus never fully or fairly represented a consensus view of the Court. Between 1957 and 1973, Burger argued, the Court had debated and compromised but had never really agreed on a national standard or test; indeed, it had never agreed on whether there should be such a test at all. In 1973 Burger, along with four other justices, returned jurisdiction to the states and in doing so left the dirty work of content censorship to ambitious local prosecutors and antiporn activists.

William O. Douglas, in a dissent joined by William Brennan, Potter Stewart, and Thurgood Marshall, bristled at the new majority's decision to hold Miller accountable to what amounted to a new standard and a new procedure for applying and enforcing that standard: "Today we leave open the way for California to send a man to prison for distributing brochures that advertise books and a movie under freshly written standards defining obscenity which until today's decision were never part of any law."[90] Conflating his due process argument with a by then familiar defense of the First Amendment (this time shared by Brennan, Stewart, and Marshall), Douglas added,

> If a constitutional amendment authorized censorship, the censor would probably be an administrative agency. Then criminal prosecutions could follow as if and when publishers defied the censor and sold their literature. Under that regime a publisher would know when he was on dangerous ground. Under the present regime—whether the old standards or the new ones are used—the criminal law becomes a trap. . . . Obscenity—which even we can't define with precision—is a

hodge podge. To send men to jail for violating standards they cannot understand, construe, and apply is a monstrous thing to do in a Nation dedicated to fair trials and due process.

In response to the civil libertarian argument voiced by Douglas in dissent, Burger offered the commonsensical argument that obscenity had no place in such a lofty debate: "In our view, to equate the free and robust exchange of ideas and political debate with commercial exploitation of obscene material demeans the grand conception of the First Amendment and its high purposes in the historic struggle for freedom."

The other four obscenity cases announced on the same day as *Miller v. California* were also decided by what *Variety* termed "a classic Nixon Court vote," five-to-four.[91] Of those cases, the most relevant to the film industry was *Paris Adult Theater I v. Slaton*. In that case, the Court found that adults-only admission policies at hard-core theaters were not enough to protect theater owners or managers from local prosecution.

In *United States v. 12 200' Reels of Super 8 mm Film*, the new majority at the Court held that Congress could exercise its commerce clause powers to proscribe importation of obscene material even if that material was intended for private use only. A similar decision was reached in *United States v. Orito* as the Court upheld the power of Congress to forbid the interstate transport of obscene materials even when safeguards were implemented to keep the materials out of the hands of minors and even when the material was transported solely for personal use. The constitutional protection of private ownership and use of pornography per *Stanley v. Georgia* got significantly muddled as the Court held that it *could be* illegal to transport obscene materials to the very consenting adults for whom ownership and use of these materials in the privacy of their homes were constitutionally protected.

The obscenity rulings handed down by the Burger Court on June 21, 1973, proved not only relevant to but helpful in the studios' ongoing attempts to regain control of the theatrical marketplace.[92] *Miller v. California* made it difficult to screen hard-core films in all but a few venues nationwide. *Paris Adult Theater I v. Slaton* made it difficult to use restrictive admission policies as a means of avoiding local bans and prosecutions. The two privacy cases—*United States v. 12 200' Reels of Super 8 mm Film* and *United States v. Orito*—made it all the more difficult to move potentially pornographic products in from overseas or from state to state. Altogether, the four decisions functionally outlawed the public exhibition of hard core and gave the MPAA exclusive access to the theatrical marketplace in all but a few selected urban markets.

Thanks to Valenti's warnings against producing and distributing films without an MPAA/CARA seal, by the time the *Miller* decision was announced the studios' product lines all fell well within the new guidelines. Hard-core and soft-core independent filmmakers, distributors, and especially exhibitors were significantly more vulnerable under the new standard. To a large extent, it was their success in the marketplace that was their undoing. From 1972 through the first half of 1973, hardcore films like *Deep Throat, The Devil in Miss Jones,* and *Behind the Green Door* enjoyed success on a scale that served only to bring more serious attention to their regulation. By 1973 the Court was inclined to view porn as a threat to impressionable audiences, a threat to once safe and pretty neighborhoods.

In a trial held two months before the Court handed down its decision in the *Miller* case, the New York City district attorney's office, in concert with Mayor John Lindsay's well-publicized anti-smut campaign, secured a local ban on screenings of *Deep Throat,* even though the film had been playing in the city since June of the previous year. New York State Criminal Court judge Joel Tyler applied the local ban only after cataloguing the film's "gymnastics, gyrations, bobbing, trundling, surging, ebb and flowing, eddying, moaning, groaning and sighing." The New World Theater, which had been showing the film to great success for almost nine months, pulled the title *Deep Throat* off its marquee and replaced it with "Judge Cuts Throat, World Mourns."[93]

As the exhibitor awaited a ruling on an appeal of the judgment, the U.S. Supreme Court announced its decision in the *Miller* case. The Supreme Court ruling dashed any hopes the theater owners may have had for a reversal of the local ban.

In concert with the New York ruling against *Deep Throat* and the precedent set in the *Miller* case, legal injunctions against screenings of *Deep Throat* were upheld in Baltimore, Beverly Hills, Memphis, Atlanta, San Antonio, St. Paul, Fort Worth, Boston, and Houston.[94] In each of these venues, local district attorneys highlighted the very local nature of contemporary community standards as elaborated in the *Miller* decision.

While the new majority at the Court supported community as opposed to national standards, exactly what might constitute a "community" (state, city, town, street?) was left vague. Expounding on an eastern Kentucky case in which Judge Robert Bork imposed a ban on

In 1973 the U.S. Supreme Court unanimously reversed a local court ruling in Georgia that banned the screening of Mike Nichols's adult melodrama *Carnal Knowledge* (Avco Embassy, 1971). The ruling seemed to suggest that so long as a film had an MPAA seal, it could not be found obscene.

Deep Throat based on a very narrow sense of the community, Justice John Paul Stevens quipped, "What is the purpose of defining the community? Should it be the economic market of a film's distribution area or a frame of reference for the jurors?"[95] Stevens's question begged an answer not from local attorneys but from studio marketers and advertisers.

Within a year of the Court's decision in *Miller v. California*, the studios' old problem with local censorship resurfaced as a simply ridiculous case, *Jenkins v. Georgia*, found its way to the Court.[96] *Jenkins v. Georgia* concerned a local attempt to enjoin the screening of the studio-made R-rated film *Carnal Knowledge*, a film with some rough language and brief nudity but no hard-core action either real or simulated. By a unanimous decision, the Court opted to reverse the Georgia ban on the film. Writing for the Court, Rehnquist argued that the film was not obscene "under the constitutional standards announced in *Miller*," and cautioned local authorities that, while the Court was inclined to leave the dirty job of censorship to the states, "juries [do not] have unbridled discretion in determining what is 'patently offensive.'" While the states were allowed some discretion in protecting the specific moral standards of their community, Rehnquist made clear, per *Miller v. California*, that "no one will be subject to prosecution for the sale or exposure of obscene materials [that do not] depict or describe patently offensive 'hard core' sexual conduct."

In a concurring opinion consisting of a single sentence, Douglas staked out his usual territory. Alone, in Black's and Fortas's absence, Douglas tersely maintained that the Georgia ban was unconstitutional because "any ban on obscenity is prohibited by the First Amendment." Brennan's separate concurring opinion, signed by Stewart and Marshall, spoke to the practical as opposed to ideological problems posed by the Court's five-to-four decision in the *Miller* case: "The Court's new formulation will not relieve us of the awesome task of making, case by case, at once the criminal and constitutional law."

The MPAA studios were at the time inclined to see Brennan's point; the Georgia ban on *Carnal Knowledge* seemed a harbinger of more such nuisance cases to come. But it wasn't. The ease with which the case was dispatched by the Court seemed only to prove Valenti, who had steadfastly warned against X-rated or hard-core product lines, right once again. There were not a whole lot of cases against studio films after 1973. His film rating system saw to that.

HOLLYWOOD v. HARD CORE: HISTORY MADE EASY AFTER 1973

If you sit by the river long enough, the body of your enemy will float by.

—an old Hindu saying

With the exception of a few venues in a few major cities, the public, theatrical exhibition of hard core was pretty much eliminated nationwide by the end of 1973. Hard-core features have since made a comeback on home video, but between 1973 and 1983 or so, between the Supreme

Court's retrenchment and the emergence of home video, the studios have had the theatrical market to themselves. And they have taken full advantage of the opportunity.

In 1974 the studios posted record profits. In 1975 Universal released *Jaws* and established a new measure for success in box office and merchandising revenues. In 1977 came *Star Wars*.

In the absence of hard core, America rediscovered Hollywood.

7

A Quick Look at Censorship in the New Hollywood

IN A JUNE 27, 1973, front-page editorial in *Variety* titled "Porno Thicket Now Jungle? Community Standards Spells Confusion," the staff writer Addison Verrill speculated on the impact of the Supreme Court's decisions in *Miller v. California, Paris Adult Theater I v. Slaton, United States v. Orito, United States v. 12 200' Reels,* and *Kaplan v. California.* The "five tough anti-pornography decisions will send shock waves through many sections of the entertainment and publishing industries," Verrill wrote.[1] Just how the studios and independents might deal with that shock, he concluded, would very much become the story of this suddenly new Hollywood.[2]

Though the Court decisions had a more direct impact on the independents, many of whom made their money producing and distributing X-rated films, studio anxiety was not without cause at the time. Particularly worrisome was a section of Burger's opinion for the Court in the *Miller* case that allowed for the regulation of "patently offensive representations or descriptions of sexual acts, normal or perverted, actual *or simulated.*"[3] Though elsewhere in the opinion Burger maintained that states could proscribe only hard-core material, the inclusion of "simulated" imagery suggested that he and at least four other justices might recognize a whole lot more material as hard-core (when they saw it!) than the liberal majority had under Chief Justice Earl Warren. For filmmakers, distributors, and exhibitors, the new criterion elaborated by Burger was disconcertingly open-ended. It made clear that obscenity was primarily a matter for states and communities to define and regulate but left vague what might constitute hard-core, bannable material.[4]

If, as Verrill feared, some states decided to proscribe films with simulated sexual activity, soft-core indie titles like *The Cheerleaders* and *The Stewardesses* as well as prestige studio pictures like *Last Tango in Paris* and *Klute* were all potentially bannable.[5] "All eyes will be on the states,"

Verrill cautioned. "It is not inconceivable to predict that some communities could ban *Ulysses* all over again."[6]

Verrill predicted "havoc and chaos" for the porn industry. In the editorial's parting gesture, Verrill quoted an unidentified "indie distributor not involved with hard-core": "[*Miller v. California*] is the biggest thing to happen to the industry since the Consent Decree and all hell is going to break loose. Hundreds of theaters will close, there'll be all sorts of different censor boards. . . . We thought we had it bad with the Memphis and Maryland censors, but we haven't seen anything yet."[7]

In the same June 27, 1973, issue, a number of smaller news stories further revealed the impact of—and the industry's concern with—the June 21 decisions. On page 6, for example, a three-paragraph piece titled "Cops Call 'Tango' Tame" told the story of a San Antonio, Texas, vice squad raid on the city's adults-only Aztec Theater. While the police ultimately found *Last Tango in Paris*, the film at issue, "tame," the possibility that the vice squad might be visiting a theater near you seemed more than adequate cause for concern.[8] Three columns to the right was an article headlined "Florida's New Law Backed: Close 'Throat,'" which heralded Florida's new, suddenly constitutional, tough antipornography law and its first victim(s): an adult theater in Orlando and *Deep Throat*, the film booked into the theater at the time.[9] A third article, the longest of the three on page 6, ran under the ominous headline "See Porno Take-Over by Underworlders." This third report ended with the following prediction from Michael Thevis, whom *Variety* dubbed "the king of pornographers": "The whole thing is ludicrous. It won't stamp out pornography, but just drive it underground. You cannot legislate morality. You just can't expect adult book stores to disappear over night. They're here to stay just like alcohol, cigarettes and wild, wild women."[10]

On the following page, clergy and various other moral crusaders weighed in mostly to say that the pornographers had just gotten what they deserved, that unrestrained trade in obscene matter was something the silent, moral majority could never have tolerated for long. Father Morton S. Hill applauded the Court's undertaking of "the job of damming the flood of filth," while Rabbi Julius G. Neuman, chairman of Morality in Media, added that the June 21 decisions were simply the Court's "inevitable reaction to the grassroots rebellion against porno."[11]

A similar piece appeared in the July 4, 1973, issue. Under the title "Pornographers Flaunted Their Wares and Embarrassed Plain Folks," *Variety* cited the popular *New York Times* columnist Russell Baker, whose sarcasm spoke volumes on the hypocrisy of the times: "A country that can tolerate, say the bombing of Cambodia without having taste offended can surely put up with a little pornography . . . [but] what the country could not tolerate was a flamboyant feast of pornography, such as we ended up with. . . . Greed was bound to bring Mr. Nixon's Supreme Court down on them in the end." As to the sudden marginality of porn, Baker affirmed that such is the fate of all guilty pleasures under capitalism: "Pornography will not be much missed. Those who want it will continue to be able to obtain it at the usual extortionate prices which the law insists we pay criminals for self-indulgence in petty vices."[12]

Two brief news items published in the August 8, 1973, issue of *Variety* reveal just how quickly porn movies were eliminated from the theatrical landscape.[13] Under the title "X's Ducked Like Boxoffice Poison; This Is the Summer of Contented R's," the trade magazine affirmed the chilling effect of the *Miller* decision. An unnamed CARA official remarked that "[Directors and producers] come to us and say, 'tell us what we have to do to get an "R,"' and they are agreeing to take out anything they have to in order to get the designation."[14] Valenti continues to argue that such a practice does not amount to censorship: after all, it's voluntary, and what local activists do to harass exhibitors screening X-rated films is none of his or the MPAA's business. But it certainly helps make everyone in the MPAA and even those who are to some extent independent of the MPAA beholden to the studio-sponsored CARA board.

The second item was offered as a kind of curio, even a gag. Running under the title "Pornography Joins Curriculum," *Variety* acknowledged the first porn movie course ever offered at an American university. The class, titled "Pornography Uncovered, Eroticism Exposed (An X-Rated Course)," was offered by the New School for Social Research in New York City. Less a course than a lecture series, the class featured weekly talks led by local veterans of obscenity battles, including Barney Rosset of Grove Press, Raymond Gauer of Citizens for Decent Literature, and *Screw* magazine's Jim Buckley and Al Goldstein.[15] The academy's confirmation of the cultural significance of porn affirmed the fact that by 1973 hard core was no longer so significant anymore.[16]

HAS THE SUPREME COURT SAVED US
FROM OBSCENITY?

The issue of obscenity as it is posed in court requires the balancing of
the offensiveness of the work in question against its social value . . . the
balancing of its aphrodisiacal properties against its formal, informa-
tional and ideological ones.

—Judge Richard A. Posner, *Sex and Reason*

A little over a month after the Supreme Court announced its decision
in *Miller v. California*, the *New York Times* ran an Arts and Leisure feature titled "Has the Supreme Court Saved Us from Obscenity?"[17] The
feature contained reactions from fifteen interested parties: the cartoonist and scenarist Jules Feiffer, the actress Joan Crawford, the
blacksploitation (and X-rated) moviemaker Melvin van Peebles, the
Deep Throat auteur Gerard Damiano, the conservative political com-
mentator William Buckley, the actress and author Chris Chase, the
writer-director Paul Mazursky, MPAA president Jack Valenti, the actress Shelley Winters, the *New Yorker* film critic and screenwriter
Penelope Gilliatt, the law professor Harry Kalven Jr., the Reverend
Malcolm Boyd (an Episcopal priest), the serially banned novelist and
essayist Henry Miller, the attorney Ephraim London, and United
Artists president David Picker.[18]

The *Times'* selection of contributors was hardly balanced or bipar-
tisan. Only Buckley seemed to have much use for the Burger Court's
retrenchment.[19] The *Times* feature seems instead, especially today,
very much the sort of thing one might find in a time capsule: what
were some interesting, mostly like-minded people in the film and culture business in 1973 thinking when they were actually thinking
about pornography?

Under the title "Art for Court's Sake," Feiffer asserted that "Movies,
which in the past were made to please banks, will in the future be made
to please courts." Feiffer predicted that the *Miller* decision would not
decrease the number of obscenity cases reaching the Court but instead
would generate a new "obscenity bureaucracy" manned by "Talmudic
authorities on community standards." At the heart of Feiffer's nightmare vision of the future of "art for court's sake" was a portable elec-
tronic, and thus wholly unsubjective and unevaluative, censorship. He
foresaw the federal financing of "an automatic . . . community bleeping

system." Such a system was not available in 1973, but it is of course much in the news these days, as Congress and the television industry continue to debate and develop the V-chip to select out films with certain images and dialogue deemed offensive to children and other impressionable audiences.[20]

At the end of his essay Feiffer wrote, "we claim to be committed to [liberty and freedom], but look close and you will see that the freedom to which we commit ourselves is freedom *from*, not freedom *to*. Freedom from those guys, freedom from weird ideas, freedom from bother, freedom from thought, freedom from equality, freedom from art, freedom from sex." A similar argument regarding obscenity and larger civil libertarian concerns lay at the heart of van Peebles's entry. The director of the controversial X-rated comedy *Sweet Sweetback's Badass Song* deftly aligned the (always political) censorship of art with larger and related issues regarding race, identity, and efforts to abridge or restrict civil rights.[21] "My shiftless behind must have slept through the whole thing," van Peebles wrote. "NEW OBSCENITY RULING!!!??? Lord, lord, new rulings and here me I haven't run into no relevant old obscenity laws." For van Peebles, the various old production codes and state and local censorship guidelines served the status quo because they reenforced white authority ("massa disguised behind a badge") and kept certain races in their places ("Tonto getting done in [long on nobility but short on victory]"). The *Miller* decision was a huge step backwards, van Peebles argued. It made legal or legitimate once again the very sort of restrictions that forced African American artists like him into marginal, counterculture enterprises and ensured that the dominant, studio product adhered to certain standards and practices—images and narratives—that were at once repressive and racist.[22]

Both veteran actresses, Joan Crawford and Shelley Winters, viewed the *Miller* decision as a return to the not so good old days of moviemaking under the watchful eye of the PCA. An anecdote told by Winters about shooting a scene under the old code spoke volumes on what she termed the "terrifying, costly and certainly artistically stultifying" effect of content censorship:

I recall *A Double Life*, during a scene in which Ronald Colman enacted *Othello* and strangled me as his fantasy Desdemona, everyone on the set had to sit down and wait an hour. The Breen Office came down to the set and gave us a decision as to how the scene could be shot so that it would be acceptable in the 48 states. After another hour . . . it was decided that if we pasted my nightgown close to my chest, above my bosoms, and the camera saw one of Mr. Colman's feet on the floor, the implications of the scene would probably be acceptable. I never understood why one foot was better than no feet or two feet. But maybe there was something about sex the Legion of Decency knows that I don't.[23]

The two attorneys, Harry Kalven Jr. and Ephraim London, expressed their discomfort with the ways the *Miller* decision effectively recriminalized pornography. Kalven predicted a "flood of new cases"—beginning with the Georgia ban against the screening of *Carnal Knowledge*—requiring the Court "to tell us which explicit treatment of sex lacks 'serious value'" and warned that the new guidelines would pose "intractable problems of administration" and more importantly would "justify the solemn intervention by the state to police the fantasies of its sexually experienced adult citizens."[24] Ephraim London, the other attorney polled, focused on the "determination of [serious, artistic] value" made by judges and jurors, individuals "without qualifications to make [such] a judgment." By way of example, London posed the following scenario: "if an unknown artist of Picasso's genius created and exhibited erotic paintings (as Picasso did), how many judges and juries would find his or her work to be of serious artistic value."[25]

United Artists president David Picker, the lone studio player in the mix, expressed concern about how the new rulings might affect theatrical exhibitors, many of whom had only just gotten used to their role in the enforcement end of the MPAA rating system. "Theater operators will be forced to run scared because of suddenly legitimized local pressure groups," Picker wrote. "Some [theater owners] will stand and fight. Some must stand and fight. And they will." Such fighting words may have been self serving at the time. The studio executive, after all, was not in the exhibition business quite yet. But he was certainly right that theater owners were once again on the front lines enforcing the new rating system for the studios.[26]

Writing on behalf of the MPAA, Valenti was at once sober and realistic. Beneath the misleading title "Censorship Is Deadly" he wrote, "It is plain that the Supreme Court decision is aimed at so-called hard-core pornography. The responsible motion picture companies and producers in this country who create theatrical entertainment films are not the target of the decision." Touting the value of "voluntary controls" adopted by "a free film industry," controls that allow adults "to make their own free choice of viewing, without imposing that choice on others," Valenti promised only good times to come, so long as the studios hung tough with the MPAA. He elaborated a personal distaste for censorship in general: "You can't put tape over the mouths of artists, handcuff them to a legal stockade, and expect creative progress to be made." Nonetheless Valenti used the *Miller* decision and the accompanying move to the Right at the Court as an excuse to publicly insist once again on studio loyalty to the new rating system.[27]

As Valenti and Picker suggest in their separate essays, after 1973 theater owners bore the brunt of local censorship at a cost of revenue, jail time for employees, and the constant anxiety and headache of dealing with informal, extralegal censorship activity. The studios, on the other hand, kept their distance from the fray and leaned all the more heavily on the new rating system, which as Valenti had promised from the start, kept them safe and profitable. After *Jenkins v. Georgia* it became clear that an R rating pretty much guaranteed that a film was not, legally speaking, hard core. On quite the other hand, films receiving an X from the CARA board, as well as films sporting self-imposed X ratings, were fair game for local prosecution. After 1973 the studios would not have had it any other way.

YOUNG v. AMERICAN MINI THEATERS

Time Sq. Sex Films Shill for Prosties.

—*Variety* headline, 1970

To what extent a city council might protect certain neighborhoods against the legal exhibition of hard-core films was a question posed in the industry trades as early as 1970. News items like "Porno Sinema Tone Hurts N.Y." and "If Legit Goes It's Kayo to N.Y. Tourism" focused ably on the macroeconomic impact of porn.[28] But the issue was not fully settled until 1976, when the constitutionality of a 1972 Detroit Anti–Skid Row Ordinance came under the scrutiny of the U.S. Supreme Court in *Young v. American Mini-Theaters.*[29]

The Detroit Anti–Skid Row Ordinance provided that "an adult theater may not (apart from a special waiver) be located within 1,000 feet of any two other 'regulated uses' or within 500 feet of a residential area." *Young v. American Mini-Theaters* concerned two separately owned theaters: the Nortown, a once legit theater that converted to hard core early in 1973, and the Pussy Cat, a gas station remodeled into a "mini-theater." Both theaters were within a thousand feet of two other "regulated uses" and the Pussy Cat was also less than five hundred feet from a residential area. A U.S. district court found in favor of the city's right to enforce the Anti–Skid Row Ordinance, but the decision was reversed by a U.S. court of appeals.

By a five-to-four vote, the Supreme Court decided to reverse the appeals court decision and found in favor of the Detroit city council. Writing for the Court (in an opinion signed in full or in part by Justices Byron White, Lewis Powell, and William Rehnquist, and Chief Justice Warren Burger), Justice John Paul Stevens argued that "the 1,000-foot restriction [did] not, in itself, create an impermissible restraint on protected communication." Stevens upheld the city's interests and rights in planning and regulating the use of property for commercial purposes and in doing so gave cities nationwide the ability to ghettoize, effectively regulate, and limit if not fully eliminate the public exhibition of hard core.

Stevens's opinion is worth a close look here because it went far beyond the specific public use questions raised in the case. In the third part of his three-part opinion, speaking for himself and three other justices, Stevens wrote, "The question whether free speech is, or is not, protected by the First Amendment often depends on the content of the speech. Thus, the line between permissible advocacy and impermissible incitation to crime or violence depends not merely on the setting in which the speech occurs, but also on exactly what the speaker had to say." Later in the same section, Stevens continued to qualify guarantees outlined in the First Amendment: "few of us would march our sons and daughters off to war to preserve the citizen's right to see 'Specified Sexual Activities' exhibited in theaters of our choice. Even though the First Amendment protects communication in this area from total suppression, we hold that the State may legitimately use the content of these materials as the basis for placing them in a different classification from other motion pictures."[30]

In a pointed dissent, Justice Potter Stewart focused specifically on Stevens's remark that "few of us" would support going to war to protect a theater owner's right to screen a dirty movie. Stewart suggested that the Bill of Rights was designed precisely to protect minoritarian interests: "For if the guarantees of the First Amendment were reserved for expression that more than a 'few of us' would take up arms to defend, then the right of free expression would be defined and circumscribed by current popular opinion. The guarantees of the Bill of Rights were designed to protect against such majoritarian limitations on individual liberty."

In a separate dissent, Justice Harry Blackmun wrote on behalf of the businessmen who, regardless of the product they hawked, were unduly and unfairly damaged by the Detroit ordinance.

> We should put ourselves for a moment in the shoes of the motion picture exhibitor. . . . His task of determining whether his own theater is "adult" [a complicated issue, in itself] is suddenly multiplied by however many neighbors he may have that arguably are within the same class. He must, in other words, know and evaluate not only his own films, but those of any competitor within 1,000 feet. And neighboring theaters are not his only worry, since the list of regulated uses also includes "adult" bookstores, "Group D" cabarets, sellers of alcoholic beverages for consumption on the premises, hotels, motels, pawnshops, pool halls, public lodging houses, "secondhand stores," shoeshine parlors, and "taxi dance halls." . . . The exhibitor's compounded task of applying the statutory definitions to himself and his neighbors, furthermore, is an ongoing one.

This unfair and impossible burden placed on small businessmen, Blackmun concluded, was further complicated by the vague and overbroad criteria established in the ordinance, which "left to the interpretation and application of law enforcement authorities" the task of *defining* as well as enforcing the law.

As Blackmun aptly pointed out in his dissent, the problem for theater owners booking hard-core films after 1973 was twofold. Local censorship guidelines posed one sort of problem. So long as local authorities employed criteria roughly consistent with the standard established in the *Miller* case, specific screenings of specific films could be enjoined and theater managers and owners fined and jailed. After the Court's decision in *Young v. American Mini Theaters*, cities were free to develop and adopt restrictive zoning practices that could force a theater owner to either change the sort of films he or she booked or be shut down in accordance with a city cleanup effort.

THE RETURN OF THE REPRESSED: LOCAL CENSORSHIP IN THE 1980S

INTERVIEWER: Are you amazed that [so many] people go to your films?
BRIAN DE PALMA: I certainly wouldn't go see them.
                    —Brian De Palma interviewed by Marcia Pally
                                    after the release of *Body Double*

The opening title sequence in Brian De Palma's breakthrough film, *Carrie*, takes us into a high school girls' locker room. The scene is shot in soft focus and slow motion with soundtrack music and effects that sound an awful lot like heavy breathing. The camera tracks, actually floats, through the steamy locker room, then locks down in the shower to focus on the film's heroine, Carrie White, who discovers in the first arrival of her menstrual blood a whole new set of problems, beginning with an escalation of the sort of peer torture she has come to expect and loathe at her high school and ending with a kind of cosmic payback in which the trickle of blood between her legs is avenged in a bloodbath that virtually annihilates her fellow classmates at the senior prom.

De Palma has shot a number of shower scenes in his career: there's the comic scene in one of his first films, *Phantom of the Paradise*, which borrows camera angles, pacing, and sound effects from Hitchcock's *Psycho*. And, more famously, there are the two violent/erotic shower scenes that frame *Dressed to Kill*, both of which carry the threat of rape and murder. The shower scenes seem at first little more than a nod to Hitchcock, to whom De Palma nods a whole lot. But even as they are a sort of *hommage*, they function within his cinema—especially in his two controversial eighties suspense pictures, *Dressed to Kill* and *Body Double*—as a deft exploration of the distinction(s) between hard core and soft core.

De Palma's complex and controversial cinema has routinely posed problems for both the CARA board and, in the wake of the *Miller* decision, local censors and grassroots organizations. First cuts of both *Dressed to Kill* and *Body Double* received X ratings from the CARA board. And while both films reached the marketplace rated R, local censors and grassroots organizations targeted local theaters exhibiting the films.

Dressed to Kill was released at the end of the 1980 summer season but it was a notorious property long before then, thanks in large part to

"The second before she screams will be the most frightening moment of your life." The first of two "killer" shower scenes in Brian De Palma's *Dressed to Kill* (Filmways, 1980).

the legendary B movie producer Samuel Z. Arkoff, the chairman of American International Pictures (AIP), who developed and coordinated the promotion and distribution of the film for Filmways. Arkoff had over two decades' experience in the B movie business and by 1980 had mounted successful exploitation circuit releases for such legendary titles as *Beach Party, The Trip, The Wild Angels, Wild in the Streets,* and *Three in the Attic.*[31] Though nominally a Filmways release, *Dressed to Kill* was Arkoff's picture. Its success at the box office and its larger success in making De Palma a notorious and bankable auteur were in large part the work of the exploitation industry veteran, who was peculiarly able to exploit the hysteria that accompanied the release of the film.

When the CARA board initially indicated that *Dressed to Kill* would probably receive an X rating, most mainstream industry executives would have panicked. But Arkoff understood that the preliminary rating was mostly good news. So long as De Palma could somehow cut the film to suit CARA—and he had to in order to cash Arkoff's check—the R-rated version of the film would be immediately notorious and easily exploitable. As per his contract with AIP, De Palma complied with CARA; he reedited the opening shower sequence (not to change its rape-fantasy content, but to airbrush out the body double's pubic hair) and in a few cases tempered the intensity of the sexual violence by shortening or selectively editing certain scenes. When De Palma complained in the press about having to cut to suit the CARA board, Jack Valenti publicly supported the censors' treatment of the film and its filmmaker: "The political climate in this country is shifting to the right, and that means more conservative attitudes towards sex and violence." As Valenti had maintained from the start, the CARA board was designed to respond to changing cultural attitudes and it was up to moviemakers to adapt to these changes. As the United States geared up for the Reagan/Bush regime, a growing distance emerged between those who made art, many of whom were young and political in the sixties, and those who constituted the retooled silent, moral majority. "A lot of creative people," Valenti observed, "are still living in the world of revolution."[32]

The print campaigns supporting the release of *Dressed to Kill* highlighted the very things that troubled the CARA board and later the local protesters as well. The first two ads appeared in the *New York Times* on August 4, 1980. The first showed an unidentified woman taking a shower, unaware of a shadowy presence lurking beside her. The ad copy accompanying the telling graphic read, "Brian De Palma, the modern master of the macabre, invites you to an evening of extreme terror." The second ad was thematically much like the first: we see a woman peeling off a stocking, unaware that a shadowy figure lurking nearby is watching her. The tag line for this second ad read, "Brian De Palma, master of the macabre, invites you to a showing of the latest fashion . . . in murder." The third and last ad ran subsequently in daily newspapers nationwide. It depicted a woman (actually a man in drag, but you had to see the film to know that) in dark glasses wielding a straight razor, which bore the reflection of actress Angie Dickinson screaming in fear. The tag line read, "The second before she screams will be the most frightening moment of your life."[33]

The first two ads were designed with the *New York Times'* readership in mind. They highlighted De Palma's auteur status (confirmed three years earlier with *Carrie*) and his reputation (off only one good film to that point) as the next Hitchcock. The third ad, which was used in pretty much every other venue nationwide, featured an exploitation-style tag line offering the familiar huckster's promise that *Dressed to Kill* was the scariest film ever. As one Filmways executive remarked in the *Los Angeles Herald Examiner*, the studio used the B movie ad slick to target a "less demanding audience," one more likely to "respond to thrills" than deft camera work and classic film allusions.[34] The three ads affirm the film's multiple appeal, its multiple demographics (those inclined to see the film because of its director as well as those inclined to see the film because it was scarier than the last scariest film ever). But while the targets for the ads may have been different, all three pictorially conflate the erotic and the violent through the familiar suspense movie poster imagery of the solitary woman under threat. Some things, we might gather from this well-orchestrated ad campaign, work for all audiences.

What to make of and do about the controversial content in *Dressed to Kill* was complicated by the fact that many mainstream critics praised the film.[35] In perhaps the most widely read opening day review, Vincent Canby of the *New York Times* touted De Palma as "an unmistakable talent" and *Dressed to Kill* as "a witty, romantic, psychological horror film."[36] Pauline Kael in the *New Yorker* applauded De Palma for defying the very boundaries of good taste that would soon get him and the film into trouble with local activists: "De Palma has perfected a near surreal poetic voyeurism—the stylized expression of a blissfully dirty mind. He doesn't use art for voyeuristic purposes; he uses voyeurism as a strategy and a theme—to fuel his satiric art."[37] Writing for *New York* magazine in an article suggestively titled "Deep Threat," David Denby similarly affirmed the film's deft mix of horror and satire: "[*Dressed to Kill*] is the first great American movie of the eighties. Violent, erotic, and wickedly funny, *Dressed to Kill* is propelled forward by scenes so juicily sensational that they pass over into absurdity. De Palma releases terror in laughter: Even at his most outrageous, Hitchcock could not have been as entertaining as this."[38]

The organized protest by antiporn groups at theaters screening the picture was slow in coming and seems in retrospect less an expression of rage against one upsetting film than astonishment and disappointment at the critics' and audience's anxiousness to take pleasure in the film's nasty content. The first protests organized by Women Against Violence Against Women (WAVAW) and Women Against Pornography (WAP) in New York, Boston, Los Angeles, and San Francisco were not staged until after *Dressed to Kill* had been on screens for well over two weeks and the film's initial grosses had already crossed the $15 million mark, two and a half times its production budget.[39]

The protests were well organized and the arguments presented by WAVAW and WAP were hard to dismiss. The film was violent and the very satire so appreciated by the critics was plenty expensive for women. But the on-street protests did little but call attention to a film already very much in the public's eye. Legend has it that Arkoff so appreciated the attention he got from the women's groups, he staged some of the protests himself, with paid actors carrying signs condemning the film. WAVAW and WAP and Arkoff's rigged protests had a significant impact on the film's first run. In the week following the first protests, *Dressed to Kill* climbed from number three to number one on *Variety*'s top fifty box office list, ahead of two of the year's biggest titles, *Airplane* and *The Empire Strikes Back*.[40]

Local efforts to obstruct the screening of other such controversial or offensive titles had pretty much the same unintended result. Street protests against *Colors* and *Basic Instinct*, for example, had the effect of making bad films important.

The few grassroots protests that worked after 1968 worked only because the industry let them work. Case in point: Martin Scorsese's *The Last Temptation of Christ*, a big-budget feature distributed by Universal that met with significant opposition first from the Religious Right and conservatives in the Republican Party and then, far more effectively, from industry players who helped kill the film not because they feared public pressure or bad public relations but just because they too objected to what the film made of the story of Jesus' life.

Like *Dressed to Kill, The Last Temptation of Christ* was notorious well before it opened theatrically. Those inclined to take sides early on used the film to say larger, uglier things about the film industry and the culturally diverse, melting-pot culture it serves. For example, in an op-ed piece first published in the *Philadelphia Inquirer* well before the mass audience had a chance to see the film, Pat Buchanan used the furor surrounding the picture to blast the mostly Jewish management at Universal and its parent company MCA for making and planning to distribute the film. Writing on behalf of "Christians, America's unfashionable majority," Buchanan wrote, "The issue is not whether *The Last Temptation of Christ* can be shown, but whether such a film should be shown. . . . Hollywood is assaulting the Christian community in a way it would never dare assault the black community, the Jewish community or the gay community."[41]

Jack Valenti countered Buchanan in a *Variety* news story titled

"MPAA Supports Universal's 'Temptation.'" "The key issue, the only issue, is whether or not self-appointed groups can prevent a film from being exhibited to the public," Valenti wrote. "The major companies of the MPAA support MCA/Universal in its absolute right to offer to the people whatever movie it chooses."[42]

It seemed safe to assume in 1988 that right-wing activists like Buchanan, Pat Robertson, and Donald Wildmon killed the film. But the key to killing Scorsese's film can be found instead in the delicate balance, forged in no small part by the new rating system, between exhibitors and distributors. In response to their own political or moral consciences, a number of key theater circuit owners, all of whom were members of NATO and thus party to the rating system arrangement between exhibitors and the MPAA studios, declined to book the film. James Edwards, for example, the owner of the Edwards chain in Orange County, refused to screen *The Last Temptation of Christ* and went on the record demanding changes in the content of the film before he would even consider booking it. In Oregon the Moyer/Act III chain, which controlled all but a handful of screens in the state, refused to show the film under any circumstances. The United Artists chain and General Cinema theaters, which combined owned almost 3,500 screens, also joined the boycott because management found the film offensive.[43] While theater owners are free to book any film they want these days, studios routinely reward theaters that "play along." But theater owners so disliked *The Last Temptation of Christ* that they were willing to jeopardize their relationship with Universal rather than screen it.

As the summer of 1988 came to a close, one was likely to find a screening of *The Last Temptation of Christ* only at a Cineplex Odeon theater—a chain owned and controlled by MCA/Universal—and at a few indie art houses. The lesson learned in the failed release of the film had less to do with obscenity or blasphemy or grassroots censorship than with the structure of the entertainment business at the end of the 1980s. Executives at Universal came to realize in 1988 that they would have had better luck with the film had they owned more theaters, a pay TV station, a video chain. Today, media conglomerates like Time Warner Turner, Viacom/Paramount, and Disney/Capital Cities/ABC can control the destiny of a film a whole lot better than Universal could back in 1988. These studios no longer have to worry about whether or not theaters will book their films. As in the good old days before the *Paramount* decision, they own them.

AN ORDINANCE OF THE CITY OF MINNEAPOLIS

Pornography is the theory, rape is the practice.
—Robin Morgan, antiporn feminist

In the fall of 1983 Catharine MacKinnon was just a visiting law professor at the University of Minnesota. By the end of the year she was the single most famous and interesting player in antiporn activism.

MacKinnon engineered the passage of a revolutionary antiporn city ordinance in Minneapolis. The ordinance broadly defined pornography as the "systematic practice of exploitation and subordination based on sex which differentially harms women." "Public harassment and private denigration . . . rape, battery and prostitution," MacKinnon alleged, all took root in the use and abuse of pornography. For conspiring to promote sexist violence, pornographers—defined broadly as anyone who made, sold, or used pornography—could and should be held liable in civil court for damages caused by individuals who commit sexually violent crimes as a consequence of the use of "their" hard-core materials.[44]

The Minneapolis ordinance did not survive a constitutional challenge. Neither did related ordinances in Indianapolis and Suffolk County, New York. Part of the problem with these ordinances was the overbroad definition of what could be categorized as obscene. While the courts and much of the general population were sympathetic with MacKinnon's desire to proscribe works that depicted women "being penetrated by animals" or works that explicitly presented women "who experience pleasure in being raped," the ordinance included and implied an equivalent pornography to any work in which "women are presented dehumanized as sexual objects, things or commodities." What the various courts overturning these ordinances recognized was that MacKinnon's criteria allowed for civil actions against virtually any film released since the turn of the century.

Though MacKinnon's attempt to use the courts to outlaw pornography failed, she succeeded in significantly complicating the censorship debate.[45] No longer can we assume that it is only those from the moral or Religious Right who want to rid the country of porn. The new players in content regulation are law professors and intellectuals like MacKinnon, Andrea Dworkin, and Susan Brownmiller, women who have little in common—with regard to women's rights, abortion, gun control—

with their new politically conservative allies Phyllis Schlafly, Jerry Fal-well, Buchanan, Robertson, and Wildmon.[46]

De Palma's R-rated *Body Double*, a film that includes a graphic de-piction of a woman being murdered (skewered at the end of a power drill) as well as a music video sequence (of Frankie Goes Hollywood's "Relax") staged to suggest a real hard-core film production, premiered a few months after the Minneapolis ordinance became a national news story. With an eye on both events, *Film Comment* published a special fea-ture.[47] Among those surveyed were porn producers and publishers, civil rights attorneys, and antiporn feminist activists.

Screw magazine publisher Al Goldstein provided the most enter-taining piece, at one point describing his newest adversaries in a very quotable sound bite: "Feminists are the new Nazis, and pornographers are their Jews." Questioning the logic in the alliance between antiporn feminists and the so-called moral majority on the Right—the strange al-liance between Schlafly and Dworkin, for example—Goldstein cannily observed, "Politics makes for strange bedfellows, and so does Puri-tanism." But like Larry Flynt, that other pornographer cum champion of the First Amendment, Goldstein is less an ideologue than a provoca-teur: "The feminists say they are anti-porn, pro-erotica, but they offer nothing in illustration of the latter. I wish they would offer up some of their erotica so I can jerk off to it. But the truth is it is all semantics; if you like it, it's pornography, but if they like it, it's erotica."[48]

The antiporn feminists polled by *Film Comment*, Dorchen Leidholdt and Janella Miller, countered Goldstein's call for First Amendment pro-tection for even the hardest-core materials with anecdotal evidence at-testing to the damage porn has done to specific, individual women. Such anecdotal evidence can be very moving and as such it persists at the heart of much of the antiporn literature. It is employed at length in the Meese Commission Report, for example, which highlighted, among other testimonials, stories of mind control and rape told by the former Linda Lovelace.[49]

The antiporn argument has a certain narrative if not factual appeal. "What looms large in the stories of women who work in pornography," writes Leidholdt,

> is not love of money and sex. Instead it is a history of being used for the sexual gratification and hatred (in porn the two are hard to sepa-rate) of someone with power over their very survival . . . the content of

pornography—the use of women as things, the conflation of sex and violence, the packaging of coercion as consent—is the content of these women's lives. Pornography mass markets their violation. It universalizes it. It turns the humiliation and abuse of a horribly exploited group of women into the blueprint of sexual relations for men and women everywhere."[50]

As several of the participants in the *Film Comment* feature pointed out, missing from the antiporn feminist argument is a plan for dealing with the problems caused by the very restrictions they seek. As Marcia Pally wrote, antiporn feminists fail to acknowledge how ordinances like the ones proposed in Minneapolis, Indianapolis, and Suffolk County might easily be "used to impound literature in favor of gay rights, a prochoice stand on abortion, or birth control." Margaret Sanger, Pally recalls, "was imprisoned for disseminating 'obscene' material."[51]

More problematic still was the strident antisex rhetoric characteristic of much of the antiporn feminist material. "Being fucked vaginally or anally," Leidholt writes, "is humiliating and usually painful."[52] That anything erotic could come of such an act, in her view, and in the view of many other antiporn feminists adhering to Dworkin's antimale, antisex screed, was simply ridiculous. Even for those inclined to accept the premise that porn is essentially a form of violence—it is of course defined by real depictions of real acts of penetration—and that women are in many ways and at many stages in the production-distribution-exhibition continuum exploited, even violated, the antisex rhetoric undermines the antiporn argument (with the general public at least) in much the same ways Goldstein's and Flynt's trashy macho bravado undermines their otherwise progressive views on the First Amendment.[53]

REGULATION BY CONTRACT

We went back four times before we got an R . . . we had to get rid of a few thrusts when he's having sex with the apple pie. The MPAA was like "Can he thrust two times instead of four?"

—Warren Zide, producer of the R-rated teen comedy
American Pie

Studio contracts routinely require the delivery of an MPAA-approved product: a G-, PG-, PG-13–, or R-rated film. The studios enforce these contracts because NC-17– and X-rated movies more often than not lose money.

Studio films these days are produced with an eye on a payoff in a multitude of parallel markets here and abroad: theatrical exhibition, video/laserdisk/DVD rental and sale, pay-per-view, premium cable, and network TV. Products must be able to move freely through all of these markets in order to be fully profitable. X- and NC-17–rated films are difficult to distribute and advertise and in some markets virtually impossible to exhibit. Many theater circuits do not book X- and NC-17–rated films as a matter of policy because it's less risky to book products that can play everywhere and it's easier on the circuit's booking bureaucracy to deal with all regional markets as if they are all basically the same. Multiplexes in malls are often prohibited by their lease agreement from screening films released without an MPAA seal. Blockbuster Video, by far the largest video rental outfit in the country, and discount houses like KMart won't handle such films either. None of the major premium North American cable channels—HBO, Showtime, the Movie Channel, and Cinemax—screen (uncut) X- or NC-17–rated films. And some huge foreign markets—almost the entire Asian continent, for example—prohibit the screening of X- and NC-17–rated American films.

The voluntary rating system was designed in part to allow filmmakers to make informed decisions as to what sort of product they would like to deliver and what sort of audience they might like to reach. But the necessity these days to produce a product that can move freely through all the various theatrical and ancillary markets has made it impossible for even the most powerful and popular auteurs to make movies independent of economically motivated corporate prohibitions on X- and NC-17–rated films. As the attorney Lois Sheinfeld so tersely put it in an opinion piece for *Film Comment*, "the voluntary nature of the Rating System—much emphasized by [then MPAA rating board chairman Richard] Heffner and Valenti . . . amounts to a 'voluntary' choice between economic suicide and self-subjection to a scheme of censorship more repressive than any government could get away with."[54] As Sheinfeld aptly contends, compulsory enforcement of the rating system is fundamentally unconstitutional. But the collusive and complex nature of the film business renders any attempt to play outside the rules at once futile and (economically speaking) suicidal.

When, for example, an early cut of Brian De Palma's 1983 remake of *Scarface* was saddled with an X rating and the director groused about having to cut his film to suit CARA, Universal executive Robert Rehme remarked succinctly to the press, "There is no way this company [will] send *Scarface* out in an X-rated version." Rehme left De Palma, the auteur but not the ostensible owner of the property, with a fairly simple choice. He could cut the film to secure an R rating or move on and let someone else at the studio do it for him. Four submissions of four versions of the film later, De Palma secured an R rating and finally took credit for a final final cut of the film.

X- and NC-17–rated films also present public relations problems for studios, which are, after all, owned by publicly traded companies. These publicly traded companies are run by high-profile executives whose public image is also a matter of some importance to stockholders and whose sense of control and power over media operations is often a matter of pride and personal interest. Hollywood films came to evince a studio style in the contract era. Audiences came to expect certain sorts of films from MGM, for example, and certain different sorts of films from Warner Brothers. Similarly, conglomerate CEOs, many of whom these days are celebrities in their own right, occasionally weigh in on matters of film content not only to exert their power but to impose some sort of personal stamp on the product. If they love a certain film they can put more of the company's resources behind its production and promotion. And if they hate a certain film, they can express their personal dislike and at the same time flex their corporate muscle by forcing cuts in the final print or, when such cuts are not made, delaying, sabotaging, or refusing to finance a film's release.

In the summer of 1996 David Cronenberg's austere and explicit NC-17–rated adaptation of J. G. Ballard's legendary experimental novel *Crash* won the Special Jury Prize at Cannes (rumor has it, over the strenuous objections of jury chairman Francis Coppola). Time Warner subsidiary Fine Line, which owned North American distribution rights to *Crash*, announced its intention to release the film in the United States a little over a month later. It planned the quick play-off to capitalize on the award and the controversy surrounding the film. But then Ted Turner, Time Warner vice chairman, saw the picture and hated it.

As Cronenberg tells the story, his bags were already packed for the New York premiere when Fine Line Pictures announced its decision to postpone the film's release until the following spring. The official reason given to Cronenberg and the press was that too many films were already in release at the time and the film could be platformed better in the lull before summer. Neither the director nor the media were inclined to buy the excuse. After all, the film was already playing to strong re-

Ted Turner delayed the release of David Cronenberg's *Crash* (Fine Line, 1996) for over six months. "Imagine the first teenager who decides to have sex while driving a hundred miles an hour," Turner remarked. "Probably [the movie] will get 'em to do that."

views and big audiences in Cronenberg's native Canada, riding strong word of mouth, essential with a limited-release NC-17 film. The decision to release the film in the spring, Cronenberg argued, was sure to kill the film's already limited chances at the U.S. box office, which, as things played out, was precisely Turner's plan.[55]

Time Warner spokesmen did their best to sugarcoat Turner's decision to delay and thus sabotage the release of *Crash*. But given a public forum, Turner himself was less inclined to shrink from the truth of the matter. Speaking at a museum luncheon in New York, Turner remarked, "I yanked [*Crash*] off the schedule. It bothered me . . . people with warped minds are going to like it, though. I mean it's pretty weird. . . . Imagine the first teenager who decides to have sex while driving a hundred miles an hour, and probably the movie will get 'em to do that."[56]

Cronenberg's reaction to Turner's museum speech was slow in coming. After all, Fine Line still owned distribution rights to *Crash* and Time Warner also controlled the director's slightly more mainstream title, *M Butterfly*. When Cronenberg finally spoke up, he kept his remarks simple and to the point: "[Turner] did what amounts to a behind the scenes censorship of my movie." Holly Hunter, one of the stars of the film, was less deferential. "It is very reminiscent of Jesse Helms," Hunter quipped. "Ted Turner's moral fascism has no place in the entertainment industry."[57]

Crash was eventually released in the spring of 1997 to little box office and in the United States at least mostly bad reviews. The NC-17 rating from CARA was never challenged by Fine Line, nor was Cronenberg compelled or even encouraged by the studio to cut the film in order to obtain an R rating. (It is hard to imagine how the film could have been cut to suit CARA. The sex scenes are integrated into the plot in such a way that small, specific cuts would have been impossible to make.)

Turner hated the film enough to lose money and in doing so sent a clear message to filmmakers working at his movie studios, at the time, the most extensive and prestigious in the business. In the fall of 1996, Turner directly controlled New Line and its subsidiary Fine Line, Castle Rock, HBO, Cinemax, TBS, and TNT, all of which were in the business of producing and distributing filmed product. And as Time Warner's second-in-command and its single biggest stockholder, Turner's input on the daily operation of Warner Brothers was no doubt significant as well.

In addition to undermining the release of *Crash*, Turner also interfered with the scheduled airing of two potentially controversial television movies: Angelica Huston's *Bastard Out of Carolina*, a candid adaptation of Dorothy Allison's semiautobiographical novel about her own sexual abuse as a child, and *Strange Justice*, another made-for-TNT film about sexual harassment based on a pro–Anita Hill book. According to

TNT president Brad Siegel, *Bastard Out of Carolina* was pulled because it was too graphic and too intense to air on a station that maintained a single schedule over all continental time zones. TNT could not screen *Bastard Out of Carolina*, Siegel pointed out, exclusively "after-hours": for example, scheduling the two-hour picture at prime time, 9:00 P.M. in the East, meant a family-hour 6:00 P.M. airing out west. Siegel took the film to Scott Sassa, president of the Turner Entertainment Group, who took it to Turner with the recommendation that TNT drop the picture entirely. Turner complied. Though Siegel affirms that TNT (which is supervised by Turner) had originally contracted the production of the film "because we [he and Turner, I suppose] felt [it contained] important subject matter," when the well-known actress screened her final cut for the studio brass, the very subject matter that attracted them to the project in the first place became the sole reason not to air the film.

When *Bastard Out of Carolina* premiered at the Cannes Film Festival, like many films screened there it was ostensibly a picture in search of a distributor. Off the festival playdate, the movie was picked up by Showtime, a premier cable outfit owned by Viacom/Paramount, the chief rival of the Time Warner subsidiary (and Turner-helmed) HBO. After the Showtime contract was signed, rumors began to circulate at Cannes that Showtime got the film only after Turner actively discouraged Time Warner subsidiaries New Line and Fine Line from taking on the project and as the hands-on director of operations at HBO, he had personally passed on the film as well.

The decision to postpone the airing of *Strange Justice* was pragmatic and political. The TNT film promised to embarrass Supreme Court justice Clarence Thomas. At the time of its scheduled release, the fall of 1996, the Court was due to rule on an important regulatory issue concerning cable television, the FCC's "must carry" licensing concession. Fearing retaliation from Thomas, Turner postponed the show. TNT's Siegel denied the rumors about Turner and Thomas, but the trades stuck by the story, which seemed too plausible not to be true.[58]

Turner's personal and political censorship of his own products had an immediate chilling effect on the Hollywood creative community. Milos Forman, who had just completed *The People vs. Larry Flynt* for Columbia, remarked, "[Turner's actions] will be a consideration for creative people when they have something that might be controversial." A similar reaction came from Paul Schrader, who wrote *Taxi Driver* (a film that outraged Turner enough to prompt an angry on-air editorial on CNN in 1982).[59] Schrader, who has faced his fair share of problems with industry and local censors (the nudity and violence in *The Comfort of Strangers*, which he wrote and directed, and the blasphemy in his script for *The Last Temptation of Christ*), predicted that Turner's dealings with *Crash, Bastard Out of Carolina*, and *Strange Justice* will put "a chill" not only into the creative community but "into the decision-making process of everyone underneath him." "He's become," Schrader concluded, "a bit of a culture czar."[60]

Turner has hardly shied away from such a label; indeed, he claims only that his contractual obligations to "everyone underneath him" make it difficult for him to succeed as much as he'd like. "The bigger I've gotten and the more successful . . . the more my standards have been compromised for the sake of the almighty dollar," Turner mused during his New York museum lecture. "My networks run a lot of programming that I'm not happy about and it bothers me."

As to the limited and uneventful release of *Crash*, Turner noted that the only reason the film ever got distributed at all was that he was contractually obligated to defer to New Line chairman Bob Shaye, and president Michael Lynne. Turner, Shaye, and Lynne have a "creative autonomy" agreement—an agreement binding enough to force the recalcitrant executive to allow the film's eventual release, but not so binding as to stop him from making sure as few people as possible got to see the picture. "The decision went above me," Turner noted during the museum lecture, then added, unironically, "I would have done well at Nuremberg, I guess, by blaming it on somebody else. I'm just a cog in the machine . . . "[61]

Two years later, the International Critics Prize winner at Cannes, Todd Solondz's *Happiness*, a black and tragic comedy that dared to humanize a pedophile, faced a fate similar to that of Cronenberg's *Crash*. *Happiness* was contracted to October films for its U.S. run and played in a limited engagement, on six screens in three cities, to convincing business (for an *indie*-film) in the first few weeks after the prestigious French festival. Then executives from October's corporate parent Universal got a look at the film and decided to take their name off and their money out of the picture. As *Entertainment Weekly* writer Degen Pener observed, "the fact that such a well-praised film was so easily jettisoned by the parent company [again at some modest financial loss, as in the case of Time Warner and *Crash*] points to a new reality for many independent film distributors. They aren't as independent as they used to be."[62]

Happiness was quickly but not so quietly sold back to its producers,

Ted Hope and James Schamus, and released under the Good Machine banner. The upside of the very independent release was that *Happiness* reached the marketplace unrated and unexpurgated. The downside was that the film was screened only very selectively and to date is still too controversial to be shown on cable television. It is unlikely that Hope and Schamus have made much money since they had to buy their film back from the Bronfman family (which owns Seagram/Universal) just to get it released at all in the United States. But there is little bitterness, at least publicly, in their account of the story. "You can understand Universal's position," Hope remarked. "This is the world we live in. I would love it if public companies worked on moral principles, but they don't, and I don't think the shareholders want them to." Solondz seemed curiously unperturbed as well. After all, signing with a prestige independent in the late 1990s means signing with the company that owns and occasionally exerts its complete control over it: "For Seagram, it's just not worth the flak and controversy that they anticipated. . . . What do they need this kind of headache for?"[63]

Solondz is right to characterize Seagram's decision to abandon his film in terms of larger economic issues. Seagram makes a lot of products that can be targeted by organized boycotts. Seagram is a publicly traded company. Severing its relationship with *Happiness* may have been somewhat embarrassing, especially to October, which could no longer claim independence, but it made good business sense "on the street," where stock prices are the one and only bottom line.

Turner's handling of *Crash, Bastard Out of Carolina,* and *Strange Justice* and Universal's refusal to honor the spirit if not the letter of October's obligation to Hope, Schamus, and Solondz are all small stories with big implications in contemporary American cinema. The so-called independents—at least those with the capital to bid on the bigger indie films like October, Miramax, Fox Searchlight, and Sony Classics, are all owned by and answerable to their conglomerate ownership.[64] That conglomerate ownership is often diffused by a respect for public ownership (Seagram's decision to jettison *Happiness* seems less a reflection of its ownership, Edgar Bronfman and Seagram, than ownership's acknowledgment of its investors' security and the potential impact of an organized boycott). More interestingly, some conglomerates are ruled by a single, iconic figure at the top: Turner, the News Corporation's Rupert Murdoch (a right-wing activist and big contributor to Newt Gingrich's archconservative political action committee), Blockbuster Video's Wayne Huizenga (who at one time had a whole lot to say about what happened at Viacom/Paramount), and Barry Diller, who in 1999 acquired October, Grammercy, and Propaganda from Universal and Polygram.

At present, Murdoch's influence can be most clearly felt on his news channels. In 1999 there was little besides "get Clinton" political talk and call-in shows to be had on his cable subsidiary. But the Fox film studios, Fox Searchlight, and the Fox television network are all under his control and all at his disposal should he ever want to use them too. At Viacom/Paramount these days, Huizenga is pretty much out of the picture, but there was a time not so long ago—1994 to be precise—when Viacom's Sumner Redstone needed Huizenga's money to outbid cable rival John Malone for control of Paramount Communications.[65] Huizenga's Blockbuster Video, by far the nation's largest video rental chain, continues to refuse to carry porn, independently released or even studio-made unrated, X, or NC-17 titles.[66] Since well over 50 percent of domestic revenues these days comes from so-called home box office (video sales, rental, pay-per-view, and cable television), getting on Blockbuster's shelves was and still is absolutely essential. Huizenga's store policies never fully influenced things at Paramount or at its premier cable stations, Showtime and the Movie Channel, but the possibility (back in 1994) that he might parlay his stock position in the company to exert such an influence over day-to-day operations at the movie studio had a sobering effect on creative people bringing their projects there and on division heads (at Paramount, Showtime, the Movie Channel, and MTV) afraid of offending the company's (at one time) single biggest shareholder.

Huizenga, much to Redstone's relief, is no longer in charge at Blockbuster. And for reasons directly related to Huizenga's policy regarding non–MPAA-approved titles, Blockbuster has hit hard times. When Redstone hired former Taco Bell executive John Anticoco to take over and save Blockbuster, industry analysts advised the new chief executive to abandon the chain's pro-family image and begin to carry X- and NC-17 rated and more importantly hard-core titles, which account for as much as 30 percent of over-the-counter rentals nationwide.[67]

Of the new moguls in charge of alternative/independent studios, Barry Diller is the most difficult to read or predict. He is deservedly a legendary Hollywood success story: he quit college at nineteen to work in the William Morris Agency mailroom and worked his way up through the ranks, eventually landing top executive posts at ABC-TV,

Paramount, and then Fox. Diller's holdings when he purchased October in the spring of 1999 included the Home Shopping Network, the
USA network, the Sci-Fi Channel, a diverse group of syndicated television shows (*Law and Order*, the *Jerry Springer Show*, *Xena: Warrior
Princess*, and *Silk Stalkings*), the online guide Citysearch, and Ticket-
master. Just how October, Grammercy, and Propaganda fit into such a
diverse set of holdings—just how Diller's powerful personality might
be manifested in or reflected by the decisions he makes on behalf of
these companies—is anybody's guess.[68]

LOLITA, 1997

Lolita: legally 18, must look 13–17, she is very much a regular American kid, but more knowing, sensual and un-inhibited than we might
expect. Possesses the sort of ambiguous beauty that can go from childlike to intensely erotic at the blink of an eye. A combination of innocence and provocation that should affect every man in the audience.
Nudity required.

—casting call for Adrian Lyne's *Lolita*

The remake of *Lolita* was first set in motion in 1990 when Carolco Pictures obtained (for $1 million) an option from the Nabokov estate to
adapt the novel. Attached to the project from the start was the director
Adrian Lyne, a savvy Hollywood player and bankable auteur whose
films included *Flashdance, 9 1/2 Weeks, Fatal Attraction*, and *Indecent Proposal*. Unlike Stanley Kubrick, who by 1962 brought a semblance of se-
riousness to the project, Lyne seemed altogether a different sort of
player, a talented Hollywood director with a canny take on the American zeitgeist and a history of pushing the rating system envelope to as-
tounding box office success.

The development of this second *Lolita* was slow.[69] Two related
"problems" delayed the onset of principal photography: (1) the screenplay, which had to remain faithful to the novel while at the same time
present Lyne and Carolco with an R-rated film, and (2) increased social
awareness of and an accompanying moral outrage (fueled by talk
shows that now dominate daytime TV) at the crime of child molestation
and abuse.

The first screenplay was written by James Deardon, the credited
screenwriter on Lyne's notorious thriller *Fatal Attraction*. Deardon, or so

the Hollywood rumor mill had it at the time, wrote a sexually explicit script, too strong for Lyne or the production company to shoot.[70] In 1994 the playwright Harold Pinter was retained, no doubt to lend credibility to the project. Pinter's version was cold, asexual, and condemning of Humbert as a sociopath and moral leper. Later in the same year, Pinter was replaced with the American playwright and screenwriter David Mamet, who, at the behest of Richard Zanuck, a veteran executive attached to the ongoing development of the project, was asked to write a relationship picture with moments of tenderness and humor. Mamet instead delivered an even more damning portrait of Humbert the pedophile.[71] Stephen Schiff, who would eventually receive credit for the screenplay, was hired in July 1995, about five years into the development of the project. Drawing liberally from his predecessors' work, Schiff quickly delivered a filmable draft.

Lolita went into production with two significant public relations problems. Both, it soon became clear, were too much for Lyne or his producers to control or combat. As with a lot of Hollywood films that take a long time to get started and feature a history of revised and discarded scripts, Lolita was tagged in the trades as an unfilmable, doomed project. The negative buzz was complicated by the fact that the topic of the screenplay—Humbert's affair with his underage stepdaughter—was, to many in the business, unfilmable and doomed in the first place.

The second problem involved timing—bad timing. Through the five years from the option sale to the start of principal photography, the news was filled with terrifying stories of abused children: the murder of JonBenet Ramsey, the abduction and murder of Polly Klaas, the rape and murder of Megan Kanka (and the law named for her that now allows police to notify residents when a convicted child molester moves into their neighborhood). Perhaps more troubling was the vaguely (and for the producers disconcertingly) worded Child Pornography Prevention Act, passed by Congress while the film languished in development, which forbade "any visual depiction that is or appears to be of a minor engaging in sexually explicit conduct."

By the time Lyne had completed a rough cut, Lolita was simply the wrong film at the wrong time. And unlike Crash and Happiness, two modestly budgeted films that ran into problems with their distributors after they were contracted for release and the producers were paid, Lolita was a $58 million picture in search of a distribution deal when Lyne submitted the film to various festivals in Europe.[72] Left holding the bag, so to speak, was a French company, Chargeurs, which had purchased the rights from Carolco and had no clout whatsoever in Hollywood. What it had instead was a film the trades and entertainment press characterized as "borderline pervy," a film "no one [in Hollywood] will touch."[73]

Lyne submitted the film to the CARA board in February 1997. By then he had already carefully considered the board's potential reaction to the film. At one point late in the process, Lyne shared supervision over the final cut with an attorney specializing in obscenity law. The nude scenes (of a nineteen-year-old body double) were excised and a number of other scenes were reworked in accordance with the new law(s). "If the lawyer felt kind of aroused we had to cut," quipped Schiff. "Having a lawyer in the editing room is something that shouldn't happen to a dog. And if it happened more often, only dogs would make films."[74]

The lawyer's practical suggestions made a difference, and *Lolita* received an R on its first CARA screening. But even with the MPAA seal of approval, Lyne found no takers for the film in Hollywood. There are, after all, several ways films get censored these days.

By the start of 1997 the studio line on Lyne's *Lolita* was that it was an expensive art picture with little chance of making much money at the box office and a much stronger likelihood of making things worse with folks in Congress who, in a flurry of election year rhetoric, had resumed blasting Hollywood. Lyne was shopping *Lolita* at the very moment players in Washington, D.C., were blaming the studios for everything from child molestation to school shootings.

When Chargeurs and its European distribution partner Pathe failed to secure a theatrical distributor for *Lolita*, Showtime, which had contracted to screen *Bastard Out of Carolina* when Turner refused to air the show on TNT, stepped in and paid $4 million for an exclusive pay-TV run. Like its chief rival HBO ("It's not TV, it's HBO!"), Showtime prides itself on airing programs (under its "No Limits" banner) that otherwise cannot be shown on network and basic cable television. Lyne put on the best face possible and applauded Showtime's courage. But even when the Samuel Goldwyn Company contracted to release the film theatrically in the United States (and Lions Gate, one of the last of the real independents, picked up the film in Canada), it was clear to Lyne and all involved in the production that like *The Last Temptation of Christ*, *Lolita* was destined to be one of those controversial films most of the American public would never get a chance to see.

There is an object lesson to be found in the limited release of *Lolita*.

Unlike the major studios, which continue to protect their public image and decline to take risks with films that might cause them trouble with the general public, Showtime successfully hawked *Lolita* as a film everyone else in the business was too "chicken" to screen. Samuel Goldwyn, on the other hand, a low-profile independent owned by MGM, quietly booked the film into selected urban markets. The U.S. release print carried the Goldwyn logo. MGM opted to leave the lion, its trademark, out of the controversy altogether.

SUMMER 1999: TWO FILMS RATED NC-17, THEN R

In a temporary world, it is fascinating to find something that endures. The reason is rather simple, in spite of almost daily criticism by those in the industry and outside of it, the [rating] system is accomplishing what it set out to do. It is providing a service to parents of young children. No other industry has made and redeemed such a pledge on a purely voluntary basis.

—Jack Valenti, MPAA president and CEO

In 1990 the MPAA issued a new rating designation, NC-17. The NC-17 was added to classify and by classification legitimize studio-produced, soft-core, adults-only films. The first film released with an NC-17 tag was Philip Kaufman's *Henry and June*, a frank if not all that graphic retelling of Henry Miller's adventures in Paris with two sexually liberated women, his wife, June, and fellow author Anaîs Nin. At the time, it seemed the perfect film to introduce the new designation: *Henry and June* was a gorgeously shot, serious bio-pic by a director with a considerable reputation.[75] It was a hard film to dismiss as just porn, but it was also a difficult and expensive art movie about an all too little known American writer with no stars and no high concept. Though the NC-17 got *Henry and June* into the legit marketplace, the film failed to make much of an impact at the box office, for reasons that had nothing to do with its rating.

The NC-17 designation is now reserved for films that fall through the cracks in the regulatory process—films that are so pervasively NC-17 that there is no way for filmmakers to cut to suit the CARA board. The most famous and the most historically important NC-17 title ever released in the United States is not *Henry and June* but *Showgirls*, a film no one was ever inclined to take seriously. *Showgirls*, even with big studio money and advertising behind it, bombed at the box office. Conventional wisdom in Hollywood today is that it is impossible to make money on an NC-17 title in theaters.

The NC-17 tag can be used to advantage in certain ancillary markets. So-called director's cuts or restored versions, often including just a minute or two of footage excised to satisfy CARA, offer additional reasons to rent or buy a video version of a film one may have already seen in a theater. Studios routinely release films in a variety of formats (video, laserdisk, DVD) and to various venues (pay-TV, pay-per-view, basic cable, network TV). The most important thing the NC-17 classification has done for the studios is that it has given them the opportunity to release the same product twice and claim, with a certain accuracy, that the two films are different enough to warrant a second look.

In the summer of 1999, two big films reached local theaters after celebrated bouts with the CARA board: Stanley Kubrick's last film, *Eyes Wide Shut,* and Trey Parker and Matt Stone's animation feature *South Park: Bigger, Louder and Uncut.* First cuts of both films received the NC-17 rating and, because of their contracts with their domestic distributors, Kubrick and Parker and Stone were compelled to cut their films in order to obtain an R rating.

Kubrick, whose film is about the impact of sexual fantasies on even the most perfect of couples and the ways sexual/erotic images both real and imagined play on all of our minds, supervised the addition of computer-generated figures to obstruct our view of the action during a long and wholly unerotic orgy scene. While Kubrick's distributor, Warner Brothers, insisted that not a single frame was cut, the effect of the computer-generated obstruction was comical.[76] Indeed, the computer-generated figures seem only to be *standing in* for the CARA board, watching the film as we watch it, putting their entire torsos in our way as we try to see what it is they can see that we can't.

When reviewers complained about the computer graphics, Warner Brothers cochairman Terry Semel offered a succinct response: "[Time Warner] is not in the NC-17 business."[77] Semel's quip is disingenuous on so many levels it is difficult to know where to start. The NC-17 cut of the Warner Brothers film, released without the computer gimmick, was in theaters in Europe at the very moment Semel made his remark. The director's cut is now available on video, laserdisk, and DVD, so Warner Brothers can cash in a second time on a film that really isn't very good the first time you see it.

South Park: Bigger, Louder and Uncut consists entirely of construction paper cutouts, crude animation that serves to highlight the animators' crude sense of humor. The film was screened by the MPAA six times. The first five times, the film was returned to Paramount with an NC-17. The sixth time proved the charm.

The dialogue between CARA and the studios is by policy confidential. The MPAA offices in New York guard CARA transcripts. All records of the rating board since its inception in 1968 are kept secret. Researchers are never granted access to official CARA materials because Jack Valenti believes that revelation, analysis, and discussion of how or why CARA rates a film R or NC-17 might compromise the board's objectivity.

In what may well have been something of a publicity gimmick, a series of confidential memos sent by the CARA board to Parker and Stone were leaked to the press. In one of the memos, reprinted in part in *Entertainment Weekly*, the filmmakers were asked to change a line of dialogue from "God fucking me up the ass" to "God's the biggest bitch of them all." After careful consideration, the board approved the use of the word "fisting," so long as its definition was excised. One board member had trouble figuring out whether or not he/she should be offended by a scene in which a cutout depiction of Winona Ryder does something seemingly unspeakable with Ping-Pong balls. Subsequent correspondence from the animators pointed out that Ryder's paddle, revealed in the last shot of the sequence, was the source of her expertise. The board accepted the explanation and okayed the scene.

The source of the leak, it turned out, was the film's executive producer, Scott Rudin, whose frustration with the board no doubt speaks for a lot of creative people in Hollywood: "The [memos were] like *Alice in Wonderland*, it was so crazy. I realize they're good people trying to do a good job, but the MPAA's not meant to be some moral arbiter of an entire culture."

Parker and Stone have proven to be savvy industry players and they have made the most of their little drama with Valenti and the CARA board.[78] "Hands down, the MPAA made our movie more graphic and subversive," the directors have boasted (and taunted) in the press. "We should send a thank-you letter to Jack Valenti. Our movie's funnier because of him." The MPAA chief doesn't argue the point: "They're trashing [the MPAA] to get attention for their film, and guess what? They have brilliantly succeeded."

However mad Valenti gets at Parker and Stone, he is no doubt happy for Paramount. *South Park* was a huge hit for the studio, even without an accurate tally of the youngsters who bought tickets at their local multiplex to G-rated films like *Tarzan* and then snuck into *South Park* when the theater manager wasn't looking. Even when filmmakers make a mockery of the process, as Parker and Stone have, the rating system is there to help everyone involved in the project to make money.

The CARA board continues to madden critics, filmgoers, occasionally even the studios. In the heat of a ratings controversy, we tend to forget that the true measure of the rating system lies not in its treatment of specific scenes in specific movies but in its maintenance of the larger network of relationships that form the new Hollywood.

In response to the New York and Los Angeles critics who railed against the MPAA's rating inconsistencies in the summer of 1999, Valenti bristled:

> When I invented this system, which is totally voluntary, it was not to placate critics—it was to protect parents. I haven't heard from a single parent who said, "Gee, I wish you'd kept that orgy in there." . . . The ratings board isn't infallible, but I don't understand why a bunch of critics are so certain that an orgy is something the rest of America would find casual. I think this system is doing exactly what it was intended to do.[79]

Valenti can afford to be so glib. The system is indeed "doing exactly what it was intended to do." As we marvel at the success of the studios these days, we need to remember that once upon a time not so very long ago the studios were not making any money. They are now. And they have Jack Valenti, the MPAA, and the film rating system to thank for it.

Appendix

THE DON'TS AND BE CAREFULS (1927)

Resolved, That those things which are included in the following list shall not appear in pictures produced by the members of this Association, irrespective of the manner in which they are treated:

1. Pointed profanity—by either title or lip—this includes the words "God," "Lord," "Jesus," "Christ" (unless they be used reverently in connection with proper religious ceremonies), "Hell," "damn," "Gawd," and every other profane and vulgar expression however it may be spelled;
2. Any licentious or suggestive nudity—in fact or in silhouette; and any lecherous or licentious notice thereof by other characters in the picture;
3. The illegal traffic in drugs;
4. Any inference of sex perversion;
5. White slavery;
6. Miscegenation (sex relationships between the white and black races);
7. Sex hygiene and venereal diseases;
8. Scenes of actual childbirth—in fact or in silhouette;
9. Children's sex organs;
10. Ridicule of the clergy;
11. Willful offense to any nation, race or creed;

And be it further resolved, That special care be exercised in the manner in which the following subjects are treated, to the end that vulgarity and suggestiveness may be eliminated and that good taste may be emphasized:

1. The use of the flag;
2. International relations (avoiding picturing in an unfavorable

light another country's religion, history, institutions, prominent people, and citizenry);

3. Arson;
4. The use of firearms;
5. Theft, robbery, safe-cracking, and dynamiting of trains, mines, building etc. (having in mind the effect which a too-detailed description of these may have upon the moron);
6. Brutality and possible gruesomeness;
7. Technique of committing murder by whatever method;
8. Methods of smuggling;
9. Third-degree methods;
10. Actual hangings or electrocutions as legal punishment for crime;
11. Sympathy for criminals;
12. Attitude toward public characters and institutions;
13. Sedition;
14. Apparent cruelty to children and animals;
15. Branding of people or animals;
16. The sale of women, or of a woman selling her virtue;
17. Rape or attempted rape;
18. First-night scenes;
19. Man and woman in bed together;
20. Deliberate seduction of girls;
21. The institution of marriage;
22. Surgical operations;
23. The use of drugs;
24. Titles or scenes having to do with law enforcement of law law-enforcing officers;
25. Excessive or lustful kissing, particularly when one character or the other is a "heavy."

THE 1930 PRODUCTION CODE

Preamble

Motion picture producers recognize the high trust and confidence which have been placed in them by the people of the world and which have made motion pictures a universal form of entertainment.

They recognize their responsibility to the public because of this trust and because entertainment and art are important influences in the life of a nation.

Hence, though regarding motion pictures primarily as entertainment without any explicit purpose of teaching or propaganda, they know that the motion picture within its own field of entertainment may be directly responsible for spiritual or moral progress, for higher types of social life, and for much correct thinking.

During the rapid transition from silent to talking pictures they realized the necessity and the opportunity of subscribing to a Code to govern the production of talking pictures and of acknowledging this responsibility.

On their part, they ask from the public and from public leaders a sympathetic understanding of their purposes and problems and a spirit of cooperation that will allow them the freedom and opportunity necessary to bring the motion picture to a still higher level of wholesome entertainment for all the people.

General Principles

1. No picture shall be produced which will lower the moral standards of those who see it. Hence the sympathy of the audience shall never be thrown to the side of crime, wrong-doing, evil or sin.
2. Correct standards of life, subject only to the requirements of drama and entertainment, shall be presented.
3. Law, natural or human, shall not be ridiculed, nor shall sympathy be created for its violation.

I. Crimes against the Law

These shall never be presented in such a way as to throw sympathy with the crime as against law and justice or to inspire others with a desire for imitation.

1. Murder
   (a) The technique of murder must be presented in a way that will not inspire imitation.
   (b) Brutal killings are not to be presented in detail.
   (c) Revenge in modern times shall not be justified.

2. Methods of crime should not be explicitly represented.
   (a) Theft, robbery, safe-cracking, and dynamiting of trains, mines, buildings, etc., should not be detailed in method.
   (b) Arson must be subject to the same safeguards.
   (c) The use of firearms should be restricted to essential.
   (d) Methods of smuggling should not be presented.
3. The illegal drug traffic must not be portrayed in such a way as to stimulate curiosity concerning the use of, or traffic in, such drugs; nor shall scenes be approved which show the use of illegal drugs, or their effects, in detail.
4. The use of liquor in American life, when not required by the plot or for proper characterization, will not be shown.

II. Sex

The sanctity of the institution of marriage and the home shall be upheld. Pictures shall not infer that low forms of sex relationship are the accepted or common thing.

1. Adultery and illicit sex, sometimes necessary plot material, must not be explicitly treated or justified, or presented attractively.
2. Scenes of passion
   (a) These should not be introduced except where they are definitely essential to the plot.
   (b) Excessive and lustful kissing, lustful embraces, suggestive postures and gestures are not to be shown.
   (c) In general, passion should be treated in such a manner as not to stimulate the lower and baser emotions.
3. Seduction or rape
   (a) These should never be more than suggested, and then only when essential for the plot. They must never be shown by explicit method.
   (b) They are never the proper subject for comedy.
4. Sex perversion or any inference to it is forbidden.
5. White slavery shall not be treated.
6. Miscegenation (sex relationship between the white and black races) is forbidden.
7. Sex hygiene and venereal diseases are not proper subjects for theatrical motion pictures.

8. Scenes of actual childbirth, in fact or in silhouette, are never to be presented.

9. Children's sex organs are never to be exposed.

III. Vulgarity

The treatment of low, disgusting, unpleasant, though not necessarily evil, subjects should be guided always by the dictates of good taste and a proper regard for the sensibilities of the audience.

IV. Obscenity

Obscenity in word, gesture, reference, song, joke or by suggestion (even when likely to be understood only by part of the audience) is forbidden.

V. Profanity

Pointed profanity and every other profane or vulgar expression, however used, is forbidden.

No approval by the Production Code Administration shall be given to the use of words and phrases in motion pictures including, but not limited to, the following:

Alley cat (applied to a woman); bat (applied to a woman); broad (applied to a woman); Bronx cheer (the sound); chippie; cocotte; God, Lord, Jesus, Christ (unless used reverently); cripes; fanny; fairy (in a vulgar sense); finger (the); fire, cries of; Gawd; goose (in a vulgar sense); "hold your hat" or "hats"; hot (applied to a woman); "in your hat"; Louse; lousy; Madam (relating to prostitution); nance, nerts; nuts (except when meaning crazy); pansy, razzberry (the sound); slut (applied to a woman); S.O.B.; son-of-a; tart; toilet gags; tom cat (applied to a man); traveling salesman and farmer's daughter jokes; whore; damn, hell (excepting when the use of said last two words shall be essential and required for portrayal, in proper historical context, of any scene or dialogue based upon historical fact or folklore, or for the presentation in proper literary context of a Biblical, or other religious quotation, or a quotation from a literary work provided that no such use shall be permitted which is intrinsically objectionable or offends good taste).

In the administration of Section V of the Production Code, the Production Code Administration may take cognizance of the fact that the following words and phrases are obviously offensive to the patrons of motion pictures in the United States and more particularly to the patrons of motion pictures in foreign countries:

Chink, Dago, Frog, Greaser, Hunkie, Kike, Nigger, Spic, Wop, Yid.

VI. Costume

1. Complete nudity is never permitted. This includes nudity in fact or in silhouette, or any licentious notice thereof by other characters in the pictures.
2. Undressing scenes should be avoided, and never used save where essential to the plot.
3. Indecent or undue exposure is forbidden.
4. Dancing costumes intended to permit undue exposure or indecent movements in the dance are forbidden.

VII. Dances

1. Dances suggesting or representing sexual actions or indecent passion are forbidden.
2. Dances which emphasize indecent movements are to be regarded as obscene.

VIII. Religion

1. No film or episode may throw ridicule on any religious faith.
2. Ministers of religion in their character as ministers of religion should not be used as comic characters or a villains.
3. Ceremonies of any definite religion should be carefully and respectfully handled.

IX. Locations

The treatment of bedrooms must be governed by good taste and delicacy.

X. National Feelings

1. The use of the flag shall be consistently respectful.

2. The history, institutions, prominent people and citizenry of all nations shall be represented fairly.

XI. Titles

Salacious, indecent, or obscene titles shall not be used.

XII. Repellent Subjects

The following subjects must be treated within the careful limits of good taste.

1. Actual hangings or electrocutions as legal punishments for crime.
2. Third-degree methods.
3. Brutality and possible gruesomeness.
4. Branding of people or animals.
5. Apparent cruelty to children or animals.
6. The sale of women, or a woman selling her virtue.
7. Surgical operations.

THE CODE OF SELF-REGULATION (REVISED EDITION, 1977)

Declaration of Principles of the Code of Self-Regulation of the Motion Picture Association

This Code is designed to keep in close harmony with the mores, the culture, the moral sense and change in our society.

The objectives of the Code are:

1. To encourage artistic expression by expanding creative freedom; and
2. To assure that the freedom which encourages the artist remains responsible and sensitive to the standards of the larger society.

Censorship is an odious enterprise. We oppose censorship and classification by governments because they are alien to the American tradition of freedom.

Much of this nation's strength and purpose is drawn from the premise that the humblest of citizens has the freedom of his own choice. Censorship destroys this freedom of choice.

It is within this framework that the Motion Picture Association continues to recognize its obligations to the society of which it is an integral part.

In our society parents are the arbiters of family conduct. Parents have the primary responsibility to guide their children in the kind of lives they lead, the character they build, the books they read, and the movies and other entertainment to which they are exposed.

The creators of motion pictures undertake a responsibility to make available pertinent information about their pictures which will assist parents to fulfill their responsibilities.

But this alone is not enough. In further recognition of our obligation to the public, and most especially to parents, we have extended the Code operation to include a nationwide voluntary film rating program which has as its prime objective a sensitive concern for children. Motion pictures will be reviewed by a Code and Rating Administration which, when it reviews a motion picture as to its conformity with the standards of the Code, will issue ratings. It is our intent that all motion pictures exhibited in the United States will carry a rating.

These ratings are:

G *All ages admitted. General audiences.*
This category includes motion pictures that in the opinion of the Code and Rating Administration would be acceptable for all audiences, without consideration of age.

PG *All ages admitted. Parental Guidance suggested. Some material may not be suitable for pre-teenagers.*
This category includes motion pictures that in the opinion of the Code and Rating Administration would be acceptable to all audiences, without consideration of age, as to which because of their theme, content and treatment, parents may wish to obtain more information for their guidance.

R *Restricted. Under 17 require accompanying parent or adult guardian.*
This category includes motion pictures that in the opinion of the Code and Rating Administration, because of their theme, content or treatment, should not be presented to persons under 17 unless accompanied by a parent or adult guardian.

X *No one under 17 admitted. (Age limit may vary in certain areas.)*
This category includes motion pictures submitted to the Code
and Rating Administration which in the opinion of the Code
and Rating Administration are rated X because of the treatment of sex, violence, crime, or profanity. Pictures rated X do
not qualify for a Code Seal. Pictures rated X should not be presented to persons under 17.

The program contemplates that any distributors outside the
membership of the Association who choose not to submit their motion pictures to the Code and Rating Administration will self-apply
the X rating.

The ratings and their meanings will be conveyed by advertising; by
displays at the theaters; and in other ways. Thus, audiences, especially
parents, will be alerted to the theme, content and treatment of movies.
Therefore, parents can determine whether a particular picture is one
which children should see at the discretion of the parent; or only when
accompanied by a parent; or should not see.

We believe self-restraint, self-regulation, to be in the American tradition. The results of self-discipline are always imperfect because that is
the nature of all things mortal. But this Code, and its administration,
will make clear that freedom of expression does not mean toleration of
license.

The test of self-restraint—the rule of reason . . . lies in the treatment
of a subject for the screen.

All members of the Motion Picture Association, as well as the National Association of Theater Owners, the International Film Importers and Distributors of America, and other independent pro-
ducer-distributors are co-operating in this endeavor. Most motion
pictures exhibited in the United States will be submitted for Code approval and rating, or for rating only, to the Code and Rating Administration. The presence of the Seal indicates to the public that a picture
has received Code approval.

We believe in and pledge our support to these deep and fundamental values in a democratic society:

Freedom of choice . . .

The right of creative man to achieve artistic excellence . . .

The importance of the role of the parent as the guide to the family's
conduct . . .

Standards for Production

In furtherance of the objectives of the Code to accord with the mores, the culture, and the moral sense of our society, the principles stated above and the following standards shall govern the Administrator in his consideration of motion pictures submitted for Code approval.

The basic dignity and value of human life shall be respected and upheld. Restraint shall be exercised in portraying the taking of life.

Evil, sin, crime and wrong-doing shall not be justified.

Special restraint shall be exercised in portraying criminal or anti-social activities in which minors participate or are involved.

Detailed and protracted acts of brutality, cruelty, physical violence, torture and abuse shall not be presented.

Indecent or undue exposure of the human body shall not be presented.

Illicit sex relationships shall not be justified. Intimate sex scenes violating common standards of decency shall not be portrayed.

Restraint and care shall be exercised in presentations dealing with sex aberrations.

Obscene speech, gestures or movements shall not be presented. Undue profanity shall not be permitted.

Religion shall not be demeaned.

Words or symbols contemptuous of racial, religious, or national groups, shall not be used so as to incite bigotry or hatred.

Excessive cruelty to animals shall not be portrayed and animals shall not be treated inhumanely.

Regulations Governing the Operation of the Motion Picture Code and Rating Administration

1. The Motion Picture Code and Rating Administration (hereinafter referred to as the Administration) is established to be composed of an Administrator and staff members, one of whom shall be experienced in the exhibition of motion pictures to the public.

2 a. All motion pictures produced or distributed by members of the Association and their subsidiaries will be submitted to the Administration for Code and Rating.

b. Non-members of the Association may submit their motion pictures to the Administration for Code approval and rating in the same manner and under the same conditions as members of the Association or may submit their motion pictures to the Administration for rating only.

3. Members and non-members who submit their motion pictures to the Administration should, prior to the commencement of the production of the motion picture, submit a script or other treatment. The administration will inform the producer in confidence whether a motion picture based upon the submitted script appears to conform to the Standards of the Code and indicate its probable rating. The final judgment of the Administration shall be made only upon the reviewing of the completed picture.

4 a. When a complete motion picture is submitted to the Administration and is approved as conforming to the Standards of the Code, it will be rated by the Administration either as G (all ages admitted—general audiences), PG (all ages admitted—parental guidance suggested), or R (restricted), according to the categories described in the Declaration of Principles.

b. Completed motion pictures submitted by non-members for rating only will be rated according to the categories described in the Declaration of Principles as G, PG, R, or X.

5. Motion pictures of member companies or their subsidiaries which are approved under the Code and rated: G, PG, or R, shall upon public release bear upon an introductory frame of every print distributed in the United States the official seal of the Association with the word "Approved" and the words "Certificate Number," followed by the number of the Certificate of Approval. Each print shall also bear a symbol of the rating assigned to it by the Administration. So far as possible the Seal of the Association and the rating shall be displayed in uniform type, size, and prominence. All prints of an approved motion picture bearing the Code seal shall be identical.

6. Motion pictures of non-member companies submitted for Code approval and rating or for rating only which receive a G, PG, or R rating shall bear such rating upon every print distributed in the Untied States, in uniform type, size, and prominence. Prints of such pictures may also display the official Seal of the Association if application is made to the Association for the Issuance of a Code Certificate number.

7. If the Administration determines that a motion picture submitted for approval and rating or rating should only should be rated X in accordance with the description of that category in the Declaration of

Principles, the symbol X must appear on all prints of the motion picture distributed in the United States in uniform type, size, and prominence and in all advertising for the picture.

8. Rating or a Rating Certificate shall condition such issuance upon the agreement by the producer or distributor that all advertising and publicity to be used for the picture shall be submitted to and approved by the Director of the Code for Advertising.

9. The producer or distributor applying for a Certificate of Approval for a picture or a Rating Certificate for those pictures receiving a rating only shall advance to the Administration at the time of application a fee in accordance with the uniform schedule of fees approved by the Board of Directors of the Association.

10. The Standards for Titles for motion pictures shall be applied by the Administration in consultation with the Director of the Code for Titles to all motion pictures submitted for approval and rating only and no motion picture for which a Certificate of Approval or Rating Certificate has been issued shall change its title without the prior approval of the Administration.

Code and Rating Appeals Board

1. A Code and Rating Appeals Board is established to be composed as follows:

(a) The President of the Motion Picture Association of America and 12 members designated by the President from the Board of Directors of the Association and executive officers of its member companies;

(b) Eight exhibitors designated by the National Association of Theater Owners from its Board of Directors;

(c) Four distributors designated by the International Film Importers and Distributors of America.

2. A pro tempore member for any particular hearing to act as a substitute for a member unable to attend may be designated in the same manner as an absent member.

3. The President of the Motion Picture Association of America shall be Chairman of the Appeals Board, and the Association shall provide its secretariat.

4. The presence of 13 members is necessary to constitute a quorum of the Appeals Board for a hearing of any appeal.

5. The Board will hear and determine appeals from:

(a) A decision of the Code and Rating Administration withholding

Code approval from a picture submitted for approval and rating and which consequently received an X rating.

(b) A decision of the Code and Rating Administration applying an X rating to a picture submitted for rating only.

On such appeals a vote of two-thirds of the members present shall be required to sustain the decision of the Administration. If the decision of the Administration is not sustained, the Board shall proceed to rate the picture appropriately by majority vote.

6. The Board will also hear and determine appeals from the decision of the Code and Rating Administration applying any rating other than X to a motion picture.

Such appeals shall be decided by majority vote. If the decision of the Administration is not sustained the Board shall proceed to rate the picture appropriately.

7. (a) An Appeal from a decision of the Administration shall be instituted by the filing of a notice of appeal addressed to the Chairman of the Appeals Board by the party which submitted the picture to the Administration.

(b) Provision shall be made for the screening by the members of the Appeals Board at the Hearing or prior thereto of a print of the motion picture identical to the one reviewed and passed upon by the Administration.

(c) The party taking the appeal and the Administration may present oral or written statements to the Board at the hearing.

(d) No member of the Appeals Board shall participate on an appeal involving a picture in which the member or any company with which he is associated has a financial interest.

(e) The appeal shall be heard and decided as expeditiously as possible and the decision shall be final.

(f) The hearing of an appeal shall commence with the screening of the motion picture involved.

(g) If either the party taking the appeal or the Code and Rating Administration desire to present oral or written statements to the Board pursuant to subparagraph (c) of Paragraph 7, any such written statement should be furnished to the Secretary at least two days before the date fixed for the hearing. The Secretary will reproduce such statements and circulate them to the members of the Appeals Board in advance or at the hearing of the appeal. Submission of written statements shall not diminish or alter the right also to present oral statements or arguments on behalf of the party taking the appeal.

(h) The Board will hear oral statements or argument on behalf of the party taking the appeal by not more than two persons, except by special permission. Oral statements or argument on behalf of the Code and Rating Administration shall be made only by the Administrator or his designated representative.

(i) Normally no more than a half hour will be allowed for oral argument to the party taking the appeal, and a like time to the Code and Rating Administration. If a party taking an appeal is of the opinion that statements or more than two persons or that additional time is necessary for adequate presentation of the appeal, he may make such a request by letter addressed to the Secretary stating the reasons why oral statements or more than two persons or more than a half hour is required for the adequate presentation of the appeal.

When such request is made by a party who is a member of the International Film Importers and Distributors of America, Inc., the Secretary shall consult with the Executive Directors or a member of the Governing Committee of that organization in determining whether and to what extent the request may be granted.

(j) In no circumstances shall the time allowed to any party for the hearing of an appeal extend beyond one hour.

A request for the participation of additional persons or for the allowance of additional time, to the extent that it is not granted, may be renewed to the Appeals Board at the commencement of the hearing of the appeal for disposition by the Appeals Board.

8. The board will also act as an advisory body on Code matters and, upon the call of the Chairman, will discuss the progress of the operation of the Code and Rating Program and review the manner of adherence to the Advertising Code.

TV PARENTAL GUIDELINES

The following categories apply to programs designed for the entire audience.

TVY All Children.
This program is designed to be appropriate for all children. Whether animated or live-action, the themes and elements in this program are specifically designed for a very young audience, including children from ages 2–6. This program is not expected to frighten younger children.

TVY7 Directed to Older Children.
This program is designed for children age 7 and above. It may be more appropriate for children who have acquired the developmental skills needed to distinguish between make-believe and reality. Themes and elements in this program may include mild fantasy violence or comedic violence, or may frighten children under the age of 7. Therefore, parents may wish to consider the suitability of this program for their very young children. Note: For those programs where fantasy violence may be more intense or more combative than other programs in this category, such programs will be designated TV-Y7-FV.

TVG General Audience.
Most parents would find this program suitable for all ages. Although this rating does not signify a program designed specifically for children, most parents may let younger children watch this program unattended. It contains little or no violence, no strong language and little or no sexual dialogue or situations.

TVPG Parental Guidance Suggested.
This program contains material that parents may find unsuitable for younger children. Many parents may want to watch it with their younger children. The theme itself may call for parental guidance and/or the program contains one or more of the following: moderate violence (V), some sexual situations (S), infrequent coarse language (L), or some suggestive dialogue (D).

TV14 Parents Strongly Cautioned.
This program contains some material that many parents would find unsuitable for children under 14 years of age. Parents are strongly urged to exercise greater care in monitoring this program and are cautioned against letting children under the age of 14 watch unattended. This program contains one or more of the following: intense violence (V), intense sexual situations (S), strong coarse language (L), or intensely suggestive dialogue (D).

TVMA Mature Audience Only.
This program is specifically designed to be viewed by adults and therefore may be unsuitable for children under 17. This program contains one or more of the following: graphic violence (V), explicit sexual activity (S), or crude indecent language (L).

Notes

NOTES TO THE INTRODUCTION

1. Armond White, "Those Who Disagree Can Kiss Jack Valenti's Ass," *NY Press and Arts Listings*, August 4–10, 1999.

2. John Cassidy, "Chaos in Hollywood: Can Science Explain Why a Movie Is a Hit or a Flop," *New Yorker*, March 31, 1997, 36.

3. Cassidy, "Chaos in Hollywood."

4. Lynda Obst, *Hello, He Lied—and Other Truths from the Hollywood Trenches* (Boston: Little, Brown, 1996), 16–17.

5. F. Scott Fitzgerald, *The Love of the Last Tycoon* (New York: Scribner's, 1993), 20.

6. Matthew J. Bruccoli, preface to *The Love of the Last Tycoon*, viii.

7. Susan Griffith and Kim Masters, *Hit and Run: How Jon Peters and Peter Guber Took Sony for a Ride in Hollywood* (New York: Simon and Schuster, 1996), 232.

8. See Jon Lewis, *Whom God Wishes to Destroy . . . Francis Coppola and the New Hollywood* (Durham: Duke University Press, 1995); "If History Has Taught Us Anything . . . Francis Coppola, Paramount Studios, and *The Godfather* Parts I, II, and III," in *Francis Ford Coppola's The Godfather Trilogy*, ed. Nick Browne (New York: Cambridge University Press, 2000), 23–56; "Disney after Disney: Family Business and the Business of Family," in *Disney Discourse: Producing the Magic Kingdom*, ed. Eric Smoodin (New York: Routledge, 1994), 87–106; "Money Matters: Hollywood in the Corporate Era," in *The New American Cinema*, ed. Jon Lewis (Durham: Duke University Press, 1998), 87–124; "Trust and Anti-Trust in the New New Hollywood," *Michigan Quarterly Review* 35, no. 1 (winter 1996): 85–105; and "The Independent Filmmaker as Tragic Hero: Francis Coppola and the New Hollywood," *Persistence of Vision*, no. 6 (1988): 26–40.

NOTES TO CHAPTER I

1. The House committee consisted of Congressmen J. Parnell Thomas (chairman), John McDowell of Pennsylvania, Richard Vail of Illinois, Richard Nixon of California, and John Rankin of Mississippi.

2. The Justice Department was particularly anxious to resume its efforts to break up the studio trusts after the war because the studios had proven

particularly unresponsive to previous consent decrees. Blind bidding and block booking continued despite prewar agreements between the studios and the Justice Department.

3. Thomas Schatz, *Boom and Bust: The American Cinema in the 1940s* (New York: Scribner's, 1997), 265.

4. Gordon Kahn, *Hollywood on Trial* (New York: Boni and Gaer, 1948), 26.

5. Kahn, *Hollywood on Trial*, 191–92.

6. The ARI report can be found in Dory Schary's papers at the University of Wisconsin, Madison. The Gallup poll results have been reprinted in a number of places, including Kahn, *Hollywood on Trial*, 177–78; and Schatz, *Boom and Bust*, 312–13. It is worth adding here that the poll data were ambiguous. The ARI poll suggested that regular moviegoers did not believe that communism was a problem in the industry. The larger Gallup poll suggested that the committee got most of its support from the least educated among the voting public, a demographic that made up a significant portion of the American population who were for some reason disinclined to go to the movies.

7. HUAC at first expressed interest in nineteen Hollywood artists, but in the first round of hearings only ten were required to appear and testify. In addition to the Hollywood Ten, the committee publicly expressed interest in Bertolt Brecht (who, after ambiguous testimony in closed session, left the United States), Richard Collins, Gordon Kahn, Howard Koch, Lewis Milestone, Larry Parks, Irving Pichel, Robert Rossen, and Waldo Salt.

8. Kahn, *Hollywood on Trial*, 189.

9. Within a year of the celebrated hearings, Thomas was found guilty of embezzling government funds and sentenced to three years in federal prison at Danbury, Connecticut. Among his fellow inmates there were Ring Lardner Jr. and Lester Cole. Though he hardly afforded the ten the courtesy let alone the right to Fifth Amendment protection, Thomas pleaded *nolo contendere*, declining to take the stand at his trial. While parole was denied for all the ten, both Thomas and fellow Red baiter (ex-)Congressman Andrew May (who was convicted on bribery charges stemming from a Defense Department scandal and served time in federal prison with Dalton Trumbo in Ashland, Kentucky) were paroled after serving less than a year.

10. *United States v. Paramount Pictures, Inc.*, 334 U.S. 131 (1948).

11. Scott's memo to Dozier and Korner is reprinted in its entirety in Larry Ceplair and Steven Englund, *The Inquisition in Hollywood: Politics in the Film Community, 1930–1960* (Garden City, NY: Anchor Press/Doubleday, 1980), 441–44.

12. The committee contended that Communist Party membership amounted to treason, but a number of formerly blacklisted writers, directors, actors, and producers were first attracted to the party in the 1930s when the Soviet Union was an ally. Many blacklistees cite as a principal reason for their interest in the party *domestic* concerns about civil rights. In his blacklist memoir,

Inside Out (New York: Knopf, 1996), Walter Bernstein makes explicit the connection between Communist Party affiliation/membership and the civil rights movement, and between the civil rights movement and Jewishness: "We were all urban, middle-class intellectuals shaped by the Depression and the war. About half of us were Jews, which did not seem to me to be disproportionate. This was where Jews belonged, wherever there was a struggle for human rights. This is what being a Jew meant" (134–35). The blacklisted screenwriter Guy Endore spoke for a significant percentage of those blacklisted in the forties and fifties when he reflected in 1964,

> I wasn't really a Communist. I didn't agree with [all of the party's doctrines]. [What] united me with it was simply the fact that they represented the most extreme protest against what I saw going on in the world. . . . I was a Communist only in the sense that I felt it would stop war and it would stop racist feelings, that it would help Jews, Negroes and so on. I wasn't a Communist in wanting the Communist Party to run the world or in wanting the ideas of Karl Marx to govern everything.

Guy Endore, *Reflections of Guy Endore*, UCLA Oral History project, 1964, 132, 140.

13. Ceplair and Englund, *The Inquisition in Hollywood*, 441–44.

14. Ceplair and Englund, *The Inquisition in Hollywood*, 318.

15. My account of Schary's testimony is based in large part on Thomas Schatz, *The Genius of the System: Hollywood Filmmaking in the Studio Era* (New York: Henry Holt, 1996), 442–49.

16. One of the victims of Hughes's cost-cutting shake-up at RKO was studio president Peter Rathvon, one of the executives responsible for green lighting *Crossfire*. Whether Rathvon was fired because of his involvement in the production of that film, and whether Schary was dumped or forced to resign for political reasons are anybody's guess these days. Hughes was an anticommunist, but at least at RKO he proved to be an unpredictable, even illogical boss. Both Rathvon and Schary were expensive managers and Hughes's treatment of them in the spring of 1948 may well have been the product of a misguided fiscal as opposed to political strategy.

17. Philip French, "No End in Sight: 100 Years of Censorship," *Index on Censorship* 24, no. 6 (1995): 24.

18. This discussion of the propaganda hearings is based in large part on Schatz, *Boom and Bust*, 38–40.

19. *Foreign Correspondent* was based on Vincent Shean's nonfiction bestseller *Personal History*, which chronicles the journalist's political awakening in fascist Spain and Germany and his role in the rescue of several Jews from Nazi tyranny. Joseph Breen, the anti-Semitic chief of the PCA, dismissed *Personal History* as "pro-Loyalist propaganda . . . pro-Jewish propaganda, and anti-Nazi

propaganda." In order to get the film made, Wanger and Hitchcock reduced Shean's personal, political story into an entertaining but relatively apolitical espionage thriller. See Schatz, *Boom and Bust*, 265–66.

20. Schatz, *Boom and Bust*, 39–40.

21. Schatz, *Boom and Bust*, 267–68.

22. An anonymous letter sent to Jack Warner after the studio announced plans to produce *Confessions of a Nazi Spy* suggests just what sort of portent: "I would suggest that after you finish the picture it would be suitable to follow with *I Am a Communist* starring Eddie Cantor and a few other Communist Jews. . . . Mr. Warner, please don't think the American people are as dumb as you think they are." The letter can be found in an MPAA file on *Confessions of a Nazi Spy* available at the Margaret Herrick Library of the Academy of Motion Picture Arts and Sciences; and in Colin Schindler, *Hollywood in Crisis: Cinema and American Society, 1929–1939* (London: Routledge, 1996), 208–9.

23. Rumors that Chaplin was (part) Jewish only increased after the release of *The Great Dictator*. Chaplin did little to quiet these rumors though they hardly helped his career or his personal security. Chaplin was only the most famous creative artist to be labeled a Jew because of his (perceived) leftist politics.

24. MPPDA document cited by Schindler in *Hollywood in Crisis*, 208. The italics are mine.

25. Schatz, *Boom and Bust*, 382.

26. Patrick McGilligan, "Tender Comrades," *Film Comment*, December 1987, 43. With Paul Buhle, McGilligan expanded these interviews under the title *Tender Comrades: A Backstory of the Hollywood Blacklist* (New York: St. Martin's, 1997).

27. Neil Gabler, *An Empire of Their Own: How the Jews Invented Hollywood* (New York: Doubleday, 1989).

28. Mayer was ousted by Nicholas Schenck after years of acrimony between Mayer and production chief Dore Schary. It takes a leap of faith to simply blame the blacklist for Mayer's exit from MGM, but the business climate created by HUAC and the *Paramount* decision exaggerated the impression that Mayer, after twenty-seven years with the studio, had outlived his usefulness. That Schenck was willing to terminate Mayer's employment at a studio that still bore Mayer's family's name reveals the growing anxiety throughout the industry in the aftershock of the HUAC hearings and the *Paramount* decision to, as Thomas Schatz so aptly puts it, "recolonize" the motion picture marketplace. See Schatz, *The Genius of the System*, 440–81.

29. Andrew Ross, *No Respect: Intellectuals and Popular Culture* (New York: Routledge, 1989), 20, 21, 25, 29.

30. Ross, *No Respect: Intellectuals and Popular Culture*, 40.

31. Robert Coover, *The Public Burning* (New York: Viking, 1976), 521–34.

32. F. Scott Fitzgerald, *The Love of the Last Tycoon* (New York: Scribner's, 1993), 92.

33. Fitzgerald, *The Love of the Last Tycoon*, 117.

34. Fitzgerald, *The Love of the Last Tycoon*, 118.

35. Fitzgerald, *The Love of the Last Tycoon*, 121.

36. Fitzgerald, *The Love of the Last Tycoon*, 121.

37. Fitzgerald, *The Love of the Last Tycoon*, 124.

38. The two opening statements admitted into evidence were provided by Alvah Bessie and Albert Maltz.

39. Kahn, *Hollywood on Trial*, 76.

40. Kahn, *Hollywood on Trial*, 98–99.

41. Kahn, *Hollywood on Trial*, 106–8.

42. Kahn, *Hollywood on Trial*, 84.

43. Kahn, *Hollywood on Trial*, 176–77.

44. See C. Wright Mills, "The Mass Society," in *Man Alone*, ed. Eric Josephson and Mary Josephson (New York: Dell, 1962), 201–27.

45. Those who chose not to change their names faced discrimination and in at least one case public ridicule. At a Directors Guild meeting in the late 1940s, C. B. DeMille gave a speech in support of the blacklist and took pleasure in trying to pronounce names like Mankiewiez as especially "Jewish."

46. Einstein viewed the committee as "nothing but a smoke screen" and said so on the record. When Crum contested that view, Einstein amended his statement (albeit slightly): "The Committee *seems* to be a smoke screen . . . [but] I would be glad to be wrong." He wasn't. See Patricia Bosworth, *Anything Your Little Heart Desires: An American Family Story* (New York: Simon and Schuster, 1997), 174–75.

47. Bosworth, *Anything Your Little Heart Desires*, 211–12.

48. Bosworth, *Anything Your Little Heart Desires*, 238–46.

49. Bosworth, *Anything Your Little Heart Desires*, 244.

50. Robert Vaughn, *Only Victims: A Study of Show Business Blacklisting* (New York: Putnam, 1972), 281. Vaughn's is one of the most widely read studies of the era. He takes his title from a conciliatory speech made by Dalton Trumbo to the membership of the Screen Writers Guild.

51. Dalton Trumbo, *Additional Dialogue: Letters of Dalton Trumbo*, ed. Helen Manfill (New York: M. Evans, 1970), 569–70. The speech was delivered on March 13, 1970.

52. Richard Schickel, "Return of the Hollywood Ten," *Film Comment*, March–April 1981, 12.

53. McGilligan, "Tender Comrades," 45.

54. Stephen Vaughn, "Political Censorship during the Cold War," in *Movie Censorship and American Culture*, ed. Francis G. Couvares (Washington, D.C.: Smithsonian Institution Press, 1996), 250.

55. Vaughn, "Political Censorship during the Cold War," 250–51.

56. Schatz, *Boom and Bust*, 293–95.

57. Schatz, *Boom and Bust*, 303.

58. This is perhaps more a conclusion than an observation and the language I use is provocative or at least colorful. Of course I don't know what was in the hearts and minds of the first-generation moguls. But their refusal to sign anti-Nazi petitions in the thirties and their abandonment of mostly Jewish writers, directors, actors, and producers during the Red Scare certainly suggest a repudiation of ethnicity and faith. As to the WASP Wall Street establishment, the moguls did answer to the New York offices and these New York offices had one eye on the stock market and the other on the banks that provided capital for studio/industry operations. Johnston's sudden turnaround in the fall of 1947—his decision on behalf of the MPAA and the industry to abandon the Hollywood Ten just days after vowing to protect them—certainly suggests that those higher up on the food chain told him to do so.

59. Kahn, *Hollywood on Trial*, 195.

60. See *Moody's Manual of Investments*, ed. John Sherman Porter (New York: Moody's Investment Service, 1947), 1880–83, 2247–53, 2907–13.

61. The analogy between the two entertainment businesses, sports and movies, is important, especially when one considers the complex relationship between labor and ownership. "Free agency" came to Hollywood in the late 1940s as an indirect result of divestiture and it empowered star-celebrities and their agents. Even a quick look at contemporary sports, all of which are now managing some form of free agency for their labor force, reveals much the same result: star athletes, represented by agents, make outrageous salaries and in the process have changed the stakes and nature of the business and its product. Of course, as in the film business, team owners make a whole lot more money than they ever did before.

62. Schickel, "Return of the Hollywood Ten," 12.

63. Schickel, "Return of the Hollywood Ten," 14.

64. Adolphe Menjou and Walt Disney, to name two.

65. This argument is made at some length in Murray Ross, *Stars and Strikes: Unionization of Hollywood* (New York: Columbia University Press, 1941), 23–47.

66. Danae Clark, *Negotiating Hollywood: The Cultural Politics of Actor's Labor* (Minneapolis: University of Minnesota Press, 1995), 43.

67. Clark, *Negotiating Hollywood*, 42.

68. Ross, *Stars and Strikes*, 44–46.

69. Gorham Kindem, "SAG, HUAC, and Postwar Hollywood," in Schatz, *Boom and Bust*, 314.

70. Kindem, "SAG, HUAC, and Postwar Hollywood," 317–18.

71. Kindem, "SAG, HUAC, and Postwar Hollywood," 317.

72. Ross, *Stars and Strikes*, 188.

73. Warner told Congressman Vail that his brother Harry "made the deal with [former U.S. ambassador] Davies" and that he (Jack) had nothing to do with the development or production of the film.

74. Hilberman has since returned the favor, generously affording damag-

ing and embarrassing material about Disney's antiunion and red-baiting activities to Marc Eliot, whose sensational biography, *Walt Disney: Hollywood's Dark Prince* (New York: Birch Lane, 1993), ably refutes the mythos of Uncle Walt.

75. The pronoun "it" seems to refer to something big, but I can't figure out precisely what.

76. Walt Disney, testimony before HUAC, October 24, 1947. See Eliot, *Walt Disney: Hollywood's Dark Prince*, 191–95.

77. This argument is made at greater length and detail by Holly Allen and Michael Denning, "The Cartoonists' Front," *South Atlantic Quarterly* 92, no. 1 (winter, 1993): 89–117.

78. Disney himself supported the theory that the strike broke the back of his animation unit. Both *Pinnochio* and *Fantasia*, ambitious and arguably terrific films, took years to make and lost money at the box office. The films lost money for two unrelated reasons: (1) they failed to capture the interest of the American public in their initial release and (2) delays in the production process left Disney with higher than expected loan payments to the bank.

79. Eliot, *Walt Disney: Hollywood's Dark Prince*, 120, 121, 135, 136, 166.

80. I discuss industry regulation in the new Hollywood at length elsewhere. See Jon Lewis, *Whom God Wishes to Destroy . . . Francis Coppola and the New Hollywood* (Durham: Duke University Press, 1995); "Trust and Anti-Trust in the New New Hollywood," *Michigan Quarterly Review* 35, no. 1 (winter 1996): 85–105; and "Money Matters: Hollywood in the Corporate Era," in *The New American Cinema*, ed. Jon Lewis (Durham: Duke University Press, 1998), 87–124.

81. Ceplair and Englund, *The Inquisition in Hollywood*, 445.

82. David Cook, *A History of Narrative Film* (New York: Norton, 1996), 453–58. Of the major film history textbooks, Cook's spends the most time on the blacklist era. According to Cook, 110 men and women testified before at least one of the three committees investigating Hollywood: the first chaired by Thomas, the second by John Wood, the third by Pat McCarren (in the Senate). Fifty-eight of the 110 witnesses named a total of 212 names. All told, Cook writes, during the blacklist "324 persons [were] fired by the studios and were no longer permitted to work in the American film industry" (457).

NOTES TO CHAPTER 2

1. Gordon Kahn, *Hollywood on Trial* (New York: Boni and Gaer, 1948), 196.

2. Kahn, *Hollywood on Trial*, 196.

3. Thomas Schatz, *Boom and Bust: The American Cinema in the 1940s* (New York: Scribner's, 1997), 288–89.

4. For a more detailed account of the MPPC and the rival independents, see Eileen Bowser, *The Transformation of Cinema, 1907–1915* (Berkeley: University of California Press, 1990), 27–36, 80–85, 217–18.

5. The MPPC standardized its product at one reel, approximately fifteen

to twenty minutes. The trust hierarchy clung to the belief that the lower-class movie audience did not have the attention span to sit through a feature-length film.

6. *Motion Picture Patents Co. v. Independent Moving Pictures Company of America*, 200 F. 411 (2nd Cir. 1912).

7. Original petition, *United States v. MPPC*, 247 U.S. 524 (1918).

8. *Binderup v. Pathe Exchange*, 263 U.S. 291 (1923).

9. Donald E. Biberman, Edward P. Pierson, Martin E. Silfen, et al., *Law and Business of the Entertainment Industries, 3d ed.* (Westport, CT: Praeger, 1996), 610.

10. Schatz, *Boom and Bust*, 17.

11. Schatz, *Boom and Bust*, 19.

12. Schatz, *Boom and Bust*, 21.

13. Schatz, *Boom and Bust*, 160–61.

14. *United States v. Crescent Amusement Co.*, 323 U.S. 173 (1944).

15. Schatz, *Boom and Bust*, 163–64.

16. Schatz, *Boom and Bust*, 324.

17. Schatz, *Boom and Bust*, 325–26.

18. *United States v. Griffith*, 334 U.S. 100 (1948); *Schine Chain Theaters v. United States*, 334 U.S. 110 (1948).

19. Justice Douglas's opinion in the *Paramount* case is reprinted in its entirety in Biberman et al., *Law and Business of the Entertainment Industries*, 611–21.

20. *United States v. Gypsum Co.*, 333 U.S. 364, 400 (1948).

21. Biberman et al., *Law and Business of the Entertainment Industries*, 614.

22. These are the numbers cited in Douglas's opinion. See Biberman et al., *Law and Business of the Entertainment Industries*, 619.

23. Films were routinely licensed to theaters under specific terms. In exchange for the right to show a film, the theater agreed to pay a certain flat fee or minimum guarantee. If ticket sales minus the "house nut" (the cost of operating the theater) exceeded the minimum, the theater then sent the studio a percentage of that amount. If a film did not do so well, the theater was obligated to pay the minimum. When films failed to earn out the guarantee, the theater operated at a loss.

24. The peculiar "genius" Douglas refers to here is of course quite different from the one elaborated in Thomas Schatz's classic film history, *The Genius of the System: Hollywood Filmmaking in the Studio Era* (New York: Henry Holt, 1996).

25. Advertising and various other forms of studio promotion were more intense with regard to choice features, and the presence of star actors in choice features certainly prefigured audience reception. But block booking and pooling arrangements did give lesser features a fair(er) chance in first run than they enjoy today.

26. Justin Wyatt, *High Concept: Movies and Marketing in Hollywood* (Austin: University of Texas Press, 1994), 66.

27. Before Walt Disney made the deal with ABC, he founded two new companies, Retlaw (that's Walter spelled backwards) and WED (Walt Elias Disney) Enterprises to better market his name as a trademark. The new companies took a separate cut out of certain lucrative Disney merchandising deals and effectively cut Walt's brother Roy and his wife, Lillian, out of the original Disneyland investment. The two companies were formed as a payback of sorts after Roy Disney refused to back Walt's plans for the amusement park. Of course, Walt was right about the park and he was also right about the value of merchandising, especially to the company that still bears his name. See Jon Lewis, "Disney after Disney: Family Business and the Business of Family," in *Disney Discourse: Producing the Magic Kingdom*, ed. Eric Smoodin (New York: Routledge, 1994), 96–99.

28. For a good summary of the transformation of the studios, see Wyatt, *High Concept: Movies and Marketing in Hollywood*, 68–72.

29. The MCA/Universal story is told at greater length in Schatz, *The Genius of the System*, 469–81.

30. Wasserman is widely credited as the agent who first negotiated profit points into star contracts with studios. For example, in the early 1950s Wasserman negotiated a deal for one of his most famous clients, James Stewart, in which the star agreed to accept less money up front in exchange for deferred profit participation. The deal was advantageous for both parties. Stewart was a box office star and his films made money. So long as his popularity held up, the percentage deal entitled Stewart (and by extension Wasserman) to share in a film's profits. Universal, Stewart's primary employer at the time, got to defer payment from the development stage (when stars are routinely paid) to well after the film's release.

31. I discuss Paramount after the Gulf and Western takeover in some detail in "If History Has Taught Us Anything . . . Francis Coppola, Paramount Pictures and *The Godfather* Parts I, II and III," in *Francis Ford Coppola's The Godfather Trilogy*, ed. Nick Browne (New York: Cambridge University Press, 2000), 23–56.

32. Wyatt, *High Concept: Movies and Marketing in Hollywood*, 71.

33. *United States v. Capitol Service, Inc.*, 756 F.2d 502 (7th Cir.), *cert. denied*, 474 U.S. 945 (1985).

34. The opinion was written by senior circuit judge George Clifton Edwards Jr.

35. Janet Wasko, *Hollywood in the Information Age: Beyond the Silver Screen* (Austin: University of Texas Press, 1995), 177–78.

36. Harris, "Squeezing the Customers," *Forbes*, July 23, 1990, 39–40.

37. Wasko, *Hollywood in the Information Age*, 179.

38. Richard Trainor, "Major Powers," *Sight and Sound*, winter 1987–88, 26.

39. I discuss at greater length the Kerkorian case and the various mergers and acquisitions that have given the new Hollywood its present shape in

"Money Matters: Hollywood in the Corporate Era," in *The New American Cinema*, ed. Jon Lewis (Durham: Duke University Press, 1998), 87–124.

40. "Needed Cash for Bank Balances, Kerkorian Sold 2% of His MGM," *Variety*, April 25, 1979, 4.

41. The CPI antitrust suit was not the first time the Justice Department had gone after Kerkorian; federal attorneys had interrogated him years earlier about his relationship with the reputed gangster Meyer Lansky, who, they alleged, helped finance Kerkorian early on in his career. Kerkorian predictably refused to testify against Lansky. In 1979 rumor had it that the government's decision to challenge the CPI deal had less to do with antitrust than retaliation.

42. James Harwood, "Trial Begins on Col. Stock Buy," *Variety*, August 22, 1979, 5.

43. "Economics Professors Unalarmed if Distribs. Shrink or Combine," *Variety*, August 15, 1979, 7.

44. James Harwood, "Dept. of Justice Draws a Defeat," *Variety*, August 22, 1979, 53. The italics are mine.

45. "Vincent Memo Defends Price as Pivotal Studio Power: Hits KK's Claims of Stark Control," *Variety*, October 8, 1980, 36.

46. A convertible debenture is an unsecured corporate bond that can be converted into common shares at the option of its owner. In this case, the convertible debenture allowed Allen to issue additional shares in order to put them in the friendly hands of in-house producer Ray Stark.

47. David McClintick's book on the David Begelman scandal, *Indecent Exposure* (New York: Dell, 1983), confirms Kerkorian's allegations. According to McClintick, when Begelman, then Columbia film studio chairman, was caught forging checks and embezzling money, Stark was powerful enough to get him (briefly) reinstated despite opposition from then CPI president (and Allen and Company employee) Alan Hirschfield.

48. Companies are said to pay "greenmail" to corporate raiders when they buy back stock at a premium in order to prevent an unwanted takeover. In 1996, Kerkorian's personal wealth was estimated at $4.36 billion, much of that earned in greenmail payoffs. See "The Superrich," edited by Graham Burton, *Forbes*, July 15, 1996, 188.

49. While MGM/UA was owned by Crédit Lyonnais, it was managed/advised by the powerful Hollywood talent agency CAA (Creative Artists Agency). Several companies bid on MGM, including Polygram, Morgan Creek, and the News Corporation, but Kerkorian's $1.3 billion—the exact amount Giancarlo Parretti had paid Kerkorian back in 1990—carried the day. At this writing, MGM executives are said to be happy about Kerkorian's return to Hollywood. One quoted in *Entertainment Weekly* succinctly explained why: "The bottom line is I get to keep my job." Once we get past the absurdity of Kerkorian buying back—or financing the buyback of—a studio he tried for almost a decade to unload, it is fair to wonder what Crédit Lyonnais executives were thinking. In

1989, when it was forced to foreclose on Parretti, Crédit Lyonnais filed suit against Kerkorian for misrepresenting the value of the property and concealing certain facts about his deal with Parretti. Apparently the French bank has learned a little since taking over the studio; in Hollywood it pays to have a short memory. See Casey Davidson, "Deals," *Entertainment Weekly*, July 26, 1996, 11.

50. Between 1978 and 1988, ten independent film companies—American International, Filmways, Weintraub, Cannon, deLaurentis, New World, Lorimar, Vista, New Century, and the Atlantic Releasing Corporation—went out of business.

51. Wasko, *Hollywood in the Information Age*, 48–49.

52. *Variety*, June 7–13, 1989, 15.

53. Advertisement, *Variety*, June 7, 1989, 15.

54. "Pending Sale of Associates First Indicates G&W May Be Considering Viacom Merger," *Variety*, May 10–18, 1989, 3. Much of the following discussion of the Time-Warner merger and Paramount's attempt to block it is discussed at greater length in Jon Lewis, "Trust and Anti-Trust in the New New Hollywood," *Michigan Quarterly Review* 35, no. 1 (winter 1996): 97–102.

55. Richard Gold, "Size Is the Ultimate Prize as Showbiz/Media Corps Fight for Supremacy," *Variety*, June 14–20, 1989, 1, 6; Richard Gold, "Will Par-Time-WCI War Victimize Creatives," *Variety*, June 21–27, 1989, 1, 4; Richard Gold, "Intense Propaganda Fight Mars Par vs. WCI War," *Variety*, June 26–July 4, 1989, 1, 5; Richard Gold, "Par's Block Looks Like a Bust as Court Backs Time Director's Stand," *Variety*, July 19–26, 1989, 1, 6; Richard Gold and Paul Harris, "Time Marches On, Grabs Warner, Outpaces Par," *Variety*, July 26–August 1, 1989, 1, 6; "Time Inc. Buyout Attempt Puts Dent in Paramount Communications Qtr.," *Variety*, September 20–26, 1989, 9.

56. Gold, "Size Is the Ultimate Prize," 1.

57. Bids are considered "hostile" when they go against the expressed wishes of management. Such bids, though, are often very good for individual shareholders, all of whom are offered a premium for their stock.

58. Gold, "Size Is the Ultimate Prize," 1, 6.

59. Gold, "Will Par-Time-WCI War Victimize Creatives," 4.

60. In a recent article in *Forbes*, Matthew Schifrin argued that the decision to turn down the PCI offer cost Time shareholders "60% of what they could otherwise have realized." See Matthew Schifrin, "The Mess at Time Warner," *Forbes*, May 20, 1996, 170.

61. Neal Gabler, "Brother Can You Spare a Million," *Esquire*, September 1995, 38.

62. See Wasko, *Hollywood in the Information Age*, 48–52. Wasko's sources are primarily Time Warner's annual reports.

63. Time Warner already owned the remaining 18 percent.

64. Mark Lander, "Time Warner and Turner Seal Merger," *New York Times*, September 23, 1995, 1, 18.

65. It is important to acknowledge here the astonishing political influence of Rupert Murdoch and John Malone, both of whom contribute strategically to conservative Republican campaigns. Time Warner Turner and the News Corporation operate free from federal regulation because they pay powerful people in Congress enough to look the other way. If this sounds like a protection racket . . .

66. See Gary Samuels, "Gore-ing Malone's Ox," *Forbes*, September 9, 1996, 52–56.

67. Bryan Burrough, "The Siege of Paramount," *Vanity Fair*, February 1994, 131.

68. Previously, the only programming mandate enforced by the FCC was that all cable systems must provide, as part of their service, network and local independent stations otherwise available over the airwaves.

69. As I put the finishing touches on this book, Time Warner Turner has just gotten a whole lot bigger and better diversified. The online provider America Online (AOL) has reached an agreement with Time Warner management to merge the two conglomerates. The deal requires AOL to ostensibly "buy" Time Warner. Because it depends on the relative stock values of AOL and Time Warner when the FCC and FTC approve the merger, the deal may well fall apart. The likelihood that the FCC and FTC will allow the deal to go through is less a statement on whether or not AOL/Time Warner is a trust than on the larger irrelevance of antitrust regulations in the entertainment and information businesses today.

70. John Cassidy, "Brotherhood of Man Dept.: Where Was Ted Turner When Levin and Murdoch Made Up?" *New Yorker*, July 21, 1997, 23.

NOTES TO CHAPTER 3

1. Kinetoscopes and early short films featured sporting events, circus acts, and scantily clad women often depicted dancing or posing by the beach. Thomas Edison's studio, which produced both kinetoscopes and films, made a number of erotic dance shorts. Annabelle Whitford, a popular dancer at the time, was perhaps the first film star and was featured in a number of Edison studio productions from 1894 to 1896. Her "serpentine dance" was reprised by a number of other attractive female dancers. Most of these films were shot by W. K. L. Dickson and William Heise for Edison.

2. Philip French, "No End in Sight: 100 Years of Censorship," *Index on Censorship* 24, no. 6 (1995): 22–23.

3. Eileen Bowser, *The Transformation of Cinema, 1907–1915* (Berkeley: University of California Press, 1990), 49.

4. My discussion here is adapted in part from French, "No End in Sight," 22.

5. Both the 1927 MPPDA list of "Don'ts and Be Carefuls" and the 1930 Pro-

duction Code Administration guidelines addressed the antisocial impact of film. The 1927 code called for "special care" in the depiction of "techniques of committing murder" ("Be Careful" number 7) as well as "methods of smuggling" (number 8). "Be Careful" number 5 warned against filmic lessons in the execution of "theft, robbery, safe-cracking, and dynamiting of trains, mines, buildings, etc." Section 1, "Crimes against the Law" in the general principles of the 1930 code similarly prohibited the depiction of techniques for murder, theft, robbery, safe cracking, and so on.

6. French, "No End in Sight," 21.

7. *Mutual Film Corporation v. Industrial Commission of Ohio*, 236 U.S. 230 (1915).

8. Richard deCordova, *Picture Personalities: The Emergence of the Star System in America* (Urbana: University of Illinois Press, 1990), 107.

9. See Lary May, *Screening Out the Past: The Birth of Mass Culture and the Motion Picture Industry* (New York: Oxford University Press, 1980).

10. deCordova, *Picture Personalities*, 108.

11. On the Arbuckle case, see David Yallop, *The Day the Laughter Stopped: The True Story of Fatty Arbuckle* (New York: St. Martin's, 1976). Some recent books on Taylor's murder have alleged that the studio coverup had little to do with the murder case itself, tales of drug use on the studio lot, or even the reputations of the two female stars rumored to be involved with Taylor (Mabel Normand and Mary Miles Minter). At stake instead was the secret of Taylor's homosexuality, evidence of which was removed by the studio before the arrival of the police at the murder scene. See Sidney Kirkpatrick, *A Cast of Killers* (New York: E. P. Dutton, 1986); and Robert Giroux, *A Deed of Death* (New York: Knopf, 1990).

12. deCordova, *Picture Personalities*, 119–24.

13. *Photoplay* published a story titled "Love Confessions of a Fat Man" the very month the scandal broke. It is possible that the magazine was on newsstands before such an inappropriate story could have been killed, but the subsequent issue's photo spread featuring Arbuckle titled "What the Well-Dressed Man Will Wear" seems significantly harder to explain or excuse. The former piece featured a quote attributed to Arbuckle that must have horrified readers at the time. In an interview conducted just weeks before Rappe's death, Arbuckle remarked, "Fat men make the best husbands because . . . it is very hard to murder or be murdered by a fat man." See deCordova, *Picture Personalities*, 127–28.

14. Cited in a variety of newspapers at the time. See the Will Hays Collection housed at Indiana State Library.

15. The unpublished memoirs are part of the Hays Collection, Indiana State Library.

16. deCordova, *Picture Personalities*, 129–32.

17. deCordova, *Picture Personalities*, 134–35.

18. From the Hays Collection, Indiana State Library.

19. The *New York Times* piece came out on July 30, 1922. See Will Hays, *The Memoirs of Will Hays* (Garden City, NY: Doubleday, 1955), 392.

20. The case was so named because it concerned efforts to prohibit the screening of Roberto Rossellini's film *The Miracle*.

21. My discussion of the *Miracle* case is based in large part on two sources: Garth Jowett, "A Significant Medium for the Communication of Ideas: The *Miracle* Decision and the Decline of Motion Picture Censorship," in *Movie Censorship and American Culture*, ed. Francis C. Couvares (Washington, D.C.: Smithsonian Institution Press, 1996), 258–76, and Frank Miller, *Censored Hollywood: Sex, Sin and Violence on Screen* (Atlanta: Turner Publishing, 1994), 146–52.

22. Not everyone, not even all Catholics, found the film offensive; indeed, in Italy *Il Popolo*, the official newspaper of the pro-Catholic Christian Democratic Party, called *The Miracle* "a beautiful thing, humanly felt, alive, true and without religious profanation." For more on the international response to the film, see Miller, *Censored Hollywood*, 148–51.

23. Miller, *Censored Hollywood*, 149–50.

24. The PCA also cautioned producers about potential problems with specific state boards. A discussion of these PCA cautionary memos is taken up later in this chapter.

25. Gerald Gardner, *The Censorship Papers: Movie Censorship Letters from the Hays Office, 1934–1968* (New York: Dodd, Mead, 1987), 108.

26. Gardner, *The Censorship Papers*, 138.

27. Gregory Black, *Hollywood Censored: Morality Codes, Catholics, and the Movies* (New York: Cambridge University Press, 1994); and Frank Walsh, *Sin and Censorship: The Catholic Church and Motion Picture Censorship* (New Haven: Yale University Press, 1996).

28. Frank Couvares, "Hollywood and the Culture Wars," *American Quarterly* 50, no. 1 (1998): 194.

29. Two books on thirties film censorship were published just as I was putting the finishing touches on this manuscript. Both discuss the early days under the production code in far more detail than I do. See Thomas Doherty, *Pre-Code Hollywood: Sex, Immorality and Insurrection in American Culture, 1930–1934* (New York: Columbia University Press, 1999); and Mark Vieira, *Sin in Soft Focus* (New York: Harry Abrams, 1999).

30. For more on censorship in the late silent and early sound periods, see Kevin Brownlow, *Behind the Mask of Innocence: Sex, Violence, Prejudice, Crime: Films of Social Conscience in the Silent Era* (New York: Knopf, 1990); and Lea Jacobs, *The Wages of Sin: Censorship and the Fallen Woman Film, 1928–1942* (Berkeley: University of California Press, 1997).

31. Couvares, "Hollywood and the Culture Wars," 197.

32. *Burstyn v. Wilson*, 343 U.S. 501 (1952).

33. While the MPAA showed little interest in publicly supporting Burstyn, it lent considerable support to the anticensorship cause in *Gelling v. Texas,* 343 U.S. 960 (1952), which involved a fine levied against W. L. Gelling, a Marshall, Texas, theater manager, for screening MPAA member Twentieth Century Fox's *Pinky.* The Supreme Court's decision in the case overturned the Texas State Supreme Court ruling upholding Gelling's conviction, and it went a long way toward encouraging other MPAA member studios to take on local censorship boards. The Ohio case was *Superior Films Inc. v. Department of Education of Ohio,* 346 U.S. 587 (1954).

34. Miller, *Censored Hollywood,* 151. State censorship laws were voided in Ohio in 1954, Massachusetts in 1955, and Pennsylvania in 1956. By the end of the decade it was clear that virtually all the state boards operated without constitutional authority and that their specific rulings would not likely be upheld on appeal.

35. Miller, *Censored Hollywood,* 49.

36. Miller, *Censored Hollywood,* 71–73.

37. That the *Paramount* decision seemed at once to dismantle the film business vis-à-vis its monopoly of exhibition and empower it in its ongoing problems with censorship agencies and boards across the country is an irony elaborated in Ira Carmen, *Movie Censorship and the Law* (Ann Arbor: University of Michigan Press, 1966), 45.

38. See Miller, *Censored Hollywood,* 161–62.

39. *The Moon Is Blue* was the thirteenth highest-grossing film of 1953.

40. W. R. Wilkinson, "Trade News," *Hollywood Reporter,* June 5, 1953.

41. Miller, *Censored Hollywood,* 165.

42. Section 1, "Crimes against the Law, Reasons Underlying Particular Applications," 1930 motion picture production code.

43. Miller, *Censored Hollywood,* 165–66.

44. I discuss *The Wild One* at greater length in Jon Lewis, *The Road to Romance and Ruin: Teen Films and Youth Culture* (New York: Routledge, 1992), 28–32.

45. Murray Schumach, *The Face on the Cutting Room Floor: The Story of Movie and Television Censorship* (New York: Da Capo Press, 1974), 45.

46. *A Streetcar Named Desire, Born Yesterday,* and *A Place in the Sun* placed fifth, sixth and seventh on the top twenty box office list for 1951. *The African Queen* was the sixth highest-grossing film for 1952. The 1953 Academy Award winner for best picture, *From Here to Eternity,* grossed over $12 million, second behind the biblical epic *The Robe.* As mentioned earlier, *The Moon Is Blue* was the thirteenth highest-grossing film of 1953.

47. Gardner, *The Censorship Papers,* 170.

48. Point 3 in the "Crimes against the Law" section reads as follows: "The illegal drug traffic must not be portrayed in such a way as to stimulate

curiosity concerning the use of, or traffic in, such drugs; nor shall scenes be approved which show the use of illegal drugs, or their effects, in detail.

49. Gardner, *The Censorship Papers*, 171.

50. For more on the release of *Tea and Sympathy*, see Miller, *Censored Holly-wood*, 173–76.

51. Miller, *Censored Hollywood*, 174.

52. Gardner, *The Censorship Papers*, 188–89.

53. Miller, *Censored Hollywood*, 174.

54. Gardner, *The Censorship Papers*, 190–91.

55. Rankin contended that Hollywood made movies that attempted "to smear and discredit the white people of the Southern states." Nothing Rankin could have seen before he made his speech in 1947 came close to the sort of smear and discredit presented in *Baby Doll*.

56. Section 6 (Costume), number 2 in the "Reasons Underlying Particular Applications" in the production code (a sub-section not included in the Appendix) notes that while "the nude or semi-nude body may be beautiful," one need take into account "the effect of the nude or semi-nude body on the normal individual." Section 6, number 5 cautions that "Transparent or translucent materials [like the Baby Doll nightie] are frequently more suggestive than actual exposure." See also note 64.

57. Section 2 (Sex) begins with an introductory paragraph regarding marriage as a sacrament not to be trifled with on film. However nasty a character Silva was, the scenario suggested that adultery in itself might not be a sin and the two characters seem to survive their indiscretion at the end of the picture. "Illicit" and/or "low forms of sex" are also proscribed in section 2, though the code includes little elaboration on the subject. It is safe to assume that in the mid-1950s the husband's voyeuristic activities, which are blatantly fetishistic and masturbatory, were beyond even the broadest interpretation of section 2 of the code.

58. The production code was divided in two. The first half lists censorship criteria; the second offers the reasons behind the proscriptions. Under the heading "Reasons Supporting Preamble of Code," the PCA endeavored to explain its larger mission to "bring the motion picture to a still higher level of wholesome entertainment for all the people," and the studio membership's recognition of "the high trust and confidence which have been placed in them by the people of the world."

59. The PCA was at first reluctant to pressure the playwright and the filmmakers to change much in the adaptation. Indeed, it was not until the Legion of Decency threatened a boycott of Radio City Music Hall, where the film was slated to premiere, that Breen urged Warners to make the four minutes' worth of cuts. See Jeremy Pascall and Clyde Jeavons, *A Pictorial History of Sex on Film* (London: Hamlyn, 1975), 114–16.

60. It is important to note that Williams and Kazan flatly refused to cut the

rape scene and made its inclusion a condition for any other cuts. In 1951 the scene was pretty shocking and the advertising department at Warner Brothers smartly exploited the groundbreaking scene in its promotion of the picture.

61. Gardner, *The Censorship Papers*, 201–2.

62. Miller, *Censored Hollywood*, 176.

63. See Larry Ceplair and Steven Englund, *The Inquisition in Hollywood* (Garden City, NY: Anchor Press/Doubleday, 1980), 447; and Robert Vaughn, *Only Victims* (New York: Putnam, 1972), 280, 284, 289. Among the names on Kazan's list was the playwright Clifford Odets, with whom the director worked in New York. Schulberg named five of the Hollywood Ten as well as fellow screenwriters Paul Jarrico, Richard Collins (who also named names), John Bright, and Waldo Salt. Cobb implicated fellow actors Lloyd Bridges, Jeff Corey, Gale Sondergaard, and Larry Parks.

64. Miller, *Censored Hollywood*, 177.

65. Miller, *Censored Hollywood*, 177.

66. The censor Jack Vizzard told Kazan that the PCA board was unanimous in finding the swing scene objectionable. Vizzard, in a personal aside, referred to the young woman's reaction to the older man's attentions as "orgiastic." Miller, *Censored Hollywood*, 178.

67. Jack Vizzard, *See No Evil: Life inside a Hollywood Censor* (New York: Simon and Schuster, 1970), 206.

68. Miller, *Censored Hollywood*, 179.

69. The first such pledge, penned earlier in 1934, was quite a bit longer and featured more colorful prose: "I condemn absolutely those salacious motion pictures, which, with other degrading agencies, are corrupting public morals and promoting a sex mania in the land." In 1957, the year after the release of *Baby Doll*, the legion subtly amended its original 1936 classification system by allowing adolescents to see A-2 films that were deemed unacceptable for children. Films like *Baby Doll*, of course, remained outside any acceptable category before and after 1956. The pledge was revised again in 1965, reduced to a single paragraph encouraging Catholics to set "a good example" and to behave "in a responsible and civic-minded manner." The legion (which became NCOMP) held on to its own separate rating system well after the MPAA instituted its system. But for the most part, after 1968 the Catholic organization abandoned the aggressive strategies it had routinely employed since 1936.

70. Richard S. Randall, *Censorship of the Movies: The Social and Political Control of a Mass Medium* (Madison: University of Wisconsin Press, 1968), 175. Randall's data are based on reported, official action as published in *Variety*, *Boxoffice*, *Motion Picture Daily*, *Motion Picture Exhibitor*, and (Martin Quigley's) *Motion Picture Herald*.

71. My discussion of informal censorship is based in large part on Randall, *Censorship of the Movies*, 169–78.

72. Randall, *Censorship of the Movies*, 170.

73. Exhibitors guarantee distributors a certain flat sum of money regardless of box office receipts. The guarantee is factored against a certain percentage of the box office. If the percentage of the film's box office revenues exceeds the guarantee, theater owners pay that amount to the distributor. If that percentage is less than the guarantee, as of course it was when local censors banned screenings of a film, theater owners were bound by contract to pay the studio the flat, guaranteed fee.

74. This discussion of the *Jacobellis* case is based in large part on unpublished interviews with Jacobellis, Zenith International Films president Daniel Frankel (who distributed the film), and Marion Kelly, a reporter who covered the story for the *Cleveland Heights Sun Press*. See Randall, *Censorship of the Movies*, 163–67.

75. This practice continues today. A number of theaters in Utah screening *Titanic* cut two scenes from the three-hour movie: the scene in the young woman's cabin as she poses nude for a portrait and a subsequent scene as the two young lovers steam up the windows of a car on one of the lower decks. These cuts—and the production of what came to be known as "the Utah version" of the picture—showed little respect for the director's vision or for the studio's copyright. See Dave Karger and Marta Murvosh, "Snip Shape," *Entertainment Weekly*, September 18, 1998, 12.

76. *The Lovers* was banned or cut in a number of markets nationwide, including Chicago, Boston, Memphis, Dayton, Portland, Oregon, and Providence, Rhode Island. Jacobellis's eventual victory at the Supreme Court implied that other local censorship regulations might not stand up to a constitutional challenge either.

77. Randall, *Censorship of the Movies*, 165.

78. Randall, *Censorship of the Movies*, 163.

79. *United States v. Kennerly*, 209 F. 119, 121 (D.C.S.D.N.Y. 1913).

80. *Butler v. Michigan*, 352 U.S. 380 (1957).

81. French, "No End in Sight," 25.

NOTES TO CHAPTER 4

1. Web site: www.mpaa.org/home.html.

2. Web site: www.mpaa.org/home.html.

3. Web site: www.mpaa.org/home.html.

4. *Who's Afraid of Virginia Woolf* won the New York Drama Critics Award in 1963.

5. Gerald Gardner, *The Censorship Papers: Movie Censorship Letters from the Hays Office, 1934–1968* (New York: Dodd, Mead, 1987), 200.

6. "A Topless Liz 'Promised' by WB," *Variety*, December 21, 1966, 1.

7. *Ginsberg v. New York*, 390 U.S. 629 (1968) and *Interstate Circuit, Inc. v. Dallas*, 390 U.S. 676 (1968).

8. In his opinion in the *Ginsberg* case, Justice William Brennan wrote, "the concept of obscenity or of unprotected matter may vary according to the group to whom the questionable material is directed or from whom it is quarantined." The concept of *variable obscenity* as it was applied by Brennan in both the *Jacobellis* and *Ginsberg* cases dates to an article by William B. Lockhart and Robert C. McLure, "Censorship and Obscenity: The Developing of Constitutional Standards," *Minnesota Law Review* 45, no. 85 (1960). For a more detailed discussion of the concept of variable obscenity, see Richard F. Hixson, *Pornography and the Justices: The Supreme Court and the Intractable Obscenity Problem* (Carbondale: Southern Illinois University Press, 1996), 61–79.

Brennan's support of a flexible, variable definition of obscenity—first outlined in his majority opinion in *Jacobellis v. Ohio* and further elaborated in the *Ginsberg* case—acknowledged the state's responsibility to safeguard its youth. But even such a commonsense argument failed to inspire unanimity at the Court. Justice Abe Fortas, in his only signed opinion in an obscenity case, objected to what he perceived as Brennan's paternalism. "To give the State a role in the rearing of children," Fortas argued, "is contrary to our traditions and to our conception of family responsibility."

9. "MPAA New Code and Ratings Rules," *Variety*, October 9, 1968, 4.

10. Valenti's initial press release can be found under the title "Personal Statement of Jack Valenti, President" in the MPAA file at the Margaret Herrick Library of the Academy of Motion Picture Arts and Sciences in Los Angeles. The memo, released "in connection with [the] announcement of new national film rating system," is dated October 7, 1968, approximately a month before the rating system took effect.

11. "Personal Statement of Jack Valenti, President."

12. Web site: www.mpaa.org/home.html.

13. For a more detailed history of local censorship in the Dallas area, see Brian O'Leary, "Local Government Regulation of the Movies: The Dallas System, 1966–1983," *Journal of Film and Video* 48. no. 3 (1996): 46–57.

14. O'Leary, "Local Government Regulation of the Movies," 50. En route to the Supreme Court, *Interstate* benefited from a confused and profoundly slow state appeals process. According to O'Leary, the Supreme Court agreed to hear the case because the justices believed that the Texas state courts had botched the suit at several stops along the way.

15. In the lone dissent, Justice John Harlan supported the city's efforts to regulate filmed material. He did so because he supported states' rights, but as his opinion reveals, he was also dismayed by the increased number of films screened at the Court. "The current approach," Harlan wrote, "has required us to spend an inordinate amount of time in the absurd business of perusing and viewing the miserable stuff that pours into the Court mostly in state cases, all to no better end than second-guessing state judges."

16. From Douglas's opinion as circulated to the Court in 1967 and cited by Hixson, *Pornography and the Justices*, 73–74.

17. The 1966 MPAA Annual Report is part of the MPAA file at the Margaret Herrick Library of the Academy of Motion Picture Arts and Sciences in Los Angeles.

18. Robert B. Frederick, "Valenti at Society of Mag Writers: Snobs Deify Foreign Film Directors Whose Name End with 'O' or 'I,'" *Variety*, September 18, 1968, 3, 17.

19. Ronald Gold, "Valenti Won't 'Blow-Up' Prod. Code for Status Films; No Church Push," *Variety*, January 11, 1967, 1, 78.

20. "'Blow-Up' B.O. Comforts Metro," *Variety*, March 22, 1967, 6.

21. "Advisory, Better Than Rigid, 'Classing,'" *Variety*, March 22, 1967, 6. This brief article was laid out directly above "'Blow-Up' B.O. Comforts Metro."

22. Ron Wise, "Illinois Court Rules in June," *Variety*, May 16, 1967, 7, 20.

23. Walter Reade would later play a significant role in the development of the 1968 rating system. Reade was the lone NATO holdout when Valenti first announced the new code. The exhibitor believed (with justification) that the rating system was inequitable, that it unfairly favored the studio distributors and left all the hard and risky work to the exhibitors. He also did not trust his competition to enforce restrictive admission policies if it meant turning people away at the box office. The self-regulatory system was bound to fail, Reade predicted, and its failure might encourage stricter extra-industry censorship. See Stuart Byron, "Adults Induced if Kids Barred," *Variety*, October 16, 1968, 5, 24, and "Reade Hangs Crepe on Ratings; NATOites Hear Him in Silence; He Sees Flop Aiding Censors," *Variety*, November 13, 1968, 17.

24. In the press release "What Everyone Should Know about the Motion Picture Code and Ratings," under the heading "Exactly what do these ratings mean?" the composition of the board is described as follows: "a competent and experienced staff with broad and lengthy backgrounds in film appraisal." Such a board would never have been practical. The only people "with broad and lengthy backgrounds in film appraisal" in 1968 were former censors themselves, hardly the sort of people Valenti wanted to include in the new system. According to Valenti, the board is now staffed by individuals who, taken as a group, accurately represent the diverse adult population. We will have to take him at his word. The identity of CARA board members is kept secret. Indeed, everything about CARA is kept secret from general population and serious researchers alike.

25. Valenti's personal statement is part of the MPAA file at the Margaret Herrick Library of the Academy of Motion Picture Arts and Sciences in Los Angeles.

26. "Rating System Should Start via MPAA in October," *Variety*, September 11, 1968, 1.

27. Frederick, "Valenti at Society of Mag Writers," 22.

28. As mentioned in chapter 2, the AOL/Time Warner deal is, at this writing, still pending.

29. Dave Kaufman, "Hollywood Unemployment at 42.8%," *Variety*, March 4, 1970, 3.

30. "Paramount Studio Buy Talks, But No Deal Yet into Focus; Realty Value Runs $29–32 Mil," *Variety*, April 8, 1970, 5.

31. See John Gregory Dunne, *The Studio* (New York: Farrar, Straus and Giroux, 1969), a satirical account of the production of *Doctor Dolittle*. Dunne's book offers an insightful look at the absurdity of Hollywood musical-comedy production at the time.

32. Pauline Kael, "*Paint Your Wagon:* Somebody Else's Success," in *Film 69/70: An Anthology by the National Association of Film Critics*, ed. Joseph Morgenstern and Stefan Kanfer (New York: Simon and Schuster, 1970), 111–15.

33. In the early 1980s I worked for Lieberman Research West, a market research firm in Century City that did a lot of work for Columbia Pictures. Back then, audience segments were separated into the following age categories: nine to fourteen, fifteen to twenty-four, twenty-five to thirty-four, thirty-five to forty-four, and then everybody else. The implication was that children under nine went to movies their parents chose and adults over forty-five went to so few films it wasn't worth the time to find out which ones. Today the demographic units have shifted. Children under nine are a now huge market and forty-five to fifty-four-year-olds (baby boomers, most of whom were in their twenties or early thirties when I left the marketing business) are a significant market segment.

34. For a more detailed account of the American Zoetrope story, see Jon Lewis, *Whom God Wishes to Destroy . . . Francis Coppola and the New Hollywood* (Durham: Duke University Press, 1995).

35. Stefan Kanfer, "Advance Obit. (introduction)," in Morgenstern and Kanfer, *Film 69/70: An Anthology by the National Association of Film Critics*, 100.

36. Kael, "*Paint Your Wagon:* Somebody Else's Success," 111, 112.

37. Joseph Morgenstern, "Hollywood: Myth, Fact and Trouble," in Morgenstern and Kanfer, *Film 69/70: An Anthology by the National Association of Film Critics*, 101.

38. Morgenstern, "Hollywood: Myth, Fact and Trouble," 105.

39. Morgenstern, "Hollywood: Myth, Fact and Trouble," 104–5.

40. My account of the American release of *I Am Curious Yellow* is based in large part on Justin Wyatt, "Selling Atrocious Behaviour: Revising Sexualities in the Marketplace for Adult Film in the 60s," in *Swinging Single: Representing Sexuality in the 1960s*, ed. Hilary Radner and Moya Luckett (Minneapolis: University of Minnesota Press, 1999).

41. "Sex Dominates B'Way First-Runs," *Variety*, March 19, 1969, 9.

42. John Simon, "Not Great, But Decent," in Morgenstern and Kanfer, *Film 69/70: An Anthology by the National Association of Film Critics*, 261–62.

43. Leonard Gross, "After Nudity, What, Indeed?" *Look*, April 29, 1969, 80–81.

44. Penelope Gilliatt, "Letter from the Flicks: Manhattan, Spring, 1969," in Morgenstern and Kanfer, *Film 69/70: An Anthology by the National Association of Film Critics*, 263.

45. Stefan Kanfer, "Dubious Yellow," *Time*, March 14, 1969, 98.

46. Vilgot Sjoman, *I Was Curious: Diary of the Making of a Film* (New York: Grove, 1969).

47. Stefan Kanfer, "Space Odyssey 1969," in Morgenstern and Kanfer, *Film 69/70: An Anthology by the National Association of Film Critics*, 41–44.

48. Penelope Gilliatt, "Into the Eye of the Storm," in Morgenstern and Kanfer, *Film 69/70: An Anthology by the National Association of Film Critics*, 36.

49. Morgenstern, "Hollywood: Myth, Fact and Trouble," 101.

50. "First Appeal on X Rating," *Variety*, November 27, 1968, 7.

51. Robert Landry, "Pics Bad Image alongside Porno," *Variety*, March 25, 1970, 5.

52. There were two notable studio-distributed X-rated films released in the first few years under the new rating system: *Midnight Cowboy*, which sported a self-imposed X (for adult content as opposed to pornographic or obscene imagery) and *Last Tango in Paris*, one of the few studio films released in the early 1970s to successfully exploit its X rating as part of its marketing strategy. UA promoted *Last Tango* with ads highlighting the film's sexual content (its explicit imagery, its frank examination of a destructive love affair), it's high-art pedigree (director Bernardo Bertolucci, one of those auteurs whose name ends in an *i* or *o*), and its star talent (Marlon Brando). Brando's participation in the project made studio executives a little nervous. It seemed to suggest that other legit stars might follow him into such explicit films. They didn't.

53. NATO Asks AO (Adults Only) to Escape Stigmatizing via X," *Variety*, March 25, 1970, 5.

54. "Protecting Public vs. Censorship," *Variety*, February 25, 1970, 7.

55. See "Curb on Ads for X-Pix Cues 'Sis' Suit by Aldrich," *Variety*, February 6, 1969, 1, 70.

56. "Protecting Public vs. Censorship," 7.

57. "Trade Ponders: X the Key to B.O.?" *Variety*, February 25, 1970, 1.

58. Gene Arneel, "Valenti Raps Loew's' "Stitch" Booking; Can't Be Both Voyeur and Respectable Biz," *Variety*, January 28, 1971, 4.

59. "Trade Ponders: X the Key to B.O.?" 1, 75.

60. Addison Verrill, "Wilsons Hate All but Profit," *Variety*, April 1, 1970, 3.

61. Arneel, "Valenti Raps Loew's' "Stitch" Booking."

62. Here again *Last Tango in Paris* seems a notable exception.

63. "X as in Paradox," *Variety*, April 1, 1970, 7.

64. "Cladgett Tidying MPAA's New Bills; 39 Wanna Tax X," *Variety*, March 25, 1970, 5.

65. Ticket prices for X-rated movies in 1970 were already higher than for mainstream pictures.

66. "Maine's Modified Censorship," *Variety*, April 1, 1970, 7.

67. "N.H. Supreme Court Kills Local Ruling Aimed at X Features," *Variety*, July 7, 1970, 20.

68. *Redrup v. New York*, 386 U.S. 767 (1967).

69. "MPAA Ratings to Now: G (43), M (29), R (22); Puzzle: X for 'Birds' but R for 'The Fox,'" *Variety*, December 4, 1968, 18.

70. Alfred Nichtenhauser, "An Open Letter to the Film Industry," *Variety*, April 6, 1970, 25.

71. Suggestions to filmmakers deemed necessary to bring a film into the G, PG, PG-13, R range were not binding. To that end, Bouras wrote, "This letter is not to be construed as an assurance that the rating of this picture can be changed from X to R." Nichtenhauser, "An Open Letter to the Film Industry," 25.

72. Nichtenhauser, "An Open Letter to the Film Industry," 25.

73. Some of Meyer's films originally rated X now sport an MPAA seal and an R rating.

74. Ed Lowry and Louis Black, "Russ Meyer Interviewed," *Film Comment*, July–August 1980, 46.

75. Roger Ebert, "Russ Meyer: Ten Years after the 'Beyond,'" *Film Comment*, July–August 1980, 44.

76. John Waters, "Out on the Edge," *Film Comment*, May–June 1981, 11.

77. Waters, "Out on the Edge," 12.

78. There is surprisingly little empirical research available on the composition of teen horror audiences; the films often have brief (or no) first run and the playoff on video, where these titles do most of their business, is especially difficult to track and code. What research there is in print affirms the obvious, that teen horror films are watched first and foremost by young men. See Bruce Austin, *The Film Audience: An International Bibliography of Research* (Metuchen, NJ: Scarecrow Press, 1983); and "Portrait of a Cult Film Audience: *The Rocky Horror Picture Show*," *Journal of Popular Film and Television*, no. 8 (1981): 43–54.

79. Charles Leerhorn, "This Year's Model," *Newsweek*, summer–fall 1990, 47.

80. Robin Wood, *Hollywood from Vietnam to Reagan* (New York: Columbia University Press, 1986), 126.

81. Wes Craven, "MPAA: The Horror in My Life," *Films in Review*, September–October 1996, 34.

82. Craven, "MPAA: The Horror in My Life," 37.

83. Legend has it that *L'Avventura* was booed at Cannes in 1960 but by the end of the year was hailed by critics and cognoscenti as a landmark film.

84. Much of my discussion of the production of *Zabriskie Point* is based on Beverly Walker, "Michelangelo and the Leviathan," *Film Comment*, September–October 1992, 36–49.

85. Walker, "Michelangelo and the Leviathan," 48.

86. Antonioni as cited by Walker, "Michelangelo and the Leviathan," 48.

87. Andrew Essex, "NC-17 Gets an F," *Entertainment Weekly*, August 13, 1999, 21.

88. "'Mature' Tending to Equate 'General,'" *Variety*, February 19, 1969, 7.

89. "MPAA Film Ratings: 1968–1981," *Variety*, November 11, 1981, 18.

90. Only 57 percent of the noncollege group and only 34 percent of those without a high school degree described themselves as frequent moviegoers.

91. Jack Valenti, "Demographics Cue Upped B.O.," *Variety*, January 3, 1973.

92. This is likely to change in the early years after the millennium. Baby boomers, the demographic targeted by the MPAA member studios after 1968, will be in that "older audience" group. This demographic, the studios' bread and butter now for over thirty years, will be too rich and too big to ignore.

93. See Lewis, *Whom God Wishes to Destroy*; and Justin Wyatt, *High Concept: Movies and Marketing in Hollywood* (Austin: University of Texas Press, 1994).

NOTES TO CHAPTER 5

1. From the start, the MPAA attached a fee to all film submissions to the CARA board. Even if the fee is considered a means by which the rating system might meet its expenses—as if the studios themselves don't have enough money to support it on their own—the symbolic or ritual aspect of the exchange of cash for a rating designation seems revelatory.

2. These two cases are discussed at length in chapter 4.

3. In the summer of 1979 the Musuem of Modern Art in New York held a five-week retrospective of films produced by Samuel Z. Arkoff for American International Pictures (AIP). That the producer of the likes of *Wild in the Streets* and *I Was a Teenage Werewolf* got a five-week run at MOMA reveals just how complex this relationship continues to be.

4. David Chute, "Wages of Sin: An Interview with David F. Friedman," *Film Comment*, August 1986, 35.

5. Muybridge's series photographs of nude women were not, technically speaking, *films*. Joseph W. Slade, "Violence in the Hard-Core Pornographic Film: A Historical Survey," *Journal of Communication* 34, no. 3 (1984): 149.

6. The dates on the films are contested by historians. These may well not be the first stag films shot, but they are the oldest still available for viewing. According to Linda Williams, the Kinsey version of *A Free Ride* is incomplete; the hard-core action that closes the film is from a 1924 stag reel titled *The Casting Couch*. Much of my discussion of these early stag films is based on Williams's work in *Hard Core: Power, Pleasure and the Frenzy of the Visible* (Berkeley: University of California Press, 1989), 58–85.

7. Williams, *Hard Core: Power, Pleasure and the Frenzy of the Visible*, 73.

8. Eric Schaefer, *Bold! Daring! Shocking! True! A History of Exploitation Films, 1919–1959* (Durham: Duke University Press, 1999).

9. David K. Frasier, *Russ Meyer: The Life and Films* (Jefferson, NC: McFarland, 1990), 5.

10. *Excelsior Pictures v. Board of Regents,* 3 N.Y. 2d 237, 144 N.E. 2d 31 (1957).

11. *Garden of Eden* showed full female nudity from behind only. Women appear bare-breasted, but frontal shots never show anything from the waist down to the knees. Men are also shown nude in full figure from behind and topless. Children are shown nude in full figure from in front and behind—a striking example of how an image might mean one thing at one point in time and something quite different at another.

12. Eddie Muller and Daniel Faris, *Grindhouse: The Forbidden World of "Adult's Only" Entertainment* (New York: St. Martin's, 1996), 62.

13. For a descriptive, entertaining, but informal survey of this second wave of exploitation pictures, see Muller and Faris, *Grindhouse: The Forbidden World of "Adult's Only" Entertainment,* 82–106.

14. Schaefer, *Bold! Daring! Shocking! True!* 337.

15. My discussion of the American release of *Ecstasy* is based in large part on Frank Miller, *Censored Hollywood: Sex, Sin and Violence on Screen* (Atlanta: Turner Publishing, 1994), 102–3.

16. For more on the ways the press highlighted the foreignness of *Ecstasy,* see Schaefer, *Bold! Daring! Shocking! True!* 158–60.

17. "*Ecstasy:* The Movie That Caused a War," *Look,* March 1937, 28–31.

18. "*Ecstasy,*" *New York Post,* April 25, 1936.

19. Joseph Mayer, *Merely Collosal* (New York: Simon and Schuster, 1953), 233–34.

20. "Sexacious Sellin' Best B.O. Slant for Foreign Language Films in U.S.," *Variety,* June 9, 1948, 18.

21. David F. Friedman with Don Nevi, *Confessions of a Trash-Film King* (Buffalo: Prometheus Books, 1990), 100.

22. For more on Babb, see David Chute, "Wages of Sin: An Interview with David F. Friedman," *Film Comment,* August 1986, 39–43; and Muller and Faris, *Grindhouse: The Forbidden World of "Adult's Only" Entertainment,* 42–44.

23. Everything was not, of course, shown in the film. The story—about a young girl who gets pregnant out of wedlock, loses her paramour to a plane crash, and then is shipped off to relatives to have the baby in secret—is hardly explicit. The characters blanch at the possibility of ever having to say the word "pregnant," let alone any other more explicit term. But the film features a series of sex hygiene reels inserted into the narrative near the film's absurd climax (in which the girl nearly dies of some mysterious complication). The sex hygiene films are indeed graphic (we see a cesarean section in real detail; we see a naked, diseased breast) but decidedly unerotic.

24. David Denby, review of *Romance, New Yorker,* October 18–25, 1999, 71.

25. Review of *Deep Throat, Variety,* June 28, 1972, 26.

26. Linda Lovelace and Mike McGrady, *Ordeal* (New York: Berkeley Press, 1980). For more on the treatment of actors in porn, see Susan Faludi, "Waiting for Wood: A Death on the New Frontier," in *Stiffed* (New York: William Morrow, 1999).

27. Advertisement, *Variety,* June 28, 1972, 25.

28. "50 Top Grossing Films," *Variety,* May 23, 1973, 15.

29. "50 Top Grossing Films," *Variety,* May 23, 1973, 15. The successful release of *Billy Jack* is an interesting story told well elsewhere. See Justin Wyatt, "From Roadshowing to Saturation Release: Majors, Independents, and Marketing/Distribution Innovations," in *The New American Cinema,* ed. Jon Lewis (Durham: Duke University Press, 1998), 73–75.

30. Review of *The Devil in Miss Jones, Variety,* February 21, 1973, 18, 24.

31. Review of *The Devil in Miss Jones,* 24. *Variety* reviewers routinely and for the most part accurately predict box office success or failure based on the ways films might be distributed and exhibited. Reviewers who write for the trades sometimes better appreciate how products move through the marketplace than studio executives (who have so much more at stake).

32. Review of *The Devil in Miss Jones,* 24.

33. For a more detailed account of the box office grosses of late sixties and early seventies hard and soft core, see Justin Wyatt, "Selling Atrocious Behaviour: Revising Sexualities in the Marketplace for Adult Film in the 60s," in *Swinging Single: Representing Sexuality in the 1960s,* ed. Hilary Radner and Moya Luckett (Minneapolis: University of Minnesota Press, 1999).

34. Much like the MPAA studios, the AFAA appreciated that it needed a strategy to avoid or subvert the local, informal, and mostly extralegal censorship of its product.

35. One of the principal arguments made against hard core in the *Final Report of the Attorney General's Commission on Pornography* (Nashville: Rutledge Hill, 1986), 291–302, was that revenues generated by hard-core films, magazines, and the like were used to finance other illegal activities pursued by organized crime.

36. Advertisement, *Variety,* June 28, 1972, 25.

37. Advertisement, *Variety,* March 18, 1970, 23. Titles with less prerelease hype or with less impressive opening week numbers could not be so easily advertised as a legit picture. Instead, these films continued to be promoted in the trades the way old-fashioned exploiters were. For example, the 1970 release *Secrets of Sex* was advertised under the banner headline "Weird Sex Film Praised by London Critics." Excerpts from reviews that seemed less laudatory than amazed followed: "Freaky . . . story of man's manic sexuality" (*Guardian*); "An unashamedly bizarre concoction of erotica" (*Films in London*); and "Sexy, sexy-violent, sexy-bizarre . . . excellent" (*Today's Cinema*). Advertisement, *Variety,* March 4, 1970, 11.

38. David Chute, "Tumescent Market for One-Armed Videophiles," *Film Comment,* September–October 1981, 68.

39. Advertisement, *Variety,* January 22, 1975, 45.

40. For those interested in *reading* more about porn, see Williams, *Hard Core: Power, Pleasure and the Frenzy of the Visible;* and "Pornographies On/Scene, or Diff'rent Strokes for Diff'rent Folks," in *Sex Exposed: Sexuality and the Pornography Debate,* ed. Lyne Segal and Mary McIntosh (London: Virago, 1992); Laura Kipnis, *Bound and Gagged: Pornography and the Politics of Fantasy in America* (Durham: Duke University Press, 1999); Constance Penley, "Crackers and Whackers: The White Trashing of Porn," in *White Trash: Race and Class in America,* ed. Matt Wray and Annalee Newitz (New York: Routledge, 1997), 89–112; Kenneth Turan and Stephen F. Zito, *Sinema: American Pornographic Films and the People Who Make Them* (New York: Praeger, 1974); Michael S. Kimmel, ed., *Men Confront Pornography* (New York: Meridian, 1990); Robert Stoller, *Porn: Myths for the Twentieth Century* (New Haven: Yale University Press, 1991); Alan Soble, *Pornography, Marxism, Feminism, and the Future of Sexuality* (New Haven: Yale University Press, 1986); Annette Kuhn, *Women's Pictures* (London: Routledge and Kegan-Paul, 1982); John Ellis, "On Pornography," *Screen* 21, no. 1 (1980); Chuck Kleinhans and Julia Lesage, "The Politics of Sexual Representation," *Jump Cut,* no. 30 (1985); Angela Carter, *The Sadeian Woman and the Ideology of Pornography* (New York: Pantheon, 1978); and B. Ruby Rich, "Anti-Porn: Soft-Issue, Hard World," *Village Voice,* July 20, 1982, 1, 16–18, 30.

41. Kipnis, *Bound and Gagged,* 163.

42. Kipnis, *Bound and Gagged,* 162.

43. Kipnis, *Bound and Gagged,* 164.

44. See my discussion of *Mutual Film Corporation v. Industrial Commission of Ohio* in chapter 3.

45. Kipnis, *Bound and Gagged,* 175.

46. Kipnis, *Bound and Gagged,* 162.

47. Kipnis, *Bound and Gagged,* 166.

48. It is ironic that the simply awful TV sitcom *Different Strokes,* which told the story of a rich white guy who adopts two black kids (out of liberal guilt), took its title from this phrase made popular by *Deep Throat.*

49. Williams, *Hard Core: Power, Pleasure and the Frenzy of the Visible,* 92–153.

50. Al DiLauro and Gerald Rabkin, *Dirty Movies: An Illustrated History of the Stag Film, 1915–1970* (New York: Chelsea House, 1976), 25.

51. Stephen Ziplow, *The Film Maker's Guide to Pornography* (New York: Drake, 1977).

52. Williams, *Hard Core: Power, Pleasure and the Frenzy of the Visible,* 107. See also W. T. J. Mitchell, *Iconology: Image, Text, Ideology* (Chicago: University of Chicago Press, 1986), 191–92.

53. Peter Boyer quoting litigator John Coale in "Big Guns," *New Yorker,* May 17, 1999, 56.

54. Williams, *Hard Core: Power, Pleasure and the Frenzy of the Visible*, 108.

55. *Roth v. United States*, 354 U.S. 476 (1957). *Jacobellis v. Ohio*, 378 U.S. 184 (1964). *Roth* will be discussed in great detail later on in this chapter.

56. I think *Cabaret* is an exception to this rule. Unlike most other musicals, the plot, theme, and characters in *Cabaret* are vividly drawn. Characters don't break into song for no good reason. The songs occur mostly in the club, where performers sing for a living, and bear certain metaphoric relation to the very serious plot and theme of the film (regarding Nazism, the political nature of art, etc.).

57. Williams, *Hard Core: Power Pleasure and the Frenzy of the Visible*, 120–52.

58. Kael's review was reprinted in its entirety in a two-page advertising spread in the *New York Times*, December 24, 1972, D5–D6.

59. See Wyatt, "Selling Atrocious Behaviour."

60. Review of *Last Tango in Paris*, *Variety*, October 18, 1972, 12.

61. Harlan Jacobson, "Climaxing Many Legal Wins, *Tango* Returns to Cincy," *Variety*, March 19, 1975, 17.

62. Some of the newspapers that featured news articles on the court battles over *Last Tango* at the same time refused to carry ads for the film because it was X-rated.

63. Review of *Last Tango in Paris*, 12.

64. "Analyzing *Emmanuelle's* B.O. Impact on the Market," *Variety*, May 7, 1975, 56.

65. Wyatt, "Selling Atrocious Behaviour." For more on high concept, see Justin Wyatt, *High Concept: Movies and Marketing in Hollywood* (Austin: University of Texas Press, 1994).

NOTES TO CHAPTER 6

1. While the terms "pornography" and "obscenity" are often used interchangeably in the popular discourse on the subject, the courts use the terms with more specificity. "Pornography" is a general term used to describe work that is brought to the attention of the courts. Obscenity is what pornography becomes when it has been proscribed by law. As Richard F. Hixson succinctly writes, obscenity is "largely defined by efforts to regulate it." See Richard F. Hixson, *Pornography and the Justices: The Supreme Court and the Intractable Obscenity Problem* (Carbondale: Southern Illinois University Press, 1996), 1–19.

2. In 1711 Massachusetts enacted a statute broadly titled "An Act against Intemperance, Immorality and Profaneness, and in Reformation of Manners." The title and text of the statute can be traced to the colony's Puritan roots. While Puritan views on the subject (and the nasty sorts of punishments promised to those who might break the law) seem extreme, even extremist, it is important to remember that the Puritan tradition continued to have a sig-

nificant impact on the framers when they wrote the First Amendment. If we are to talk about the framers' intent, we should note that while they were fearful of abridging self-expression as it regarded freedom of religious expression (since religious persecution was the reason so many colonists had left Europe), they were also aware of what the Puritans, indeed many Protestants, had to say about pornography and the erotic in general. The Puritans had a history of endorsing if not enacting censorship regulations dating at least as far back as the seventeenth century in England. Apropos the notion that regulation is only as good as those who get to do the regulating: the Massachusetts obscenity statute also prohibited the possession of writings containing Quaker opinions.

3. *Province Laws*, 1711–12, ch. 6, section 19.

4. *Laws of Vermont*, 1824, ch. 23, number 1, section 23.

5. 5 Stat 566. The ostensible targets here were French postcards.

6. 15 Stat 50. The primary distribution apparatus for pictorial pornography in 1865 was the U.S. mail. Early successes in banning pornography—spearheaded by the antipornography activist Anthony Comstock—sidestepped the intractable First Amendment debate and instead focused on the right of the government to regulate the U.S. mail service.

7. *Queen v. Read*, 11 Mod. Rep. 142 (1708).

8. *King v. Curl*, 2 Stra. 788 (1720).

9. 16 and 17 Vic., c. 107 (1853).

10. 20 and 21 Vic., c. 83 (1857).

11. 20 and 21 Vic., c. 83 (1857).

12. *Queen v. Hicklin*, L.R., 3 Q.B. 360 (1868).

13. My discussion of Anthony Comstock's role in the evolution of a legal standard of obscenity in the United States in based on an argument presented in James C. Foster and Susan M. Leeson, *Constitutional Law: Cases in Context* (Englewood Cliffs, NJ: Prentice Hall, 1998).

14. *Rosen v. United States*, 161 U.S. 29 (1896). In *Ex Parte Jackson*, 96 U.S. 727 (1878), the Supreme Court upheld the government's constitutional right to regulate the mails (per the Comstock Act). But it was not until the *Rosen* case that the Court first weighed in on the subject of obscenity.

15. Justice John Marshall Harlan should not be confused with his grandson, Justice John Harlan, who sat on the Supreme Court for sixteen terms from the mid-1950s until his retirement in 1971.

16. *Swearingen v. United States*, 161 U.S. 446 (1896).

17. Swearingen described his unnamed adversary as "meaner, filthier, rottener than the rottenest strumpet that prowls the streets by night . . . a black-hearted coward [who would] sell a mother's honor with less hesitancy and for much less silver than Judas betrayed the savior, who would pimp and fatten on a sister's shame with as much unction as a buzzard gluts on carrion."

18. In finding for Swearingen, the Court purposefully elaborated that written or pictorial material might be unpleasant, nasty, or even libelous, but it was obscene only if it was erotic in nature and appealed primarily to the prurient interests of one or more groups within the larger mass audience. Such a view was consistent with the intent and spirit of Judge Cockburn's opinion in *Queen v. Hicklin*, and was based on a distrust and disdain for the uneducated and unsophisticated masses.

19. The *Mutual* case is discussed at length in chapter 2.

20. *United States v. Kennerly*, 209 F. 119 (D.C.S.D.N.Y. 1913).

21. Hand also authored the landmark opinion in the Latham Loop patents case *Motion Picture Patents Co. v. Independent Moving Pictures Company of America*, 200 F.411 (2nd Cir. 1912), a decision that precipitated the demise of the Motion Pictures Patents Company.

22. *United States v. One Book Called* Ulysses *by James Joyce*, 5 F. Supp. 182 (D.N.Y. 1933). *Ulysses* proved to be a very significant book in the history of literary censorship. See Paul Vanderham, *James Joyce and Censorship: The Trials of* Ulysses (New York: New York University Press, 1998).

23. My discussion of *United States v. One Book Called* Ulysses *by James Joyce* is based on Hixson, *Pornography and the Justices*, 11–14. Woolsey's opinion in *United States v. One Book Called* Ulysses *by James Joyce* reveals the judge's personal take on the novel, which he read in its entirety before examining the specific "passages [about] which the government particularly complain[ed]." (This was unusual at the time.) Like a lot of educated Americans, Woolsey admired the book "taken as a whole" and argued that "in spite of its unusual frankness" it should not be proscribed as legally obscene. Woolsey's admiration for Joyce's novel and his conviction that the government should not be in the business of censoring great and important works of literary fiction led him to question not only the utility of the *Hicklin* standard but also the larger system of censorship that the standard upheld.

24. *United States v. One Book Entitled* Ulysses *by James Joyce*, 72 F. 2d 705 (1934).

25. An interesting side note: Samuel Roth, the New York bookseller involved in the landmark case, *Roth v. United States* in 1957, was once arrested and jailed for selling a pirated edition of Joyce's *Ulysses*, the first version sold in the United States.

26. *United States v. Levine*, 83 F. 2d 156 (1936).

27. *Commonwealth v. Gordon*, 66 D.C 101 (1949).

28. Hixson, *Pornography and the Justices*, 16–19. *People v. Doubleday*, 297 N.Y. 687, 77 N.E. 2d 6 (1947). See also *People v. Doubleday*, 335 U.S. 848 (1948).

29. At issue was one particular section of the book titled "The Princess with the Golden Hair."

30. Without offering a written opinion, the Court of Special Sessions af-

firmed the lower court decision that the publisher and its bookstores had violated the New York state penal code, section 1141: "A person who sells . . . or has in his possession with intent to sell, lend, distribute or give away, or to show . . . any obscene, lewd, lascivious, filthy, indecent, disgusting book . . . or who . . . prints, utters, publishes, or in any manner manufactures, or prepares any such book . . . is guilty of a misdemeanor."

31. The Supreme Court split four to four on *People v. Doubleday*, with Felix Frankfurter not participating in the decision. The conviction was therefore allowed to stand.

32. While the New York court—and for that matter the Supreme Court as well—rendered its decisions in *People v. Doubleday* without written opinion, it is worth taking a look at Judge Nathan D. Perlman's articulate dissent, registered at the very start of the lengthy and complex legal struggle over Wilson's book. Recalling Woolsey's opinion in *United States v. One Book Called* Ulysses *by James Joyce* and Learned Hand's opinion in *United States v. Levine*, Perlman called for a little common sense:

> To adopt a standard of obscenity which would disregard the interests of the mature and ignore the positive and vital contribution which books can make in their lives, is to needlessly sacrifice the welfare of a vast portion of our community. . . . The public is entitled to the benefit of the writer's insight and that right may not be lightly disregarded by excluding from consideration all interests but those of the young and immature.

In 1959, two years after the Court "defined" obscenity in *Roth v. United States*, *Memoirs of Hecate County* was published in a new edition and sold without incident.

33. *Butler v. Michigan*, 352 U.S. 380 (1957).

34. In his opinion in the *Butler* case Frankfurter made no effort to define obscenity or to formulate a relevant standard or test, but he implied a willingness on the part of the majority of the Court to establish guidelines by which adults might have access to materials that would have been found obscene under previous guidelines.

35. *Interstate Circuit v. Dallas*, 390 U.S. 676 (1968).

36. In the seven years between *Roth v. United States* and *Jacobellis v. Ohio* only one significant obscenity case, *Manual Enterprises, Inc. v. Day*, 370 U.S. 478 (1962), seemed to signal progress toward a national obscenity standard. The *Manual Enterprises* case concerned the seizure by the Alexandria, Virginia, postmaster of a single bulk mailing of hundreds of magazines published for gay men. A lower court in Virginia upheld the ban. But by a vote of six to one (with Justices Frankfurter and White not participating), the U.S. Supreme Court reversed the state judgment, maintaining that the Alexandria postmaster was not

within his rights as elaborated in the Comstock Act or his job description when he refused to deliver the magazines.

In one of two significant opinions written for the majority, Justices Harlan and Stewart, both social conservatives, avoided the central issue regarding the U.S. mail service's role in the case and instead focused on the three magazines themselves, which they found to be lacking in "patent offensiveness" or "indecency," as per the state statute. Justice Brennan and Chief Justice Warren took a different tack, remarking that the postmaster general was not "authorized" to evaluate the material at all. In doing so, Brennan and Warren implied that the proposed national standard might render the Comstock Act moot.

37. The background on *Roth* presented here is based on Foster and Leeson, *Constitutional Law: Cases in Context*, vol. 2.

38. Like Guccione and Flynt, Roth was a provocateur. By the time his 1955 conviction was heard by the Supreme Court, Roth had over thirty years of experience fighting state censorship, including a renowned battle with the postmaster general Arthur E. Summerfield, who vigilantly pursued enforcement of the Comstock Act during the Eisenhower administration.

39. Hixson, *Pornography and the Justices*, 23–24.

40. The briefs challenged the constitutionality of the specific obscenity statutes at issue in both the *Roth* and *Alberts* cases as well as larger questions regarding obscenity law and enforcement in general. The briefs argued that (1) with regard to the *Hicklin* standard, "no reliable evidence put on at [either] trial show that obscene publications or pictures have any appreciable effect on conduct," and (2) with regard to the clarity of criteria imposed at trial, "criminal obscenity statutes [in specific here and in general] violate the Due Process Clause of the Fifth Amendment. Due process requires that an individual know with certainty whether action is criminal before engaging in the conduct."

41. The operative California criteria are derived from *People v. Wepplo*, 78 Cal. App. 2d Supp. 959, 178 P.2d 853 (1947).

42. For *Harlan, Roth* was less about obscenity per se than the constitutionality of the specific New York and California state statutes and the more general constitutional right of the states to draft and enforce obscenity statutes enjoining the publication/distribution of materials "obnoxious to the moral fabric of society." That subjective criteria inevitably attend such statutory determinations, Harlan concluded, compelled the Court to turn the entire matter over to local authorities: "the very division of opinion on the subject [of obscenity] counsels us to respect the choice made by the state [to draft and enforce obscenity statutes]."

The only time the federal government was compelled to interfere with the states' right to draft and enforce obscenity laws was when such laws became so permissive as to allow the screening or sale of materials objectively determined by the Court to be hard-core.

43. *Burstyn v. Wilson*, 343 U.S. 501 (1952), *Gelling v. Texas*, 343 U.S. 960 (1952), and *Superior Films v. Department of Education of Ohio*, 346 U.S. 587 (1954).

44. The phrase "a varying meaning from time to time" is taken verbatim from Hand's opinion in *United States v. Kennerly*.

45. Rembar successfully litigated the lifting of the ban on *Tropic of Cancer* and *Lady Chatterley's Lover* and for a while defended the legendary comedian Lenny Bruce.

46. Hixson, *Pornography and the Justices*, 53.

47. *A Book Named John Cleland's Memoirs of a Woman of Pleasure v. Attorney General of Massachusetts*, 383 U.S. 413 (1966).

48. Justices Black and Stewart concurred by simply affirming their respective (dissenting) opinions in *Ginzburg v. United States*, 383 U.S. 463 (1966), and *Mishkin v. New York*, 383 U.S. 502 (1966). Their decision not to sign on to Brennan's opinion even though they concurred with his decision in the case revealed how little support Brennan had in his pursuit of a national standard.

49. Though the literary experts argued convincingly that *Memoirs of a Woman of Pleasure* was not "utterly without redeeming social value," Putnam's advertising scheme for the book raised some new problems for those on the Court who supported a lifting of the ban. The advertising campaign highlighted the book's erotic content and not its literary and/or literary historical value. The attorneys for the state of Massachusetts argued persuasively that the advertising folks at Putnam had in effect defined or at least described *Memoirs* in terms that highlighted the fact that the book was indeed (legally) obscene. Brennan dismissed "the circumstances of production, sale, and publicity" as irrelevant. "All possible uses of the book must . . . be considered," Brennan concluded, "and the mere risk that the book might be exploited by panderers because it so perversely treats sexual matters cannot alter the fact—given the view of the Massachusetts court attributing to *Memoirs* a modicum of literary or historical value—that the book will have redeeming social importance in the hands of those who publish or distribute it on the basis of that value."

50. *Bridges v. California*, 314 U.S. 252 (1941).

51. A final and telling challenge was issued in Harlan's, Clark's, and White's separate dissenting opinions. All three focused on Brennan's efforts to develop national criteria and expressed reservations about how he seemed to be assembling material from a series of related opinions (*Jacobellis, Roth,* and *Memoirs*). Clark argued that the *Roth* test was fairly simple: "material is obscene and not constitutionally protected against regulation and proscription if to the average person, applying contemporary community standards, the dominant theme of the material taken as a whole appeals to prurient interest." While he supported such a definition, he and his fellow dissenters did not abide by and indeed resented the suggestion that the *Roth* test was somehow, suddenly a combination of two similar opinions in two different cases.

52. Hixson, *Pornography and the Justices*, 73.

53. Hixson, *Pornography and the Justices*, 75.

54. Foster and Leeson, *Constitutional Law: Cases in Context.*

55. Bob Woodward and Scott Armstrong, *The Brethren: Inside the Supreme Court* (New York: Avon, 1979), 234.

56. The commission lineup, appointed by Johnson, included William B. Lockhart, Frederick Wagman, Edward Elson, Thomas Gill, Edward Greenwood, Morton Hill, G. William Jones, Kenneth B. Keating, Joseph Klapper, Otto Larsen, Irving Lehrman, Freeman Lewis, Winfrey Link, Morris Lipton, Thomas Lynch, Barbara Scott, Cathryn Spelts, and Marvin Wolfgang.

57. Kenneth Keating and Charles H. Keating Jr. are not related.

58. The entire report was published as *The Report of the Commission on Obscenity and Pornography* (New York: New York Times Books, 1970). Keating's long and detailed rebuttal is published in full at the end of the book (578–664).

59. Published as *Final Report of the Attorney General's Commission on Pornography.*

60. The difficulty in predicting precisely how Justices White or Black might vote on key civil rights issues, for example, led Nixon to the conclusion that neither jurist could be trusted as his chief justice.

61. *Brown v. Board of Education* and *Brown v. Board of Education II; Miranda v. Arizona;* and *Ginsberg v. New York* and *Interstate Circuit v. Dallas.*

62. Warren's politics were hardly a secret. He had been a three-term governor of California and a vice presidential nominee.

63. Eisenhower also selected the liberal justice William Brennan, a more conciliatory figure on the Court than Warren. That said, Brennan was a staunch opponent of capital punishment and the eventual broker if not author of the landmark decision in *Roe v. Wade.*

64. Woodward and Armstrong, *The Brethren*, 5.

65. Justice William O. Douglas struck Nixon as a radical civil libertarian. Hugo Black was less colorful than Douglas but no less of a problem on First Amendment issues. Abe Fortas, William Brennan, and Thurgood Marshall were liberals, especially on civil rights issues. Byron White and John Harlan were conservative Republicans, but Nixon didn't trust them, especially with regard to school desegregation. Potter Stewart was the only acceptable candidate to replace Earl Warren as chief justice, but he turned Nixon down. Warren Burger, though new to the Court in 1968, became chief justice by default.

66. Woodward and Armstrong, *The Brethren: Inside the Supreme Court*, 14–24.

67. Woodward and Armstrong contend that Douglas's lifestyle additionally bothered Nixon. Douglas was on his fourth marriage at the time, to a woman forty-five years his junior.

68. Woodward and Armstrong cite a memo from FBI director J. Edgar Hoover to attorney general John Mitchell confirming that the Justice Department was funneling information/dirt on Fortas to the *Life* magazine writer

William Lambert. Woodward and Armstrong, *The Brethren: Inside the Supreme Court*, 14.

69. If Fortas was survived by his wife, Wolfson promised to pay her instead.

70. Woodward and Armstrong, *The Brethren: Inside the Supreme Court*, 16.

71. Nixon appreciated the fact that the South won him the election in 1968 and planned to use the Haynsworth nomination to pay the region back for its support.

72. The failure to replace Fortas in a timely fashion proved to be a significant if temporary setback for the Nixon administration as a key civil rights case, *Alexander v. Holmes County Board of Education*, reached the eight-man Court. With the recent addition of Burger, the Court was evenly split. Brennan, Douglas, Black, and Marshall formed a liberal bloc. Burger joined Harlan, Stewart, and White on the Right.

Alexander v. Holmes County Board of Education was an important case. It concerned the state of Mississippi's continued refusal to comply with mandated school desegregation. The eight-man Court split four to four. Brennan, Douglas, Black, and Marshall expressed outrage at the state's request for yet another delay in what had been fifteen years of stalls and noncompliance. Burger, Harlan, Stewart, and White did not necessarily approve of Mississippi's position but argued that the matter at hand was none of their business. They had had their say on the subject of school desegregation and the state's refusal to comply with the federal law was a problem of enforcement (as opposed to ideology) and thus a problem for the Fifth Circuit Court of Appeals. Brennan brokered a compromise, which worked very much to the liberals' advantage. The Court's two-page *per curiam* insisted on immediate compliance. The decision was a major victory for civil rights advocates at the time. But it also served to highlight the importance, with regard to the ideological balance of the Court, of the next Nixon appointee.

73. Woodward and Armstrong, *The Brethren: Inside the Supreme Court*, 83.

74. I am not convinced that appointees necessarily change all that much after reaching the Court, that presidents are necessarily betrayed by the decisions their appointees make in important cases. Blackmun, as Nixon had hoped, proved to be a dependable conservative player on the Court, with one important exception, *Roe v. Wade*. Blackmun's decision to join the liberal minority in that case (and in doing so establishing a slim majority in favor of a woman's right to an abortion) surprised Nixon and other Washington players. But Blackmun's experience at the Mayo Clinic—his understanding of how doctors viewed the controversial issue—proved more important than his otherwise conservative civil rights record.

75. Woodward and Armstrong, *The Brethren: Inside the Supreme Court*, 97–99.

76. Black died just two days after Harlan submitted his resignation, eight

days after he had submitted his own. Woodward and Armstrong, *The Brethren: Inside the Supreme Court*, 184–85.

77. Mitchell's failure to alert Nixon to the problems posed by Haynsworth and Carswell led Nixon to turn to Dean.

78. Powell was in one very specific way a significant compromise. As president of the Richmond, Virginia, school board, Powell had kept schools open in defiance of segregationist pressure to close them down rather than comply with *Brown v. Board of Education*. By 1971, some three years after the election, Nixon perhaps felt a less pressing need to appoint an anti-integrationist just to satisfy his political supporters in the South, especially since Powell was a social conservative on most counts and a well-respected jurist in a southern state (Virginia).

79. Woodward and Armstrong, *The Brethren: Inside the Supreme Court*, 185–91.

80. *Stanley v, Georgia*, 394 U.S. 557 (1969).

81. *Cain v. Kentucky*, 397 U.S. 319 (1970).

82. *Walker v. Ohio*, 398 U.S. 434 (1970).

83. *Hoyt v. Minnesota*, 399 U.S. 524 (1970).

84. *United States v. Reidel*, 402 U.S. 351 (1971); *United States v. Thirty-seven Photographs*, 402 U.S. 363 (1971). Black, joined by Douglas in a strong dissent in *United States v. Thirty-seven Photographs*, wrote, "The right to read and view any literature and pictures at home is hollow indeed if it does not include a right to carry that material in one's luggage when entering the country."

In *Grove Press v. Maryland State Board of Censors*, 401 U.S. 480 (1971), the Court upheld the state ban on *I Am Curious Yellow* because Douglas, who had once published with Evergreen, a Grove imprint, had to recuse himself. In his absence, the court split four to four; the tie allowed the Maryland judgment to stand. The ironic effect of *Stanley* is explored at length in Hixson, *Pornography and the Justices*, 99–107.

85. Richard F. Hixson, *Pornography and the Justices: The Supreme Court and the Intractable Obscenity Problem*, 107.

86. *Miller v. California*, 423 U.S. 15 (1973). *Paris Adult Theater I v. Slaton*, 423 U.S. 49 (1973). *United States v. 12 200′ Reels of Super 8 mm Film*, 413 U.S. 113 (1973). *United States v. Orito*, 413 U.S. 139 (1973); *Kaplan v. California*, 413 U.S. 115 (1973).

87. "Show Biz's Fig-Leaf Crisis: High Court Hands Reins over Porno to Local Judges," *Variety*, June 27, 1973, 1, 78.

88. The brief also argued that the California state courts had "committed a reversible error" by failing to prove that the materials in question were obscene by even local community standards. The ACLU challenged the expertise of the one state witness, a police officer, and the unscientific, unrepresentative "survey" used by the state to at once define the community's standards and to label Miller's mailer and the texts it advertised obscene.

89. The italics are mine. The deletion of the term "utterly" was the single most significant difference between the *Roth* and *Miller* standards.

90. The Court did not actually uphold the state court's decision but instead returned the case to the state with stricter guidelines. Douglas's point, then, was that Miller was being held accountable *post facto* to what were essentially new standards.

91. "Show Biz's Fig-Leaf Crisis," 1.

92. In *Kaplan v. California*, the Nixon majority held that a book containing words alone (and no pictures or illustrations of any sort) could be found obscene. While this did not impact the film industry directly, it did reveal just how seriously the Burger Court took its role in the regulation of pornographic material.

93. See Addison Verrill, "No-Jury, 10 Day Throat Trial; Obscene Ruling by Judge Tyler Foreshadows Fine of $2,000,000," *Variety*, March 7, 1973, 6; and "In 'Greatest Money Notice' Ruling, Judge Tyler Cuts *Deep Throat* Film," *Variety*, March 7, 1973, 1, 33.

94. The 1976 Memphis verdict against sixteen *Deep Throat* defendants (including star Harry Reems) was perhaps the most famous and significant of these cases. The assistant United States attorney Larry Parrish, who succeeded, at least at first, in securing huge fines and even jail time for the film's producers, performers, distributors, and exhibitors, became a celebrity of sorts. He appeared on talk shows and was interviewed in national magazines. In the late 1970s and then even more so during the Reagan-Bush years, porn became the issue *du jour* for politically ambitious and/or celebrity-hungry local, state, and federal prosecutors. See also Justin Wyatt, "Selling Atrocious Behaviour: Revising Sexualities in the Marketplace for Adult Film in the 60s," in *Swinging Single: Representing Sexuality in the 1960s*, ed. Hilary Radner and Moya Luckett (Minneapolis: University of Minnesota Press, 1999).

95. "Bork 'Confesses' Error in Kentucky *Deep Throat* Case," *Variety*, November 3, 1976, 30. Bork chose to define "community" in the narrowest of terms, refusing to acknowledge that the community in question was quite near Cincinnati, where the film was not banned at the time.

96. *Jenkins v. Georgia*, 418 U.S. 153 (1973). The Court voted unanimously to reverse the ban on screenings of *Carnal Knowledge*. Such unanimity was and is rare in obscenity cases—testimony to the absurd criteria used by the local jurisdiction in the case.

NOTES TO CHAPTER 7

1. Addison Verrill, "Porno Thicket Now Jungle? Community Standards Spells Confusion," *Variety*, June 27, 1973, 5.

2. In a *New York Times* opinion piece published about a month later, the controversial novelist Henry Miller—not the Miller in the pivotal California

case, though he no doubt wished he was—also predicted a difficult adjustment period for the majors. Miller thought the anxiety might do the treacherous Hollywood players some good. "As for the impact on the film industry, my guess is that [the studios] will panic. Let them panic, say I, it will be good for their souls." Henry Miller, "Absurd and Unworkable," *New York Times*, August 5, 1973, sec. 2, 16.

3. The italics are mine.

4. It also left uncertain when and how the Court might review or overturn local decisions. After *Redrup v. New York*, the Court routinely reversed local and state decisions after close review of the materials at hand. Burger seemed to suggest in *Miller* that the states had a free hand in defining their own community standards so long as the criteria were reasonable and rational.

5. At the New York Museum of Modern Art, Warner Brothers president Frank Wells, a former entertainment lawyer, opined that the museum, and not the public movie theater, might someday be the only place to see certain contemporary films, like Warner Brothers' own recent release, *Klute*. See "Frank Wells Re. Porno Decisions," *Variety*, July 4, 1973, 6.

6. Verrill, "Porno Thicket Now Jungle?"

7. Verrill, "Porno Thicket Now Jungle?"

8. "Cops Call 'Tango' Tame," *Variety*, June 27, 1973, 6.

9. "Florida's New Law Backed: Close 'Throat,'" *Variety*, June 27, 1973, 6.

10. "See Porno Take-Over By Underworlders," *Variety*, June 27, 1973, 6. Thevis's prediction regarding the increasingly extralegal, clandestine nature of porn after 1973 seems to have come to pass, at least so far as the anecdotal evidence gathered by the Meese Commission suggests. Of particular interest to the Meese Commission members was the role of organized crime in the production and distribution of pornography—an allegation the committee never bothered to connect to the criminalization of porn by the Court after June 1973. See *Final Report of the Attorney General's Commission on Pornography* (Nashville: Rutledge Hill, 1986), 291–302.

11. Robert J. Landry, "Morality in Media Clergy Chiefs Elated: Long Urged End to That 'Redeeming Social Value' Escape," *Variety*, June 27, 1973, 7.

12. "Pornographers Flaunted Their Wares and Embarrassed Plain Folks—Baker," *Variety*, July 4, 1973, 6. The July 4, 1973, issue of *Variety* ran with the headline "Justice Dept.'s Porno Stance: Impossible Burden Removed; Case Load Eased." The article, by Larry Richie, focused on Nixon's realignment of the Court and posed the accurate if not obvious argument that *Miller v. California* reflected the will of the Court's conservative majority to get out of the business of evaluating specific movies, books, and magazines once and for all.

13. When videocassettes first hit the market in the early 1980s, porn titles—many of which could not be publicly screened in theaters in most U.S. communities—were quite suddenly in vogue again.

14. "X's Ducked Like Boxoffice Poison; This Is the Summer of Contented

R's," *Variety*, August 8, 1973, 3.

15. "Pornography Joins Curriculum," *Variety*, August 8, 1973, 3.

16. As an academic I think I'm in as good a position as anyone to make this point.

17. "Has the Supreme Court Saved Us from Obscenity?" *New York Times*, August 5, 1973, sec. 2, 1, 11, 16.

18. Though Feiffer is far better known as a cartoonist, he wrote *Carnal Knowledge*, the studio film that first put the *Miller* standard to the test in *Jenkins v. Georgia*.

19. "I vigorously applaud the decision of the Supreme Court," Buckley wrote in an essay focusing mostly on the Court's effort to distinguish between pornography and art. William Buckley, "Obscenity Is Commerce," *New York Times*, August 5, 1973, sec. 2, 11.

20. Jules Feiffer, "Art for Court's Sake," *New York Times*, August 5, 1973, sec. 2, 1. On all digital converter boxes provided by the cable TV conglomerate ATT/TCI, parents can block programming based on the MPAA/CARA system as well as the new TV rating code. Though the technology is not inside the TV (like a V-chip), it is in the converter/tuner box that precedes the signal's entrance into the television set.

21. Nixon made the connection as well. His efforts to realign the Court had less to do (directly at least) with revisiting the obscenity issue than with supporting states' rights efforts in the South to delay implementation of integration. Van Peebles's focus on race was of course predictable, but his opinion found support from a somewhat unlikely fellow contributor, the Reverend Malcolm Boyd. "Ours is a society that does tragic things," Boyd wrote, "obscene things, in the contexts of power, greed, racism and war."

22. Melvin van Peebles, "Rulings? Not Mine," *New York Times*, August 5, 1973, sec. 2, 11.

23. Shelley Winters, "A Feeling of Deja Vu," *New York Times*, August 5, 1973, sec. 2, 11.

24. Harry Kalven Jr., "A Step Backward," *New York Times*, August 5, 1973, sec. 2, 11.

25. Ephraim London, "Very Real Danger," *New York Times*, August 5, 1973, sec. 2, 16.

26. David Picker, "Some Must Fight," *New York Times*, August 5, 1973, sec. 2, 16.

27. Jack Valenti, "Censorship Is Deadly," *New York Times*, August 5, 1973, sec. 2, 1.

28. Abel Green, "Porno Sinema Tone Hurts N.Y.," *Variety*, March 11, 1970, 1, 74. "If Legit Goes It's Kayo to N.Y. Tourism," *Variety*, January 5, 1972.

29. *Young v. American Mini Theaters, Inc.*, 427 U.S. 50 (1976).

30. Powell took exception to this section of Stevens's opinion. He con-

curred with Stevens et al. that the city of Detroit was within its rights to "inno-vatively" regulate land use, contending that "Without stable neighborhoods, both residential and commercial, large sections of a modern city quickly can de-teriorate into an urban jungle with tragic consequences to social, environmen-tal, and economic values." But because he found that the case did not hinge on free speech protections in any material way, Powell decided against signing on to the third section of Stevens's opinion, much of which focused on First Amendment issues.

31. *Dressed to Kill* reached the marketplace in a period of transition for the two companies that owned it, AIP and Filmways, independents with very dif-ferent ideas about the future of the film business. As the seventies came to a close, Arkoff decided to move AIP slightly up-budget and contracted to pro-duce and release three ambitious features: *Love at First Bite* (a vampire film spoof), *The Amityville Horror* (a medium-budget exploitation film based on a best-selling nonfiction book), and De Palma's lurid psycho-thriller, *Dressed to Kill*. Though all three films did well at the box office, especially considering their sub-$6 million budgets (less than half the studio average at the time), Arkoff soon discovered that his company was not well enough capitalized to bring the films to term. Movies are financed on short-term credit and in 1980 short-term credit cost in the neighborhood of 20 percent. In order to complete and distribute the three films, Arkoff decided to merge AIP with Filmways. Filmways was run at the time by Richard Bloch, who from the start had plans for AIP/Filmways that did not include Arkoff. At the time of the merger, Arkoff wanted to continue to make up-budget exploiters. Bloch dreamed of turning Filmways into a major studio specializing in prestige pictures. About six months after the merger, Bloch exploited a dispute over valuations of the two companies to oust Arkoff. But before he allowed himself to be bought off, Arkoff engineered the release of *Dressed to Kill*. For more on the AIP/Filmways story, see Jon Lewis, *Whom God Wishes to Destroy . . . Francis Coppola and the New Hollywood* (Durham: Duke University Press, 1995), 33–37.

32. Peter Wood, "How a Film Changes from an 'X' to an 'R,'" *New York Times*, July 20, 1980, sec. C, 1.

33. Charles Lyons, *The New Censors: Movies and the Culture Wars* (Philadel-phia: Temple University Press, 1997), 69–70.

34. Gregg Kilday, "Dressing Down," *Los Angeles Herald Examiner*, August 18, 1980.

35. See Marcia Pally et. al., "Sex, Violence and Brian De Palma," *Film Com-ment* 21, no. 5 (September–October 1985): 9–13.

36. Vincent Canby, "Dressed to Kill: De Palma Mystery," *New York Times*, July 25, 1980, sec. C.

37. Pauline Kael, "Master Spy, Master Seducer," *New Yorker*, August 4, 1980, 68.

38. David Denby, "Deep Threat," *New York*, July 28, 1980, 44.

39. Lyons, *The New Censors: Movies and the Culture Wars*, 74–80.

40. Lyons, *The New Censors: Movies and the Culture Wars*, 79.

41. Pat Buchanan, "Anything for a Buck: Hollywood's Sleazy Image of Christ," *Philadelphia Inquirer*, July 27, 1988, sec. A.

42. "MPAA Supports Universal's 'Temptation,'" *Variety*, July 27, 1988, 3.

43. Lyons, *The New Censors: Movies and the Culture Wars*, 170.

44. "An Ordinance of the City of Minneapolis" was reprinted in full in *Film Comment*, December 1984, 31.

45. In *American Booksellers v. Hudnut*, 771 F.2d 323 (1986), the Supreme Court affirmed a federal appeals court decision holding that antiporn "civil rights" ordinances constituted a form of "thought control" and as such violated the First Amendment.

46. See Catharine MacKinnon, *Feminism Unmodified: Discourses on Life and Law* (Cambridge: Harvard University Press, 1987); Andrea Dworkin, *Pornography: Men Possessing Women* (New York: Dutton, 1991); Susan Griffin, *Pornography and Silence: Culture's Revenge against Nature* (New York: Harper and Row, 1981); and Susan Brownmiller, *Against Our Will: Men, Women and Rape* (New York: Simon and Schuster, 1975).

47. "Pornography: Love or Death," *Film Comment*, December 1984, 29–49. The contributors to this feature "midsection" included the film critic David Denby, the law professor Alan Dershowitz, the media researchers Edward Donnerstein and Daniel Linz, *Screw* magazine editor Al Goldstein, WAP founding member Dorchen Leidholdt, the media researchers Neil Malamuth and Jan Lindstrom, the Minneapolis-based antiporn activist Janella Miller, *Film Comment* writer Marcia Pally, the psychiatrist and chairperson of the National Coalition on Television Violence Thomas Radecki, the prostitutes' rights activist Margo St. James, the attorney and professor Lois Sheinfeld, and the anticensorship feminist Ann Snitow.

48. Here Goldstein, perhaps unwittingly, is calling attention to one of the key issues in the feminist debate on porn. The binary of pornography and erotica is elaborated and analyzed at length by Susan Sontag in her influential essay "The Pornographic Imagination." See Susan Sontag, *Styles of Radical Will* (New York: Doubleday, 1969), 35–73.

49. *Final Report of the Attorney General's Commission on Pornography*, 224–46, 465–71, 472–76. See Linda Lovelace and Mike McGrady, *Ordeal* (New York: Berkeley Press, 1980).

50. "Pornography: Love or Death," 38.

51. "Pornography: Love or Death," 43.

52. "Pornography: Love or Death," 38.

53. For a deft critique of the antiporn feminist argument, see Andrew Ross, "The Popularity of Pornography," in *No Respect: Intellectuals and Popular Culture* (New York: Routledge, 1989), 171–208.

54. Lois P. Sheinfeld, "Ratings: The Big Chill," *Film Comment*, June 1986, 13.

55. Pener, "Ted's Civil War," *Entertainment Weekly*, November 22, 1996, 19.

56. Pener, "Ted's Civil War," 22.

57. Pener, "Ted's Civil War," 19.

58. Pener, "Ted's Civil War," 19, 22.

59. Tonight, as I am finishing this manuscript, *Taxi Driver* is scheduled to air on Turner Classic Movies. Perhaps it is hard for Turner to keep track of such things, running so many companies and sports teams as he does.

60. Pener, "Ted's Civil War," 24.

61. Pener, "Ted's Civil War," 24.

62. Pener, "What Price Happiness?" *Entertainment Weekly*, October 30, 1998, 20.

63. Pener, "What Price Happiness?" 21.

64. Miramax is owned by the Disney Corporation, which balked in 1995 at its subsidiary's release of the unrated *Kids*. Disney executives insisted that the film be released under the Shining Excalibur banner, with no reference anywhere on the print to Miramax or Disney. Fox Searchlight is owned by the News Corporation and Sony Classics is owned by Sony.

65. For a more detailed account of the Viacom purchase of Paramount and of Redstone's skirmish with Malone, see Jon Lewis, "Money Matters: Hollywood in the Corporate Era," in *The New American Cinema*, ed. Jon Lewis (Durham: Duke University Press, 1998), 107–10.

66. As late as 1997, one out of every four video stores in the United States was a Blockbuster.

67. Ty Burr, "Blockbusted," *Entertainment Weekly*, August 15, 1997, 42.

68. See Josh Young, "A Killer Deal," *Entertainment Weekly*, May 21, 1999, 17.

69. My account of the development of this second *Lolita* is based in large part on an as yet unpublished manuscript titled "The Majors and the Minor: The Commercial Aesthetic of Adrian Lyne's *Lolita*," by Kevin Sandler.

70. For more on the various scripts, see Christopher C. Hudgins, "*Lolita* 1995: The Four Filmscripts," *Literature/Film Quarterly* 25, no. 1 (1997): 23–27.

71. Lyne especially disliked Mamet's version. See Charles Fleming, "Nabokov Cocktail," *Vanity Fair*, January 1997, 120. Lyne told Fleming, "Mamet's version was really awful. Humbert Humbert was an ordinary filthy pedophile—thoroughly unpleasant."

72. Jerome Seydoux of Pathe (which handled the release of the film in Europe and ended up shouldering some of the debt when the film failed to interest a U.S. distributor) claimed that the budget was more like $62 million. See Michael Williams and Rex Weiner, "Lolita Tryst Proves Costly," *Variety*, September 15, 1997, 35.

73. Benjamin Svetky, *Entertainment Weekly*, August 9, 1996, 1; Giles Whittellm, "Steamy *Lolita* Scares Off Americans," *London Times*, August 7, 1996, 9.

74. Bob van Voris, "Coming Soon: Lolita—the Lawyers Cut," *Recorder,* August 13, 1996, 70.

75. Kaufman also directed *The Right Stuff* and *The Unbearable Lightness of Being.*

76. Though Kubrick died before the film was released, he is said to have supervised the post-production of the orgy scene himself. After all, he was contractually obligated to deliver an R-rated film, at least for theatrical release in the United States. No doubt the director would have appreciated the studios' ad copy, which claimed that not a single frame of his film was *cut* to suit the censors.

77. Andrew Essex, "NC-17 Gets an F," *Entertainment Weekly*, August 13, 1999, 21.

78. The feeling is mutual: Valenti called the animators "hairballs" in *Entertainment Weekly*. See David Hochman, "Putting the R in Park," *Entertainment Weekly*, July 9, 1999, 16.

79. Essex, "NC-17 Gets an F," 20–21.

Index

About the Author

Jon Lewis is Professor of English at Oregon State University where he has taught film and cultural studies since 1983. His books include *Whom God Wishes to Destroy . . . Francis Coppola and the New Hollywood, The Road to Romance and Ruin: Teen Films and Youth Culture,* and (as editor) *The New American Cinema.*